# Professional Selling
## A Relationship Approach

# Professional Selling:

## A Relationship Approach

**Maurice G. Clabaugh, Jr.**
University of Montevallo

**Jessie L. Forbes**
University of Montevallo

**West Publishing Company**
St. Paul    New York    Los Angeles    San Francisco

Copyediting:      *June Gomez*
Text Designer:    *John Edeen*
Composition:      *Parkwood Composition Service*
Artwork:          *Precision Graphics; human drawings by Cyndie C. H. Wooley*
Cover Image:      *David Bishop*
Cover Design:     *John Edeen*

Copyright 1992    By WEST PUBLISHING COMPANY
                  50 W. Kellogg Boulevard
                  P.O. Box 64526
                  St. Paul, MN 55164-0526

**Library of Congress Cataloging-in-Publication Data**

Clabaugh, Maurice G.
  Professional selling: a relationship approach / Maurice G. Clabaugh, Jr., Jessie L. Forbes
    p.    cm.

  Includes bibliographical references (p.    ) and index.
  ISBN 0-314-88422-X
  1. Selling.  2. Selling—Case studies   I. Forbes, Jessie L.
  II. Title.
HF5438.25.C52 1992                        91-16667

658.8'5—dc20                              CIP

## Photo Credits

**Page 6** Courtesy of Dale Carnegie & Associates, Inc.  **Page 12** © Andy Sacks/Tony Stone Worldwide.  **Page 20** Guy Gilette/Photo Researchers.  **Page 31** © The Stock Market/Mug Shots.  **Page 33** Courtesy of IBM.  **Page 43** © David Frazier/Tony Stone Worldwide.  **Page 56** © Wynn Miller/Tony Stone Worldwide.  **Page 59** Frost Publishing/Honeywell.  **Page 69** © The Stock Market/George Disarie, 1989.  **Page 81**© The Stock Market/JS Productions.  **Page 82** © The Stock Market/Mug Shots.  **Page 85** © David Powers, 1986/Stock, Boston.

*—Continued on page following Index*

To Grandma Workman, whose life exemplified the relationship principle, and to Kathy, Jason, Jerod, and Jenna for their encouragement, understanding, and sacrifice which made this dream a reality.

—mgc

To Nelson, Lyles, and Mallory
—jlf

# Brief Contents

# Contents

**PART**    **II**

**Learning Selling Skills**   51

**P A R T ▶ III**

## Applying Selling Skills    165

## 7    Prospecting For Relationships    167

**P A R T**  IV

**Strengthening
Relationships**    379

**14   Building Quality Relationships**    381

# Preface

For the career-oriented student, few topics are more exciting and dynamic than selling. Studying the subject paves the way for diversified career opportunities. The keys to sales excellence lie buried within each individual salesperson. Once you have a positive attitude, enthusiasm, the desire to help people satisfy their needs, and the drive to succeed, combined with basic relationship selling principles, the necessary elements for success are in place.

## Approach of the Text

This text uses an applied theory approach and emphasizes relationship development for career growth. Although the material is addressed from a pragmatic, how-to point of view, we have not sacrificed the behavioral theories which support the application of the selling tools. We address the issues that you may face when looking at employment in the area of sales. The approach we have used assumes no prior knowledge of selling. Thus the material is presented in a simple, straightforward language. We have defined all terms carefully, provided many real-life examples, and supported every-day application of sales tools with theoretical background.

The competitive spirit of the sales arena may make customers wary of a salesperson's presentation, since the customers feel that if the salesperson wins by selling, they must lose by being persuaded to buy. In relationship selling, however, the salesperson has the clients' needs as the uppermost reason for selling. The salesperson wins because satisfied clients bestow their future trust back with the same salesperson. The clients, on the other hand, win because the salesperson is genuinely dedicated to serving their needs and creatively solving their problems.

This book builds on the principles and qualities which inspire sales excellence. The text is structured to accomplish three major objectives:

1. To provide the basic selling tools to the reader in such a manner that the novice salesperson will understand what tool to use in a given

situation, how to use that tool, and the theoretical background which supports the reason for choosing that particular tool;

2. To provide a structure by which a salesperson can reinforce, reevaluate, and restructure sales techniques in a continuing effort to improve selling effectiveness;

3. To introduce the relationship sales approach.

## Organization of the Text

This text contains 17 chapters, organized into Parts I through IV. The format and language of the text are similar to training materials you might experience in an entry-level sales position. However, we have added theoretical support for the usage of selling tools, so that you will not only know what methods to use in specific situations, but that you will also know why it is the best tool to use.

The book follows a logical career-path sequence. In a selling career, the sales trainee begins experiencing the selling situation through classroom training sessions. Trainees then progress to on-the-job training, actually selling to clients. Finally, salespeople move into sales management. This text follows the same format. Part I, *Preparing To Sell*, takes a macro approach to the selling environment with a look at the opportunities and positions of the selling profession (Chapter 1), followed by an overview of the history of selling (Chapter 2).

*Learning Selling Skills*, Part II, emphasizes the skill areas needed for successful selling. By using the materials from a sales training program, students learn: about the selling skills and product knowledge gained in sales training programs (Chapter 3); about talking ("creating and transmitting sales messages") (Chapter 4); and about listening ("receiving verbal and nonverbal messages") (Chapter 5). Insight into understanding buyer behavior, both for the organization and the household, is emphasized in Chapter 6.

In Part III, *Applying Selling Skills*, the skills learned in Part II are applied into planning and implementing the sales dialogue. Prospecting (Chapter 7), and strategy formulation (Chapter 8) are essential elements in preparing to meet customers. Additional chapters in this section take you step by step through the sales dialogue from contact (Chapter 9); dramatizing the sales presentation (Chapter 10); conflict resolution and negotiation (Chapter 11); closing (Chapter 12); and, finally, with postsale activities (Chapter 13). Each chapter shows you how to apply the theories presented earlier. This section emphasizes the basic application of relationship selling techniques—"reading customers," determining their needs, satisfying those needs efficiently and successfully, and following up the sale to be certain customers remain satisfied.

In Part IV, *Strengthening the Relationship,* you are taken beyond the dialogue, since the salesperson's job is not finished with the closing of the sale. Areas of discussion include developing a stronger relationship with yourself (Chapter 14), and with your company, clients and society—through a discussion of ethics and legal aspects of selling (Chapter 15), and managing your time (Chapter 16). For those who may wish to look beyond a career in sales, this part concludes with a brief discussion of sales management (Chapter 17).

## How To Study Selling With This Text

Look carefully at the first three pages of each chapter. The information provided here is valuable. It highlights the topics covered in the chapter, shows how the information fits with past information, and spells out specific learning objectives. You can use these objectives to guide your understanding of the material, since they provide a good preview and review.

We have tried to make the book interesting and exciting by including experiences from practitioners. *In the Field* capsules at the beginning of each chapter and the *Partnerships* examples within the chapters are presented to illustrate the real-life usage of the material. Additionally, we have included *Technology Bulletins* to make you aware of the impact technology is having on the field of sales.

To help you relate what you have read to real-life situations, this text offers several helps. Each chapter includes *Discussion Questions* to make you think about the material you have just read. Following the discussion questions in each chapter is *Decision Crossroads: Ethical Issues.* This unique feature applies the chapter material to everyday ethical situations faced by professional salespeople. These ethical situations conclude with questions for discussion that identify contemporary issues. *Key Terms* are highlighted at the end of each chapter to reinforce the concepts you should understand from reading the material. Also included in each chapter are two *Cases* that let you confront real sales problems. Working with this material, you can see selling in action with illustrations of both good and bad sales examples. You can make decisions and judge someone else's actions. Applying the material in this text should lead the reader to sales excellence.

## Supplementary Support Materials

A comprehensive package of ancillary materials is available to support your course. These ancillaries have been prepared by the main text authors to be used in many combinations to accommodate various approaches and teaching styles.

- **Instructor's Manual.**   Prepared by the authors, the *Instructor's Manual* contains separate sections on teaching formats, suggested syllabi, role playing and sales presentation suggestions, and suggested alternative video/films sections. Each chapter includes *Learning Objectives,* definitions of *Key Terms,* an extended lecture outline with indications of where transparencies could be used, answers to *Discussion Questions,* answers to *Decision Crossroads: Ethical Issues,* and solutions for the two Cases that conclude each chapter. The manual is designed so that instructors can use the material during class lectures and discussions.
- **Transparency Masters.**   Ninety transparencies masters are provided. These masters consist of key text figures, as well as new figures not presented in the text. The masters are designed to supplement and support the text material. Key concepts and flow charts are provided to make it possible for students to easily grasp key concepts.
- **Test Bank.**   A thorough, class tested test bank containing over 850 multiple choice, true and false, and essay questions is provided. Each chapter includes questions from each range of difficulty. The questions are designed to test the student's knowledge of the most salient points of each chapter.
- **WESTEST 2.0.**   WESTEST 2.0 is a computer version of the printed Test Bank, available for PCs and the Macintosh. This supplement gives instructors an easy-to-use testing program with multiple choice, true/false, and essay questions.
- **Relationship Selling Video.**   Provided to qualified adopters, this video was prepared in cooperation with Wilson Learning Corporation, a leader in sales training. It contains twenty-six segments illustrating the process of selling. The video is optional, but is designed to illustrate key concepts and techniques. Segments illustrate a variety of techniques reinforcing the material in the text. The video segments vary in length from 1–10 minutes, and present selling situations in several industries.
- **Relationship Selling Video Instructor's Guide.**   An instructor's guide accompanies the Relationship Selling video. It describes each segment of the tape by giving its purpose, approximate time, a brief outline, and a description of the accompanying material in other supplements that may be used to support the video segment. It provides an overview of each segment with suggestions for in-class use.

- **Experimental Exercises in Relationship Selling.**  Consisting of seventy-five exercises, this book is designed to provide practical selling exercises for the student. One-third of the exercises have been prepared to work closely with video segments from the Relationship Selling video. Exercises include observations of sales situations, interviews, self-analysis, video analysis, and role-playing, all of which are combined with written exercises. This ancillary is for instructors who want more "hands-on" material than is provided in *Professional Selling: A Relationship Approach*. It is comprehensive and covers a range of topics including careers, the stages of the dialogue, self-improvement skills, and sales management. An instructor's manual for the Exercise book provides guidance on how to effectively use the exercises to supplement *Professional Selling: A Relationship Approach*. The manual provides answers to the questions in each exercise.
- **Practical Selling: A Case Approach.**  A case book with ninety-one cases provides material for those instructors who have found inadequate case coverage in current texts. *Practical Selling* can be used as a stand-alone text, or to supplement *Professional Selling: A Relationship Approach*. Its coverage parallels the material in the text.

  *Practical Selling* provides cases on careers , sales training, communications, buyer behavior, sales dialogues (7 chapters), self-improvement, time management, and overcoming problems in sales. Each chapter begins with Learning Objectives, a section on concepts of selling, then a continuing case on Eli Lilly and Company, which follows a student from career selection to ethical issues she faces. Each chapter concludes with six additional cases containing an equal mix of business-to-business and retail cases. The dialogue cases provide the opportunity to examine the interaction between a salesperson and a client. An instructor's manual, which provides alternative case solutions accompanies the casebook. Discussion questions end each case, and are provided with suggested answers.

## Acknowledgments

Finally, the authors are indebted to many people who have assisted us through out this experience. Our sincere appreciation is extended to the following people who graciously assisted in the preparations of the manuscript: Duane Bachmann, Central Missouri State University; James Boespflug, Arapahoe Community College; Dayle Dietz, North Dakota School of

Science; Gary Donnelly, Casper College; Dean Flowers, Northeast Wisconsin Technical College; Donald Hackett, Wichita State University; Michael Harford, Morehead State University; Kay Keck, University of Georgia; Alicia Lupinacci, Tarrant County Junior College; Jack Maroun, Hermiker County Community College; Don McCollum, Portland Community College; John R. Mitchell, Southeastern Louisiana University; David Syzmanski, Texas A&M University; Dan Weilbaker, Bowling Green State University; Curtis Youngman, Salt Lake Community College; Bernie Yavets, Alma College.

We are especially indebted to our editors, Rick Leyh and Tom Hilt, who brought focus to the text and offered many suggestions to encourage excellence.

Also, a special note of thanks to Penny Allen, Judy Perkins, Sharon McCoy, Melanie Sherrill, and Ellen Shepard for their assistance in preparing the manuscript and its revisions.

# Professional Selling
## A Relationship Approach

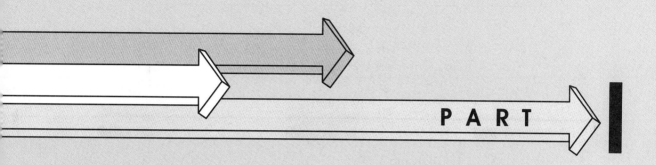

# Preparing to Sell

Before we know where we are going, we should have some idea of where we have been. Likewise, before examining the arena of selling, we need to have some background information. Part I of the text provides you with an overview of selling. Chapter 1 examines the selling profession from a career perspective, while Chapter 2 takes a historical look at the development of the profession.

## Chapter Outline

Benefits of a Sales Career

Sales Opportunities: A Market Channels
    Perspective
    Business-to-Business Sales
    Trade Sales
    Consumer Sales

Sales Career Advancement

## CHAPTER 1

# Opportunities in Professional Selling

**Learning Objectives**

After reading this chapter, you should be able to:

- Describe general characteristics of sales jobs
- Understand sales opportunities in three marketing channels
- Describe the general career path of a salesperson

## IN THE FIELD

In 1986 Ronald Shaw was promoted to president of Pilot Pen Company of America. With his arrival earlier as national sales manager, Pilot's U.S. sales jumped from $1 million to $52 million in just 11 years.

His first selling job was in an interview with Bic Pen Company. "I was hired because of my spunk, because I didn't meet the age requirements," he said. After four months, he was promoted to regional manager and seven years later was made national sales manager. He retained that position for six years before being replaced by Bruno Bich, son of Bic's Chairman of the Board and company president. Shaw was recruited by Pilot Pen Company. After much negotiation, Shaw was named national sales manager of this "little known company" for a lower salary in lieu of a percentage of sales. Although his title was the same as at Bic, he was responsible for selling, marketing, advertising, and packaging. More responsibility on less salary was not a setback for Mr. Shaw but was seen as a challenge. Because of his performance and insight, he was made vice president of marketing eight months into the job. And in 1986 he was named president of the U.S. subsidiary. Today Pilot is a leading contender in the specialty pen market.

Shaw's most significant contribution to his company was his attitude, something he says he developed during his earliest days. "I just always felt there wasn't anything in the world that I couldn't go after. If you told me 'NO,' it would only make me want it more. I think that characteristic has stayed with me right through my business career."

*Source:* Bill Kelley, "Take My Pens, Please," *Sales and Marketing Management* 139 (July 1987). Reprinted with permission of *Sales and Marketing Management.* © 1987.

You may be surprised to learn that everyone sells. But think about it: perhaps you remember selling Kool-Aid® to passers-by; selling magazines to raise money for your school; selling the "sensible" car your parents gave you to buy a sportier model; or helping at your family's garage sale. Indeed, anyone who is interacting with one or more people in a negotiating process is selling. Larry Adler (see the *Partnerships* box) shows that selling may begin at an early age.

Other examples of selling are college graduates who "sell" themselves to recruiters for jobs, employees who sell themselves to bosses for raises, one sex to the opposite sex to be mates, and peers to other peers in conversations for acceptance and approval. Small businesspeople, students, politicians, and laborers sell products, services, and ideas. A woman

## PARTNERSHIPS

*He went beyond the lemonade stand into doing other things. In fact he's hard to keep down. He works long hours and he works late. I try to keep him down a little more than he would like.*   **Rebecca Adler Goldstein**

Ms. Goldstein is speaking of her son Larry Adler. Larry, a fourteen-year-old, has grossed $100,000 since going into the ``rent-a-kid'' business, a lawn-mowing venture. At age 9, with a loan of $19, he started this lawn-mowing service. Today, Larry has 60 employees and now calls the business Larry Adler & Associates/The Kid Rep. Larry decided to diversify into distributorship after buying 10,000 small plastic baskets, filling them with candy, and selling them to gift shops. ``I'm a kid, so I know what a kid wants,'' he says. ``Everything I sold to stores they sold,'' he continues. Kid Rep, founded last year, handles products for children from 50 companies. His third subsidiary, Kidcorp, is a consulting service for youngsters. Through it he hopes to give seminars on topics such as how a young person can start a business. Where does this ninth grader see himself going? Like Ron Shaw, Larry wants to be successful (in less than five years, he hopes). And, as one might expect, he plans to be a business major in college.

*Source:* Pam McClintock, ``The Kid Rep Doesn't Kid Around,'' *Sales and Marketing Management* 140 (June 1988). Reprinted by permission of *Sales and Marketing Management.* © June 1988.

may sell her spouse on the new dress she has just purchased, and an accountant may sell a client on adopting new and better procedures. Writers of this century, such as Dale Carnegie and Earl Nightingale, are known for their books and talks persuading people to improve self-image and "get high on themselves." This, too, is a form of sales because the writers are selling readers on believing in themselves.

This chapter examines the career possibilities available to those who want to take such informal selling one step further. In the following pages we discuss opportunities in *professional selling*. Many people who look at selling as a career do not realize all the available opportunities this career offers. To provide this information for you, we present an overview of selling from a **marketing channels perspective**—how products get from the manufacturer to the consumer. This chapter assesses the selling environment, showing the characteristics of sales opportunities, types of positions available, and their unique features and growth opportunities.

Lamb points out how choosing a career or making any choice can be measured by one's satisfaction with the selection.

**marketing channels perspective**

> The measure of choosing well is whether a man likes what
> he has chosen.
>
> **Lamb**

Before you chose a career, you should investigate the characteristics of that career. This chapter can help you look at sales positions. It first presents a brief overview of the benefits of a sales career, followed by a discussion of the types of sales positions. An interview with a practitioner illustrates each sales job.

## Benefits of a Sales Career

What benefits can you expect from a career in selling?

**straight salary**

**straight commission**

1. *Earnings.* Today many people evaluate a career according to the compensation or earning potential and the benefits it offers. Diverse methods of compensation make it difficult, however, to compare the monetary rewards of sales positions. Many salespeople work on **straight salary** (an annual wage such as $25,000 a year); others work on salary plus commission ($20,000 and 2 percent of sales); and others on **straight commission** (5 percent of sales). Successful salespeople make good incomes; and in many commission selling jobs, the amount sellers make is largely based on their own efforts. According to David Komansky, national sales manager at Merrill Lynch, "Merrill Lynch has one of the best training programs of anyone in the securities industry. It can take a first-time entrant, and within a reasonable period of hard work, crank out a salesperson who will produce in excess of $200,000 in three years."[1] In determining their total compensation, some salespeople add fringe benefits, such as a company auto or regional cost-of-living differentials. Figure 1–1 shows a brief analysis of sales compensation for various levels of sales positions. In comparison with individuals in other management positions, salespeople fare quite well.
2. *Respect of customers.* Since many customers rely heavily on the people who sell them products, salespeople can build long-term relationships by providing accurate, honest information and superior service. These relationships grow to mutual respect, forging a bond of trust between customer and sales representative.
3. *Security.* Selling can provide a secure career financially, along with job safety. Good salespeople are valuable assets to their companies. Sales managers are aware that successful salespeople have job mobility; therefore successful sellers are important to their companies. **Job mobility** is the ability to advance in an organization or to move to jobs in other companies. The usual practice within a company is to promote people who are successful marketers to higher positions of manage-

**job mobility**

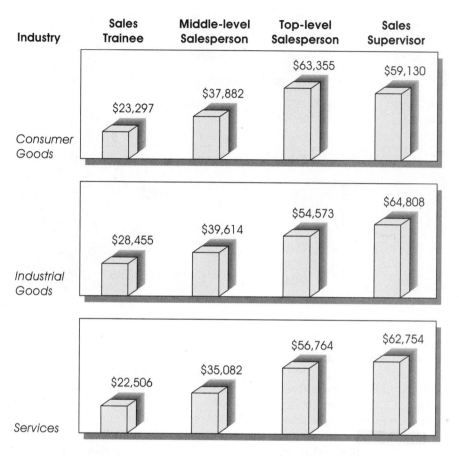

| Industry | Sales Trainee | Middle-level Salesperson | Top-level Salesperson | Sales Supervisor |
|---|---|---|---|---|
| Consumer Goods | $23,297 | $37,882 | $63,355 | $59,130 |
| Industrial Goods | $28,455 | $39,614 | $54,573 | $64,808 |
| Services | $22,506 | $35,082 | $56,764 | $62,754 |

**Figure 1–1**
**Sales Compensation**
*Note:* Compensation includes salary, commission, and bonus.
*Source:* Reprinted by permission of *Sales & Marketing Management.* Copyright: Survey of Selling Costs, February 26, 1990.

ment, as illustrated by Ronald Shaw (see *In the Field*). However, for the successful salesperson, job opportunities abound outside the company. The flexible schedule and independence of a sales job provide time for those seeking new job opportunities to investigate other opportunities, if desired. Many opportunities come to salespersons, because of their reputation for success, without their actively seeking a new position.

4. *Rewards.* Results of selling are easily measured, and companies are eager to recognize good salespeople. Their accomplishments are noted externally with **extrinsic rewards** by the company: cash awards, expense-paid trips, plaques, promotions, and election to company-sponsored achievement clubs such as the President's Golden Sales Circle at B.F. Goodrich. Internally salespeople gain self-respect, pride, and confidence from accomplishing personal and company sales goals **(intrinsic rewards)**. A sales career is ideal for people who desire reinforcement (recognition) for their efforts. With face-to-face interaction, selling provides feedback on the seller's activities as they occur. Since a sale

**extrinsic rewards**

**intrinsic rewards**

Salespeople may receive many different kinds of awards for sales excellence.

is not always made immediately, verbal or nonverbal feedback, or both, provide reinforcement, positive or negative, for the salesperson's attempts. Making a sale, and thus solving a customer's problem, reinforces the representative's good work and builds pride and self-confidence. Daniel Cronin (see *Partnerships*) shows one way of giving feedback to help salespeople.

5. *Independence.* Few occupations provide the degree of independence found in selling. Most salespeople have control over their daily routines. Although supervised, they are not under the direct eye of a supervisor for most of the day. With the exceptions of **telemarketing** (selling over the phone) and retail selling, most salespeople operate **autonomously,** acting as independent agents for a company.

**telemarketing**

**autonomously**

Company ties are maintained through reports and memorandums rather than through face-to-face supervision. This is not to say that a company sends salespeople out to "sink or swim" on their own but that outside salespeople are free from close supervision.

6. *Challenge.* Selling offers a variety of challenges because of the ever-changing nature of the position. A wide range of services and products offered to many buyers, each with a distinct personality, fills the sales job with unique opportunities to interest and challenge the salesperson.

**quotas**

Selling teems with challenge: each prospect is different; conditions in the marketplace constantly change; **quotas** (expected sales per year) change; and products change. The sales job is anything but boring. The challenges of increasing sales, solving problems for customers, and matching wits with competitors add zest to the day-to-day routine.

---

## PARTNERSHIPS

When Daniel A. Cronin was president of MacBick, Billerica, Massachusetts, the medical products company had only 25 salespeople. Each day he had the order processing department pull copies of all orders turned in for new accounts. He'd take his felt tip pen and write "Nice order, DAC." He knew a great deal about the care and feeding of new salespeople. A note from the president did wonders for the morale of salespeople making five calls a day trying to sell virtually unknown products with a company name that no one could remember.

*Source:* Jack Falvey, "The Care and Feeding of New Sales People," *Sales and Marketing Management* 142 (Feb. 1990). Reprinted by permission of *Sales and Marketing Management.* © February 1990.

---

7. *Advancement.* Entry-level sales positions are gateways to higher level sales and nonsales positions in most companies. Sales experiences are valuable preparation for these advancements.
8. *Travel.* The amount of travel depends on the number of customers in an area, its size, and the degree of management the territory needs. Many salespeople travel, but most are home every night or perhaps are away from home only a few nights a month. Some salespeople serve very small territories, such as representatives for Xerox copiers in the Chicago Loop, where a territory may be merely one city block. A Proctor and Gamble (P&G) territory in Indianapolis is only one half of the city. Therefore, both the Xerox and P&G salespeople in these territories travel less than do many commuting office workers in the same cities. Of course, *retail salespeople,* those who sell to the ultimate consumer in their stores, travel only rarely.

If a seller is motivated by the benefits gained from a sales position, excellence then becomes the ultimate goal of the sales professional. To the sales manager, excellence may mean surpassing the quotas. To the customer, it may mean assistance in finding the best product to solve the problem. To the sales representative, excellence means achieving one's highest potential.

## Sales Opportunities: A Market Channels Perspective

Goods and services move from producer to consumers through marketing channel intermediaries. These **marketing channel intermediaries**—man-

**marketing channel intermediaries**

ufacturers, wholesalers, distributors and retailers—perform several functions, such as buying, selling, storing, transporting, sorting, risk taking, financing, and information development, for other channel members.[2] Therefore each marketing intermediary provides sales career opportunities.

Just as sales compensation, benefits, and potential are diverse, so are the types of selling and opportunities within sales. In this text sales career opportunities are classified into three categories based on where they operate in the market channels: **business-to-business selling** (selling to businesses and industry), also known as **industrial sales; trade sales** (selling for resale); and **consumer sales,** or **retail selling** (selling to consumers), as shown in Table 1–1. The first two categories sell goods or services to companies for their own consumption or production or sell products to be resold to other businesses; consumer sales markets to the retail consumer exclusively.

**business-to-business selling**
**industrial sales**
**trade sales**
**consumer sales**
**retail selling**

## Business-to-Business Sales

The business-to-business sales position, or industrial selling, involves selling equipment, components, and supplies to manufacturers of goods, to other business establishments, or to governmental customers who further distribute goods to ultimate consumers at the national or local level.[3] Industrial salespeople may sell intangibles, such as worker's compensation insurance or motivational programs, or tangibles, such as machine tools or packaging equipment, business forms, or ingredients for the manufac-

**Table 1-1**
**Sales Career Opportunities: A Marketing Channels Perspective**

| Category | Customers |
|---|---|
| *Business-to-business selling* | 1. Standardized commodity buyers<br>2. Manufacturers of industrial goods (industrial sales)<br>Manufacturers of consumer goods<br>3. Governmental agencies |
| *Trade selling*<br>*(selling goods for resale)* | 1. Wholesalers<br>2. Distributors<br>3. Retailers |
| *Consumer selling*<br>*(retail sales)* | 1. Ultimate consumer |

turer's product. There are three types of industrial customers: purchasers of standardized commodities to be used as is (e.g., lime, which is used in water purification); buyers of manufactured equipment, components, and supplies for the production of other goods (e.g., a machine to stitch together the leather for shoes); and governmental agencies (e.g., highway departments), which buy both commodities and manufactured goods. A company specializing in industrial sales generally has a specialized sales force for each type of customer, since a company tends to specialize in one part of the marketing channel, that is, suppliers of commodities concentrate on selling raw goods to manufacturers of industrial and consumer products. Industrial goods manufacturers concentrate on selling their products to manufacturers who use these goods to make other products. In both cases industrial salespeople are involved; however, a salesperson would rarely sell both commodities and manufactured products for the same company. Table 1–2 shows who the customers are in business-to-business selling.

## Buyers of Standardized Commodities

Industrial selling often involves selling large quantities of raw goods, which are **standardized commodities,** such as bauxite, sand, coal, fertilizer, and wheat; that is, they are alike regardless of who is selling them. Selling standardized products requires emphasizing service and price to differentiate between offerings, since there are few differences between the products.

**standardized commodities**

However, J. Donald Staunton, of National Starch and Chemical says, ''There's no such thing as a commodity. Look hard enough and you

Table 1-2
**Business-to-Business Selling**

| Business-to-Business Customers |
|---|
| ***Buyers of Raw Goods:*** |
| Manufacturers of industrial goods (buyers of raw goods for processing) |
| Government agencies (national, regional, and local municipalities) |
| ***Buyers of Processed Goods:*** |
| Manufacturers of industrial goods (buyers of capital equipment, manufactured goods, and components and supplies) |
| Government agencies (national, regional, and local municipalities) |
| Consumer goods manufacturers |

Sales presentations are often made on the job site to ensure that the standard commodity fits the buyer's needs.

will find a differential—delivery, for instance, or packaging—to create value. Price becomes academic, if you can reduce customer costs. That's the object of selling value."[4] After establishing a relationship with a company, personal visits are made periodically, perhaps semiannually, with additional contacts by telephone made by support personnel or salespeople themselves. In contrast, sellers stress product attributes when selling manufactured goods, such as autos or typewriters.

**purchasing agents**

Companies which buy certain commodities are concentrated in small geographic areas. Their buyers are called **purchasing agents.** For example, the tire industry centers around Akron, Ohio, and the steel industry around Gary, Indiana and Pittsburgh, Pennsylvania. This concentration minimizes the amount of travel for the industrial salesperson.

**procuring agents**

While purchasing agents in private industry can buy products directly from the salesperson, their counterparts in government, called **procuring agents,** usually do not make the final buying decisions. Governmental customers, both at the local level (state and county government agencies and municipalities) and at the national level, buy standardized goods and raw materials, such as supplies for streets, water-treatment plants, and sewage-treatment plants. By law, governmental customers usually buy goods through a bidding process. Once the industrial salesperson obtains a specification list of the agency's requirements, the home office generally supplies a bid for the goods needed. Bids are opened by the governmental agency at a preset time and location. In theory this practice means that the government buys at the lowest possible price, from the best supplier available, while minimizing the emotional and personal appeal of each individual salesperson.[5]

## TECHNOLOGY BULLETIN

### Computer Program Update

IndustriaLogic, a computer software program, contains a menu that lists a series of questions similar or even identical to the ones expert sellers use. These questions help novice, *inside* salespeople probe for the same level of application-specific detail that their more experienced counterparts obtain. Levi Hill, President of Hill Systems, Inc., is offering distributors a way to enhance selling efforts of their inside salespeople through artificial intelligence programs such as IndustriaLogic. To increase the efficiency of inside salespeople, distributors of industrial goods must transform their people from order takers to professional sellers. Levi Hill's company provides the path for this goal. ''The beauty of IndustriaLogic is that it is programmed to keep asking follow-up questions until it has enough information to solve a customer's problem, much like an expert would,'' Hill explains. Levi's company is providing a service rather than goods to people who use the product to provide better services to their customers—field selling at its best.

*Source:* Reprinted from *Industrial Distribution*, January 1990, Cahners Publishing Co.

### Buyers of Manufactured Goods

Selling manufactured goods, processed materials, or capital goods to governmental agencies, industrial users, and manufacturers of consumer products is another type of industrial selling.[6] Rather than selling raw goods, as discussed above, this type of industrial selling involves products that have been processed by others into equipment, components, or supplies. For example, buying the wiring and light bulbs that are to be put in refrigerators is buying manufactured goods.

The governmental buyers in this area are the same customers who buy manufactured raw goods from the industrial salesperson. However, when they purchase from an industrial salesperson, they are purchasing capital goods and processed goods. They purchase a variety of products—from office equipment, automobiles, and train engines to cheese, sugar, and gasoline. Again, government buyers rely on the bid system to minimize emotional buying and to maximize savings.

The industrial user, like the governmental buyer, purchases goods to be used in manufacturing or processing of other industrial goods. These sales may include coke, used to make steel, or tin sheeting for making tin cans, each of which is further processed before its ultimate consumption.

Another buyer for industrial salespeople is the manufacturer of consumer products. These manufacturers process goods that are used by

**ultimate consumer**

the ultimate consumer. The particular goods they buy are not unlike the goods purchased by the industrial user except that they are used to make products for the "end user"—the **ultimate consumer.** Manufacturers of consumer goods buy such goods as microchips to make electronic equipment, processed potatoes to make Pringles®, brewers' yeast to make beer, or bottling equipment to bottle soft drinks.

For example, an industrial salesperson for United Silicon, a raw goods manufacturer, would sell (industrial sales—commodity) silicon to Micro Bits, a manufacturer of microchips, an industrial good. The industrial salesperson for Micro Bits would sell microchips (industrial sales—manufactured goods) to Data Point, a manufacturer of microcircuits. Data Point, an assembler of processed goods, is not only an industrial user but also is involved in industrial sales because it sells its manufactured product to a consumer calculator manufacturer. A Data Point industrial salesperson would sell the completed circuits to Commodore, a manufacturer of consumer calculators.

Additionally, purchasing agents for manufacturing firms depend on the industrial salesperson for information and support. Because products they buy are less standardized, salespeople use creativity to fulfill the specialized needs of the industrial goods manufacturer and the manufacturer of consumer goods. Industrial sellers try to find ways to fit the needs of their buyers better than the competitors. For example, an industrial salesperson teamed with his or her company's research and development division finds a way to make one component for a customer's product replace the three components currently being used. Both parties win in this relationship. This creativity, however, must not surpass the need of these buyers for continuity and consistency of supply to keep the assembly lines rolling.

### Industrial Selling Attributes

Job attributes of business-to-business selling are:

1. *Supervision.* One must be a self-starter who needs very little supervision. Industrial selling requires being away from the home office for long periods of time without direct supervision. In fact, most of the supervision in the industrial sales job occurs by telephone or mail. The selling hours of the industrial salesperson are spent in creative selling, which requires helping a customer solve problems, soliciting orders, and servicing the customers' needs. In addition, industrial salespersons spend many working hours performing public relations tasks.
2. *Travel.* Geographic concentration of business customers somewhat limits the salesperson's need to travel. "Silicon Valley" in California, car manufacturing in Michigan, furniture manufacturing in North Carolina, and textile factories in South Carolina are all such examples. The

industrial salesperson is continually out in the territory, making these sellers highly visible to their company, competitors, and customers.

3. *Visibility.* The dollar sales are quite high, so each sale a representative makes is visible to the upper echelon of the company. Other companies also notice competing representatives' expertise as they vie for industrial sales dollars. For example, a total of 941 coal and lignite mining companies in the United States shipped $16.6 billion of their products in 1988.[7]

4. *Compensation.* Remuneration of industrial salespeople reflects the high dollar volume of their sales. Industrial sales ranks among the highest paid areas of the profession, ranging in 1989 from an average of $28,455 for an entry-level sales trainee to $54,573 for a top-level salesperson.[8] The industrial salesperson usually has two valuable fringe benefits— an expense account and an automobile furnished by the company.[9]

5. *Growth.* Expected growth in industrial sales positions in the first half of the 1990s is projected as follows: telecommunications, 60.8%; printing, 43.6%; construction, 47.2%; chemicals, 42.1%.[10]

---

## Profile: Industrial Sales

**Commodity sales.**    Here are some words from Bill Brown, who sells re-sorcinol, a raw good used in the making of paper, for Reichhold Chemical, a division of INSPEC Corporation. As one of four company salespeople, his territory is the Western Hemisphere.

> Since we are a very established company (market share about 80 percent), my job is to see that we keep servicing customers by meeting their delivery needs. Resorcinol is a commodity-type good. Therefore my differential advantage over the competition is getting my customers the best contractual agreement I can. I try to be a liaison between the client and INSPEC while making a profit. Although I travel a great deal of the time, most of my customers are concentrated, of course, where there are paper mills. I have the opportunity to travel and meet clients in various countries, but I still am able to work out of my home 30 percent of the time. I guess what I enjoy most about this career is the relationships I have developed with my clients over the years. I help them solve their problems and make better paper products.[11]

**Manufactured Goods.**    Charlotte Barrett Jacobs, national account manager, Pitney Bowes, sells mailing systems, shipping systems, electronic inserters, copiers, and mailing room furniture to a limited number of accounts (national headquarters of 16 companies). She finds applications for

Pitney Bowes's wide line of products in other departments of these companies. She stresses the importance of maintaining good rapport with the present users so that they will not only suggest applications elsewhere but also serve as "satisfied users" in recommending the products to others.[12]

---

## Trade Sales

Selling consumer goods to the trade, trade sales, involves two types of organizations: wholesalers/distributors and retailers, as shown in Table 1–3. Consumer goods can be sold by their manufacturers either direct to wholesalers/distributors or direct to retailers. Trade sales are also made by the wholesaler to the retailer.

### Sales to Wholesalers/Distributors

**wholesalers/ distributors**

**Wholesalers/distributors** "add value" to a product by performing the duties of "breaking bulk," "creating an assortment," then reselling goods to other channel members;[13] that is, by buying a different mixture of goods than their competitors (other wholesalers), wholesalers create a unique assortment of products. Buying quantities smaller than manufacturers produce is called **"breaking bulk,"** a function that reduces the discrepancy between the amount produced and the amount needed by consumers.

**breaking bulk**

The needs of the wholesale buyer differ from those of the industrial buyer. More emphasis is placed on the amount of profit on a product **(markup)** and its salability, or how well it will sell to retailers **(turnover)**.

**markup turnover**

Table 1-3
**Trade Selling**

| Trade Sales Customers |
| --- |
| *Consumer Goods Manufacturer's Salespeople:* |
| Sell direct to wholesalers/distributors of consumer goods |
| Do detail, or missionary, sales for wholesale/distributors to their retailers of consumer goods |
| *Consumer Goods Wholesaler/Distributor Salespeople:* |
| Sell direct to retailers of consumer goods |

Product continuity, consistency, and the willingness to help solve wholesalers' problems are important when a wholesaler buys a trade seller's goods.

Wholesalers provide credit, storage, promotion, and transportation to retailers who buy their goods. If they provide these services more efficiently than a manufacturer, wholesalers are assured a niche in the market. They are available when a manufacturer is unwilling or a retailer is unable to accept the responsibility for these functions in the marketplace.

Wholesalers sell more than retail products; they sell maintenance equipment and supplies to users in industry for plant and equipment maintenance. Such products include paper goods, floor wax, light bulbs, and buffers. Buyers of maintenance equipment and supplies seek the same qualities that an industrial purchasing agent is seeking: continuity of supply and quality at the lowest price.

## Trade Sales To Retailers

A **retailer** is the only marketing channel intermediary that sells goods directly to the ultimate consumer. Any time a sale is made to the ultimate consumer, the retail function is being performed, regardless of the name the firm calls itself.[14] Trade sales are made by a wholesaler performing its functions of breaking bulk and creating an assortment, as discussed above, or directly by a consumer goods manufacturer. When a manufacturer of goods sells directly to a retailer, eliminating the wholesaler, the manufacturer or the retailer generally accepts the wholesaling functions. Sometimes they divide the wholesaler's functions between them. In any event the wholesaler's functions are not eliminated but are absorbed by another channel intermediary. Yamaha, for instance, sells the pianos it manufacturers directly to retail dealers.

**retailer**

In addition to quality, continuity of supply, and price, the retail buyer needs information that facilitates the resale of the product to consumers. Therefore the trade salesperson is involved in teaching retail buyers and salespeople the desirable features and benefits of the product, which are then conveyed to the consumer. Furthermore, the retail buyer is interested in the amount of sales that can be expected from a product, so the trade salesperson emphasizes not only features of the product, the product assortment, but also the amount of retail markup and the expected turnover.

## Dual Roles of Trade Sales

Although two possible channels for consumer goods sales exist, rarely do trade salespeople get involved in selling directly to both wholesaler and retailer in the same territory. By selling their products directly to retailers who sell the product and the wholesaler who carries the goods in the same territory, trade salespeople would be competing against their own customer's (wholesaler's) sales, which would defeat the purpose of having a wholesale/distributor. However, the trade sellers may perform detail selling activities for the wholesaler, even though they are paid by the manufacturer. This type of selling is called **missionary,** or **detail selling.**[15]

**missionary (detail) selling**

For example, a salesperson working for a consumer goods manufacturer such as Colgate would sell to drug and grocery store wholesalers as a primary sales responsibility. A secondary sales responsibility would include calls on retailers to help the wholesalers promote Colgate products. Any sales that are made are given to the wholesaler to be delivered from its stock.

Missionary selling is used by manufacturers who want a more aggressive sales promotion effort with retailers than a wholesaler often provides. Missionary sales may be conducted by a separate sales force or as a secondary responsibility for a manufacturer's representative, as is most often the case.

### Attributes of Trade Sales

Trade selling requirements differ somewhat from those of other sales positions:

1. *Supervision.* Sales to the trade tend to require more creativity to solve the more complex client problems than do industrial sales. Therefore companies wish to maintain closer contact with the salesperson. For example, many wholesale salespeople work a five-day week in a territory or route. Representatives frequently contact their home offices; they call on customers and wholesalers often, sometimes daily, and have more direct supervision than many other nonretail salespeople.
2. *Travel.* A person in trade sales should be achievement oriented and enjoy some travel. Territories generally cover only a portion of a state or at most a single state, since customers who use their products are often concentrated in certain locales. Most trade salespeople work a scheduled territory, so accounts are called on more frequently and more regularly with higher levels of personalized service than in industrial sales. For example, a salesperson for Broyhill Furniture would cover only the dealers in Illinois.
3. *Compensation.* Pay schedules vary from company to company. Manufacturers' salespeople generally receive lucrative salaries often combined with a bonus for achieving the company's goals. They may be paid on a straight commission based on a higher percentage and lower volume than industrial sales. Fringe benefits abound and often include travel and entertainment expenses. Unlike manufacturers' salespeople,

many wholesale sellers are compensated by straight commission with less liberal fringe benefits because of the lower percentage of profit wholesalers possess. Nonetheless, many sellers to the trade can make a very good living. In 1989 they averaged an annual income of $23,297 for a sales trainee to $63,355 for a top-level salesperson.[16]

4. *Growth.* It is predicted that the growth in wholesale sales positions in the early part of the 1990s will be approximately 37.9%.[17]

---

### Profile: Trade Sales

In the 12th annual Top Salesperson Competition sponsored by *Purchasing* magazine, good salespeople made a difference. In the balloting, three of the top ten winners were women, two of whom are involved in trade sales. Deborah Martin, Roadway Inc., of Jackson, Tennessee, was recognized as a "hard-working professional who knows her product and is very assertive." She takes it upon herself to train and educate customers who may not be familiar with the details of tariffs and other transportation minutiae. "We have saved thousands of dollars in the past two years," says one of her customers, "because of what she taught me."

Another winner, Sally Monnich of Brownell Electro in Memphis, Tennessee, was nominated for the award by a client. "Her expertise with Just-In-Time (inventory program) has made our transition from our past system almost effortless and without cost increases," said one of her customers. In fact, her knowledge of her own and our product line has resulted in "continuous updating and refining of specifications." Result: over $400,000 in cost savings reported by one senior buyer. It is easy to see how these two top salespeople have applied the relationship selling philosophy and have developed partnerships with their customers.[18]

---

## Consumer Sales

Consumer sales jobs differ greatly from the other types of selling positions, as shown in Table 1–4. Generally called retail selling because they involve selling to the ultimate consumer, these jobs may be in-house selling (in the retail store—Macy's, e.g.). or specialty selling (in the home, door to door, out of store—Avon or Amway, e.g.).

When a manufacturer sells directly to the ultimate consumer, a large, separate sales organization is established, and it is technically called direct marketing, or **direct sales,** a form of consumer sales. In this capacity the manufacturer performs a dual role: producing products and retailing them directly to the consumer. The latter role is retail sales by definition. Working conditions differ from other selling situations, since the staff in a retail store controls the sales environment. The customer enters the retail

**direct sales**

**Table 1-4**
**Consumer Sales**

| Retail Selling |
| --- |
| Retail sales to customers who go to a retail store |
| Retail sales to customers who invite retail salespeople into their homes (specialty selling) |
| Direct sales—Manufacturer sells direct to the consumer (door to door or mail order) |

store (salesperson's realm) instead of the salesperson entering the customer's office, as would be the case in trade selling or business-to-business sales. In some jobs the consumer salesperson goes door to door (direct marketing) to sell or makes house calls by appointment, such as carpet or drapery sales.

Retail firms include those as exclusive as Neiman-Marcus, Tiffany's, and Saks Fifth Avenue, and as "down to earth" as the Main Street hardware and the local pizza shop. Though representing a wide spectrum, these businesses can display characteristics of sales excellence.

### Attributes of Consumer Sales

1. *Supervision.* The in-house retail selling job affords the sales employee a high degree of supervision; that is, store management is always available to help with problems. As a result, retail sellers have less need to be as independent or as self-sufficient as those engaged in other areas of sales.

   Direct selling (in the home) is demanding in that it requires a representative with initiative and only intermittent need for supervision. Customers control the selling environment in their homes as a purchasing agent does in a business. Sometimes this environment can become hostile toward salespeople or can make them feel like intruders. If the salesperson is trained adequately, however, this should not be a barrier.

   Offering a wide variety of products, retail salespeople display a high degree of creativity and product information to help satisfy customers' needs. Knowledge about the product is imperative for effective consumer sales.[19]

2. *Travel.* Whereas industrial and trade salespeople go to the customer's establishment to make a sale, most retail sales are made in a store environment. Since the client comes to the establishment, in-store sell-

ing can be enjoyable to a person who prefers not to travel but who still wants the challenge of dealing with people.

Direct selling, or door-to-door selling, places the salesperson directly in the customer's home. Examples of products or services most likely sold this way are encyclopedias, vacuum cleaners, household products, life insurance, and burial plots.

3. *Compensation.* Retail salespeople may work between forty and sixty hours a week with a variety of people and make a good living. Some who sell "big ticket" items, such as jewelry, carpet, furniture, or cars, are paid on commission. Since personnel have greater motivation to sell these more expensive goods, consumer salespeople are limited only by their abilities. Efficient, career-oriented salespeople often are moved into a management position within the first year or two of employment and are therefore salaried as manager trainees. Entry-level positions are lower paid, however, than other types of selling, even though career salespeople in this area compete quite well with top-level salespeople in other areas.

Relationship sellers at Saks Fifth Avenue provide personal attention.

The direct salesperson may work long hours, making appointments by phone before or after traditional working hours, when prospective buyers are at home. Many life insurance representatives, for example, may work from 10 A.M. to 10 P.M. five or six days a week. Spending these long hours, however, can bring good compensation. Since the number of sales closed may be low, direct sales commission rates are quite high, possibly 40 percent of the retail selling price, as in sales of Amway products and Current greeting cards.

4. *Growth.* Of all the sales positions analyzed by Sales Consultants International, retail sales positions were expected to grow in the early 1990s by 61.8 percent. This was 21.3 percent over the national average of 40.5 percent for projected growth in all sales positions during this period of time.[20]

## Profile: Consumer Sales

Harry Davis has worked for J. C. Penney Corporation in Atlanta, Georgia for over ten years. Harry reports:

> Although some retail sales jobs require limited training
> and sophistication, as salesperson in the Interiors
> department, I need considerable product knowledge,
> strong interpersonal skills, and the ability to work with a
> diversity of customers. Jobs like mine pay commission, and
> my income was limited only by my skills and the
> economy. When the economy was strong, I made very
> good money; and when it was weak, we all struggled. The

hours were not any longer than other types of selling, and in my department I got to leave the store and visit clients' homes. My travel was minimal, and I was home every night. Nights and weekends that I had to work weren't the best, but I have been made a manager now. And I enjoy working with Penney's people in this position.[21]

From this analysis you can compare these three areas to determine which type of sales best matches your personality and would be most desirable as a career goal. After looking at the specific sales jobs, you then need to look at opportunities for advancement in your career.

## Sales Career Advancement

A career in sales provides a variety of alternatives. Many companies in industrial or trade sales begin new employees' careers at the entry-level position of sales trainee. Then, as shown in Figure 1–2, the sales trainee progresses to salesperson.

Advancement from the salesperson position can be into a career sales, sales management, or other marketing managerial position inside the company. Those who choose the career-selling path advance from salesperson to senior salesperson, who handles major accounts in a district; to territorial salesperson, who handles major accounts in a region; to a national account manager, who handles only major national accounts, such as Sears or ITT, like Charlotte Jacobs of Pitney Bowes (see *Profile*).[22]

Alternatives to career sales are positions in sales management or other senior level positions inside the company, such as market research, product management, promotion, or distribution. Advancement in the sales management track follows a similar upward path as that of career salesperson but concentrates on managing salespeople in a district, region, or at the national level as opposed to selling directly to clients. The third path involves moving into other areas of marketing, such as market research, product management, promotion, or distribution management.

Advancement in consumer sales can be illustrated with a department store example. Trainees advance through the sales ranks of a department store from assistant department manager to store management through a variety of buyer and managerial positions. However, with each management position, less and less time is devoted to selling to customers and more time is spent in "selling to store personnel" the benefits of its operational procedures.

In retail selling, men and women with the requisite self-motivation, creativity, energy, and risk-taking and decision-making abilities

**Figure 1–2**
**Career Opportunities in Sales (Non-Retail)**

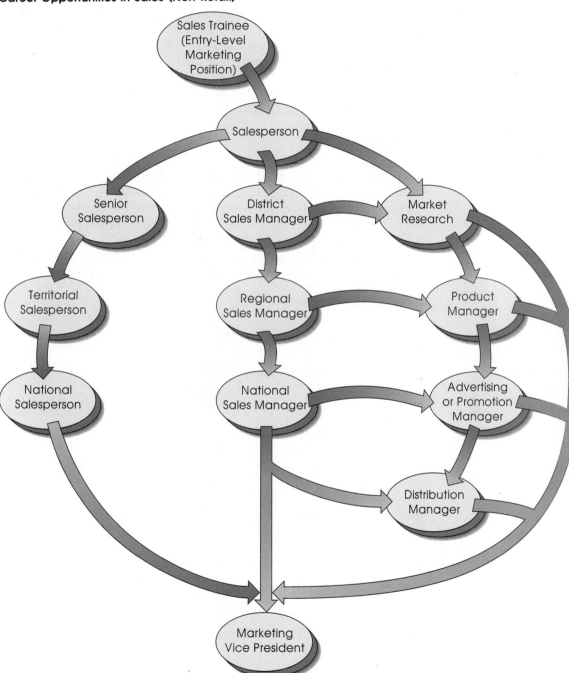

progress from assistant department manager to a high-level executive position as store merchandise managers. The assistant department manager sells on the floor as well as provides managerial support for the department manager. Macy's, like other department stores, alternates assignments between buying positions and sales floor supervisory jobs. All employees in the management training program receive a background in both buying and selling.

## Summary

Selling involves a variety of tasks that are performed in several types of jobs. Sales jobs offer mobility, independence, challenge, recognition, and generous compensation. Careers are available in the areas of industrial, trade, and consumer sales. When deciding to work in one particular marketing channel or another, a person should consider the job attributes of supervision, travel, compensation, and growth. Advancement opportunities exist for those persons who work toward sales excellence.

## Key Terms

marketing channel perspective
straight salary
straight commission
job mobility
extrinsic rewards
intrinsic rewards
telemarketing
autonomously
quotas
marketing channel intermediaries
business-to-business selling
industrial sales
trade sales

consumer sales
retail selling
standardized commodities
purchasing agents
procuring agents
ultimate consumer
wholesalers/distributors
breaking bulk
markup
turnover
retailer
missionary (detail) selling
direct sales

## Discussion Questions

1. List general characteristics of sales jobs.
2. How are sales careers in the three marketing channels alike? How are they different?

3. What career steps might you take if you were a retail salesperson?
4. To be an effective salesperson, list some essential characteristics you would need.

## Decision Crossroads: Ethical Issues

1. If a person takes a new position with company B after working several years for rival company A, should he or she use the privileged information gained on the past job with company A? Support your reasoning.
2. Do you feel it is unethical to ignore helping a fellow salesperson get out of a sales slump? Why?
3. Would you pass helpful information about a client to another salesperson in your company if you knew it would help that person get promoted to the managerial position you want? Why?

## Case 1-1   B. F. Goodrich

Graduating from the University of Cincinnati with a degree in chemistry, Ray Sherry knew what career he wanted. He wanted to sell chemicals. Ray was unsure that he could compete with the business students who had sales training but was confident that with a good foundation of product knowledge and company support, he could be successful at selling. He decided that he would maximize his strengths and minimize his weakness, so he interviewed with chemical companies for a job as a chemist. After working as a chemist for Dow Chemical company, he accepted a position working for B. F. Goodrich, plastics division, as a chemical supervisor. He obtained the job because of a recommendation of a relative already working with the company.

One day, eighteen months later, Ray noticed a position opening for a selling position posted on the bulletin board. It was for the plastics division. He felt he was ready to begin selling and prepared to apply for the job. But he was unsure how to approach the interviewer; it was a long time since he had really interviewed for a job, and he really wanted this one. Ray made an appointment with the interviewer in the personnel office for Tuesday of next week so that way he would have almost a week to prepare.

Discussion:

1. If you were Ray, how would you prepare for the interview? Be specific.

2. What questions should Ray be prepared to ask the interviewer?
3. Should Ray look for other chemical sales jobs just in case he does not get this one? If so, how would you suggest that Ray go about preparing for a career in chemical sales?
4. What would you consider before you took a selling job with a company? What questions would you ask the recruiter? What questions would you ask yourself?

## Case 1–2    **Eli Lilly & Company**

It was graduation day at Ohio University. All the festivities of the day filled the atmosphere with bittersweet feelings—the excitement of new beginnings and the sadness of losing contact with old friends. It was easy to get caught up in the happiness of the day and forget the fear of the unknown that followed the walk across the stage. As Julie Edelen stood in line to receive her degree, fear of her unknown future began to make her nervous. She realized she was moving up the stairs to the stage. Suddenly she noticed only one more step. Snapped into the reality of the moment, her fears were again forgotten. As "Julie Kay Edelen" came across the public address system she said a short prayer: "Please, God, don't let me stumble on the last step; help me remember to shake with my right hand and take the diploma with the left." She crossed the stage and returned to her seat.

The parties and packing to leave campus after graduation eased the fear of going home with no job. Picking up her mail on Friday, she noticed two long envelopes, one from Eli Lilly Pharmaceuticals, the other from Du Pont Chemical. Fearing rejection, she opened the first. Du Pont Chemical, an *offer*!!! "A really good one," she thinks. "I can start, ah—in two weeks." There was no hesitation now about opening the Lilly envelope. "At least I have a job," she thinks. "So what if its the only offer; it's a job. Eli Lilly wants me too!!!" Julie jumps for joy. "I have a choice!!!"

Both offers were within $200 dollars of each other monetarily and each had fringe benefits that were equal. The main difference was in their sales training programs. Lilly had a step-by-step program of classroom training mixed with on-the-job training that lasted for a year before the salesperson had his or her own territory. Training was quite extensive, with a lot of emphasis on sales principles, product knowledge, and learning the "Lilly" way. Although it was a large company, Julie felt there was a place for her.

Du Pont had what her sales professor described as a "fast-track" approach to sales training. They offered extensive training in product knowledge and sales principles, all in a six-month period. Each successful trainee was placed in his or her own territory after the six-months training period. Julie was anxious to prove herself, but she wondered if she could "learn it all" in six months?

**Discussion:**

1. If you were Julie, which offer would you take?
2. What would you look for in a company? From personal investigation at your library, decide which company fits your career goals better.
3. What traits would the different companies be looking for in a salesperson?

**Chapter Outline**

Relationship Selling
  Differential Advantage
  Trust
  Saves Time

Selling Styles
  Customer Orientation
  Self-Orientation

Reasons to Practice Relationship Selling

A Historical Perspective of Selling
  Preindustrialization Period (Pre-1920)
  Industrialization Period (1920–1950)
  Post-War Era: (1950–1965)
  Revitalization of Consumerism (1965–Present)

The Future of this Sales Evolution

Traits of Effective Relationship Salespeople

# The Evolution of Relationship Selling

## Learning Objectives

After reading this chapter, you should be able to:

- Understand a definition of selling
- Describe some benefits of a selling career
- Trace the history of sales to the present time
- Compare and contrast styles of selling: hard sell, persuasive, problem solving, and relationship selling
- Explain the importance of other-oriented, relationship selling
- Recognize the characteristics of effective relationship salespeople.

## IN THE FIELD

After completing a marketing degree at Youngstown State University (YSU) in Ohio, Mary Worthington took a sales position with a railroad. Completing the company's training program, she was assigned to work with a senior salesperson in the Pittsburgh territory, where rail transportation is rebounding after several years of decline.

Mary met with several YSU students and faculty at a recent Pittsburgh American Marketing Association last summer. She chuckled about wearing a sweater to the air-conditioned meeting site because she was still a little cold from working in a client's refrigerated warehouse the night before. It seems that she had gotten a large food processor to agree to try a large rail shipment rather than a truck shipment, as was previously done. Mary was fearful that something might go wrong with this shipment, so she decided to personally oversee the loading of the rail cars.

She brought insulated underwear and ski clothing to the processing plant because the refrigerated cars were loaded and switched in a refrigerated warehouse during the night. Mary checked the temperature of each car, approved the necessary paper work, rode with the switch engineer, and worked with the operations people for a perfectly controlled shipment. Everyone appreciated Mary's help, and she took great pride in knowing that her efforts restored a lost customer with major shipping volume.[1]

selling

**Selling** is usually thought of as a face-to-face, interactive dialogue between two or more people. Understanding and using sales techniques efficiently enhances the probability of making a sale and receiving the benefits which result from those sales efforts. Selling is a complex subject partly because of the variety of products sold, the technical aspects of some of those products, and the different types of customer personalities. Moreover, there is more than one way to sell.

Chapter 2, after looking at Relationship Selling in depth, takes a look at some of the "ways" selling has historically been used. This history lesson reveals the "evolution" of sales, an evolution that has brought us to Relationship Selling.

## Relationship Selling

When Mary Worthington (see *In the Field*) thought about a selling career, she never even considered selling transportation services. She had learned the rudiments of selling in the classroom, but using these principles to sell transportation services was a challenge. Nonetheless, she succeeded, and her goals were achieved through hard work, personal attention to details, and building trust with clients. She learned the necessity of going beyond the job description items to build a relationship with her clients rather than just taking an order. Through her actions, Mary epitomizes relationship selling.

Over the years, the selling environment has changed and the variety of available products has multiplied. Thus buyers need more information on which to base a decision. Many companies, such as Mars Candy Company, Gulf Oil, and Entre Computer Centers, responded to these changes by adopting a new selling style—relationship selling. **Relationship selling (consultative approach)** is defined as a *continuing alliance* in which the salesperson helps the client achieve maximum satisfaction in the allocation of customer resources. To do so, the salesperson satisfies customers' needs for information, thereby adding value to the customers' decision process. According to Chonko and Tanner, relationship selling "is based on the idea that no single sale and no one contact is more important than the collective contacts that make up the long-term relation between the salesperson and the prospective qualified buyer."[2] Relationship selling differs from other types of selling because it concentrates on (1) adding (value) to the customer's decision process; (2) providing accurate and complete information about *all* products that could solve the customer's needs; and (3) building a long-term relationship in the process. It concentrates on the long-term client relationship as opposed to the short-term sale. Mary Worthington exemplifies the relationship salesperson. She went beyond the customer's order to personally oversee the load-

**relationship selling (consultative approach)**

Relationship selling does not always take place in a one-to-one setting.

ing of the railcars—gaining her customer's trust and building a relationship.

Relationship selling goes beyond just solving problems. Leaving behind an approach that manipulates customers to buy, the relationship seller becomes more consumer oriented by adopting a double-win philosophy.

**double-win philosophy**

In his book *The Double Win*, Waitley defines the double win as follows: "If I help you win, I win, too."[3] From this nonmanipulative approach, the clients achieve satisfaction (i.e., win), appreciate the services performed by the salesperson, and build trust in and gain respect for the seller; therefore they purchase more over time. Thus the client wins and the salesperson wins (a **Double-win philosophy**) and the development of a relationship is enhanced. This "helping" orientation aids customers in solving problems by providing *complete* product information and minimizing the time used for information gathering. Figure 2–1 depicts the basis of the consultative approach to relationship selling.

**win-lose philosophy**

Relationship selling can be contrasted to persuasive selling in which a **win-lose philosophy** exists. If the salesperson *wins* by persuading the customer to buy, the buyer *loses,* since the purchase may be made because of the persuasive abilities of the salesperson rather than to solve a client's need. When sellers spend their days persuading people with exploitation and manipulation, it is no wonder customers have lost their tolerance for the domineering salesperson who seeks to manipulate them for his or her own goals. The customer may not be completely satisfied, so this competitive philosophy changes from a win-lose to a lose-lose situation.

Figure 2–1
**Foundations of Relationship Selling**

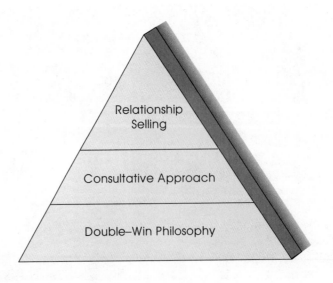

Unlike a persuasive selling concept, which concentrates on the seller's problems of "moving merchandise," relationship selling "employs a customer-oriented approach that employs truthful, nonmanipulative tactics which satisfy the long-term needs of both the consumer and the selling firm."[4] The **marketing concept** holds that the key to achieving organizational goals consists in determining the needs and wants of customers and delivering the desired satisfactions more efficiently and effectively than competitors.[5] Relationship selling fulfills the marketing concept with its "client-helping" orientation. The foundation of a double-win philosophy and consultative approach gives the relationship seller the freedom to increase sales to enjoy selling by:

**marketing concept**

- Avoiding tension-inducing pressure
- Building long-term relationships of mutual trust
- Maintaining client-helping orientation (e.g., **nonmanipulative methods**)[6]

**nonmanipulative methods**

## Differential Advantage

To help clients in today's highly competitive business environment, sellers seek differential advantages to sell products and services. A **differential advantage** is a unique trait used as a basis for vying in the marketplace. Fewer innovative product advantages exist today; therefore even relating the best features of a product may not increase its sales. Many products have identical features that produce similar prices, and quality is often assumed to be equal unless proven otherwise. With products, prices, promotions, and locations for products being similar, what is left to sell? Only one thing: the seller's customer orientation and a long-term relationship as their own differential advantage. For example, business owner Donna Jones practices this helping philosophy in her Tandem Computer business. She does not just meet the prospective buyers and start showing them equipment. Rather she meets them in their offices, where they share coffee or a soft drink. She listens carefully as they talk about their needs, business environment, price constraints, and any special considerations. Then Donna becomes a consultative salesperson who is helping clients find a machine exactly suited to their needs. In addition, Donna saves the clients' time by eliminating those machines that are not appropriate for them. Does this philosophy win for Donna? Consider that she sells over $4 million in business machines each year; that one year she sold $10 million; and that she has been named top salesperson in her company for two years! The majority of her business comes from referrals from satisfied buyers, showing that Donna's clients win too—a long-term relationship has developed in an area where one-time sales are prevalent.

Developing a differential advantage other than those intrinsic in the product is developing an attitude toward situations that allows a sales-

**differential advantage**

Demonstrating superior product knowledge to prospects establishes a trusting relationship between the client and the salesperson.

person to view products from a client's perspective. Products are viewed as a bundle of satisfiers that can quench the customer's bundle of wants. Capable relationship salespeople must have product knowledge as well as a feeling for the needs, values, and viewpoints of their clients. In addition, introspection is needed to determine how resources (ideas, time, insight, recommendations) can best be delivered to meet clients' needs. Salespeople focus attention on managing two key relationships: (1) the relationship of the client to the problem or opportunity over which the client is seeking to exert control, and (2) the relationship of the salesperson to the client to be helped.[7] It is the continuation of this consultative approach and double-win philosophy that is the foundation of relationship selling and thus allows it to occur.

## Trust

Trust is basic to successful relationship selling. By providing accurate information to help the client solve problems, the salesperson lays the foundation for a trusting relationship between buyer and seller. The salesperson strengthens this relationship by being a continuing source of accurate, pertinent information.

**trust link**

Kotler illustrates not only the helping relationship, but also the **trust link** when he states:

> The consultant's key task is to understand the client and the client's problems. That understanding allows the creation of a credible working *relationship* within which ideas may be shared and acted on.[8]

The salesperson should feel that "the consulting relationship is in essence a phenomenon of 'community'—a sharing and exchange of information and action. The breadth and depth of that exchange will reflect in an important way the consultant's belief about what is real and what is valuable."[9]

Relationship selling means putting greater emphasis on personal negotiation and creative communications between people than any other selling style. It means selling yourself first and realizing that sales and profits will follow. As illustrated at Young and Vann Tool Distributors, "The job of an outside salesperson in the 1990s is to identify customers who are changing their purchasing practices from the lowest price to total cost, and tie them to our company," says William Vann. "To do this, the outside salesperson may have to go beyond purchasing and past the shop floor and call on financial and data processing managers. The idea is to look at the entire package and solve problems customers are having with inventory, production and receivables," he says.[10]

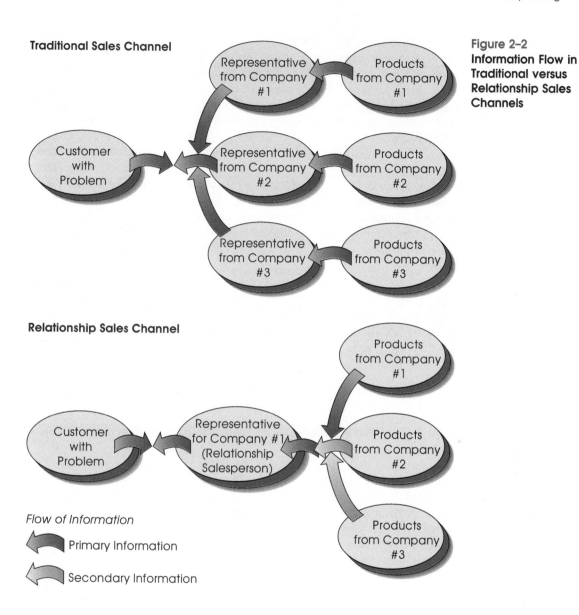

**Traditional Sales Channel**

**Relationship Sales Channel**

*Flow of Information*

Primary Information

Secondary Information

**Figure 2–2**
**Information Flow in Traditional versus Relationship Sales Channels**

## Saves Time

As consumers demand more information and as companies see the inroads relationship selling is making in increasing the market share, more and more salespeople using this technique have made manipulative techniques obsolete. The time-saving importance to the client of the helping relationship formed by being an informational source is illustrated in Figure 2–2.

In the traditional sales channel (i.e., nonrelationship) most company representatives know much about their product and little about other companies' products. This means customers must talk to, as shown in Figure 2–2, three salespeople from three different companies to gather the maximum amount of information on three different products. This time-consuming method often produces confusing and conflicting information.

In contrast, the relationship selling channel emphasizes communicating the maximum amount of information in the minimal time. For a Maytag representative to develop a relationship, he or she would have
**primary information**    **primary** (first-hand) **information** about Maytag washers gleaned from the
**secondary**    Maytag company. The sales representative would also possess **secondary**
**information**    (second-hand) **information** concerning competitors' washers that he or she had obtained from such sources as customers, competitors, and trade shows.

Secondary information is a key factor in relationship selling. It allows the salesperson to compare and contrast benefits of various products. As a clearinghouse of information, the efficient relationship salesperson provides one-stop shopping, permitting the client to minimize decision-making time by talking to a salesperson early in the buying process.

## Selling Styles

As mentioned earlier, Relationship Selling is the result of an evolution in sales. Indeed, only recently have large numbers of companies recognized the need for and the advantages of a relationship approach to selling. Earlier selling styles were often based on the needs of the salesperson rather than on customer's needs. If you view various selling styles according to the amount of customer orientation salespeople show, a continuum is evident, as shown in Figure 2–3.

### Customer Orientation

The right side of the continuum shows the customer being influenced by selling styles that implement the marketing concept. These salespeople seek to help customers solve their individual problems rather than just
**other-orientation**    make a sale. **Other-orientation** is an attitude of concern more for satisfying the customers' needs than for promoting one's product, regardless of the circumstances. Seeking to help, the salesperson views the customer as an equal to be treated with care and respect. For these types of salespeople, customer satisfaction is the motive for selling products; and profit

## Figure 2–3   A Selling Style Continuum

The selling style continuum shows an evaluation of selling styles according to a customer's view of the salesperson's orientation. For example, a salesperson viewed as using a persuasive style would be self-oriented, while a problem-solving approach would require a salesperson to be more customer-oriented.

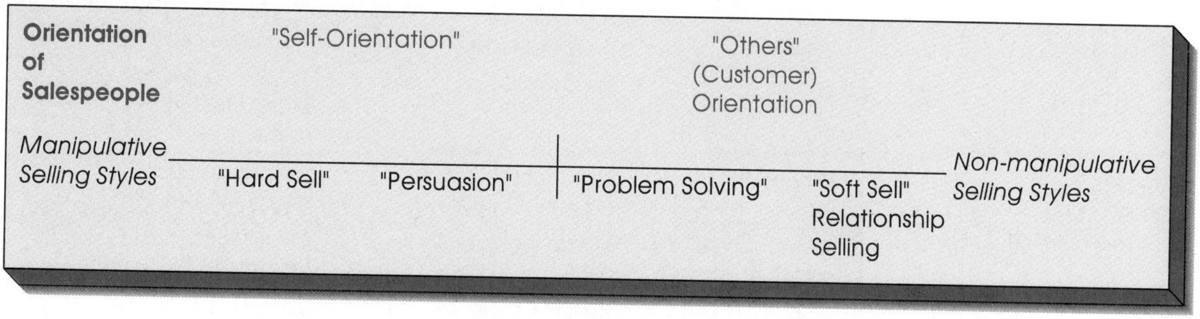

| Orientation of Salespeople | "Self-Orientation" | | "Others" (Customer) Orientation | | |
|---|---|---|---|---|---|
| Manipulative Selling Styles | "Hard Sell" | "Persuasion" | "Problem Solving" | "Soft Sell" Relationship Selling | Non-manipulative Selling Styles |

becomes a natural by-product of customer satisfaction.[11] For instance, the other-oriented salesperson works to help you find the washing machine that fits the small space in your apartment, fits your budget, and does a thorough job of washing your clothes so that you are pleased with the purchase. You will go to this same salesperson when you need another such product because a relationship built on trust has been established. Other-orientation selling styles include relationship selling, as discussed earlier, and problem-solving selling.

### Problem-Solving Selling

The **problem-solving style** involves less two-way communication in the form of information-seeking questions between the salesperson and the customer than in relationship selling. The problem-solving salesperson could be equated with a surgeon who must diagnose the problem and prescribe the right solution. This approach requires the salesperson to develop a presentation using more of a questioning (listening) attitude than a persuasive (telling) attitude, as Table 2–1 shows.[12] However, problem-solving salespeople are trying to show how *their* product best solves the customer's problem more than any others in the market. Their emphasis is on solving the problem with *their* product rather than just satisfying the customer's needs in the best possible way. Therefore with a problem-solving style, the tendency is to concentrate on the immediate problem rather than to build a long-term relationship.

**problem-solving style**

## Self-Orientation

As seen through a customer's eyes, the left side of the continuum in Figure 2–3 emphasizes different selling styles—the self-oriented styles. The **self-**

**self-oriented**

Table 2-1
**Two Ways to Consider Sales**

|  | Self-Orientation | Customer-Orientation |
|---|---|---|
| *Goal* | A signed order | A satisfied customer |
| *Scope* | Sell as much as possible | Give complete service even after making the sale |
| *Procedure* | Sell as much as possible on each contact | Probe with questions, define the problem |
| *Comparative excerpts from sales dialogues* | ``I can increase your profits by 30 percent.'' <br><br> ``Let me show you this fabulous line.'' | ``If this line would increase your profits 30 percent, would you be interested?'' <br><br> ``Tell me about your plans.'' |

**oriented** approach of the hard-sell and the persuasive styles means that the salesperson treats customers as objects. The manipulative, self-oriented salesperson *uses* the customer to meet his or her own ends.

Some people equate these manipulative styles, the hard-sell and persuasive styles, with negative connotations of selling. To them, salespeople are "fast talkers," "often unethical," and have the "gift of gab." **Manipulative methods** result from salespeople's self-serving motives. Thus helping you find the right washing machine for your apartment is secondary to the salesperson's desire of earning commission.[13]

Persuasive selling has fewer elements of the self-oriented style than the hard-sell style. Customers are convinced to buy goods or services through the persuasive efforts of the salesperson. Here salespeople try to convince you that their particular clothes washer is better than any other washer on the market. Although persuasive-style salespeople move toward the problem-solving efforts encouraged by the marketing concept, they are still using their own gain as the reason for making a sale. Refer to Table 2–1, which shows the differences in the self-oriented and customer-oriented sales styles.

Customers have used a personal, problem-solving approach to *buying* for years. In fact, they enter the marketplace to solve problems. Salespeople are learning a problem-solving selling style from their customers; they are learning that buying is a problem-solving process that can no longer be solved by rote presentations, hard-sell tactics, or use of

**manipulative methods**

impersonal persuasion. Tom Reilly, President of Sales Motivational Services, points out the advantages of changing the selling style:

> Those who fail to adapt will fall to the wayside. For those
> who adapt, the future is bright. It will be an era of
> challenge, fulfillment, prosperity, and growth.

# Reasons to Practice Relationship Selling

For those who hesitate about selling because they feel they will need to be too aggressive, impersonal, and uncaring about clients' needs, relationship selling can reassure them that the opposite approach is possible. Table 2–2 contrasts traits of relationship and nonrelationship sellers. The relationship salesperson gets involved in client needs; stresses meeting needs after the sale; gets involved in future planning with clients; is creative in solving problems; builds trust with clients; and becomes an information source for the client. Contrarily, nonrelationship sellers are self-oriented and are involved in enhancing their lives, not solving the client's needs.

**Table 2-2**
**Traits of Relationship versus Nonrelationship Sellers**

| The Relationship Salesperson | The Nonrelationship Salesperson (Hard Sell and Persuasive) |
| --- | --- |
| Solves client's problems rather than maximizing commissions | Sells the product that makes the most commission |
| Stresses customer service beyond the product purchase | Pushes to get a signed order |
| Plans with clients to minimize problems that may occur in the future. | Maximizes sales efforts each day to reach monthly quotas |
| Seeks new ways to meet client's needs with currently available products | Emphasizes how products fit recurring problems that clients in the industry face |
| Builds trust through customer satisfaction gained in the follow-through after the sale | Feels customer satisfaction is expressed by a client's purchasing a product, not by following up on the sale |

But salespeople have not always used a relationship approach. The evolution of relationship selling occurred over several years. To better appreciate this, we take the advice of Oliver Wendell Holmes, Jr.:

> When I want to understand what is happening today or try to decide what will happen tomorrow, I look back.

We now look back at the history of selling and selling styles.

## A Historical Perspective of Selling

Looking at the past allows one to assess advantages and disadvantages of an era and to gain knowledge that can point to trends for future success. A look at the history of sales can show how selling has changed and can yield insight into the future of the profession.[14] Historically we could trace the profession of selling to Biblical times. Egyptian, Phoenician, Greek, and Roman empires have well-documented activities on expanding trade. This text, however, generalizes only on the current century in the United States. Table 2–3 shows a historical perspective of selling philosophies and selling styles.

**Table 2-3**
**A Historical Interpolation of Selling**

|  | Business Philosophy | Prevalent Selling Styles |
|---|---|---|
| Preindustrialization (Pre-1920) | "Make the goods!" | Less emphasis on selling |
| Industrialization (1920–1950) | "Sell the product!" | Hard-sell approach |
| Post-War (1950–1965) | "Market the product!" | Persuasive approach |
| Revitalization of Consumerism (1965–Present) | "Satisfy the customer!" | Problem-solving approach |
| Future Evolution (1990–...) | "Help the customer!" | Consultative approach (relationship selling) |

## Preindustrialization Period (Pre-1920)

The period before 1920 was dominated by consumers' demands for manufactured goods that far exceeded companies' abilities to supply them. The agrarian society in the United States was changing. People were moving to the city for jobs that paid better than farm labor. Lifestyles changed. Manufacturers now had a labor force with which to fill this growing demand for manufactured goods. The business philosophy of the time was to fulfill the demand before someone else did—"make the goods!" No longer was the largest part of the population self-reliant. City dwellers had become dependent on others for goods and services. Generally everything produced could be sold with little effort. Emphasis therefore was on manufacturing goods rather than selling them. Competition existed but was not as intense as it is today.

## Industrialization Period (1920–1950)

Rapid expansion of manufacturing plants and of the rail network made great strides in reversing the excess demand of the previous era. Industrial capacity and corporate farms were efficiently generating surplus between 1920 and 1950. The importance of the salesperson was becoming evident: the salesperson emerged as the principal contact between business and the customer. Competition forced a business manager's focus away from production to stress *selling* as a primary function of business.

      The business philosophy most prevalent between 1920 and 1950 was "sell the product!" Sales training efforts centered around **hard-sell** tactics, typified by the back-slapping, high-pressure salesperson who won't take no for an answer. Other salespeople depended on a memorized or "canned" sales presentation. Both tactics were impersonal, and resentment grew among consumers toward these depersonalized approaches.

**hard sell**

## Post-War Era (1950–1965)

After World War II, a trend toward *personal selling* began to emerge. **Personal selling** can be defined as an interpersonal, persuasive process designed to influence the buying decision process. The business environment had changed from a seller's market to a buyer's market. With the rise of the marketing concept, all parts of the organization were beginning to be geared toward solving the customer's problems.[15] The American economy began to be **"market oriented,"** that is, the economy was controlled by the marketplace, not the manufacturers. In this type of economy, economic

**personal selling**

**market oriented**

decisions are determined for the most part by the consumers in the marketplace rather than by political leaders. All members of the economy—consumers, workers, and producers—have considerable latitude of choice in the marketplace; and profit incentives eliminate inefficient producers and stimulate growth. The marketing concept holds that the key to achieving organizational goals consists in determining the needs and wants of customers and delivering the desired satisfactions more efficiently and effectively than competitors.[16] Competition was intense and led to an evolution from the hard-sell to less "power-selling" tactics.

**persuasive approach**

**persuasion**

The prevalent selling style of the postwar era was a muted version of the hard-sell, the **persuasive approach.** Rather than overpowering customers with "pushiness," salespeople relied on the power of persuasion. According to Webster's *New World Dictionary,* **persuasion** is an open appeal, either rational or emotional, to influence someone into action or belief. Salespeople tried to persuade buyers that their products would solve customers' problems better than a competitor's product. Customers had a choice of which products to buy, and the hard-sell approach was no longer acceptable. The persuasive approach retained the emphasis on emotional appeals used in the hard-sell, which some customers still found offensive. New selling styles began to evolve more rapidly.

## Revitalization of Consumerism (1965–Present)

Unfortunately not all businesses adopted the marketing concept. Some firms saw marketing from only the external viewpoint—getting the right product, to the right person, in the right place, at the right price, at the right time. Since marketing involves both external factors (product, promotion, place, price, and time) and internal factors (customers' needs and wants) sellers needed to devote more time to defining and fulfilling customers' desires. In the last 25 years this has happened. Increased attention to consumers has increased the cost of selling. Indeed, costs of industrial sales calls (including inflation) increased in ten years from less than $100 per call in 1980 to $250 per call in 1989.[17]

In this period, consumers have also become more vocal about their likes and dislikes, and protests against consumer abuses in the marketplace have become more common than ever before. On the national level, more consumer protection laws were passed between 1965 and 1985 than in the entire U.S. history through 1964.[18] In this most recent period, the hue and cry of the consumer has been for satisfaction; therefore business philosophy has been *"satisfy the customer!"*

As lists of competing suppliers grew, salespeople found "selling harder" did not work; they had to learn to "sell smarter." Today's salespeople no longer concentrate on just increasing sales volume, but instead they focus on segmenting the buyers into "most qualified buyers" in terms of appropriate needs and profitability as well as individualized customer satisfaction and problem solving.[19] With problem solving, the purpose of the sales call is not just to satisfy the salesperson's need to make a sale, but also to satisfy *customers'* problems, unfulfilled needs, and wants. People buy services or products most often because they feel that they and their problems are understood by the seller, not because the buyer is made to understand the product by an insistent salesperson.[20] The problem-solving approach used by salespeople more closely follows the total marketing concept.

## The Future of this Sales Evolution

New sales approaches have evolved, as we have seen, because of changing business conditions. Predicting the future accurately, if not impossible, is difficult at best. Looking at continuing trends in buying behavior, how-

The future of sales will bring increased demands from customers for more information in a timely fashion.

ever, makes the prediction much easier. Some trends as described below seem fairly obvious.[21] These are:

1. *Buyers will remain vocal.* Most buyers are not willing to "sit down and shut up" concerning consumer abuses and their wants.[22] Consumerism is a business condition with which to be reckoned.

2. *Buyers will continue to demand more information.* One of the most frequently heard buyer complaints is lack of enough information to make an accurate judgment.[23] To meet the specific needs of the buyer, sellers will combine their efforts with other experts in their company to face problems in a team effort,[24] as Mike Blades and Bob Helscher have done (see *Partnerships*). More professional training and certification of organizational buyers present greater opportunities for professional sales efforts.

3. *Time will become a more important factor in the buying decision process.* The advent of mail-order shopping, direct marketing, and telemarketing

## PARTNERSHIPS

*There is no question that Mike Blades has done a fantastic job organizing the branch and helping it reach its potential. But a significant part of the Tampa branch's success stems from Bill Jones' willingness to make field calls with our salespeople.*

**Bob Helscher, President of Allied Fastener & Tool**

Tampa's branch of Allied Tool is consistently able to win big construction jobs because of help from Mike Blades, Branch Manager, and W. E. "Bill" Jones, District Manager for ITW Ramset/Redhead manufacturing company. The Tampa branch's sales grew 20 percent in 1989 under Mike's supervision. Both Blades and Jones agree that the key to their success depends on the business relationship between them. They both took the time to define clearly each other's role in the partnership. Blades says this team-oriented strategy with ITW Ramset/Redhead is the reason why he and his staff have won a number of major orders for Ramset/Redhead products with contractors. "We've been very successful promoting the partnership idea," says Blades. "Customers understand that as a distributor, Allied provides the local support, and ITW supplies the strength of a large national manufacturer."

*Source:* Steve Zurier, "Team Effort Earns Construction Sales," *Industrial Distribution* (May 1990). Reprinted from *Industrial Distribution*, May 1990, Cahners Publishing Company.

have helped buyers to minimize the time spent making purchase decisions. Since time is important to clients, salespeople strive to help buyers minimize the amount of time spent between the recognition of a problem and a purchase decision.[25] For example, a Maytag salesperson who has information on all the washing machines available can minimize the amount of time a buyer searches for the correct machine.

All of these trends point in the direction of relationship selling as they demand that salespeople, to achieve sales effectiveness, adapt their presentations to the client's problems.

Two examples of such adaptation are the telephone companies and the industrial distribution industry. For the most part, the telephone company helps the customer determine the problem and then designs a system to fit the present needs. As for the industrial distribution industry, rather than just selling clients standard products, industrial distributors have progressed into helping them develop inventory control systems which minimize the inventory needed, in hopes of building longer relationships.

In the future, such examples will be more common, as sales approaches will become more relationship-oriented. Indicators point toward a more helping relationship between salesperson and buyers.[26] Salespeople will be involved in establishing and managing relationships between themselves and clients.[27] The strength of these relationships will be based on the efficiency of the salesperson to adapt to a consultative, relationship stance geared to the client's needs rather than just selling products.[28]

A recent Forum Corporation study shows current outstanding sales achievers make every call count by:

- Focusing on customer needs
- Being frank about their product performance
- Asking smart questions: they don't presume to know everything
- Managing their own company's resources to the customer's advantage
- Acting as the buyer's partner to build a bridge to profitability
- Planning strategies from the customer's point of view.[29]

All of these features indicate the use of relationship selling by outstanding sales achievers. Each of the qualities of sales achievers in the Forum study shows the growing need to adopt relationship selling. To achieve sales goals in the future, salespeople will have to have more knowledge concerning their products as well as the competition. Use of high-technology selling tools such as fax machines, laptop or notebook computers, and electronic data interchange will be necessary to keep up-to-the-minute sales information on customers. Sales gains will come from

## TECHNOLOGY BULLETIN

### Computers

In what is the largest installation to date of sales-oriented, full-function portable PCs, Chrysler will spend $5 million outfitting 600 account managers (salespeople) with laptops. The program goal, says Paul Berrigan, Chrysler's manager of sales information, "is to give the account managers the information they need to make effective calls on dealers." Special application software written by Chrysler staff enables them to use the laptops (Grid Systems' GridCase 3) to download information. All Software is user-friendly, menu-driven for use by first-time users. They can download information from as many as 10 different databases that are a part of Chrysler's Professional Analysis and Communication System. When preparing for a call on a dealer, the sales manager can download information, as current as sales up to the previous day. The laptops were the natural choice "because the managers are on the road most of the time and we wanted them to have access to information all of the time. Also, because the laptop is available to them all the time, we felt the new technology would be accepted faster than with the intermittent use of a desktop or transportable."

*Source:* Thayer C. Taylor, "The Computer in Sales and Marketing," *Sales and Marketing Management* 142 (June 1986): 82.

better time management to allow more selling time, better understanding of international business, and the development of better relationships with customers. For those who adapt to these trends, the future is bright.

To examine exactly what characteristics will be necessary for this adaptation, we now look at the traits of effective relationship salespeople.

## Traits of Effective Relationship Salespeople

How a person sells is important to success, but individual traits are equally important. Some personal traits are important to success in relationship selling. Successful salespersons are *determined* to get ahead. Their ambition and willingness to work long hours, often under discouraging circumstances, give them spirit and pride in achieving goals. The *patience* and *perseverance* of an effective seller complement his or her determination. The persevering salesperson uses patience in calling on qualified prospects repeatedly and regularly, never knowing when the prospect will say "yes" to buying a product.[30]

A salesperson needs the *initiative* of a self-starter.[31] Personal goals, rather than those of sales managers, motivate the self-starter. By performing without close supervision, salespeople with this orientation learn to rely on their own resources rather than the resources of others. They constantly search for ways to improve both themselves and their companies.

*Enthusiasm* is another priceless quality. Enthusiasm reflects the salesperson's interest in the product, the company, and the customer, and plays a vital role in a demonstration or sales presentation. If the salesperson cannot be enthusiastic about the company and its products, how can the customer be enthusiastic about them? Happily, this quality is infectious; it builds self-confidence within the salesperson, and promotes the customer's confidence in the salesperson, the company, and its product.

Knowledge and experience result in the development and nurturing of *confidence*. This requires believing in oneself and having a healthy respect for one's own capabilities. Confidence allows the salesperson to overcome the fear of being rejected—the fear of the customer's saying "no." A confident salesperson continues to the next call even if the last customer happened to say "no" to purchasing.

*Sincerity* is essential to gaining the prospect's continuing trust and confidence.[32] Prospects can often distinguish the sincere from the insincere, and they usually buy from sales representatives who are honest and committed to serving them. Salespeople who demonstrate hypocrisy or insincerity reduce their chances of obtaining an order, since the link of trust between a customer and a salesperson is built on honesty and sincerity. Each of these traits—determination, initiative, enthusiasm, confidence, and sincerity—contributes to effectiveness in sales.[33]

> Many salespeople say that they like working with people. That's not enough to succeed. Sales success only begins when we enjoy serving people.
>
> **Gerhard Gschwandtner**

## Summary

Selling is a face-to-face, interactive dialogue between two or more people. At some point in their lives, all people sell either a product, a service, or an idea.

Relationship selling is a helping, nonmanipulative, consultative role. The salesperson's motive is to add value to the customer's decision process by providing information about products and services available in the marketplace to best satisfy the customers' needs and wants and develop a long-term relationship. This relationship is built on a trusting, nonmanipulative two-way interaction between the client and the salesperson. Because of the abundance of products and services, customers seek more and better information, resulting in a trend toward relationship selling.

A look at the history of selling reveals that changes in market conditions shifted the emphasis from a self-orientation selling style to an other-oriented selling style. Movement continues today from a problem-solving approach to a more customer-oriented approach—relationship selling.

## Key Terms

selling
relationship selling (consultative
  approach)
double-win philosophy
win-lose philosophy
differential advantage
marketing concept
nonmanipulative methods
trust link
primary information

secondary information
other-orientation
problem-solving style
self-oriented
manipulative methods
hard sell
personal selling
market oriented
persuasive approach
persuasion

## Discussion Questions

1. Define selling.

2. Describe the selling environment before 1920. What were the major attributes of salespersons of that time?

3. How did the industrialization and post-war eras change the selling environment? What changes did salespeople make?

4. Explain business conditions since the 1960s and their effects on a selling career. What changes are expected for the future?

5. Compare and contrast the self-orientation and other-orientation sales styles. Which is better? Why?

6. What is the relationship selling philosophy?

7. Explain the difference between problem-solving selling and relationship selling.

# Decision Crossroads: Ethical Issues

In the classroom portion of the sales training program at A. B. Graphics, Michele Pollard learned about the company's emphasis on building strong relationships with its customers. Now in the second portion of the training, her sales manager, Jose Casanova, was stressing different things. He expressed the following sentiments:

> Do what you have to do to make your sales goals. That relationship stuff is nice, but you are rewarded on the bottom line, sales. Relationship selling depends on long-run partnerships, and sales goals depend on short-run objectives. Look Michele, it all boils down to this: 'gravy yeah, gravy nay.' You sell, you eat; you don't sell, you don't eat. Relationships come later. You have to decide.

Discussion:

1. Would you choose to follow Mr. Casanova's approach or the company's approach? What is your reasoning?
2. What are possible repercussions of your choice?

## Case 2-1   **Mead Corporation**

Bob Meredith, salesperson for Mead Corporation, makers of printing machines and supplies, has worked with Carl Ramsey of Ramsey Printing for over a year concerning Carl's need for a new printing machine. Bob realized during his evaluation of the available printing machines that would fit Carl's needs that his own product was overpriced. Therefore he was not averse to Carl's purchase of the Ziggler Machine. Bob switched his sales emphasis to providing supplies—negative film and paper—that were of better quality and at a lower price than Ziggler's. Rather than protesting Carl's purchase of a competitor's machine, Bob agreed that the Ziggler machine was the best buy and proceeded to show how his supplies and services could improve the quality of Carl's product and his profits.

Discussion:

1. Should Bob have justified the purchase price of his equipment as being superior and pushed for a close? Closed by appealing to Carl's friendship?
2. Do you feel Bob's attitude built trust between he and Carl?
3. What do you think Bob's sales manager's reaction would be if he or she were listening to the above conversation?

## Case 2-2  **Doug Marx's Career Choice**

The clock on the wall read 2:45 P.M. Doug was startled from a doze in his sales class when Dr. Hawes asked a question of him. "What do you want to do with your life, Doug?" he asked. Startled, Doug had to admit that he was not paying attention but that he would think about it. "You bet you will," said the professor, "because for tomorrow's assignment, I want you to give me two pages of how you are going to find out if selling is a career for you after you get out of college. That is *if you do!*" he continued. "That goes for the whole class. Class dismissed," stated Dr. Hawes. Doug quickly set up an appointment at the guidance and counseling office on campus to use the computerized career guidance program. He knew it would give him a five-page printout that would be a good resource for Dr. Hawes' paper.

### Discussion:

1. Evaluate Doug's procedure to respond to Dr. Hawes' paper.
2. How would you decide if selling is a good career choice for you? What sources would you use? Which sources are the best?
3. What qualities of a sales career fit what you are looking for in a career. What qualities do you think are necessary to be a successful salesperson? Why?
4. Do you have the qualities that it takes to make sales a successful career? If not, do you want to develop them? Is it possible to develop them?

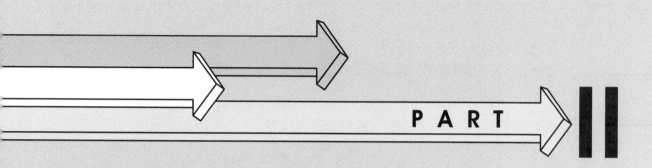

# Learning Selling Skills

Part I presented an overview of career opportunities in sales, discussed the history of sales, and examined the selling profession and selling styles with emphasis on a consultative approach to relationship selling. Following a career path format, Part II first examines how salespeople are trained, how they gain product knowledge, and selling's place in marketing theory. Next it examines communication skills that help buyers and sellers in the decision process. Finally it examines how and why people purchase items.

**Chapter Outline**

An Overview of Sales Training Programs

Components of Initial Sales Training
- Company Knowledge
- Product Knowledge
- Promotion and Price Knowledge
- Policies
- Knowledge of Competitors
- Selling Techniques
- Marketing Theory
- Buyer Behavior Theory
- Dialogue Skills

Accomplishments of Sales Training

Beyond the Formal, Initial Sales Training
- Sales Refresher Training
- Sources of Information

Sales Training Program Implementation

# Gaining Product Information and Selling Skills

**Learning Objectives**

This chapter provides information on how to gain selling skills in sales training; after reading it, you should be able to:

- Discuss the purposes of sales training programs
- Understand phases of sales training programs
- Describe theory and skill components of training programs
- Explain the importance of information about a company and its products
- Explain the importance of information about competitors and their products
- Recognize sources of information.

## IN THE FIELD

If ever there was a corporation that relationships built, it is Comdisco, a $1 billion-a-year computer leasing company in Chicago. Chief Executive Kenneth N. Pontikes, age 47, a former IBM salesman who founded the company in 1969, had a theory about selling: the way to win is to build long-term relationships instead of chasing transactions. So he recruited the best salespeople he could find and instructed them not to "hustle" for sales. "Just let people get to know us," he said. Pontikes did not want to hear his salespeople boasting when they closed a deal. He just wanted to know how they did it: did the customer want a long-term relationship, or did the salesman get lucky? Was this strategy successful? Comdisco's return on equity has averaged 28 percent over the last five years. And their two top salespeople, each of whom started out with a $20,000 salary, now earn over $500,000 a year, four times more than IBM's best salespeople make. Using a consultative approach to develop a long-term relationship is paying off for the company and its salespeople.

*Source:* Monci Jo Williams, *Fortune.* © 1987 Time Inc. All rights reserved.

This chapter discusses the skills salespeople are expected to use to be successful. As will be seen, these skills are developed during sales training.

A person joining a company's sales force often is full of anxieties and fears. The novice asks: Will I be successful? Do I have enough confidence in myself? What do I remember from college? Anyone beginning a career in selling can have feelings of inadequacy and fear of the unknown, as can people in other careers. Most of these fears come from facing situations of uncertainty and thereby risking failure. But good **sales training** and being well informed minimize these fears and prevent poor selling traits (see *In the Field*) from occurring in you.

**sales training**

Companies realize that growing business depends on successful salespeople to ensure their success, so they generally provide sales training programs to cultivate their salespeople. These programs are designed to instill self-confidence by teaching people the foundations for successful selling and the tools with which to stimulate productivity. Sales training and product knowledge reduce anxieties and fears as beginners develop sales skills that increase their efficiency in helping customers, as shown by the following statement:

> Since our largest single expense is people, first on your list of improving productivity must be the stimulation of people.   **Mervin G. Morris, Chairman, Mervyn's of California**[1]

The "stimulation of people" that Mr. Morris mentioned is one of management's chief concerns in training salespeople. Salespeople need training in the skills of selling to be successful. Researchers have identified significant qualities necessary for an effective professional salesperson. These are:

- One must want to succeed.
- One must get along with people.
- One must exercise self-discipline.
- One must develop selling skills.
- One must have product knowledge.
- One must have the ability to listen and to empathize with the customer.[2]

The desire to succeed is necessary for achievement, since personal motivation compels action. It is hard to teach, but self-motivation, as self-discipline, can be learned. Knowing how to get along with people also is essential in any marketing career but is especially so for a salesperson who must listen and empathize in face-to-face contacts with customers.

Training programs focus on developing one's product knowledge and sales skills and then communicating product knowledge. Companies design their sales training programs to educate the beginner on the basics and to provide refresher training for the experienced salesperson. Beginners need to understand how knowledge gained in sales training is valuable in building effective sales skills. Sales productivity then comes from the application of these key skills.

## An Overview of Sales Training Programs

Roerig Division of Pfizer, Inc., a pharmaceutical company, spends $40,000 annually in training each new salesperson.[3] Why would a company devote so much time, energy, and money to increasing its personnel's sales effectiveness and efficiency? Through sales training, sales managers can develop a more productive staff, thus increasing sales revenues.

Most sales training programs consist of two phases. These are: *phase 1,* initial sales training; and *phase 2,* sales refresher training.

Although sales training programs differ from company to company, all cover some common topics. The **initial sales training** program places greatest emphasis on product knowledge, selling techniques, and on learning about the company and its competitors. Some training programs include the use of mentors, experienced successful salespeople, to help newcomers learn about the company (see Technology Bulletin). Ap-

**initial sales training**

Sales training is an
important part of
effective professional
selling.

plication of theory about how a buyer makes a decision, communications
skills, personal motivators, and routine company information receive less
attention. Phase 1 at Roche Biomedical Laboratories starts with classroom
training, as described below by Karen McFadden, division sales manager
for Roche.

> We start with a formal training process. We orient the new
> employees to our business standards and professional
> selling skills necessary to sell in our industry. This is
> followed by several weeks in the field with different
> representatives to give the trainees a flavor of the various
> styles and selling techniques they might use. This phase
> typically lasts for less than one year.[4]

**sales refresher
training**

The second phase of sales training takes place a year or more after
the initial phase has ended. In phase 2, **sales refresher training,** the focus
shifts to improving sales techniques by correcting inefficient sales skills
that may have developed and learning new sales motivating techniques.
Lighter emphasis is placed on new product information and competitive
changes in the marketplace. Phase 2 generally lasts for less than one month
and occurs periodically during a sales career. Since this text follows a

**career path format**

**career path format** (how you progress from initial sales job to advanced
positions), interest at this time is primarily in phase one—the initial sales
program.

## TECHNOLOGY BULLETIN

### Training

Ask recruiters and trainers what's hot and they all agree—mentor programs. Mentor programs allow novice salespeople to work with experienced, successful salespeople as a part of their sales training experiences. Schering-Plough, Colgate, Johnson & Johnson, AT&T, Pathfinder software, Bellcore, and Pacific Bell are sophisticated users of mentor programs. Programs, usually 12 months in length, are intended for new hires who are likely to have problems settling in. The goal is to make the new hires at home in their jobs, teach them corporate culture, and provide them with a source to go to for advice. Each individual is paired with a ''mentor'' who ideally is a good motivator and teacher and who reflects the company's values. Schering-Plough credits its program for winning some of the nation's best qualified new hires.

*Source:* Arthur Bragg, ''Is A Mentor Program in Your Future,'' *Sales and Marketing Management* 141 (July 1990):20. Reprinted by permission: © Feb. 1990.

## Components of Initial Sales Training ▬▬▬▬

Initial sales training sessions concentrate on knowledge of company history, products, promotions, prices, and policies; competition knowledge; and sales techniques; that is, the dialogue between customers and sales representatives (discussed in detail in *Part III*). Initial sessions also cover the basics of marketing, buyer behavior theory, and communication skills to show beginners how the many aspects of sales mesh and to orient newcomers to the sales environment. The makeup of such a program is shown in Table 3–1.

## Company Knowledge

Since salespeople are placed in direct competition in their territories with other firms' salespeople, they must understand their own company's history of growth and development. Its past goals, its present status, and its future outlook constitute important information for a salesperson. This knowledge provides not only background but also direction for the individual's sales and career planning. For example, John Deere set new goals directed toward more involvement in the lawn equipment industry, which included phasing out its involvement in the all-terrain vehicle business.

Table 3-1
**Composition of Initial Sales Training Program**

| Heavy Emphasis | Light Emphasis |
|---|---|
| *Company knowledge concerning:* | |
| Company history | Marketing theory |
| Products | Buyer behavior theory |
| Promotion | Company organization |
| Price | Dialogue skills |
| Policies | |
| *Competitive knowledge concerning:* | |
| (Same elements as *Company Knowledge* (above) | |
| *Selling techniques of:* | |
| Prospecting | |
| Strategy formulation | |
| Prospect contact and needs assessment | |
| Presentation | |
| Need fulfillment or conflict resolution or both | |
| Closes | |
| Follow-up | |

Knowing about this change, salespeople concentrated their efforts on the lawn and garden equipment area.

Other important topics concerning a company are when the company was founded; by whom; why it was founded; and the principles on which it was founded. More important, however, are facts concerning company plant capacity, industry sales ranking, and trademarks. These facts help one analyze the company's position in comparison to its competitors, and they can be used to form a solid sales presentation.

## Product Knowledge

When people speak of a salesperson's superior product knowledge, they often are speaking about more than knowledge of a particular good or service. They are talking about the total knowledge a salesperson possesses. In this sense, when people discuss a person's **product knowledge,**

**product knowledge**

it includes information about company history, product information, present and future product promotions, and the firm's pricing policies. Sales productivity has been directly correlated to the knowledge a salesperson uses, and this is important because:

- Customers demand facts that are translated into benefits of purchasing the good or service.
- Competition and customers force knowledgeable salespeople to compare products.
- Knowledge concerning product offerings instills customer confidence plus salesperson self-confidence.

Salespeople representing their company are expected to be experts on the products they sell. Some buyers may want to know detailed information on the manufacture of a product such as hydraulic hoses. They may ask what materials are used, how it is made, and what is done to ensure quality control. Other buyers may believe the company's name speaks for its value. To be prepared for all buyers, the salespeople must know specifications on component parts and materials; how the product is made; policies of delivery, credit, warranties, maintenance, and pricing; and product promotions.

Knowing product features is insufficient. To be effective the salesperson must also learn what the client needs, what benefits they are seek-

Salespeople representing their company are expected to be experts on the products they sell.

customer benefits

ing, and how products satisfy specific needs. Salespeople rely on extensive product knowledge to help them convert features of a product into **customer benefits** (i.e., what the consumer gets from the purchase) during the sales presentation. Buyers are not interested in factual knowledge unless it relates to fulfilling their needs, as shown in Table 3–2.

FAB technique

Knowing how to translate one's knowledge about a product's features into customer benefits, called the **FAB (features, advantages, and benefits) technique,** helps a sales representative make up for other shortcomings. All salespeople should use the FAB technique. Salespeople practice benefit statements until they become second nature; success depends on it. Since each customer is different, the representative listens to a client's answers to the questions. These answers provide insights into product attributes most beneficial to satisfying that customer's needs.

As discussed in Chapter 2, knowing what distinguishes their product from competitors' products is called a differential advantage. One such differential product advantage is performance, and performance features are always discussed during sales presentations. Good salespeople learn to present features in terms the buyer can understand, namely, benefits they are seeking, such as the following:

- Car sellers talk about gas mileage and reliability to buyers looking for economy and reliable transportation.
- Paint sellers talk about durability, spreadability, and coverage as well as markup and turnover on the product.
- Electronic field representatives talk to television dealers discussing clarity and quality of the picture of the product as well as the brand acceptance consumers have.

Table 3-2
**Features, Advantages, and Benefits of a Zenith Laptop Computer**

| Feature | Advantage | Benefit to Client |
|---|---|---|
| Weighs 9¼ lb. | Provides portability | Increased productivity of the system and increased return on investment |
| Full-size, backlit, black-on-white LCD screen | Displays 25 lines by 80 characters | Easy readability, reduces eye fatigue, increases productivity |
| 386 chip with a 80386 processor | Provides latest state-of-the-art microcomputer technology | Faster solutions to most modern business and professional needs |

- Photocopy representatives mention speed in copies per minute, quality, and dependability.

Customers understand these terms because they represent performance benefits they want to receive from the product. Benefits are used for product comparisons.

## Promotion and Price Knowledge

Salespeople have to know the history of the company's promotional policies plus current and future promotions. The ability to use this knowledge often makes the difference between happy and unhappy customers or between a sale and a rejection. A menswear representative showing Arrow shirts, for example, should be aware that in eight weeks the company is going to reduce shirt prices to dealers for its annual two-for-one sale. The buyer may delay a large order to take advantage of this offer.

    Knowledge of pricing policies is important because the salesperson is often responsible for quoting **price,** which legally binds the company. Since salespeople often have flexibility in adjusting price to meet customer demands or the competition, knowledge of pricing terms is imperative. Common expressions in quoting and discounting price are: **price**

- **List price.** The published base retail price (listed in price sheets and catalogues) from which buyers receive discounts. **list price**
- **Net price.** The price clients pay after all discounts and allowances are deducted. For comparative purposes, buyers often use this price to evaluate suppliers. **net price**
- **Zone price.** The price based on geographic location. **zone price**
- **FOB price.** FOB (free—or freight—on board) means that the freight is paid by the shipper to the location designated after the FOB term. **FOB price**
  - **FOB shipping point.** Means shipping costs are assumed by the buyer when it is loaded on board the transportation unit. **FOB shipping point**
  - **FOB destination.** Means that the seller pays the freight to the buyer's designated location. **FOB destination**
- **Quantity discounts.** Used to entice one to make larger purchases. One-time reductions in price are **noncumulative quantity discounts.** A Johnson Wax representative might offer 2 dozen cans of Pledge® for every 24 dozen the buyer purchases. Discounts received for buying a certain amount over time are designed to induce continued purchasing. Such discounts are called **cumulative quantity discounts.** Levi Strauss may give an additional 12 percent discount when a purchaser accumulates purchases of $12,000 in womens blue jean jackets. **quantity discounts** / **noncumulative quantity discounts** / **cumulative quantity discounts**

**trade discounts**

- **Trade discounts.** Used to compensate marketing middlemen (wholesalers and retailers) for the services they perform. This discount is usually stated off the list price. The wholesaler may be offered a 60 percent discount off the list price, or the manufacturer may sell directly to the retailer at a 50 percent discount. The wholesaler's price to its retail customers is 10 percent above its cost, or 50 percent off the list price. Trade discounts provide sufficient margins to cover the costs and a reasonable profit for the functions rendered by the middlemen.

**cash discounts**

- **Cash discounts.** Earned by the buyers who pay their bills early within a stated time period. For example, a company who purchases goods with the cash discount terms of 2/10, n/30 (2 percent in 10 days, net in 30 days) may deduct a 2 percent discount from the net price if the company pays the bill within ten days of the invoice or the stated period listed on the invoice. Otherwise the total is due in 30 days.

**promotional allowances**

- **Promotional allowances.** Monetary or free goods (e.g., $100 promotional allowance or buy 12 cases, get 1 case free) compensation used to promote the products in the marketplace. In considering prices for advertising, some companies will share part of the advertising costs for their productions with retail stores (called **cooperative, or co-op advertising**), provided the retailer's advertisements comply with the company's co-op advertising specifications.

**cooperative (co-op) advertising**

Price actually consists of one or more discounts or allowances made for specific purposes. Prices will vary within the same industry and therefore can be a differential advantage. Sales trainees need complete understanding of their company's pricing policies. Does the company sell for a set price, or can the salesperson negotiate? Can the salesperson give additional discounts, take trade-ins, or change prices for a buyer who purchases goods out of season?

## Policies

To ensure consistent decisions throughout the organization, companies implement policies to control such factors as prices, promotions, guarantees, and sales expense reimbursement. Knowing the company's policies prevents misunderstandings. For example, if a representative says yes to a customer's request to return goods 45 days after receipt when company policy is 30 days, the company can refuse to accept the returned merchandise. The salesperson looks incompetent to both sales manager and customer. After paying freight costs on the ill-advised returned goods to and from the factory, the angry customer may never buy from the salesperson again.

In addition, purchasing agents for manufacturing companies look for such other features as service and delivery. Service distinguishes products in the market. It implies the company's commitment to satisfied customers. A manufacturer must have dependable service for its plants or it cannot effectively schedule its work force. Factory-trained personnel available on short notice present further evidence of the company's integrity and its desire to maintain the product's reputation. Warranties are another example of service differential advantages. Curtis Mathes television sets, for instance, come with extended four-year picture-tube warranties, which is more than that offered by most competitors.

Shorter delivery time could be a differential advantage, but a word of caution is necessary because a salesperson who misstates a shipment date can expect a dissatisfied customer when predictions are not met. Manufacturers, farmers, and truckers are examples of people who cannot afford delays caused by equipment failure or slow service, so they are interested in a company's delivery record.

As a key to understanding company policies, salespeople must understand, too, the inner workings of their company and its organization. Every company has an organizational chart depicting its formal structure, and salespeople should be familiar with it. They need to know the names of department heads and management employees. Knowing the names of order processors and shipping department officials may help the seller expedite delivery for a customer. Being helpful and kind to all company personnel builds team spirit and a willingness to cooperate when a salesperson needs help in meeting a customer's needs.

## Knowledge of Competitors

Knowing about one's own company is not enough; the seller must have knowledge of competitors. A **competitor** is anyone who supplies goods or services that have the benefits a customer desires, so a thorough salesperson considers a customer's needs when trying to determine competition. The same information gathered about one's own company should be collected in reference to all of its competitors, both strong and weak, and their products, promotions, and prices. It is common for buyers to ask, "How does your product compare to the one I'm presently using?" Salespeople must know the relationship between their products and the other products in the market and be able to discuss the features, advantages, and benefits of the comparison.

**competitor**

Probably the quickest way a salesperson can become invaluable to a customer is to deliver complete, comparative product information in a sales presentation. Since the salesperson is presenting a company's products for a customer's decision, comparisons of competitors' products help customers consider the features and benefits of each to reach a more objective decision.

*Example:* Alice Miller entered a Dayton-Hudson department store and asked the salesperson in the furniture department, Don Davis, to show her an extra-firm mattress. Ms. Miller told the salesperson that she suffered from backaches and was buying a mattress on a physician's advice. Also, she said she had shopped at two other retailers, where she had seen competitive brands. Being a well-informed mattress salesman, Don soon discovered, through his questions, that Ms. Miller had limited her choice to Sealy Posturepedic and Simmons Beautyrest. He began using his product knowledge to explain that these two top-of-the-line mattresses were quite different in construction. However, both were designed to help alleviate problems similar to hers. Don continued, explaining facts about the mattresses and their benefits to her.

Alice Miller bought the mattress from Don, not because he was the only one who handled them but because he was the only one who contrasted features and benefits of the two mattresses and gave her information that made her decision easier.

Information about competitors' promotions can also be helpful, although it may be hard to get in advance. Many companies have promotions at traditional times (e.g., the January white sales, year-end clearances, and inventory sales). A wise salesperson should remember competitor's past promotions when scheduling a sale to be sure to give the customer the best bargain available.

**value-added sales presentation**

Most salespeople would like to know the policies of competitors because complete knowledge about all products that would fill the client's need or solve the problem helps deliver a **value-added sales presentation.** No salesperson can know everything, but salespeople should provide information to clarify the client's decision process. When a salesperson is unable to answer several questions during the dialogue, credibility suffers. After all, if the seller does not care enough to be informed, why should a customer care enough to buy the product? This information helps minimize decision-making frustrations for the customer. Unfortunately, complete information about competitors' policies is not readily available, although some may be obtained indirectly through customer contacts and by experience in the field.

## Selling Techniques

Initial training programs spend considerable time teaching the beginner the techniques of the sales process. These techniques of prospecting, strategy formulation, customer contact and need assessment, presentation, sales resistance, closing and follow-up provide a company perspective to the salespeople selling the products. A thorough initiation on finding prospects, planning sales presentations, and executing them together with learning procedures for follow-up comprise most of the initial sales training. Each of these areas is discussed in detail in Part III of the text. Learning sales techniques now, before entering a company as a sales trainee, will help you reduce the fear of uncertainty, minimize the risk of failure, and build self-confidence.

## Marketing Theory

The marketing concept can be thought of as the mortar that binds sales skills into an integrated, solid foundation for a career. Marketing includes all the activities involved in ''moving'' goods from the producer to the consumer—identifying needs, developing products, pricing, promoting, and distributing need-satisfying goods to the marketplace.

Marketing is built on two basic concepts: consumer orientation and profitability. Foremost among these is the idea that all company plans, policies, and operating procedures—the marketing mix—should be oriented toward satisfying a customer's needs. The second premise is that profitable sales volume, making the best use of physical and human resources, is a primary operating goal as firms consider alternative strategies to satisfy consumers.

Companies form strategies to verbalize their efforts to achieve these dual objectives, as shown in Figure 3–1. A **marketing strategy** is a comprehensive plan for using the **marketing mix variables:** product, price, distribution, and promotion. Strategies specify how a particular company plans to mix its marketing variables to meet customer needs. **marketing strategy**
**marketing mix**
**variables**

Since marketing does not take place in a controlled environment, strategies must allow for possible changes in the competitive, legal, political, economic, cultural, social, and technological environments in which all firms operate as well as changes in customer needs. Although innovations are being made in marketing strategies, the success or failure of the total marketing effort often hinges on the efforts of salespeople. The sales force is the one-to-one liaison between the company and the marketplace (the customers). Salespeople must understand both marketing theory and buyer behavior to communicate product knowledge effectively.

## Buyer Behavior Theory

Half of the customer–salesperson dialogue comes from prospective customers: how they think; what drives they have; what they, as individuals,

Figure 3-1
**The Marketing Environment**

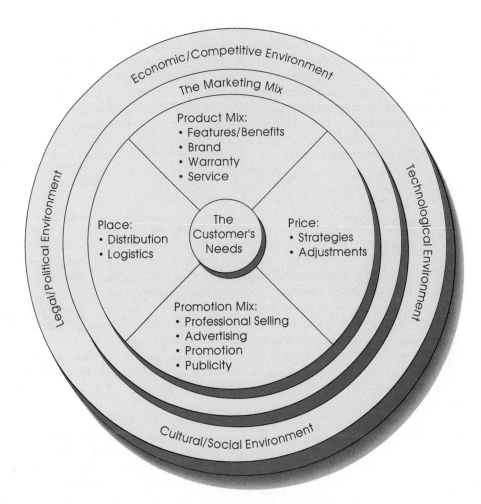

Economic/Competitive Environment

The Marketing Mix

Product Mix:
• Features/Benefits
• Brand
• Warranty
• Service

Place:
• Distribution
• Logistics

The Customer's Needs

Price:
• Strategies
• Adjustments

Promotion Mix:
• Professional Selling
• Advertising
• Promotion
• Publicity

Legal/Political Environment

Technological Environment

Cultural/Social Environment

want; what specific problems or incentives bring them into the marketplace. (Specifics of buyer behavior are discussed in Chapter 6.) These are all important types of information for a salesperson to know. This knowledge will more ably equip the salesperson to recognize and to help solve a customer's problem, which, after all, should be the basic reason for the sale. The better sales representatives know their customers' needs, the better their ability to render service to those customers.

## Dialogue Skills

One's knowledge is only as effective as his or her ability to communicate that knowledge. Sales training helps representatives develop skills needed to communicate a product's potential to satisfy a need. Therefore the sales-person often becomes an integral part of the **promotional mix** component of the marketing strategy. After all, the salesperson's ability to make a sale will depend on effective communication. The techniques of dialogue, talking, and listening are discussed in Chapters 4 and 5, respectively. Training programs emphasize dialogue techniques during the practicing of sales presentations.

**promotional mix**

## Accomplishments of Sales Training

Training should develop traits in a salesperson that are appealing to the customers. The best way to know what the customers want is to ask them. One training expert explains: "We teach our students to find out what customers' needs and wants are and how to satisfy them rather than teach how to get rid of whatever product of which they have a surplus. Good salespeople try to satisfy customers' needs, not salespeople's needs."[5]

Another philosophy toward training and hiring is expressed in the 1986 Annual Report of Parisian, Inc., a retail fashion clothier based in Birmingham, Alabama. Parisian says: "The culture of Parisian is not surprising when you consider the kind of people associated with the Company. We start by hiring nice people who already understand how customers want to be treated and then give them all the training and support that we can."[6] Another training program is described in *Partnerships.*

## Beyond the Formal, Initial Sales Training

Training and learning go beyond the formal, initial training program. Learning never ends! It is a continual, lifelong process. A salesperson who lacks accurate, up-to-date product knowledge cannot be successful.

## Sales Refresher Training

After selling for a while, sellers wish to increase their productivity. A variety of programs mainly concentrating on improving sales techniques, obtaining new product knowledge, and learning motivational techniques are offered or made available by most companies to their sales personnel. Some companies provide refresher training internally; others send their people to seminars, conferences, and schools to get this specialized train-

## PARTNERSHIPS

Thomas Golisano, president of Paychex Inc., a payroll-processing company, describes its sales training program as eight (not so) easy weeks. His comments follow:

"Weeks 1 and 2. So as not to 'culture shock' them, the trainees' first two weeks are spent orienting themselves to the atmosphere and routine in their home offices. One of the things we love to have them do is stay at night and watch the computer work.
Weeks 3 through 5. The recruits gather at the training center in Rochester, New York, where they're put up for three weeks and taught the technical intricacies of payroll accounting and reporting. If it were purely up to me, I would keep them longer. But we cram as much into them as we can before this session winds up with a comprehensive examination.
Weeks 6 and 7. The survivors (about one in 15 fails the technical test) return to their branches for sales presentation coaching by their managers.
Week 8. Back to Rochester for seven rigorous days, these to sharpen sales skills such as reading body language and dealing with client's personality types. Videotaping is used extensively."

*Source:* Robert A. Mamis, "How to Manage Your Sales Force," *Inc.* 12 (January 1990):121.

ing. Xerox Corporation, one of two winners in 1989 of the Malcolm Baldridge National Quality Award and known for many years as having an excellent sales force, has packaged its sales training program, "Professional Selling Skills" (PSS). PSS is now a separate sales training company that has an impressive list of clients who have used their services for specialized initial and refresher sales training.[7] Even if a company provides this refresher training, most salespeople know that they must become more productive if they are going to achieve their goals. Keeping knowledgeable and well informed is the key to success.

## Sources of Information

**information sources**

"Survival of the fittest" in this case belongs to the best-informed salesperson. Information is available not only from sales training but also from various other **information sources,** such as work experience, conventions, plant visits, sales meetings, research and testing bulletins, other salespeople, handbooks and company publications, professional journals, and trade association reports, to name a few. A salesperson can never learn

Efficiency in sales depends both on having basic knowledge, and on knowing where to get information quickly.

all that is needed from any one source. Although information is generally provided by the company in its training program, it is the responsibility of the salesperson to obtain the knowledge necessary to be effective, even if it is not provided by the company. Efficiency in sales depends both on having basic knowledge and knowing where to get other information quickly. Much can be learned from company sources, independent agencies, and personal sources.

### Company Sources

Manufacturers often supply wholesalers and retailers with literature that gives product specifications and illustrates features and benefits to prospects. These **company sources** of product knowledge are disseminated by promotional literature, tape cassettes, videotapes, sales-training texts or manuals, newsletters, and advertising copy. For instance, new trainees at Pfizer Pharmaceutical may spend more hours studying during their introductory sales training materials than they did during their college years.[8]

     Information is supplied in a formal manner at **sales meetings** and conferences. Held in the off-selling season, these sales meetings detail upcoming promotional campaigns, new product introductions, and information concerning corporate and policy changes. Such meetings motivate the sales force by establishing pride in the company and self-esteem within the individual.

**company sources**

**sales meetings**

### Independent Sources

If customers tend to discount claims made by the representative's company, independent sources of information can aid the salesperson. A company could test its own products and report on their superiority; but if an independent research agency, such as Consumers Union, tests and recommends them, the claims gain credibility.

**independent sources**

Many companies subscribe to **independent sources** for information research efforts, then make the results available to their salespeople. Examples of research firms are A. C. Nielsen Retail Audits, Starch Reports, and Sami Report. Libraries are full of material that should be of interest to a salesperson. Trade associations, magazine articles, media advertisements, and annual reports, for example, offer much useful information.

Information from outside the company is widely available, but it takes extra effort to seek it out. Successful salespeople will make that extra effort, since they know that the more knowledge they bring to the sales presentation, the better their chances for success.

### Personal Sources

There is no substitute for an alert salesperson. Often people say that a sale was just luck, but luck can occur only when opportunity meets preparedness. Gathering knowledge is a means of being prepared. The astute salesperson knows that much can be learned through personal contacts and initiative. Fellow salespeople, sales managers, repair personnel, and

**personal sources**

customers are all potential **personal sources** of information.

Sales managers can answer questions or at least tell you where to get the answers. Repair personnel can spot potential problems or supply information when a machine needs to be replaced. The customer is an expert on customer problems and often is well versed on competitive offerings and sales techniques. Even the competition's salespeople can reveal information about customers they cannot serve.

To be efficient, salespeople need personal, reliable libraries. Basic textbooks such as this one, motivational booklets and tapes, and company publications collected over the years build permanent, accessible libraries that, when necessary, can be sources of motivation and self-taught refresher courses.

## Sales Training Program Implementation

Companies realize that sales training is vital to the future prosperity of business. In 1989 an estimated $9 billion dollars was spent on various

## PARTNERSHIPS

*"Train your people in every aspect of your business and your customer's business. Your people can't be too good at what they do."* As highly skilled and motivated people become increasingly harder to find, training becomes an essential, competitive tool. Most salespeople opt for selling over more time in training; but to be effective, salespeople need to know how their customers think; that takes training.  **Advice to business owners from F. Michael Hruby, Marketing Consultant**

*Source:* "17 Tips (Not Just) for Industrial Marketers," *Sales and Marketing Management* 142 (May 1990). Reprinted by permission of *Sales and Marketing Management*, © May 1990.

personnel activities with a substantial amount of this spent on sales training.[9] Reporting companies, in an annual survey made by *Sales and Marketing Management* in 1990, averaged more than $28,800 (salary plus expenses for the trainee *only*) spent for each person receiving training.[10] Still few, if any, consistent patterns in sales training emerge.

Training can be offered in a variety of forms, but most programs combine classroom experience with on-the-job training, returning to the classroom for "tuning up" and then going into the field. The purpose of all training is to ensure growing sales. Typical of training programs is that of Procter and Gamble. At first the trainees may feel as if they have returned to school. They study books and literature, participate in group discussions, take tests, and practice sales skills with videotaped role plays, audiotape case presentations, and case work. Sales trainees also observe a sales manager or an experienced salesperson in action. By the end of the program, the trainee should be comfortable with sales skills and product information and should have the confidence to meet an actual customer.[11] Training at Lee Patterson Co., a paint spray distributorship, takes a different turn. All salespeople attend the PSS course marketed by Xerox, regularly attend supplier-sponsored product training sessions, and are encouraged to take business courses at local colleges or universities. "Business skills are increasingly important to me," says Patterson. "I want everyone on my staff to know what a P&L statement is and how to access a Dun & Bradstreet report and to understand the role distribution plays in the economy."[12] F. Michael Hruby echoes the importance of a thorough training program in the *Partnerships* box.

Responsibility for success (or lack of it) lies with the individual, not with the company's sales training program.[13] Those who strongly desire to succeed would do well to listen to the wisdom of Helen Keller, who advised that, "The best educated human being is one who understands most about the life in which he is placed."[14]

## Summary

Inputs into the buyer/seller dialogue consist of communication skills of both parties and specialized inputs of each participant. As one of the seller's inputs, the sales training program gives salespeople the opportunity to gain self-confidence, which leads to increased sales volume for the person and increased revenue for the company.

Among the theories and skills learned in sales classes are the marketing concept, buyer-behavior theory, communication skills, and specific company and product information. Sources of this information for salespeople include company sources, sales meetings and conferences, independent sources, and personal sources.

The training programs vary in content and duration depending partly on whether the students are beginners, seasoned veterans, or those moving into management. They also vary from company to company and product to product.

Sales effectiveness is a personal responsibility. Those who receive little or no training from their employers can take the initiative to gain product knowledge and sales skills independently and become well-informed representatives.

## Key Terms

sales training
initial sales training
sales refresher training
career path format
product knowledge
customer benefits
FAB technique
price
   *list price*
   *net price*
   *zone price*
   *FOB price:*
   *FOB shipping point*
   *FOB destination*
   *quantity discounts:*
   *noncumulative quantity*
     *discounts*

*cumulative quantity discounts*
*trade discounts*
*cash discounts*
*promotional allowances*
cooperative (co-op) advertising
competitor
value-added sales presentation
marketing strategy
marketing mix variables
promotional mix
information sources
   *company sources*
   *sales meetings*
   *independent sources*
   *personal sources*

## Discussion Questions

1.  What is the purpose of sales training?
2.  What key areas form the foundation of effective professional selling?
3.  On which of the above key areas does all successful selling rest?
4.  Sales training programs consist of what two phases in the progression of a career?
5.  What general topics are emphasized in phase 1, initial training?
6.  If you subscribe to the marketing concept, why would you consider the persuasive, self-oriented salesperson unsuccessful?
7.  Evaluate the sources of information for salespeople.
8.  What information does one need about his or her competition?

## Decision Crossroads: Ethical Issues

Under pressure from his manager to increase sales, Robert Kuen was feeling inadequate to meet the challenge. He had not received enough information about the competitors in the company's training program. Now out in the field, Robert found this lack of knowledge to be a detriment to closing a sale. While visiting J. K. Sager Co., the purchasing agent, Kay Berger, and Robert were discussing why she was buying from his competitor. During this discussion Kay was called out of her office on another matter and was gone for over five minutes. Robert could see copies of her invoices on her desk.

**Discussion:**

1. Under the pressure to get competitive information: If you were Robert, would you pick up and read the invoices? Read the invoices from where you are seated? Casually look around the room and "inadvertently" peek at the invoices without handling them?
2. Should Robert have made arrangements with Kay to leave her office while she was gone to prohibit any possibility of indiscretion?
3. When Robert establishes good rapport with Kay, should he ask for the information he is seeking?

## Case 3–1  Redken Hair Products

Upon moving recently to a little town outside of Charleston, South Carolina, Mrs. LeVan wanted to find new ways to meet her career objectives.

She had never done any selling but felt that she had the ability to sell. The extra money would help in the expenses of her and her husband's new home.

Mrs. LeVan found an ad in the newspaper for a new sales representative for Redken Hair Products. Having no previous experience other than using and liking their products, she was excited about the possible opportunity and went for an interview. Redken personnel managers were impressed by her enthusiasm and hired her on the spot. Mrs. LeVan went through three months of training and knew her products well. She was ready to go out and sell. The product to be sold was an introductory brand of Redken shampoo and conditioner called Aussie Mega shampoo and Aussie Three-Minute Miracle Conditioner with papaya plant enrichments. Mrs. LeVan organized herself with free samples, brochures, and her phone number book. She knew, through observation, which stores were the best prospects. Mrs. Jett of Bloomingdales' department store was her first customer.

At 10 A.M. Monday morning, Mrs. LeVan knocked on the door of Mrs. Jett's office. Mrs. Jett, looking as if she'd been disturbed by the knock, opened the door. She was dressed professionally and had a well-appointed office with a tidy desk and pictures of her family that provided a "homey" atmosphere. Without offering Mrs. LeVan a seat, Mrs. Jett asked her to be "quick about it," adding "I have an appointment in five minutes." Mrs. LeVan introduced herself and began with some small talk about her office. Mrs. Jett seemed to be disinterested and asked her to come back some other time.

Mrs. LeVan began to tell her about Redken in general and about their products currently on the market. She then began to tell her about the new product.

Mrs. Jett was distant and hard to reach. She wanted to skip the details and get on with it. She looked at her watch. Mrs. LeVan nervously gave basic information about how well the product works and the price and offered her a free sample. Mrs. Jett apologized for her bluntness and excused herself as she ushered Mrs. LeVan out the door.

As Mrs. LeVan sat in her car, she analyzed the call. She was very frustrated and felt that she had gotten nowhere.

Discussion:

1. If you were Mrs. LeVan, what would you have wanted included in your sales training program to minimize these feelings?
2. What could Redken do to enhance Mrs. LeVan's sales calls?
3. Outline a sales training program that would be appropriate for this type of product and salesperson.

## Case 3–2  **Business Systems Machines**

Business Systems Machines Incorporated has been the leading seller in the copying machine area for the last fifteen years. Its training process includes three weeks of training, learning product knowledge. The training also includes three additional weeks on how to present the product to the sales manager. After these six weeks, each salesperson is given a specific company with which to establish a professional relationship. When the seller has developed rapport with the customer, he or she is then ready to cover more ground.

Danny Holmes has now met the necessary training requirements and is in the act of establishing his own line of consumers. Mr. Holmes is about to meet with Ms. Sutton, the purchasing agent for Michigan Mutual Insurance Co. This is a walk in; neither the seller nor the buyer have ever met. Mr. Holmes pulls up to Michigan Mutual Insurance Company, nicely groomed and feeling very motivated. He reaches for his briefcase filled with the history of Michigan Mutual and its copy machine business.

Ms. Sutton, unaware of Mr. Holmes' visit, looks up and notices a nicely groomed young man standing before her. Ms. Sutton is frequently faced with surprise visits from salesmen and by now knows exactly how to handle them. She invites Mr. Holmes to take a seat, paying attention to his style of professional dress. Unlike other salesmen, Ms. Sutton feels Mr. Holmes is well prepared. Ms. Sutton quickly notices that Mr. Holmes is very organized and gives him her attention.

Mr. Holmes has been in Ms. Sutton's office for fifteen minutes with introductions and small talk. Now that he has her attention, he proceeds to tell her about the new F-150 copy machine.

**Discussion:**

1. Did Mr. Holmes, being a newly hired salesperson, use the right approach in acquiring a new prospect in the commercial market? Why?
2. Evaluate the sales training program of Business Systems? What improvements would you recommend? Would you pay more attention to a professional salesperson or a nonprofessional salesperson? Why?
3. Will Mr. Holmes have a better chance at introducing his new style copier if he focuses on Michigan Mutual's previous buying patterns of copier machines? Why or why not?

**Chapter Outline**

Importance of Effective Communication

Components of Communication
- Encoding
- Transmitting
- Decoding
- Responding

Barriers to Effective Encoding
- External Sources of Noise
- Internal Sources of Noise

Communication Styles and Personalities
- Determining Communication Styles
- Adapting Communicative Styles
- Neurolinguistic Programming

Communication Style Conflict

## CHAPTER 4

# Communicating: Creating and Transmitting the Sales Message

**Learning Objectives**

After reading this material, the reader should be able to:

- Recognize why effective communication is important to sellers
- Identify the components of communication
- Discuss the interaction between each component
- Explain barriers to effective encoding and decoding
- Differentiate between Jung's four communicative personalities
- Identify communication styles, one's own and the prospect's
- Modify the communication styles to achieve more ``commonness'' between the salesperson and the prospect.

## IN THE FIELD

Michael Zinman exemplifies the words ''good communicator.'' His job depends on it. In fact, communication is the core of his business. Earthworm Tractor Company, Ardsley, New York, is buyer, seller, and trader of construction goods. They compete directly with Caterpillar in earthmoving equipment. Michael, as chairman of Earthworm, bought a Caterpillar tractor in Japan and sold it to a Caterpillar dealer in the Midwest. Says Michael, ''We perfect markets. We buy where prices are relatively low compared to the world market and sell to markets where prices are high. I just pick up the phone and call 100 gas and oil companies and say 'Let me speak to your purchasing department' and ask them if they have any stuff they bought that's for sale.'' The success of the company depends on his ability to adapt his communication to different sellers and buyers of equipment. They purchase construction equipment such as engines and compressors that were never installed for whatever reasons by the original buyers and then sell the ''new'' equipment to buyers at a considerably lower price than newly specified equipment would cost. But price is not the reason this $35 million company survives. Its life depends on Michael's communication abilities both in buying and selling equipment in this specialized market.

*Source:* Bill Kelley, ''How to Undercut a Caterpillar,'' *Sales and Marketing Management* 140 (March 1988). Reprinted with permission, © March 1988.

The last chapter generally described the selling skills you would receive in a sales training program. Dialogue is the connector between sales training and the implementation of selling skills.

A successful sales dialogue results when the sales representative and the buyer communicate ideas effectively to each other. The buyer describes the need; the seller listens. The seller describes how a product meets that need; the buyer listens. Therefore the salesperson and the buyer apply two essential communication skills: verbalizing and listening. This chapter discusses talking (creating and sending the message).

People communicate their thoughts and ideas to inform, to influence, and to collaborate with others. Professional selling is the process of providing information and collaborating with prospects to solve problems in buying the right product or service or to act upon an idea through the use of person-to-person communication.[1] As shown in the ''In the Field'' example, Mike Zinman's effectiveness depends on his ability to adapt his communication style to each buyer and seller. It is this person-to-person interaction that makes professional selling a unique element in the promotional mix of a company.

## Importance of Effective Communication ▪▬▬▬▬▬▬▬▬▬▬▬

Just because the message may never be received does not mean it is not worth sending.

**Segahi (Translated by David Stockton)**

The word "communication" is derived from the Latin root word *communis*, meaning common. **Communication** is the two-way exchange of information. Effective communication, then, implies commonness of experiences. Each person, the communicator and the receiver, has experiences, educational backgrounds, socioeconomic statuses, cultural biases, and social skills that accumulate to comprise one's character and personality. This accumulation of experiences is called a **"relevant field."** Because each person's relevant field is unique, efforts must be made to develop an overlap between the relevant fields of the communicator and the receiver. This intertwining of relevant fields, this commonness, allows the message to be created and interpreted in terms that each of the parties will understand.[2]

**communication**

**relevant field**

The success of the professional sales representative depends directly on the ability to communicate. The immediacy of this person-to-person exchange of thoughts and feelings allows "editing," or "instant replays" during the sales presentation through explanation and repositioning. Therefore knowing how to perfect communication skills is essential; and successful sales professionals understand the communication process, minimize barriers to effective communication, and apply these concepts.

## Components of Communication ▪▬▬▬▬▬▬▬▬

The communication process is a circuit involving two entities: communicators and receivers. The message flows from communicator to receiver, and feedback flows from receiver to sender. Figure 4–1 illustrates how the components in the process interact, with emphasis on the salesperson's message.

The necessary components or elements of communication are (1) encoding by the salesperson, (2) transmitting the sales message, (3) decoding by the client, (4) responding. Bypassing any element in the process or the inefficient use of any element may cause only a mild distortion of meanings. However, it could result in a complete failure to communicate.

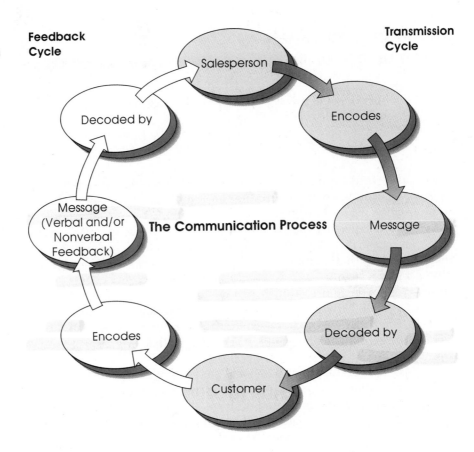

**Figure 4–1**
**The Communication Process**

## Encoding

The communication process begins as a salesperson transmits an idea to buyers. To convey information, a salesperson must transform it into a common system of symbols, signs, or words—**encoding.** Generally a salesperson uses words combined in sentences to form the message, a sales presentation.

**encoding**

## Transmitting

The sales presentation, once encoded by a salesperson, is transmitted to the client receiver. This message is composed not only of verbal and nonverbal signals (**body language**) but also of the medium used to transmit its content. For example, advertising, sales promotion, and public relations specialists use the print media of newspaper or magazines or the audio-

**body language**

Seeing a computer software package demonstrated while having it explained by the salesperson encodes the information to the customer better than simply reading it in a manual.

visual media of radio and television, while sales representatives use a personal medium of face-to-face dialogue along with nonverbal communication, illustrations, and demonstration to transmit sales presentations. This person-to-person transmission distinguishes professional selling from all other types of promotion. As seen in *Technology Bulletin*, the Panaboard is an innovative way to transmit a message.

## TECHNOLOGY BULLETIN

### Electronic Print Board

The Panaboard is an electronic board that can make up to 99 letter-sized copies of anything on its 30-by-47-inch writing surface At the touch of a button, any writing on the board can be translated onto copies for all attendees. In addition, the Panaboard can copy materials taped to its surface, such as oversized charts, maps, or floor plans. Its price is $2,495. Panaboard would be most helpful in sales presentations to a group of buyers, at sales trade shows, or in sales training situations.

*Source:* "Tools of the Trade," *Successful Meetings* 39 (October 1990): 127.

## Decoding

decodes

The client **decodes,** or interprets, the transmitted sales presentation. Does the message mean the same to the client as it meant to the salesperson? It should if the salesperson encoded the message in terms that are familiar to the client.

## Responding

feedback

The client, after obtaining and decoding the message, reacts in some manner. This reaction, called **feedback,** might be a verbal message or a nonverbal one, as in body position and facial expression, which is transmitted back to the salesperson. Feedback tells the salesperson whether the message was understood or whether the message should be reencoded and retransmitted for clarity purposes.

   If you become a salesperson, you will develop your own verbal communication style, learn how to classify a prospect's verbal style, and also learn how to modify your personal style to be more compatible with your prospect. Compatibility increases credibility and can help you be more sensitive to influences on the prospect's buying decision. The prospect's reaction to your presentation provides feedback for you. If the pros-

Salespeople know when they are really communicating with clients by evaluating verbal and nonverbal feedback.

pect buys the product, you receive positive reinforcement. If the prospect does not buy the product, you then realize that a barrier exists in the selling process. This barrier may be caused by improper product selection to fit a client's needs or poor communication or both. Effective communication depends on removal of the barriers that obstruct communication of information.

# Barriers to Effective Encoding

Although the communication process seems relatively simple, many circumstances may disrupt the communication flow. These barriers can be grouped under a general name—noise. **Noise** is any interference in the communication process. It can originate from sources outside the process or from any component within the communication process. Table 4–1 shows many of the external and internal sources of noise that particularly affect the sales dialogue.

**noise**

## External Sources of Noise

Most external sources of noise come from the environment surrounding the sales process. Obviously the selling environment influences the effectiveness of the communication. Abnormal temperatures, light levels, noise levels, and obnoxious odors all distract the salesperson and client and interfere with the communication. External noise is often beyond the control of salespeople, although they should attempt to minimize or to remove these barriers if possible.

Table 4–1
**Sources of "Noise"**

| External Sources of Noise | Internal Sources of Noise |
|---|---|
| Uncomfortable levels of temperature (too high or too low) | Predispositions (psychological contracts) |
| Odor (body odor, smoke, stale air, chemical smells, as in factory settings) | Incompatible relevant fields |
| | Incompatible language (jargon) |
| Environmental noise (piercing sounds, other conversations) | Medium bias (stereotyping) |
| Uncomfortable levels of light (too much or too little) | Message bias |

Selling on the site can present many distractions, such as job-related noise, which the salesperson must overcome.

## Internal Sources of Noise

Those barriers to communication that are generated by a person are called internal sources of noise. A salesperson who wishes to communicate with a prospect brings to the exchange not only the feelings to be expressed but also a set of expectations of how the prospect will act or react.

### Predispositions

**predispositions**

**psychological contract**

Collectively these expectations, **predispositions,** or personal attitudes concerning another person's actions are termed a "psychological contract." A **psychological contract** consists of expected verbal remarks and body language messages sent by means of body positions, gestures, and facial expressions. Both the salesperson and the client develop a psychological contract or a set of expectations concerning other participants involved in the sales exchange.[3]

These expectations are often generalized in the form of **stereotyp-**    stereotyping
**ing.** "Blondes have more fun;" "Germans are methodical, but unimaginative;" and "Irish have hot tempers" are common examples of generalizations used to classify groups of people—stereotyping. Stereotypical impressions of salespeople include descriptions of salespeople as "back-slapping, cigar-smoking, arm-twisting, foot-in-the-door" operators who "won't take no for an answer" as they "peddle," "drum," or "hard sell" their products. Professional salespeople combat such impressions through honest, trustworthy, informative presentations built on fulfilling clients' needs.

Overcoming the preconceived notions of clients is the responsibility of the seller. Few clients disclose their expectations verbally. Thus when the salesperson does not meet the clients' expectations, these unmet expectations become "noise" and inhibit effective communication. With experience and practice, a seller learns to ask probing questions that elicit information about the buyer's expectations of the seller. Knowing what prospects expect of the sales representative increases communication effectiveness, since the representative can better fulfill the psychologic contract and can better analyze the verbal and nonverbal behaviors of the prospect.

## Incompatible Language and Relevant Fields

As another source of noise, one's relevant field is composed of experiences, training, and environmental backgrounds that cause that person to act as he or she does.

Separate relevant fields surround the receiver and communicator, as shown in Figure 4–2; but these fields should overlap at the message. This overlap illustrates the "commonness" needed for effective communication. Common areas, such as similar experiences, feelings, or purposes, allow the relevant fields to mesh for more effective communication.

For example, a person from the southern part of the United States communicates in the language of the South. Southern influences and experiences have become a part of that individual's relevant field. If that person travels north and asks where "hushpuppies" can be bought, he or she will be sent to a shoe store rather than to a restaurant. In the North "Hushpuppies" is the name brand for shoes, whereas in the South "hush-puppies" is fried cornbread which is usually served with fish dinners. Since the encoding was not adapted to the language of the location where it was decoded, attempts to communicate effectively are hampered.

A seller may fail to communicate because of such obstacles as age gap or educational gap. A seller must "speak the customer's language,"

Figure 4–2
**Relevant Fields in the
Communication
Process**

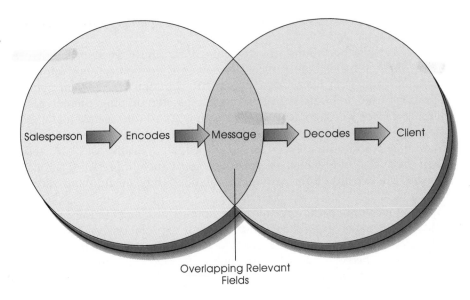

Overlapping Relevant
Fields

**incompatible
language**

speaking neither "over the head of the customer" or "beneath the individual." Inattention results when the seller talks above the buyer's capacity, while talking "down" to prospects demeans and alienates them. Table 4–2 shows examples of **incompatible language** that may lose the sale.

### Message Bias

**biases**

**Biases** are defined as the partiality, or prejudice, toward one's own thinking or way of doing things. During encoding, biases may create communication noise. People seek to express their feelings with words, but words themselves have only the meanings people attach to them. If the seller is unable to encode information with the precise word, noise—bias in message—can occur. Most words have denotative and connotative meanings. **Denotation** indicates the definitive meaning of the term; **connotation** refers to the associations that are added to the term as the result of personal experience or usage. The word "home," for example, usually denotes a place where one lives. To one person, the word "home" has the connotation of a place that is comfortable and intimate, while to another person, the same word may connote abuse, misery, and loneliness. The failure to elaborate and to include definitions in the message (denotation) is illustrated in the *Partnerships* example. A salesperson therefore wisely notes words that have negative connotations and encodes sales messages carefully, making no assumptions concerning how the words "should be taken."

**denotation
connotation**

Table 4–2
**Examples of Incompatible Language**   These are examples of trying to
reach clients when actually the salesperson is presenting the sales
message in inappropriate language. To communicate effectively, the
salesperson should talk the language of the client, not above or below it.

---

*Talking Under*

A car salesperson is talking to a young female customer about a used car.
- ''Well, sweetie, this is a good little machine driven by a conservative
  grandmother. Your boyfriend would probably know all the technical
  reasons why this is a super buy, but I'll just give you the bottom line: it's a
  winner at a rock-bottom price.''

*Talking Above*

A microcomputer salesperson is communicating to an unknowledgeable
customer about a new computer.
- ''This model 100 uses an 8 bit 80C85 CMOS microprocessor with a built-in
  300-baud modem. Other features include a parallel printer interface; four
  cursor keys; four command keys; and eight function keys for only $2495.''

---

# Communication Styles and Personalities

A key to understanding communication styles/personalities comes from
a basic knowledge of psychologist Carl Jung's psychological types. Jung's
theory of personality types shows that "if people differ systematically in
what they perceive and [in] conclusions they come to, they may as a result
show corresponding differences in their interests, values, needs, and motivations."[4] Thus much of what appears to be random behavioral differences are actually orderly and consistent parts of a person's communication style.

## Determining Communication Styles

Salespeople get the most help from the portion of Jung's study that focuses
on the *perception mode* (intuitor/sensor) and on the *informational mode*
(thinker/feeler). The **perception mode** discusses the processes by which
one becomes aware of objects, occurrences, or ideas, while the **information
mode** deals with how one processes the information gathered in the perception mode.

    In the perception mode, information is *perceived* by our five senses
on a continuum from a *sensor* who uses a predominate sense—hearing,
seeing, smelling, touching, tasting—to an *intuitor* who uses multiple senses

**perception mode**
**information mode**

## PARTNERSHIPS

*"Communicate to each decider the message that will address his or her chief concerns."*

**F. Michael Hruby, Technological Marketing Group**

The sales force of a major lighting controls firm once approached every customer with the same message: "Our system is cheap and easy to operate." What they failed to communicate to top management was that this system would **save money** by keeping the lights off when no one was in the building. Additionally, they failed to communicate to the building engineers that it would not leave those who were working late in the dark. Feeling that their needs would not be met by the system, executives didn't buy it.

Ironically, the benefits that went unmentioned were exactly what both the executives and engineers had been saying they wanted all along. The failure to get the sale was not the benefits of the product itself but rather a denotative problem, that is, the need to define terms and elaborate on the benefits of purchasing.

*Source:* F. Michael Hruby, "17 Tips (Not Just) for Industrial Marketers," *Sales and Marketing Management* 142 (May 1990). Reprinted by permission, © 1990.

to determine that the "whole is worth more than the sum of its parts." Using intuition, we know something is true, yet we don't always know why. This feeling is known as having a "sixth sense" or a "gut" feeling.

In the information mode, processing information is dependent upon logical analysis of the consequences of our actions (thinking) or is dependent on our feeling capacities. Feeling capacities cause us to consider situations on the basis of our likes and dislikes rather than depending on logic.[5] The information mode is also illustrated by a continuum, as seen in Figure 4–3.

Since each person gathers information and makes decisions from it, each person has a position on *both* the perception continuum and informational continuum. Therefore a person can be an intuitor/thinker, intuitor/feeler, sensor/thinker, or a sensor/feeler but cannot be a intuitor/sensor or a thinker/feeler (two things on the same continuum). One trait is dominant on each continuum.

Based on Jung's elements of personality, distinct communicative personalities occur both in the perceptive and informational mode. Each **personality types**    person has characteristics of the **personality types** listed below:

▪ *Perception Mode.*

**intuitor**    1. **Intuitors.** Intuitor types have a tendency toward generalizations and often grow impatient when confronted

**Figure 4–3   Jung's Archetype Continuum of the Information Mode**

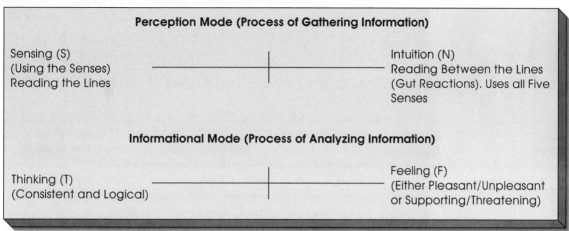

with specific exceptions or details that must be worked through to make a proposal applicable. They often have an ability to see relationships between objects and events that others fail to see. In their "thinking processes," they are basically future oriented individuals. Much energy gets directed toward issues involving "where we are headed."

2. **Sensors.** Sensors have the characteristics of being result oriented, assertive, pragmatic, and of desiring to "do it now." Sensors place high value on action, preferring to get things done without unnecessary deliberations. They are implementors more than idea people. Sensors tend to demonstrate a direct, down-to-earth, energetic approach to their work and lives. In their thinking processes, sensors tend to be oriented to the present. They respond readily to their immediate environment. Sensors tend to respond to packaged proposals for which they can see an immediate application.

*sensor*

*Informational Mode.*

1. **Thinkers.** Individuals favoring this style have the basic characteristics of being logical, prudent, objective, analytical, rational, and of preferring alternatives in their thinking. Thinkers place high value on logic and systematic inquiry. They tend to develop a variety of solutions to problems, weigh them carefully, and act on the basis of systematic analysis of data.

**thinker**

2. **Feelers.** Feelers have the basic characteristics of being empathetic, of understanding their own experiences, and of being emotional and responsive to their own feelings as well

**feeler**

as the feelings of others. Placing high value on human interaction, they try to understand and analyze their own emotions and those of others. Feelers are often quite astute in "reading between the lines" in the behavior of others.

## Adapting Communicative Styles

To use one's knowledge of style characteristics successfully, you, as a future salesperson, must put two skills into practice: (1) diagnosing styles, your own and the buyer's; and (2) adapting your own communication style to the prospect's style for greater efficiency.

When diagnosing styles of a prospect, you determine the decision maker's interests and activities along with those environmental influences affecting the decision. After the diagnosis, you adapt the presentation message by communicating in the client's style to enhance the understanding. Modifying the sales focus is not falsifying or "buttering up." It allows you to speak the buyer's language, thereby enhancing the buyer's understanding to realize that someone else sees the problem similarly (an overlapping of relevant fields). This overlap of relevant fields builds a trust bond in the relationship.

Because people constantly show both visual and verbal clues of their communicative styles, professional salespersons learn to "read" these clues efficiently. Clues are not exact measures of individual styles but merely hint of the dominant communication style. Thus, sellers can rarely classify the buyers in only one category on the basis of these clues (see Table 4–3).

## Neurolinguistic Programming

**neurolinguistic programming (NLP)**

Another view of communication style, **neurolinguistic programming (NLP),** is based on recognizing and then appealing to the dominant modes of perception used by another person.[6] NLP correlates well with Jung's sensor personality. After years of study, NLP found that sensory people fit into three basic groups: visuals, auditories, and kinesthetics, each with separate body language.[7] Table 4–4 highlights some of this body language.

### Visuals

Visuals are *sensors* who understand more from what they see than what they hear or sense. Visuals prospects rely heavily on their ability to "see" things. They like brochures, pictures, and images that portray information. Visuals take words and translate them into pictures, and they conjure up images while you are communicating, so that they comprehend very rapidly. Visuals make up approximately 35 percent of all prospects.

Table 4–3
**Indicators of Possible Communication Style**

| Personality Type | Verbal | | Nonverbal | |
|---|---|---|---|---|
| | General | Specific | Personal | Spatial |
| Intuitor | Talk of general principles and ``long-range'' effects.'' **Time orientation:** Future. | Impatient with details. Talks in passive voice. Uses words: ``unique,'' ``Idea,'' ``premise,'' ``hypothesis.'' | Avoids eye contact during dialogue. Looks into space. Avoids physical contact. Forgets social comforts. | **Office:** sparsely decorated. **Books:** general nature. **Desk:** uncluttered top. **Pictures:** abstracts of landscapes. |
| Sensor (visual and auditory traits) | Calls rather than writes. Time is of the essence. **Time orientation:** Present. | Uses active tense. Eliminates unnecessary details to relate to one or two specific matters. Uses short sentences. Uses words: ``skip the details,'' ``take charge'' | Always behind schedule. Abrupt hand gestures. Has direct eye contact. | **Office:** disarranged and disorganized. **Books:** synopses, ``how to'' or supportive material. **Desk:** cluttered. **Pictures:** action. |
| Thinker | Very precise usage of terminology.Uses great detail. **Time Orientation:** Past, Present, and Future. | Very specific questions. Uses present tense in speaking. Uses words: ``I think'' ``organized,'' ``options.'' | Rearranges items on desk. Defines own personal area. Uses calculator for discussion of costs. Uses charts and graphs for supportive evidence. | **Office:** neat. **Books:** philosophical types and technical. **Desk:** orderly ``piles.'' **Pictures:** charts and printouts displayed. |
| Feeler | Fills in motive of others. Likes personalized small talk. **Time orientation:** Past. | Personalize with listener's name. ``Name dropper.'' Relates experiences. Uses words: ``I feel....'' | Closed eye contact. ``Physical touching.'' Will sit next to person rather than behind a desk. Personable approach. | **Office:** filled with ``live-in'' look. **Books:** human interest. **Desk:** ``arranged.'' **Pictures:** human interest or family photos. |

Visuals relate to words that correlate to vision and that help to form mental pictures, such as show, clear, bright, looks, picture, see. "I see what you are saying," and "Well, let's keep this in focus," are examples of phrases that visuals may say. Sellers talk with visual sensors using "pictorial" words and illustrations that appeal to their sense of vision.

Table 4–4
**Neurolinguistic Eye Cues Indicating Thought Processes**

| Eye Cues | Meaning |
|---|---|
| *Visual Sensor* | |
| Looking up and left | Visualizing (remembering from the past; picturing the past mentally) |
| Looking up and right | Visualizing (constructing image of future events) |
| Looking straight ahead, unfocused, staring into space | Thinking about the present |
| *Auditory Sensor* | |
| Looking sideways to the left | Hearing sounds from the past (memories) |
| Looking sideways to the right | Constructing future conversations: thinking of the right words |
| Looking down to the left | Holding an internal conversation with oneself; trying out sounds |
| *Kinesthetic* | |
| Looking down and to the right | Remembering past feelings |

*Source:* From Kerry L. Johnson, *Subliminal Selling Skills* (New York: Anacom, 1988), 8–9.

Visual sensors can be identified from their words and actions. A visual person looks up and to the right when thinking about information concerning the future, looks up and to the left when thinking about the past, and looks straight ahead, unfocused, as if staring off into space, when thinking about the present. They have good eye contact, good visual memory, are affected by colors, and are good with directions.

## Auditories

auditories

Sensors who buy, not because of what they see but from how a salesperson talks about his or her products, are called **auditories.** They listen more closely to how a salesperson says things rather than to what he or she says. Auditories are interested in voice tones, inflections, pitch, tone, and timbre. They buy more quickly over the phone than face to face because the expressions they read are in the voice rather than in traditional body gestures. Auditories make up approximately 25 percent of prospect populations.

Words that auditories respond to are tone, static, hear, rings, sounds, say. Auditories have a vocabulary of their own that expresses the words above, such as: "Don't speak to me in that tone"; "Sounds good to me"; "Say, can you come back and see me at 4 P.M. today?" They like low, rhythmic, and smooth voices. Auditories are more aware of sounds, delivery, pace, and pitch than are visuals and kinesthetics.

Nonverbal expressions of the auditory sensor's eyes are different from the visual sensor. Auditories look straight across and to the right when thinking about the future, to the left side when thinking about past information, and down left when constructing new information. Indicators of auditories are rhythmic speech; lower, smooth voice; and communicating to themselves. They like concerts and music—things that stimulate hearing.

### Kinesthetics

Getting a "gut" feeling about who to buy from is a characteristic of **kinesthetics.** They buy because of visceral feelings (an intuitive, instinctive, emotional basis rather than an intellectual one) or deep emotions formed about sellers. They establish trust as a result of their feelings and feel "hot" or "cold" about someone very quickly during a conversation. Kinesthetics are capable of experiencing deep emotions even during a conversation and desire to touch and feel your ideas. Kinesthetics (*intuitors*) compose approximately 40 percent of prospects.[8]

**kinesthetics**

Words that appeal to kinesthetics are those that express the sense of touch: touch base, grab, handle, rub, feel, etc. "It really feels good" (as she tries on a dress) and "Well, that really rubs me the wrong way" are examples of kinesthetic phrases. The salesperson must realize that there is no right or wrong way to talk to a kinesthetic. Understanding them is most important.

Since kinesthetic persons get information more from touch, feel, emotions, attitudes, and hunches than from what you say, you must be aware of your presence. Eye contact is very important, even though kinesthetic persons often look down and to the right when they are thinking. Their decisions are based not on what they see or hear when you are with them but on how they feel around you. Remember, kinesthetics get intuitive feelings, positive or negative, in your presence; pause frequently during conversations to get a feeling of what's transpiring; and like physically touching people and things. They often get more information from what they touch and feel than from what they hear or see.

Jung's classification of personalities and neurolinguistic programming are compatible classification schemes. With these plans people are classified according to the category they fit best. Table 4–2 illustrates verbal and nonverbal clues exhibited by people in each category. For simplicity of discussion here, we discuss visuals and auditories as sensors, since both rely most heavily on a single sensory organ to gather information. Knowledge and usage of Table 4–5 helps salespeople to modify their style to communicate more effectively with prospects.

## Communication Style Conflict

Just as a compatible communication style increases the possibility of closing a sale, a conflict between styles can decrease the probability of making a sale. Consider briefly the reactions one might have to a conflicting style as shown in Table 4–5. This table shows how one style of communicator perceives other styles and how conflict may arise from the incompatibility. For example, a receiver who is classified as a feeler would evaluate senders of other styles in the following way:

| Style | Evaluation of Feelers |
|---|---|
| *Intuitor* | Cold, condescending, self-involved |
| *Sensor* | Overbearing, self-involved, lacking trust in others |
| *Thinker* | Cold, unemotional, insensitive, not emphatic, overly reliant on hard facts |
| *Feeler* | Most compatible, attractive |

Obviously conflict arises when the salesperson fails to tolerate the prospect's different style. With practice, this conflict can be lessened by a seller who is adaptable to different types of communicators.

Figure 4–4 shows five people positioned on a communications-style matrix. Each person's position on the matrix describes the communication/personality style. In this example each person is in a quadrant that describes that person as follows: A and S are thinkers/sensors, B is a thinker/intuitor, C is a feeler/sensor, and D is a feeler/intuitor. The farther one is from where the axes intercept, the more dominant the factor; that is, although A and S are in the same quadrant, thinkers/sensors, A is more dominant a sensor than S, but both are equal in logic (thinking) because they are similarly high on the thinking axis. You, as salesperson S, a thinker/sensor, are compatible with person A, also a thinker/sensor, and no communication changes are indicated. When you (S) call on person B, however, you would adapt by discussing things in a thinking mode (terms of logic, basic facts, etc.) that you have in common. In relating to person C, you would communicate in the terms of sensing; that is, the information communicated would appeal to person C's senses by being very visual, dramatic, and repetitive. You would have the hardest time adapting to customer D because you have no common communication

Table 4–5    Reactions to the Different Styles

| Salesperson's Style | Generalizations of Client's Basic Style by Salesperson | | | | Client's Generalizations of Salesperson's Style |
|---|---|---|---|---|---|
| | Intuitor | Sensor | Thinker | Feeler | |
| Intuitor | Most compatible | Nit-picking Overly serious and rigid Overly cautious Too involved in detail to grasp basic principles | | | Impulsive/impatient: likes solving new problems; dislikes routine, works in spurts rather than continuous; reaches conclusions quickly; patient with complicated situations; follows inspirations—good or bad; can make errors in fact; dislikes precision. Future time orientation. |
| Sensor | Too theoretical Impractical Verbose Non-doer | Most compatible | | | Standardized/routine: dislikes new problems; likes established ways; likes repetition; works at steady pace; reaches conclusion step by step; patient with details and impatient with complications; distrust inspiration; good at precise work. Present time orientation. |
| Thinker | | | Most compatible | Overreacting Overpersonalizing issues Too casual Subjective Manipulative | Impersonal/task oriented: controls emotions and uncomfortable with feelings; may unknowingly hurt other's feelings; likes order and analysis; does not need harmony; needs fair treatment; can reprimand or fire people when necessary; tends to be firm minded. Past, present, and future time orientation. |
| Feeler | | | Cold Unemotional Insensitive Not emphatic Overreliance on hard facts | Most compatible | Emotional/people oriented: tends to be aware of other people and their feelings; enjoys pleasing others; likes harmony; decisions influenced by other's opinions; needs occasional praise; responds to other's values; tends to be sympathetic. Past time orientation. |

Note: To read chart: If the salesperson is a thinker and the client is a feeler, the salesperson sees the client as one who overreacts, overpersonalizes issues, is too casual, is very subjective and tends to be manipulative. Likewise, the client sees the salesperson as one who is impersonal and task oriented. The seller controls emotion and often hurts others' feelings unknowingly. This salesperson can relate to the past, present, and future. He or she desires fair treatment, likes order and analysis of situations, but doesn't need harmony so much. He or she tends to be firm minded.

Figure 4–4
**Communication Style
Positioning Matrix**

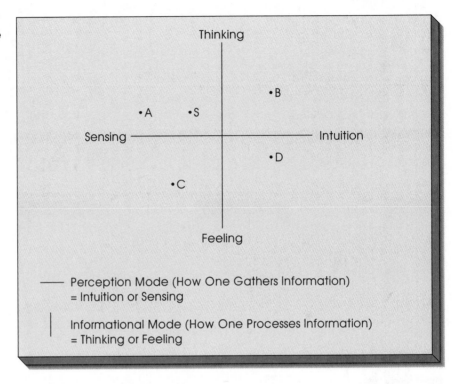

Perception Mode (How One Gathers Information)
= Intuition or Sensing

Informational Mode (How One Processes Information)
= Thinking or Feeling

traits. Customer D is an intuitor/feeler, and you are a thinker/sensor—just the opposite. Therefore you would have to adapt your communication of the presentation into the language of feelings and intuition.

Compatible communication styles are the most attractive, while different styles promote conflict. Therefore more sales are made between prospects and salespeople who are similar. Whereas the salesperson can influence a prospect through "attractiveness" or through fulfilling the psychological contract, it is this identification of mutual similarities (relevant fields) that forms the prospect's favorable opinion, establishes credibility, and builds strong relationships.

## Summary

Professional selling is the process of informing and aiding a customer to find goods or services that satisfy the prospect's needs through personal communication. Therefore sales representatives must not only know the theory of communication but also know how to identify the barriers to effective communication. After identifying the barriers, the salesperson develops strategies that attack the interference or "noise" that prohibits effective communicating. Overcoming external and internal barriers allows the salesperson to concentrate on "reading" the prospect.

Reading a prospect is achieved by perfecting the ability to discern communication styles. Each individual communicates a style that reflects that person's personality. Because the professional salesperson modifies the presentation for each prospect, knowledge of one's own style and the ability to classify others' styles are necessary. Communicating in a style compatible with that of the prospect helps the seller achieve the highest possible level of relationship.

## Key Terms

communication
relevant field
encoding
body language
decodes
feedback
noise
predispositions
psychological contract
stereotyping
incompatible language
biases
denotation

connotation
perception mode
information mode
personality types
   *intuitor*
   *sensor*
   *thinker*
   *feeler*
neurolinguistic programming
   (NLP)
auditories
kinesthetics

## Discussion Questions

1. What are the components of the communication process? What happens if one or more of the elements is removed?
2. How does the communicator begin to communicate his or her feelings to another person or a group of people?
3. What is a relevant field? How can it be used to enhance the communication process?
4. What is the general name given to barriers in the communication process? Where does it originate, and what can be the result?
5. Give some examples of both external and internal sources of noise.

6. Explain the concept of a "psychological contract."
7. What is message bias and how does it occur?
8. What is denotation? Connotation?
9. Describe the perception process.
10. Describe each of Jung's four communicative personalities. Show how a person who is classified as a "feeler" personality evaluates and relates to the other personality styles.

## Decision Crossroads: Ethical Issues

1. How can Jung's psychological types and neurolinguistic programming be used unethically?
2. Some sales people use a technique called mirroring. Mirroring involves reflecting a client's behavior, both verbally and nonverbally. It is believed that this type of activity—talking in the clients' terms and imitating their behavior—increases a salesperson's believability during a dialogue. Can salespeople draw a distinction between mirroring and manipulation of the client? If so, how?

## Case 4–1   IBM Company

Doug Marx has been with IBM for two years since graduating from college. He could be characterized as intelligent, hard working, and professional. Conversationally Doug seems to be impatient with details, discusses long-range implications, avoids eye contact while looking for the "long-range effects," and is considered lacking in the social graces of "IBM people." His car is a very spartan Chevy Nova with the minimum of comforts. He has often stated to his friends that his "car, like his office, is very functional and should be neat and uncluttered and should not distract from its real purpose." After one year in the sales training program with IBM, Doug was assigned to a territory in the Southeastern part of the United States and became responsible for introducing the IBM Super PC 20 to computer stores such as Bohman's.

John Bohman is the owner and manager of the soon-to-be-opened Bohman's, a hardware-software retail store. He makes all the buying decisions and is currently reviewing several lines of competing computers. Although not planning to limit his selection to one brand, John is very cost conscious, as a result of the high expenses involved in this type of enterprise. He is known for his tough, shrewd, but honest business dealings. Prior company knowledge of this customer is nonexistent; therefore

Doug must gather this information immediately before and during the presentation.

Upon entering the store, Doug was greeted by John and was asked to wait a few moments in his office at the rear of the store. Doug noticed that the store had an unusual "home" atmosphere. It was a nonthreatening atmosphere that invited you to relax and not rush. While he waited in John's office, several minutes passed. Doug observed that the office was like the store. It was neat, orderly, and filled with books that were technical as well as philosophical. One wall was highlighted with charts and graphs of sales projections. With the exception of a picture of what seemed to be John's family, a calculator, and a personal computer (PC), the desk was decorated with just a desk pad and a pencil holder.

Just as Doug was revising his sales call plan, John entered the office.

| | |
|---|---|
| *Bohman* | Sorry to keep you waiting (extending his hand in greeting). |
| *Marx* | (Jumping to his feet with a startled look on his face) You scared the hell out of me (gasping for breath and gathering his composure)! I'm Doug Marx, your IBM salesperson. I'm here today to sell you the new IBM PC 20. No computer store that is viable in the marketplace can be without it. |
| *Bohman* | (with a frown on his face as he sits down and begins to rearrange the few items on his desk): Well, Marx, I'm afraid that you have got this *all* wrong. You are not my IBM salesperson (speaking in a louder tone with a touch of hostility). Let's get the details straight. I don't carry any computers, as of yet, so you are *not my IBM salesperson*. And I take exception to your comment about viable computer stores. I know that it is the position of IBM. But that is typical of their shortsighted attitude toward the marketplace. |
| *Marx* | Well, I didn't mean to insult you. What I meant to say was . . . (Bohman interrupts). |
| *Bohman* | I am sorry if I was abrupt, but I am tired of salesmen coming in here telling me what I should think, how I should be organized, and what my options are. I am very capable of doing that myself. |

| | |
|---|---|
| *Marx* | I can see that by the unique atmosphere you have in your showroom. What do you have planned for the space in the northwest corner? |
| *Bohman* | (Standing up and walking to a chart on the wall, Bohman speaks in great detail for five minutes about his showroom.) |
| *Marx* | I can see that you are very proud of your showroom. I would like to acquaint you with how IBM's Super PC 20 will enhance your business. I will only take a limited amount of your time. Is this the appropriate time? |
| *Bohman* | Well, it is as good as any. But I don't have all day. |

### Discussion:

1. Analyze the situation of the call. What should Doug be aware of?
2. Plan a brief outline of the preapproach strategy that Doug could use from his information before he enters John's office. How would you change the presentation after waiting for John? After communicating with John?
3. Analyze John and Doug. What communication styles are they exhibiting? What should Doug do to communicate more effectively with John?

## Case 4–2   O'Brien Paints

Jerry Bates has been selling paints and varnishes to industry for many years. Although he's not a chemist, he knows a great deal about the various types of finishes—their capabilities and limitations. So when the purchasing agent for an electric motor manufacturer said the company was going to use a new lightweight housing for their small motors and asked what types of paint should be used, Jerry didn't hesitate to make a recommendation. On his next call the purchasing agent said: "I shouldn't even talk to you. You made me look bad recommending that paint for the small motor housings. We never could stop it from peeling, so we decided to let them stay their natural color, unpainted. I can't say they look so good, though."

**Discussion:**

1. List each of Jerry's alternatives in answering the purchasing agent's comments. What is the outcome of each alternative?
2. Recommend to Jerry what to do that would maximize the trust relationship between him and the purchasing agent.
3. Write a dialogue for Jerry's answer.

**Chapter Outline**

The Need to Listen

Levels of Listening

Effective Listening Skills
     Active Listening

Barriers to Effective Listening
     Attention Levels
     Value Levels
     Source Credibility
     Communication Styles
     Defensive Listening

Improving Listening Skills
     Improving Effective Listening
     Improving Active Listening

"Reading" the Client

Elements of Body Language
     Facial Elements
     Body Elements
     Body Position

Verbal/Nonverbal Listening: An Example

Verbal/Nonverbal Listening: Conflict

## CHAPTER 5

# Listening to Verbal and Nonverbal Messages

**Learning Objectives**

After completing Chapter 5, you should be able to:

- Explain the need to listen
- Explain three levels of listening
- Evaluate one's own listening habits
- Describe an active listener and list ways to improve active listening
- Define defensive listening and discuss ways to overcome it
- Explain the various elements of body language
- Discuss feelings expressed through body language
- Show understanding of the messages expressed nonverbally
- Explain the cautions necessary in interpreting nonverbal messages.

## IN THE FIELD

"A sales effort is an *exchange* of communication. You are not a guest lecturer. No matter how good your product is and how well prepared you are, you will not succeed if you are insensitive to the vibrations your client is sending," says Janis Drew of the *Los Angeles Times.*

"Having empathy, which allows the representative to read the prospect, is an important component of good selling," she continues. "For example, if you determine that an individual is highly intelligent and well informed, elevate your sales story to its highest level. Use your vocabulary, and don't be afraid to move rapidly to the close. But if the person appears to be slow or dull, be careful to stress each point before moving to the next. If someone is preoccupied and you can't pull him out of it, be sensitive to this rigidity and arrange for a later appointment."

*Source:* Porter Henry, *Secrets of the Master Sellers* (New York: American Management Association, 1987), 1940.

Selling is a two-way process. The salesperson talks, the customer listens; the customer talks, and the salesperson listens. Listening is essential for effective communication. It is necessary in all of our daily activities, but it is even more important to persons such as salespeople who make their living through communication, as Janis Drew (*In the Field*) has shown.

Donald Peterson's statement, which follows, shows how important he feels good listeners are:

Good listeners will outlast fast talkers in the changing areas of marketing and communications. Survival in a rapidly changing market requires not only that we adapt to change but that we anticipate change. To do this, we have to understand the people we serve—their needs and desires, their hopes and dreams, their fears and misgivings, their habits and hobbies, and the way they live. It means caring enough to ask questions and to listen and to respond in ways that make sense.

**Donald E. Peterson, Ford Motor Company**[1]

As with Willy Loman in Arthur Miller's *Death of a Salesman*, the seller who sees sales communication only as passing information from salesperson to customer is wrong. Today's consultative salesperson, using the relationship approach, is more of a receiver than a transmitter and must understand that communication in selling is a two-way interaction. Figure 5–1 repeats the Communication Process diagram shown in Chapter 4, but emphasizes the feedback portion of the process. From the perspective of salespeople who are talking, they are the communicators, and customers are the listeners. In the listening cycle, the customer becomes the communicator, and the salesperson is the listener.

## The Need to Listen

Most Americans are not good listeners. White-collar workers devote 42 percent of their day to listening, yet comprehension tests show that most listen at only a 50 percent rate of efficiency.[2] Listening is a trait we admire. A survey by Communispond Inc. identified listening as the number one problem of salespeople. Only 28 percent of the responding buyers replied

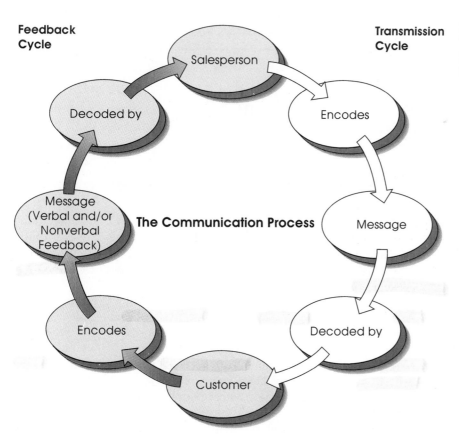

**Feedback Cycle**

**Transmission Cycle**

Salesperson

Encodes

Decoded by

The Communication Process

Message

Message (Verbal and/or Nonverbal Feedback)

Encodes

Decoded by

Customer

Figure 5–1
**The Communication Process—A Feedback Perspective**

## PARTNERSHIPS

Phillip Cooper, former President of David Edwards Ltd., a Baltimore-based furniture manufacturer, redirected the goals of his company based on the input of the customers. The former strategy was simply to manufacture high-quality, upholstered furniture for the contract market. They depended on specifications from interior designers, many of whom were also customers. To get a better indication of the needs of the market, Cooper decided to meet with 12 prominent local designers and to ask their opinions, not of his company in particular but of the industry in general. The initial meeting was so successful that Cooper arranged a tour of 27 cities and held similar meetings with designers across the country. The program was a smashing success. The company modified its products, policies, and procedures from the information their customers gave them. The results were impressive: company officials estimated sales increased 25 to 45 percent in the first six months following implementation of the plan. It does pay to listen to the client.

*Source:* Steve Zurier, ''Get Out and Listen to Your Customers,'' *Industrial Distribution* 77 (Nov. 1988). Reprinted with permission from Cahner Publication Co.

that their salesperson listened.[3] The *Partnerships* example shows the difference that listening to customers made in one company.

## Levels of Listening

When salespeople are able to gain genuine acceptance by a customer, they can be powerful helping agents. To gain this acceptance, however, both customer and sales representative must communicate, and that requires **effective listening.** Effective listening is the highest form of the three levels of listening:

**effective listening**

1. *Noise.* At this level very little, if any, comprehension takes place. Noise comes from internal and external distractions in the receiver's environment.

**hearing**

2. *Hearing.* At the **hearing** level comprehension is accomplished to a limited degree. Bits and pieces of information are received and acted upon. At some point of conversation, most people's attention reverts to the noise level. The time of concentration is called attention span; and it varies according to age, interests, and intelligence. People tend to use the hearing level as a transitional phase between noise and listening.

3. *Effective listening.* This is the highest level of listening. It is as if every word the person is saying is of utmost value. People achieve this level briefly until they begin processing new information in their minds; then the hearing level resumes. Later, listening may regress to the noise level.[4] All sellers are capable of being good listeners, but many remain at the hearing level, at best.

## Effective Listening Skills

As consultative, relationship sellers strive to increase their skills inventory, they learn traits of active, nondefensive listening.

## Active Listening

Effective listening, the highest level, is active rather than passive. In **active listening,** the listener directs the flow of the conversation. In the sales situation, active or reflective listening, as it may be called, differs from **passive listening** in that it encourages the customer to take charge of the conversation rather than being directed by the seller's comments.[5] Active-listener salespeople can strengthen their differential advantage over competitors by urging the talker to relate needs and feelings. The salesperson with the skill to uncover those needs is the one most likely to satisfy the customer and make the sale. The following are traits of an active listener:

- Listener responds to the talker's statements in a positive, supportive manner to encourage free-flowing communication: "I can see why you think our delivery schedules need to be improved."
- Listener seeks clarification by asking questions. Irrelevant issues can often be eliminated by summarizing key points and asking, "Is this what you mean?"
- Listener provides information that is new to the customer without lecturing. Here, care must be taken to avoid disguising manipulation under a cloak of guidance. Moreover, a seller who is providing information might be tempted to manipulate clients by ignoring the weakness of a product and overselling its positive features. This self-oriented technique can backfire in the form of a dissatisfied customer. "Let me tell you what we have begun to do in improving delivery schedules."
- Listener personalizes and uses verbal reinforcers. People like to hear their names, so a wise salesperson responds to a customer's comment by addressing that person by name. (Use

**active listening**

**passive listening**

the first name if you have established an informal relationship; otherwise wait until the customer suggests using a first-name basis.) In addition, using verbal reinforcers such as "I see" and "Yes" when appropriate provides direction and encourages the customer to explain in greater depth. "Yes, Ms. Cataldo, I see what you mean."

- Listener recognizes that communication is serious and takes the customer seriously. The humorous response is appropriate only when it supports the customer. Since each person's idea of humor is different, it is easy to offend the customer with attempts at humor. So it is usually best to forego the humorous quip.

- Listener praises the customer for frankness. When a customer expresses feelings, a representative should praise that person's candidness. The seller's affirming and reinforcing such expressions encourages the customer to open up. The sales representative needs to know about the client's inner feelings, since they reflect the values, social principles, goals, and standards that comprise that person's code of behavior. "Thank you for letting us know about this situation and for giving us some good suggestions."

- Listener uses open-ended questions, that is, the seller increases the amount of dialogue between the client and himself or herself by asking questions that require more than a yes or no answer. For example, Kathy Johnson, a saleswoman for Vanity Fair Ladies Wear, could ask why the buyer preferred the "Night Light" line over the traditional line. The buyer begins a dialogue, since a yes or no answer would be incorrect.

Being an active listener requires practice and concentration. One will become more comfortable with active listening through usage. Then other levels of listening will be considered ineffective and will be gradually discarded.

## Barriers to Effective Listening

Since the listening (decoding) process takes place in the mind of the receiver, factors such as attention levels, incongruent value levels, source credibility, and defensive listening may affect the effectiveness of listening.

## Attention Levels

The selective attention of the receiver can cause noise. The message that the buyer receives is the only message that can be acted upon.[6] Because everyone is bombarded with thousands of stimuli each minute and must assimilate a multitude of facts, each person screens out what seems to be irrelevant or, in essence, practices **selective perception,** as shown in Figure 5–2. The selective perception process is shown as a funnel. Here, receivers of information, both the salesperson and the client, choose what they will expose themselves to (**selective exposure).** Of that to which they expose themselves, they decide, consciously or subconsciously, to what extent and to whom they are going to pay attention (**selective attention**). Of that which one pays attention to, a small amount is comprehended (**selective comprehension),** and of that comprehended, a smaller amount is retained in memory (**selective retention**). For example, you read for 30 minutes or hear a 30-minute lecture. You choose which parts of the reading or speech you will concentrate on. From those parts, you select what portions you deem important enough or interesting enough to remember.

As each stage progresses to the next stage, irrelevant information is squeezed out and ignored. Buyers make value judgments about the importance of the sales message to their existence and well-being. When buyers deem the information to be highly valuable and pertinent, they remember it. When they consider the information to be irrelevant or not immediately pertinent, or when retrieval of the information is no longer needed, buyers screen it out and forget it. So if a customer screens out a

**selective perception**

**selective exposure**

**selective attention**
**selective comprehension**
**selective retention**

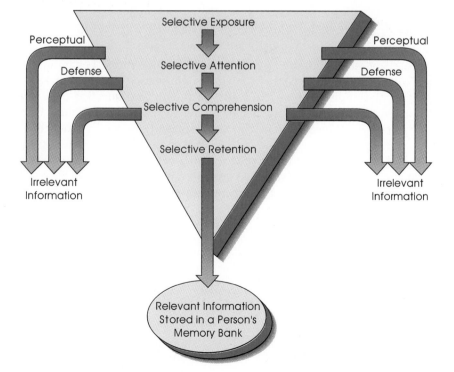

Figure 5–2
**Selective Perception Process**

In today's electronic society, cellular phones are an excellent sales tool. However, if a call comes during a conversation, it can distract participants. Such distractions make it harder to keep the client's attention, particularly when some customers insist on maintaining constant cellular phone contact with the office.

salesperson's message, is inattentive, or perceives the message to be unnecessary, the customer cannot respond. Discovering what is important to a prospect can aid the seller in keeping the buyer's attention.

## Value Levels

Because a message consists of total verbal and nonverbal behavior, the buyer must not only overcome problems of imprecise wording and selective listening but also must make value judgments and question the credibility of sources. Value judgments here refer to the personal values held by the person. Salespeople develop sales presentations around their own values and the perceived values of the prospect. When the value judgments of the salesperson and the prospect are not alike (**incongruent value levels**), the message will be screened out and ignored. Faced with different value judgments, the prospect often concludes, "The sales representative was only interested in selling the product, not in solving my problems." For instance, the Ford salesperson may tout the features of the car's sound system when the young adult client is more interested in economy and dependability.

**incongruent value levels**

## Source Credibility

**source credibility**

A correlative of value judgment is source credibility. **Source credibility** is the extent to which one is perceived as knowing the right answer and being willing to communicate it—how much believability this person has.[7] The degree of knowledge, intelligence, and technical expertise displayed by the salesperson is part of his or her believability.

*Trustworthiness*—a component of credibility—is shown by the sincerity the seller conveys. Although essential, trustworthiness cannot be specifically taught in a classroom. The more expertise and evidence of trustworthiness a salesperson seems to possess, the higher the prospect's perception of the salesperson's credibility.[8] To show such qualities, the consultative salesperson customizes the sales presentation in an honest and sincere manner to meet the needs of each buyer. The individualized presentation emphasizes solving that buyer's problems, thereby increasing the value of the presentation to the prospect. Close adherence to a prospect's values by forming a believable and trustworthy source maximizes effective communication by penetrating the prospect's perceptual defenses.

## Communication Styles

An additional barrier to listening examines the way sellers and buyers communicate. Your communication style reflects your basic personality. If you communicate your personality in a style incompatible with the buyer's personality/communication style, you have formed a barrier to effective listening. This barrier is removed by adapting your communication style to one compatible with the buyer, or the buyer won't listen.

## Defensive Listening

For a variety of reasons, people sometimes make us feel defensive when they speak. This is a prevalent, though incorrect, listening response.

Usually, **defensive listening** occurs when the listener considers the speaker's remarks to be a psychological threat. Once people begin to be defensive, they are apt to develop the habit of interpreting any comment or question as an insult or threat. For example:

**defensive listening**

| | |
|---|---|
| *Buyer's remark* | John, where have you been? I expected you to call on me last week. |
| *Salesperson's defensive response* | What do you think I am, Superman? I had other sales calls to make. |
| *Buyer's remark* | Did you get my Hanes hosiery inventory straightened out? |

| | |
|---|---|
| *Salesperson's defensive response* | It's not my fault. George (the former salesperson) messed it up before he was transferred. Don't blame me. |

These responses indicate a defensive attitude that may hinder further communication. Chronic defensive listeners fail to maintain harmonious relationships with superiors, peers, and customers, since their retorts usually have a "sting."

## Improving Listening Skills

Certain skills can aid anyone to be a better listener: effective listening skills, active rather than passive listening skills, and nondefensive listening skills. Table 5–1 presents ten steps for effective listening. A study by Princeton Research and Consulting Center asked sales and marketing executives to name the training topics they consider most critical for salespeople. At the top of the list was effective listening. A rash of recent surveys done with customers agree that salespeople often don't listen to what the client is saying either "up front" or innately through body language.[9] Perhaps the importance of listening is best expressed by J. C. Penney in the *Partnerships* that follows.

### Improving Effective Listening

Good listening, like the communication process, is circular. The first and last steps tell the salesperson who should be listening to stop talking.

Good listeners shift from talking or planning what to say to adopting a patient, receptive attitude. If the buyer is uncomfortable in conversation because of the people present or the physical or emotional circumstances, the salesperson can try to put the speaker at ease by being relaxed, informal, and reassuring.

**Table 5–1**
**Ten Steps to Good Listening**

| | |
|---|---|
| 1. Stop talking. | 6. Be patient. |
| 2. Put the talker at ease. | 7. Hold your temper. |
| 3. Show the talker you want to listen. | 8. Go easy on argument and criticism. |
| 4. Remove distractions. | 9. Ask questions. |
| 5. Empathize. | 10. Stop talking. |

*Source:* Frank Van der Wert, "Learn to Really Listen," *American Salesman* 134 (Jan. 1989). Reprinted by permission. ©, The National Research Bureau, Inc., 424 North Third St., Burlington, Iowa 52601-5224

## PARTNERSHIPS

*''Listening is not something that comes naturally; it is an acquired art. For most of us, listening, whether in a social conversation or around the table at a conference, is just a pause we feel obligated to grant a speaker until we again have a chance to air our own opinions. This is not real listening, in any sense of the word. Listening is not a passive activity during which we let our own thoughts intrude upon what someone else is saying. To actively listen to another person requires willpower, concentration, and great mental effort.''*

**J.C. Penney**

*Source:* Frank Van der Wert, ''Learn to Really Listen,'' *American Salesman* 34 (Jan. 1989). Reprinted by permission, © The National Research Bureau, Inc., 424 North Third St., Burlington, IA 52601-5224.

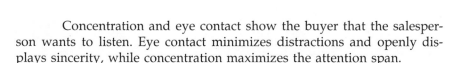

Concentration and eye contact show the buyer that the salesperson wants to listen. Eye contact minimizes distractions and openly displays sincerity, while concentration maximizes the attention span.

A correlative to showing that one wants to listen is to remove distractions. We live in a hectic, noisy age in which we are constantly bombarded by extraneous sights and sounds. A good listener develops the ability to ignore distracting stimuli. Good listeners instinctively monitor the environment to ensure that it is conducive to listening. If the distraction cannot be avoided by closing a door, turning off noisy equipment, or moving closer to the speaker, the active listener overcomes it with increased concentration.

The next task is to establish a bond—find some common ground. Since people communicate feelings, the strength of the bond between communicators determines how deeply they can express those feelings. Here the key to effective listening is empathy, the capacity to participate in someone else's feelings.

Often the salesperson faces the problem of hearing repetitious, controversial, or objectionable material. The advice to be patient and to not interrupt directs the salesperson to allow the buyer to complete a statement without challenge or interruption, and the salesperson discharges any negative feelings harmlessly. If the speaker is interrupted or challenged, tempers may flare, causing the communication to come to an abrupt halt. Patience on the part of the salesperson will defuse a confrontational situation. Asking questions enables the salesperson to clarify particular points of the conversation. Clarification forces the speaker to restate, possibly to rethink, certain ideas to improve communication.

Finally, each party must be willing to stop talking. For the salesperson or buyer to be receptive to future communications, the present dialogue must cease.

## Improving Active Listening

We can greatly improve participative listening skills by avoiding lazy, habitual responses. For example: we must not prejudge the customer's conversation to be routine or dull. After the first few sentences, the poor listener decides this talk is boring and simply "tunes out." A good listener may be equally unimpressed with the significance of what is being discussed but may still attempt to determine if any of the concepts have value. Land's End (see *Technology Bulletin*) knows the value of good listeners in its direct-mail business.

Good listeners should not evaluate the client's remarks in advance. They should listen to the customer's ideas. Sellers who react too

---

### TECHNOLOGY BULLETIN

**Dial 1-800...**

Toll-free service has been around since AT&T introduced it in 1967. Then it was strictly a tool for large companies. Companies like Lands' End give testimony to the uses of 800 numbers in direct marketing. Lands' End, a leisure-wear cataloguer with sales of $545 million, has 1,500 employees working the phones offering nationwide, 24-hour, seven-days-a-week service. It has an on-line computerized telephone system for order taking, stocking, and inventory control and routinely answers 30,000 calls a day and up to 80,000 daily during gift season. Success for Lands' End is "having someone on the end of the phone who has what the customer wants and is able and willing to serve him or her," says Mike Gillespie, Lands' End customer service director. One 800 number handles everything—ordertaking, complaints, exchanges, whatever. Gillespie says the bottom line for any successful cataloguing operation is "answering every call with a human voice and providing what the customer wants 97 percent of the time."

*Source:* Daniel Rosen, "Expanding Your Sales Operation? Just Dial 1-800..." Sales and Marketing Management 142 (July 1990): 82–101.

quickly to a client's points because of their own biases and attitudes often "turn off" the customer.

Concentrating on the buyer's delivery is also a mistake. Attention should be given instead to the content of the message. Good listeners are interested in learning what the client knows about the subject under discussion.

Another distraction may be caused by the difference in speaking and listening speeds. The average speaker talks at a rate of approximately 125 to 160 words a minute. Most people can listen and think easily at about four times this rate, or 450 to 480 words a minute.[10] The average listener, then, has three quarters of his or her listening time to evaluate, accept, reject, summarize, or contest whatever is being said. Poor listeners may allow their concentration to wander, while good listeners use the excess thinking capacity to examine what is being said, how it is being said, and to attempt to anticipate the next point. Listening to verbal messages is important, but so is listening to nonverbal ones, as the following statement points out:

> The ability to read a potential customer's body language is essential to successful selling. Body language can alert successful salespeople to any doubts or suspicions that must be removed before the sale can be closed.
>
> **Roland M. Charles Jr., GTE Mobilnet, Inc.**[11]

Actively listening to the client's answers to need-analyzing questions is one of the most important elements of relationship selling.

## "Reading" the Client ▐▬▬▬▬▬▬▬▬▬▬▬▬▬▬▬▬▬▬▬▬

**nonverbal
communication**

Most people think of **nonverbal communication** as body language. *Body language* is composed of a combination of body features that "express" the inner feelings of a person. A salesperson reads this body language to see if it is consistent with the verbal responses a customer is sending. Although it is dangerous to generalize and draw conclusions from each gesture of body position, body language is one means, though not a scientific one, to verify a customer's feelings.

Just as listening to the verbal remarks made by a customer gives a salesperson clues to the customer's feelings, observing the customer's nonverbal language also gives valuable hints. Since body language is silent, "listening" in this case means using the eyes instead of the ears to discern what someone is feeling. Birdwhistell tells us how important nonverbal signals are: "In ordinary conversation between two persons, words convey less than 35 percent of meaning. The remaining 65 percent of meaning is transmitted through nonverbal communication."[12] Carr-Ruffino[13] reports in her study that only 7 percent of the respondents felt the verbal impact of a conversation was more important versus 93 percent who felt nonverbal communication was more important in a conversation. Of the 93 percent who felt the nonverbal communication influenced communication most, 38 percent paid attention to voice tone and 55 percent watched facial expressions.

**gesture**

Understanding nonverbal communication gives additional insights into the significance of gestures. A **gesture** is any form of nonverbal expression of feelings and may include eye movement, facial expression, and body position. Often salespeople only vaguely understand customers' gestures, if indeed they observe them at all. This is unfortunate, since understanding these gestures is an important tool in the understanding of one's customer.

A word of caution is to be noted here. Reading body language is the process of reading a set of gestures. One gesture by itself is insufficient to make a definite statement; combined gestures, on the other hand, often give a very accurate picture of one's inner feelings.[14] The correct reading of these gestures gives the seller valuable insight into how the customer is receiving the presentation.

You must exercise care when reading a person. Only after many experiences can you hope to develop a reliable degree of accuracy. Since it takes skill and practice to read gestures on a conscious level, you should practice reading at least ten people a week to increase your skill. Nonverbal messages are signposts pointing to customer feelings, and the smart seller realizes that accurate readings of these signs can increase the ability to meet customer's needs.

## Elements of Body Language

Most of us are fairly adept at reading the expressions of the mouth, recognizing, for example, compressed lips as a denotation of anger or a lifted corner of the mouth as a sign of uncertainty. Other signs also appear: dryness in the mouth is a tension indicator; an abnormal amount of lip and tongue movement is a hint that the customer is anxious about something.[15]

Generally body language expresses reinforcement for what is being said. But contradictory body language is more dramatic to notice. Most people do not know how to deceive with their bodies; therefore most body language is involuntary or uncontrollable behavior and is usually more reliable than verbal behavior.[16] When reading body language, the salesperson must pay attention to three generalized areas: elements concerning the face, body, and body position.

## Facial Elements

Easily the most controversial of all areas of nonverbal communication is the area of facial expression. Writers point out the importance of the face when they say, "The face provides one of the most visible signs of emotional content and feeling available in the grammar of nonverbal communications."[17] Because they are most easily observed, facial expressions are the most easily misinterpreted. The typical patterns of facial expression, according to Gschwandtner, are shown in Figure 5–3. From this example, two things are clear. First, facial expressions of inner feelings change as the person's feelings change. As we see in Figure 5–3, the customer has moved from shutting the seller out (*Illustration 1*) to accepting the presentation enthusiastically (*Illustration 4*), and the customer has changed his facial expression.

Second, the elements of facial expression (eyes, mouth, head position, nose, brow, etc.) are outward signs of inward feelings. The human face is a highly expressive organ that conveys a tremendous amount of information to be carefully observed, including the subtle grading within a general emotional state. For the expert, the combinations of movement of mouth, eyes, and forehead form a signaling screen capable of rapidly conveying several ideas a minute.[18]

To illustrate the various messages that can come from facial expression, consider only those that come from the eyes. Rapid eye movement, blinking, is a sign of tension and anxiety that may well mean that the subject is trying to hide something. Eyes that remain closed while a salesperson is speaking may indicate that the subject is shutting out the remarks. The common belief that someone who may be lying is shifty

Figure 5–3
**Facial Expression
Patterns**

*Illustration 1:* Prospect's eyes are downcast, covered by lids. Face is turned away. Smile is thin lipped, restricted to the mouth, with nostrils not flared and eye creases not deepened. Translation: Salesperson is being shut out.

*Illustration 2:* Mouth is relaxed with a mechanical smile. Chin is forward. Eyes are still averted but visible. Translation: Prospect is considering salesperson's presentation.

*Illustration 3:* Prospect's eyes engage salesperson's for several seconds at a time. A slight, one-sided smile extends at least to nose level. Brows are drawn together. Translation: Prospect is weighing salesperson's proposal.

*Illustration 4:* Prospect's head is shifted to same level as salesperson's. Smile is relaxed, includes mouth, nostrils, and eyes. Eyes are fully visible. Brows are clear or have slight horizontal lines. Translation: Prospect is enthusiastic—the sale is virtually made.

eyed and cannot maintain eye contact could be quite true, with the exception of the liar who realizes this and overemphasizes eye contact in an effort to convince others of his or her sincerity. The pupil of the eye dilates when something pleasant is seen or heard and contracts at unpleasantness—this movement is visible to the observer.

Finally, sellers must use their own judgment when finding the receiver's eyes moving away on certain questions. A certain amount of eye movement is normal, but discerning observers can spot a tendency to look away when discussing sensitive areas.[19] Other facial elements are equally indicative of inner feelings, and further reading on this subject should prove helpful to aspiring salespersons.

## Body Elements

The hands, arms, torso, legs, and feet are all instruments of body language. A large number of hand gestures have no specific function in a conversation and will often reveal the customer's inner feelings about a topic. The most common gesture is probably a hand-to-head movement made as if to brush the hair or a movement actually made to brush the hair—a normal, tension-relieving movement (see Figure 5–4). Noting the frequency of its appearance will give an idea of the emotional state of the customer. Nervousness causes sweating, and gestures made to wipe away sweat—either real of imaginary—or to dry the palms of the hands are excellent telltales. Cold hands show nervousness also. A number of other grooming gestures may have some importance if they are repetitive or if they appear in clusters. Ten brushes to the hair during an interview might be normal for one person or an indication of extreme nervousness in another. The salesperson must observe sharply to establish patterns.

The position of a person's arms during dialogue should also be watched. Crossed arms, when combined with other gestures, may show

Hand-to-head movement is a common body element signal with little specific function other than relieving tension.

Figure 5–4
**A Common Body Element Gesture**

resistance. Remember that many people cross their arms simply for comfort. One hand holding the other may indicate restraint—the subject is physically holding back. A similar desire to keep certain information repressed may cause some people to cover their mouth with the hand while speaking.[20]

Other parts of the body can be as expressive of inner feelings as the arms and hands. More importantly, however, the seller must be sensitive and adaptable to the messages sent by the client's facial and body expressions. As Freud says, "He that has eyes to see and ears to hear may convince himself that no mortal can keep a secret. If his lips are silent, he chatters with his fingertips; betrayal oozes out of him at every pore."[21]

Other body elements are noted by Cleese.[22] The face and figure of the person you're calling upon may suggest different sales approaches to use. For the timid or fearful (tense posture, peaked brows, hunched shoulders, pulled-in chin, wide eyes), a reassuring presence is indicated. If your client seems depressed (lethargic manner, deep folds from mouth to chin, drooping eyes, saucer brows), light humor and quiet enthusiasm may put that person in a receptive mood.

For the irritable customer (tense, jerky movements; brows drawn together and raised at the corners; pursed or tightly smiling mouth; numerous, fine, under-the-eye lines), crisp efficiency and seriousness will probably prove the best course. The officious or disdainful prospect (peaked brows, lifted chin, folded arms), is likely to respond to calm confidence mixed with deference.[23]

Body language speaks loudly to the attentive salesperson. By their expressions and body position, the people in this room are telling the salesperson their various feelings about what is being said. Even though only one gentleman is raising a question, the seller should be aware that many have questions concerning the material being presented.

## Body Position

A view of the entire body is necessary for accurate reading of body language. Body position consists of three positions: greeting position, standing position, and sitting position. The greeting position's most prominent element is the handshake. Many people consider themselves experts in analyzing character and attitude from a handshake, probably because perspiring palms usually indicate nervousness.[24] The flaccid or "dead-fish" handshake is equally unpopular, although there may be mitigating circumstances. Many athletes are overly cautious about controlling their strength when shaking hands and as a result use very little pressure. Skilled artists, such as musicians and surgeons, are very concerned about their hands and will take defensive measures to protect them. But in the United States, for example, there is something vaguely un-American about a flaccid handshake.

Typically American is what we term the politician's handshake. During election campaigns it is used by candidates for offices ranging from dogcatcher to president. The usual form is to grasp a hand with the right hand and cup it with the left, as shown in Figure 5–5, *Illustration 1.* Almost as popular is shaking with the right while grasping the other person's right forearm or right shoulder with the left hand. For two friends to greet in this manner is acceptable. But most people feel very uncomfortable when someone whom they do not know well shakes hands with them in this manner. They tend to see the gesture as insincere and falsely ingratiating; yet many politicians persist in using it.

Women, when expressing sincere feelings to other women, particularly during a crisis, do not shake hands. They gently hold the other's hands in theirs and with congruous facial expressions communicate their deep sympathy, as seen in Figure 5–5, *Illustration 2.* Often an embrace that endorses their attitude will follow. Very seldom will a woman use this gesture with a man. It seems to be especially reserved for communication with her own sex.

The standing position is indicative of feelings also. Even a person's walk shows feelings. Dejected people shuffle along with their hands in their pockets, seldom looking up or noticing where they are going. The preoccupied person takes a meditative pose while walking—head down, hands clasped behind the back, walking at a slow pace, as shown in Figure 5–5, *Illustration 3.* The stance we take explains much about our feelings to the astute observer.

Like the greeting and standing positions, the sitting position is indicative of inner feelings. Experts advise us that

> A basic sign of attitude is a man's seated posture. A
> slightly forward lean indicates relaxed interest; a stiffly
> erect pose shows wariness; a backward sprawl, disrespect.

**Figure 5–5**
**Body Positions**

*Illustration 1:* Typically American is the politician's handshake. This is the most appropriate greeting between people who are not strangers.

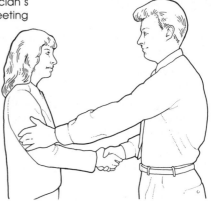

*Illustration 2:* This greeting assumes familiarity between people, and is typically used between women to communicate sincere feelings.

*Illustration 3:* Meditative stance is used when one is preoccupied in thought.

A salesman should first decide whether his prospect's posture is habitual or whether it is a specific response to the sales call. Notice the man's position when you arrive, and be alert for changes in it during the visit. While some customers are experienced enough in the use of words and expressions to make it difficult for a salesman to know how he's doing, there are always cues to follow.[25]

Fidgeting or other movement may indicate nervousness. Moving a chair farther away in gradual movements may mean that the client does not want to cooperate or has a lack of confidence.

Some people who have had little training in interpreting nonverbal communication find it difficult not to jump to conclusions about others after seeing only their facial expressions or the way they sit, stand, walk, or shake hands. It is good advice to reserve your judgment about the nonverbal messages. Instead, begin by focusing on gaining experience in "reading" people and learning about their attitudes.

## Verbal/Nonverbal Listening: An Example

Verbal and nonverbal behaviors may be helpful or harmful to the customer-salesperson dialogue. In many typical sales transactions, both parties adopt the "I-am-going-to-win-and-you-are-going-to-lose" attitude. This causes an elevation of emotional reactions. Let us outline such a harmful situation: Mr. Morris, the buyer, sits back, away from the desk, folds his arms, crosses his legs, and suspiciously says, "What do you want to talk about?" Jerry White, the seller, might respond by sitting up on the edge of his chair, feet in a sprinter's position, body leaning forward in a take-charge attitude, waving his hands and using his index finger to drive home his point. Mr. White's initial gestural advances can cause the buyer to become suspicious, especially if Morris is one of those who bitterly resents a hard-sell approach. The "tell-you-what-I-am-going-to-do" (hard-sell) approach obviously causes Morris to withdraw and become defensive.

Instead of changing to an alternate plan or trying to motivate Morris to get involved, White now becomes insecure because his ideas are not being accepted. At this point White's gestures tend to be defensive. He may push himself away from the desk, twist his body in a silhouette, cross his legs and arms, then ask Morris such ineffective questions as, "Don't you understand the problem?" or "Why are you being so unreasonable?" This line of questioning only serves to drive the two further apart.

When this stage has been reached, there are very few instances in which either a buyer or a seller is expert enough to restructure or wind down the emotions to solve their problem and reach an agreement. A "let's-call-it-off-or-postpone-it" attitude prevails. Often the atmosphere becomes so negatively charged that each side starts accusing the other of causing the breakdown. In day-to-day situations, this is the point at which we tend to rationalize that, "It was the other guy's fault we didn't settle," and "How can we do business with people like that?"

Experienced salespeople know how important it is to "close the gap" between buyer and seller, so they usually manage to have available some photographs, reports, or other visual presentations. With these they try to move around the desk, either to the same side as the buyer or at a right angle to the buyer. If the buyer reacts to the salesperson's moving closer by crossing the arms or by making some other defensive gesture, this should be taken as evidence of displeasure. The salesperson should take care to return to his or her original position on the opposite side of the desk. Some people are extremely sensitive about their position of dominance behind a desk and will fight to maintain their images.

Figure 5–6 represents gesture clusters that might be seen in a typical buyer/seller relationship. The buyer is leaning far back in the chair, away from the seller, and is steepling the hands. With coat buttoned and legs crossed, the buyer swings one foot as if impatient with what is being said. A slight scowl indicates unreadiness to buy or to accept what the seller is offering.

The seller is leaning forward in an action-oriented position. Gesturing with the upturned palms of the hands, a simple smile and unbuttoned coat indicate that the seller is being open and desires the buyer to feel comfortable. Having reached the critical stage of the sales presentation, the seller knows that it is time to be careful. If the seller says the wrong thing now, the buyer may signal this by crossing the arms over the chest or recrossing the legs so that the elevated foot points away from the seller and toward the nearest exit.[26]

**Figure 5–6**
**Typical Buyer/Seller Gesture Clusters**

## Verbal/Nonverbal Listening: Conflict

Conflict may arise when the listener indicates a desire to interrupt and speak. The urge to interrupt is greatly increased whenever the speaker says something that affects the listener emotionally. If the speaker motivates the listener to a point where the listener wants involvement, the reception suffers because the listener now wants to change roles. If, on the other hand, the speaker emotionally triggers the listener with negative words or anxiety-producing statements, he or she runs the risk of being tuned out and turned off.

Finally, if the speaker does not motivate, involve, or in any way stimulate listeners, the audience may fall asleep without closing its eyes. Being consciously aware of nonverbal messages is essential for eliminating some of these difficulties.[27]

Listening for verbal and nonverbal messages totally involves the listener's mind in the attempt to elicit every ounce of meaning from the client's message. Remember how much it hurt when we discovered that someone we really wanted to hear us was not listening? Disappointing as it may have been, the experience can help us realize how important it is that we become good listeners.

## Summary

Most people expose only a portion of their attitudes, values, and goals, but many people do give clues to their feelings through verbal and nonverbal signals. Interpreting these messages requires listening skills and sensitivity to the nonverbal messages communicated through facial elements, body elements, and body position.

Listening completes the communication cycle and therefore is of ultimate importance if one is to be an effective communicator. When combined with the empathy and caring of the relationship salesperson, listening can provide insights into the client's attitudes and needs.

Effective listening is the highest level of the three levels of listening and is active and nondefensive. Improving listening skills is imperative for all humans, not just for those who plan a sales career.

## Key Terms

effective listening
hearing
active listening
passive listening
selective perception
selective exposure
selective attention

selective comprehension
selective retention
incongruent value levels
source credibility
defensive listening
nonverbal communication
gesture

## Discussion Questions

1. Identify and discuss three levels of listening.

2. Describe active or reflective listening. How can one improve his or her active listening skills.

3. What is defensive listening? Give an example of a defensive response to the question: Why is my order late?

4. How can one overcome defensive communication? Give an example of a nondefensive reply to the question: Why is my order late?

5. What nonverbal messages may be communicated by the receiver's mouth?

6. Discuss the nonverbal messages expressed by one's face, gestures, and body position.

7. What cautions should be exercised by those attempting to "read" another's body language?

8. Why might nonverbal communications be truer indicators of a customer's inner feelings than his or her verbal communications?

9. In nonverbal communication, how would you "read" or interpret the following:
   a. rapid eye movement?
   b. closed eyes?
   c. shifty eyes?
   d. excessive eye contact?
   e. dilated pupils?

10. Using body language, how would you interpret gestures of the following body elements:
    a. excessive hand gestures?
    b. rubbing/wiping of palms?
    c. cold hands?
    d. crossed arms?
    e. one hand holding the other?
    f. subject covering mouth while speaking?

11. If you were the salesperson, how would you describe your initial impression of a prospective customer if you observed the following facial and body expressions:
    a. tense posture, peaked brows, hunched shoulders, pulled-in chin, and wide eyes?
    b. lethargic manner, deep folds from mouth to chin, drooping eyes, and saucer brows?
    c. tense, jerky movements and brows drawn together and raised at the corners, pursed or tightly smiling mouth, and numerous, fine, under-the-eye lines?

    d. peaked brows, lifted chin, folded arms?

What sales approach would you use for each of the above?

12. Which of the body positions—greeting position, standing position, or sitting position—is a basic sign of attitude?

13. What attitude is indicated by
    a. a slight lean forward?
    b. a stiffly erect pose?
    c. fidgeting or movement?
    d. a backward sprawl?
    e. moving a chair farther and farther away in gradual movements?

14. What feelings can be detected from a person's walk?

15. If a buyer is one who typically resents a hard sell, what might his reaction be to the "tell-you-what-I'm-going-to-do" approach?

16. What is indicated by the following gesture clusters?:
    a. The buyer is leaning back in his chair, away from the seller. His coat is buttoned and his legs are crossed while he swings one foot. He has a slight scowl on his face.
    b. The seller is leaning forward in an action-oriented position. He has upturned palms, a simple smile, and an unbuttoned coat.

17. What may result when verbal words and nonverbal gestures conflict?

## Decision Crossroads: Ethical Issues

One of the applications of neurolinguistic programming, after determining the client's type, is to mirror/match his or her actions. Verbal matching uses words like those that the client uses to express his or her views. Nonverbal mirroring is matching the client's body movements with your own. For example, during a presentation, Jody, while listening to a client speak, crossed her arms when the client crossed his. And she continued to match his nonverbal reactions with her nonverbal reactions throughout the sales presentation. Jody felt that this mirroring of nonverbal communication together with matching the client's verbal language created incredible rapport.

### Discussion:

1. Do you feel that mirroring/matching is appropriate for relationship sellers? If appropriate, in what instances?
2. Do you feel use of this technique would be manipulative?
3. What do you see as dangers of this technique? As rewards?

## Case 5-1 **Lyle Lumber Company**

Dan Platt is a salesman for the leading printer in his city. One day recently he received a call from the manager of the Lyle Lumber Company, who told him to "get right over here so I can show you what a lousy job those printers of yours did on my folders."

Dan wasted no time getting to the lumber yard, and for 15 minutes he didn't open his mouth as Mason, the manager, lambasted him about the stupid people who couldn't spell the simplest of words and who'd made Lyle Lumber a laughing stock. The error, it seemed, was on the third page of a four-page folder that the lumber company was mailing with its monthly statements. The word "building" had been spelled without the "d".

"One of my best customers was quite sarcastic," Mason said. "He even asked if I could spell my own name." The dressing down was ended with a demand to know what Dan intended to do about it.

### Discussion:

1. What answer can Dan give to Lyle Lumber? Evaluate Mason's response to each alternative.
2. Knowing that Mr. Mason proofread the material before the final print, what answer would you give?
3. Write a dialogue that you would use if you were Dan and wanted to keep the Lyle Lumber account.

## Case 5-2 **Xerox**

Active listening is an important part of selling. For example:

| | |
|---|---|
| *Customer* | "Your price is too high." |
| *Salesperson* | "I don't think you will feel that way after you hear all that you are getting for your dollar." (unsatisfactory response to price) |
| *or* | |
| | "I take it you feel that for the value received, you are paying too much." (better way to ferret out a hidden objection) |

Read the following dialogue between Mel Henson, the Xerox sales representative, and Jean Johnson of Consolidated Shipping. What is the customer really saying?

| | |
|---|---|
| *Jean* | "Right. Canon is offering essentially the same features for less money." |
| *Mel* | "Then I take it you have decided to do business with Canon copiers." (The salesman is taking the customer's implication and making it explicit. If the salesman tried to compare value, he might miss the customer's point.) |
| *Jean* | "I am thinking about it." |
| *Mel* | "Then you still haven't decided. Are there possibly some merits in considering our product over Canon's?" (The salesperson is picking up on the doubt he sees in the customer. He asks the question designed to find out what she is really feeling.) |
| *Jean* | "Yes, I have to be honest with you. I really like doing business with you personally, Mel, and with Xerox. I think you'll have a tough time, however, convincing my boss that the extra money is justified." |
| *Mel* | "I can understand your problem. Would it be helpful to get our heads together and come up with a proposal that will anticipate your boss's reservations? |
| *Jean* | "Sure. I need all the help I can get." |

Discussion:

1. What is Jean's real resistance—price or fear of her boss?
2. As an active listener, what are some phrases you might consider?

# PART II

## Learning Selling Skills

**Chapter Outline**

Overview of Buying Situations
Multiple Influences on the Buying Center
>The Decision Maker's External Environment
>The Decision Maker's Internal Environment

The Decision Maker
The Decision Process
>Problem Recognition
>Determination and Description of Characteristics
>and Quantity Needed
>Search for Potential Sources
>Acquisition, Analysis of Proposals, and Selection
>of Supplier
>Selection of Order Routine and Feedback
>Evaluation

Differences in Buying Centers
>Market Differences
>Buyer Differences

## CHAPTER 6

# The Buying Decision Process

**Learning Objectives**

After reading this chapter, the reader should be able to:

- Define organizational and household buying
- Compare and contrast organizational buying with household buying
- Describe the process of each buying center
- Recognize multiple buying influences on organizational and household buying units
- Describe elements of the decision-making process
- Recognize how communication skills and image affect buying
- Contrast the household's various environments
- Recognize environmental influences of household buying
- Compare and contrast the decision process for the household center in purchasing an automobile and for a business in buying a computer, for example.

## IN THE FIELD

Domestic expenditures for new plant and equipment were over $163 billion in 1988. In the $47 billion difference between 1983 and 1988 figures, you will find plenty of evidence showing how distributors profit by adding significant value to standard off-the-shelf valves. McArdle-Dresco's value-added valve market focuses on the type of people who are responsible for plant and maintenance engineering. As explained by Jack Wright, vice president of sales, "we take valves off the shelf, machine and/or modify them, then add accessories to meet a specific need. The customer has a result he wants to achieve." Joseph Pendrack, president, says "customers say 'help me with this problem. I'll be indebted (loyal) to you.' Loyalty does two things. It makes the distributor more valuable to his suppliers. And second, it is easier to become part of his or her thinking process."

To be successful at helping customers, McArdle-Dresco combined engineering talent, a corporate policy oriented toward long-term customer relations, and five outside salespeople. McArdle reports that 22 percent of the firm's overall sales are derived from this arrangement. As Wright says, "you have to go through a fair amount of customer development . . . to get the respect" that leads to success.

Creating a partnership with a customer, he explains, often involves taking buyers to the vendor's manufacturing site. Sometimes salespeople establish credibility with customer principals by visiting them with the vendor to demonstrate basic qualifications and compatibility. "We want to create a setting wherein the manufacturer can tell the customer that we're doing the right things," Wright says. McArdle-Dresco is successful in understanding how organizations' buying centers operate.

*Source:* George M. Fodor , "Adding Value to Valves," *Industrial Distribution* 77 (December 1988). Reprinted with permission from *Industrial Distribution*, Cahners Publishing.

Since customers' needs are the basic foundations of relationship selling, understanding their behavior in the marketplace is very important to salespeople. In Chapter 6 the basic building blocks of buyer behavior theory are discussed in detail.

> The chain of influence in most industrial buying situations
> is long, involved, and even mysterious.
>
> C. E. Walsh

## Overview of Buying Situations ▰▰▰▰▰

Any behavior of a prospect in the marketplace is considered buyer be-havior. The buying process consists of several elements: (1) multiple buy-ing influences in the environments surrounding the purchase decision; (2) a decision maker (called the buying center); (3) a decision process; and (4) a salient need. Since the buying process generalizes the occurrences for all buying decisions, it is easier to look at buyer behavior as it occurs in the marketplace, as purchasing by an organization or by a household.

**Organizational buying** refers to a firm purchasing goods and ser-vices to be used in making other goods as well as purchasing goods to be resold. Manufacturers of industrial or consumer goods, wholesalers, and retailers are organizational buyers.

**organizational buying**

Traditionally organizational buying has been viewed as a single unit—the actions of one purchasing agent. Although this is an easy way to explain a firm's buying process, it is highly inaccurate and insufficient.[1] Organizational buying often results from a decision process encompassing input from many different people and is not performed in isolation by a single individual. "Organizational buying is seen as a decision-making process carried out by individuals in interaction with others in the context of a formal organization.[2]

Observations since 1960 suggest that the buying center concept should explain more than organizational buying, since it can as easily be applied to a homemaker as to a purchasing agent.[3] A **household** is an individual or group of people who share a common dwelling.[4] Tradition-ally families constituted households. In today's society, however, not all households are families. In 1990, the **nuclear family** (father, mother, and

**household**

**nuclear family**

Organizational buying is influenced by various interest groups. These groups send representatives to form a buying committee, and often participate in the presentation of a product proposal by a salesperson.

children living together) accounted for only 27.1 percent of the households in the United States.[5] Changes in American culture have made it more accurate to refer to these groups as households because it implies no assumptions concerning marital status, children, or employment of the members. Singles living alone, single parents, same-sex couples, unmarried couples living together, adults with children living with other adults, extended families, and larger groups living under the same roof constitute households.

In some respects organizational buying is like household buying. For instance, organizational buyers and household buyers are similar because they each are affected by multiple buying influences that are internal and external to the decision maker. Too, each type of buying has multiple buying influences (situational, cultural and social) which affect the decision, and each has a similar decision process. Finally, both types of buying involve people (although in different capacities). In other respects, however, their needs, responsibilities, and backgrounds are different. Organizational buying is more structured than household buying. For example, buying for an organization is a detached, less emotional, less personalized transaction by a professional buyer involving more specifications, profitability and productivity factors, and supply considerations.

Furthermore, organizations spend more money on single purchases than do households. To illustrate the total size of the market, for a simple pair of wool slacks, wool must be purchased, made into wool thread, and then made into cloth, each step being performed by different manufacturers. The clothing manufacturer buys cloth, zippers, thread, snaps and buttons, machinery, and services before the slacks are made and then sold to retailers.

The interpersonal relationships among members involved, directly or indirectly, with purchases are important to a salesperson. Individuals involved with and influencing buying decisions have different responsibilities and roles according to the situation surrounding the purchase decision. Identification of each individual's role, shown by each person's own expectations and those of others, his or her behavior, and his or her relationship to others, is needed if one is to understand the participation of those in the buying decision process. Considerable interaction takes place between individuals, and they are often required to decide jointly between alternatives.[6] Thus the nature of buying is seen as *transactional* (involving exchanges), *interdependent* (dependent upon input from others), and *relational* (decisions involving participation with others).

## Multiple Influences on the Buying Center

buying center

To analyze buying thoroughly, one must examine both the buyer's action and the influence on the decision. A **buying center** is an aggregation of people involved in all stages of any one purchase decision.[7] The buying center, as illustrated in Figure 6–1, is organized into two main components—the decision-making unit and the environments in which decisions are made. The arrows show the flow of information and interaction between components of the buying center. Double arrows indicate two-way flow—the interaction between two components influencing both parties' actions. This type of influence exists between each environmental component, between the decision maker's environment and the decision maker.

Five multiple buying influencer roles that culturally surround the buying center have been identified. They are:

1. **Buyers** (generally the purchasing agent but not always), who have the authority for contacting suppliers                                    **buyers**
2. **Influencers,** who affect decisions by providing information and criteria for making evaluations                                            **influencers**
3. **Deciders,** who choose among alternatives                           **deciders**
4. **Users,** who work with the products and services purchased          **users**
5. **Gatekeepers** (generally purchasing agents), who control the flow of information to and from buying centers.[8]                  **gatekeepers**

While the buying center concept is not the only way to view organizational purchasing, it does allow us to view the direct and indirect involvements of all the participants in the buying decision. Showing the influences on the organizational buyer can explain single or multiple decisions that take place over an extended time.

A multiple buying influence situation can be illustrated using hospital decision making. The Johns Hopkins Hospital administrator may be

Buyers are influenced by the people directly involved in the discussion, and by people who are gathering information behind the scenes. It is necessary to communicate with all the participants, active and passive, in the buying decision.

Figure 6–1
**Organizational Buying Center**

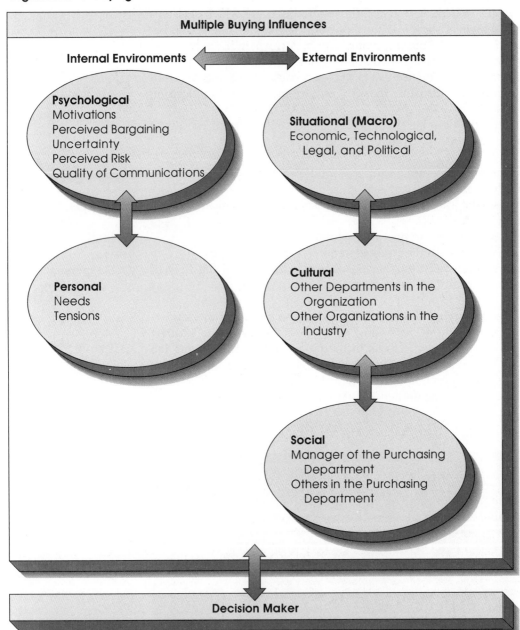

**Multiple Buying Influences**

**Internal Environments** ⟷ **External Environments**

**Psychological**
Motivations
Perceived Bargaining
Uncertainty
Perceived Risk
Quality of Communications

**Situational (Macro)**
Economic, Technological,
Legal, and Political

**Personal**
Needs
Tensions

**Cultural**
Other Departments in the
Organization
Other Organizations in the
Industry

**Social**
Manager of the Purchasing
Department
Others in the Purchasing
Department

**Decision Maker**

charged with the formal purchasing authority but is influenced by others. Updating office equipment, supplies, and medical treatment apparatus may involve the hospital administrator, doctors, and nurses. In these situations the nurses (influencers, users) often exert pressure on the purchase authority, since the administrator lacks the expertise of a nurse and since physicians have severe time restraints. Knowing who holds the power in the decision process helps the salesperson to adapt to the needs of the organization.

Multiple buying influences have changed the way a modern household makes purchases. Here the buying center has broken away from the traditional roles each member played in the buying process. Previously, specific, designated people were initiators of buying, information gatherers, or decision makers, according to their position in the family unit. Now the salesperson can no longer assume that the male or female head of household decides which product to buy. In today's household various members influence the decision of what to buy as they assume the roles of buyer, influencer, decider, user, and gatekeeper. In a single-person household outside influences may have more effect on the purchase decision.

## The Decision Maker's External Environment

Organizational buyers and household members make decisions within the buying center framework, which is composed of two elements: multiple buying influences and the decision maker. The multiple buying influences are categorized into two subenvironments, the external environment and the internal environment. The external environment is composed of the situations surrounding the buying center, the social and cultural environments surrounding the decision maker that influence purchasing decisions. Internal environments are those influences that emanate inside the decision maker. These internal environments of personal and psychological influences can alter a buyer's behavior; thus they are part of the multiple buying influences. Each subenvironment in the organizational buying center, shown in Figure 6–1, interacts with and influences the others. One should understand, however, that all possible variables that could affect the sale cannot be included.

For comparison, Figure 6–2 illustrates the components that compose the household "buying center." As in organizational buying, the two main factors that influence the household purchase decision are the multiple buying influence environments and the decision maker.

### The Macroenvironment/Situational

Organizations and households are influenced by a number of national and global factors—economic and competitive, political and legal, and tech-

**Figure 6–2**
**Household Buying Center**

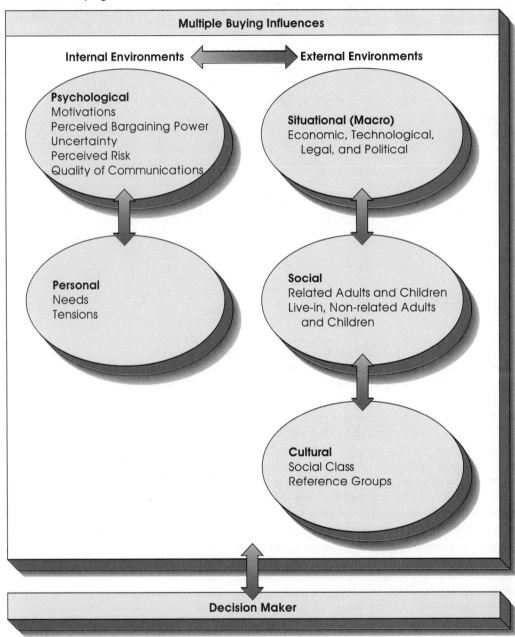

nological—called **macroenvironments,** or *situational influences,* which sur-    **macroenvironments**
round the buying decision. Changes brought about by these factors are,
to a large extent, uncontrollable. Since no country can be an "island unto
itself," the actions in one country affect many other countries, most noticeably through imports and exports. For instance, technological advances
allowed Japan and Taiwan to miniaturize transistor radios and calculators,
thereby reducing costs and forcing changes in purchasing agents' decisions on these types of goods. Also, the price of gold directly influences
such business activities as the purchase of goods and the viability of foreign competition.

Purchasing agents must consider the world as their marketplace;
therefore any change in an uncontrollable variable in this environment
could change a decision. Since firms evaluate purchasing agents on their
ability to maintain a continuous supply of goods and services that meet
specifications for low price and minimal inventories, these buyers must
keep abreast of the changes in the uncontrollable macroenvironment.
Salespeople also should be informed of environmental changes to be able
to correlate their offerings to the purchasing agents' needs, thus making
the decisions more efficient and accurate.[9]

Like the organization, each household consciously or unconsciously evaluates the dynamics of each part of the macroenvironment
before a decision is made. These noncontrollable variables have the same
effect as they do on the organization. For example, households evaluate
economic factors of personal, disposable, and discretionary income: inflation, personal employment, and energy and product shortages. Political
and legal environments affect household decision making because controversy and abuses in the marketplace are publicized and attract consumer
attention. Finally, technological changes in cable television and telemarketing are changing households' purchasing habits.[10]

## The Cultural Environment

Fewer and fewer buys are made exclusively by purchasing agents, especially on new buying or capital goods decisions. As pointed out by Harry
McGill of McGill Hose and Coupling, "Today's purchasing managers are
more knowledgeable because they are better trained and they consult
more people than ever before making a major purchase."[11] In purchase
situations in which the firm has no previous experience, **new buy,** a pur-    **new buy**
chasing agent relies on input from various departments in the company
that will be affected by the purchase. Also, the decision maker will receive
advice from others outside his or her own company who have solved
similar problems. These influences are considered **cultural influences,**    **cultural influences**
since they involve more than the agent's own company.

The amount and type of influence other departments have on the
decision process depend on a firm's organization structure and its policies.

In some firms interdepartmental participation is encouraged. Decentralized decision making allows maximum input from the departments affected by the purchasing agent's decisions without overly complicating the buyer's role in minor decisions. Decentralization does, however, require the salesperson to present information to one or more persons at a time, and it generally requires a longer selling time from the initial inquiry to the actual purchase of the goods.[12]

Organizational variables that control other departments' influences are:

- *Formalization of the buying procedure.* To what degree has the company developed a policy on the purchasing department's procedures? More formalized policies generally specify who should help make the decision and when.
- *Centralization of authority, responsibility, and power.* Strong, independent buying centers seem to be less influenced by members of other departments.[13]
- *Size of the organization.* The larger the organization is, the more formal is the structure.
- *Complexity of the buying task.* A new buying situation for a technical good will require more dependence on other departments in the decision process.
- *Type of good.* Technical goods require more dependence on interdepartmental influences by a purchasing agent than basic goods such as raw material for production or maintenance products such as toilet paper or floor wax.[14]

One difference between cultural and macroenvironmental influences is that cultural influences are relevant to one company or event, whereas the macroenvironmental influences are more generalized and are felt by all firms.

Cultural influences also affect household buyers, since most decision makers are persuaded to some degree by other households. Reference and social groups impart informal or perhaps formal approval of the purchase of goods. For example, extended family groups, which could include father, mother, in-laws, and other relatives, may influence which brand of automobile a person buys. One might purchase from General Motors because "everyone in the family drives a GM car." Generally groups affect buyer behavior by providing information and standards of behavior, by sharing what they know about a product, or by telling others how they should act.

The relative importance of the group to the decision maker determines its influence in the buying decision. The amount of interpersonal influence a group has on an individual household's purchase depends upon the size of the group and its authority, responsibility, and power.[15]

In very large groups, an individual household would have less impact on the purchases of the organization. The reciprocal is often true also. The degree of influence an outside group has is dependent upon how much an individual identifies with the group, the type of good being sought, and the complexity of the buying situation.[16] The more uncertainty surrounding a purchase decision, the more a purchaser generally seeks to minimize the risk by checking with reference group members. Often buying requires a consensus decision in which the whole group decides what will be purchased. Some examples are fraternity or sorority party favors, club jackets, and the types of automobiles in a car club.

**Status groups** reflect a community's expectations for lifestyles among each social class, and they restrict behavior between individuals of different groups. Social grouping is hierarchical; it restricts interpersonal communication between groups of people.[17] To a large extent the image people have of their groups and themselves determines which products they find appealing and which stores they patronize. Even so, social grouping is less important to a salesperson than knowing a customer's feeling toward status.

**status groups**

Indicators of social status include occupation, personal performance within the occupation, possessions, value orientation, interpersonal interactions, and class consciousness. Status-conscious customers purchase accordingly. Clothing, home furnishings, and amount and use of leisure time have been found to be highly influenced by one's social group.[18] Multiple buying influences also come from these groups, who may have the same or different values and whose criteria influence the buyer's choice.

The need to belong appeals to both the social and psychological needs of each person. Often people buy products to fulfill more dominant social needs as opposed to buying a product that is better suited to their personal needs.[19] Wanting to belong to a group that wears Liz Claiborne clothes or Rolex watches is a cultural influence that prompts one to buy those items. For example, teenagers may want to belong to a peer group so badly that they will spend their entire clothing budget on one "designer outfit" rather than buying three outfits that are less socially significant. In this case, designer clothes reflect an internalized need that supersedes the need for economy.

## The Social Environment

Members of a buying center who participate in the purchase decision from within the purchasing department itself are considered **social influences.** Support for and communication between individual purchasing department members vary with the organizational climate in each firm.

**social influences**

The most ideal climate for making decisions to buy innovative products appears to be a very decentralized, heterogeneous, "project team'' operating with little bureaucratic interaction. This type of climate encourages conflict, but consensus and cooperation are primary decision mechanisms. This climate is particularly useful for new buys. The interpersonal relationships among organizational members and within the purchasing department are specifically important to a salesperson. To analyze the influence of purchasing department members, the salesperson must consider the same variables that controlled the other departmental influences: formalization and size, centralization, complexity, and type of good.

The formalization of procedures often dictates the degree to which other members of a buying department will participate in a particular decision. Formalization correlates to the size of the organization.[20] Larger firms can have more formal procedures that allow more than one person to analyze data and to provide background information. Also, larger firms may also have computerized ordering and feedback systems to determine buyer efficiency, along with vendor rating systems to determine a supplier's efficiency.[21]

Centralization of authority, responsibility, and power are present in some firms such as chain department stores. Because their buying offices are centralized, all merchandise for resale is purchased through one main office. This structure gives the buying center a great deal of authority and power. Some decisions may require the expertise of more than one buyer; however, most buyers in this situation work autonomously. Although buyers assume large responsibilities, most purchasing departments have an interdepartmental structure that requires each buyer to be responsible to a higher authority. The organizational hierarchy may impose restrictions upon the individual buyer, especially budgetary restraints. The organization sets the budget for each buying area and thereby restricts a purchasing agent's open-to-buy situations. Other organizational restraints such as **reciprocity** (I'll buy from you if you'll buy from me) do occur and influence a buyer's decision process.

**reciprocity**

A complex buying task requires input from numerous sources and considerable personnel support. The organization may be structured to allow more experienced purchasing agents to handle the complex tasks and less experienced personnel to handle routine repurchases. Some buyers may be involved in information searches on larger, more complex projects. The more complex the task, the more likely it is that specialized personnel will work on the project.

It is easy to see that the purchasing department's influence on an individual purchasing agent's decision will vary according to the type of good being bought. Goods purchased routinely would receive little, if any, influence from the department, while specialized, new-buy goods may have several departmental and nondepartmental supervisors checking on the progress of a particular purchase decision.

An influencer's dominance in the purchasing department tends to increase on projects where day-to-day contact occurs. Although this phenomenon is not undesirable, a salesperson must be aware of these social forces that influence a decision. Thus they better assist the purchasing agent.

The social environment in which a household makes decisions is similar to the organization's social environment. This environment is composed of all the people living in the household, including related adults; children; and live-in, nonrelated adults and children. Except for single-person households, purchasing behavior is a function subject to the influence of multiple users. Single-person households' purchases are more prone to influence from others.

Each member of the household buying center has some role in the buying decision. Prescribing specific functional roles to household members is difficult because each member may perform different roles depending on the occasion and type of product.[22] Each household member can perform the functional roles of buyer of different products, influencer of the decision, decision maker, user of the product, or gatekeeper (screener) of information at various times. For example, a wife may assume the role of influencer and user on a car purchase, decider on grocery purchases, influencer on a purchase of clothes for her husband, and decider on clothes purchases for the younger children.

Degree of participation by household members is not an either/or proposition. Many times one spouse will narrow down the alternatives (gatekeeper), and the other spouse helps make or makes the decision between alternatives (decider). How much a member uses a product plays a major influence in the decision-making process. Other considerations are the complexity of the purchase task—new buy, **modified rebuy** (when a product or service is needed to replace an existing one), or **straight rebuy** (much previous experience is available and no new alternatives are considered)—type of good, and its price.[23] Understanding compromise situations and the household's decision making increases the salesperson's insight into the roles people are playing during the sales dialogue.

**modified rebuy**
**straight rebuy**

## The Decision Maker's Internal Environment

The buying function is more complex than it initially appears. It involves many people, often with vastly different views; it often is a protracted activity lasting several months; and it may be influenced by factors that are largely related to the quality and price of the product being sold.[24]

Organizational buying is structured to minimize the problems of emotional decisions and impulse buying that are associated with a consumer purchase. Even though a firm's buying structure minimizes individual decisions for the most part, the buying center is built around an individual buyer.

In organizational buying, the role of the purchasing agent is determined in part by the interaction with others, both within and outside the buying office. Purchasing agents are both seekers of status and advocates of professional advancement.[25] They push to improve their own performance (personal influences), their department's work (social influences), and their understanding by other departments (cultural influences).

Influenced by lateral negotiations between departments, skillful and ambitious buyers use formal and informal communication to influence the terms of purchase requisitions. In this manner the purchasing agent introduces two-way flow, thereby increasing status. As gatekeepers of information, purchasing agents can structure the outcome of the purchase decision through the control of information to maintain or to improve their political position in the organization. No matter what interactive position an agent appears to fill, he or she remains an individual with personal and professional needs.

### Personal Influences

**needs**
**want**
**drive (desire)**

**Needs and Tensions.** **Needs** are basic forces, physiological and psychological, that motivate individuals to do something, whereas a **want** is a means for satisfying needs. A **drive,** or **desire,** is a strong stimulus that causes the tension that individuals try to reduce. The existence of both

Household buyers often have hidden needs which must be discovered by the retail salesperson before a solution is offered.

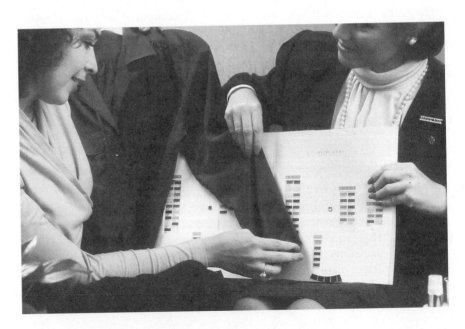

**Table 6–1**
**Need Motivators**

| Physiological Needs | Psychological Needs | Wants |
|---|---|---|
| Food/drink | Affiliation | Acceptance |
| Self-preservation | Aggression | Achievement |
| Warmth/coolness | Beauty | Affection |
| Clothing | Companionship | Appreciation |
| Activity/rest | Conserving | Comfort |
| Shelter | Discovery | Dependence |
| | Distinction | Fame |
| | Discriminating | Happiness |
| | Dominance | Identification |
| | Emulation | Prestige |
| | Imitation | Recognition |
| | Independence | Respect |
| | Individualism | Satisfaction |
| | Love | Security |
| | Nurturing | Self-confidence |
| | Order | Sociability |
| | Personal fulfillment | Status |
| | Power | Sympathy |
| | Pride | |
| | Security | |
| | Self-expression | |
| | Symmetry | |
| | Striving | |
| | Understanding | |

physiological and psychological needs is well documented (Table 6–1). Some authors, such as Maslow, have even developed a hierarchy of needs.[26] The important point here is that *various needs exist, and tension or frustration occurs when a need is not being met;* thus it motivates a buyer to action.

External information perceived through one's senses of seeing, hearing, touching, smelling, and tasting can motivate internal needs, desires, or wants. Because thousands of bits of information bombard a person each minute, people use a selective perception process to prevent information overload. The screening of relevant from irrelevant information is a defense mechanism used to enhance the learning process, and it determines what is seen and felt.[27]

In the organization, a purchasing agent's job also involves supplying the needs of the firm. Purchasing motives that promote actions to buy are generally separated into **functional motives (task related)** and **psychological motives (nontask related)**. The actions of purchasing managers were considered entirely functional or task oriented by early re-

**functional motives (task related)**

**psychological motives (nontask related)**

searchers who operated under the *economic man concept* (driven mainly by price motives). Their functional motives were price, quality, and services from a supplier.[28]

While functional motives are dominant, *psychological motives* such as habit, emotional stress, caution, and confidence of price level do have an impact on the buying decision. Both types of motives affect the outcome of a specific purchase decision.[29] A salesperson who tries to satisfy her customers' functional and psychological needs is Cecile Satterwhite (see *Partnerships*).

### Psychological Influences

**psychological influences**

**Psychological influences** have several components that are internal to the decision maker and outside influences of the buyer's decision. Psychological factors that influence the household are motivation, perceived bargaining power, uncertainty, perceived risk, and quality of communications.

**motivation**

**Motivation.**   When the tension level rises to the point of recognition, a person begins to think about satisfying that need. This recognition becomes **motivation.** However, if the tension level rises too high, it becomes so frustrating that one has to block out the tension to survive. For example, needing to do well on a particular test to pass a course can become so

## PARTNERSHIPS

Many people think of selling shoes as unexciting work, but that's not true for Cecile Satterwhite, Leon's Fashions, Tyler, Texas. Cecile sells $600,000 of shoes each year while doubling as store buyer. These sales earn her about $100,000 annually. The reason is the way she treats each customer, many of whom will have only Cecile wait on them. Her secret: ``we just kill 'em with kindness,'' she says. She gives her current customer her complete, undivided attention. Even though she has half a dozen clients waiting to see her, Cecile does not even look away. If the shoe doesn't fit, she won't let you buy it and will stop you from purchasing one that ``doesn't look pretty on your foot.'' Cecile says, ``If you buy that shoe, don't tell a soul that I waited on you.'' She has been known to bring out as many as 300 pairs of shoes to satisfy the needs of a client and kneels down to put each shoe on and take it off. She started working at Leon's at the age of 20 and now at age 66 gets ``antsy'' because Leon's is closed on Sundays. ``I do love to sell,'' Cecile says. ``It's exciting. It gets into your blood.''

*Source:* Monci Jo Williams, ``America's Best Salesmen,'' *Fortune* 116 (October 26, 1987). © 1987, Time Inc. All Rights Reserved.

tension filled that an overload of information (studying all night) causes a mental block. Students temporarily forget what they know about a subject, even after studying very hard.

According to Ryan and Holbrook, once a need reaches the recognition stage, the person is motivated to satisfy it. This motivation can come from internal personal factors, such as values or feelings (psychological needs), or from physiological needs, such as hunger or thirst. Sellers know that conflict can occur between decision makers and their environments both within and outside of a department.[30] For example, Susan Choice can lose a computer sale to a competitor by failing to realize that Jaime Beuller's decision is based on political rather than functional motives. The purchasing agent, J. Beuller, could be involved in a complex exchange of information and politics with several other members of the buying center. S. Choice's awareness of potential conflict in the buying center can help her to avoid mistakes and thus to make sales.

**Bargaining Power.**   Bargaining power is directly related to the degrees to which the parties in the negotiation see themselves and the other parties as experts—the amount of expertise each is perceived as having. **Expert power** is the belief that one has some unique ability to perform necessary activities. Expert power is influential because people trust knowledgeable individuals, whether they are selling or buying.

**expert power**

Another influence is the degree to which each party trusts and identifies with the opposite party, which is called **referent power.** A salesperson with referent power (trust) can exert influence in numerous situations under many differing circumstances.[31]

**referent power**

The stronger a salesperson's perceived referent and expert power, the more trustworthy this individual becomes to a particular buyer. The perceived bargaining power is directly related, therefore, to the degree of expertness each party sees and the extent to which to trust the other.

Each buyer, organizational and household, has power to negotiate. Consciously or unconsciously, you may perceive yourself as a person who likes or dislikes "haggling" or negotiating. If you see yourself as a negotiator and feel it is important to negotiate in buying, you probably stress your bargaining power. Your power to bargain, however, is only as strong as the seller's willingness to negotiate. Just as with the organizational buyer, the negotiating power of the buyer depends upon his or her interests.[32] Your bargaining power depends upon your **self-concept**—how you view yourself—the importance of the purchase, and the willingness to win.[33]

**self-concept**

Higher bargaining power tends to make a purchasing agent more independent. This autonomy, or **self-perception,** affects the agent's ability to find answers to relevant purchasing questions and affects the degree of agent dependence upon other individuals for information and decisions.

**self-perception**

Associated with self-concept and wanting to win is the importance of the purchase to the buyer. For most people, buying a bicycle is not as important as purchasing an automobile. Therefore less intense negotiation is present.

**Amount of Uncertainty.**    The degree of uncertainty surrounding a purchase influences a buyer's behavior. A new buying situation poses risks because the organization has no previous purchasing experience in the area. In this situation purchasing agents generally seek a great deal of information from a variety of sources and may consider many alternatives.[34]

Of the three buy classes—new buy, modified rebuy, and straight rebuy—uncertainty is maximized in the new buy and is minimal in the straight rebuy.

A modified rebuy occurs when a product or service is needed to replace an existing one. This situation requires that new information and alternative products and services be considered along with those currently used and experiences from similar purchases. The buying task is not completely new, but an alternative may be purchased. Uncertainty is reduced by experience.

Straight rebuy conditions exist when much previous purchasing experience is available and no new alternatives are considered. The firm simply "reorders" from the last supplier. Minimum uncertainty exists.

Uncertainty can be minimized by the buying center's gathering of information concerning the purchase. In many cases the risk of purchasing a product or service can be reduced by gathering additional information. One study concluded that industrial buyers' preference for informational sources varies according to the amount of uncertainty. In new-buy situations, buyers were found to prefer personal communication, such as that from salespeople and friends, over mass communications media such as advertising and direct mail, as sources of information.[35] The influence of relationship selling with its emphasis on providing information to the buyer's decision process has a large impact by providing valuable information.

**risk**

**Perceived Risk.**    **Risk** can be perceived in financial, physical, social, performance, and psychological well-being and loss of time.[36] A prospect faced with a need may perceive certain risks associated with filling that need. Perceived risks that influence the organizational buyer also affect the household buyer, except these risks are personal rather than detached.[37]

All behavior involves risk because any action of a consumer produces consequences that are not anticipated fully. To cope with these hazards, consumers tend to develop risk-reducing strategies that enable them to make more confident decisions. A common risk-reduction strategy involves seeking additional information from a number of sources.[38] Thus the relationship salesperson helps customers reduce their risks by providing information to reduce risk.

As purchasing agents strive to minimize the risks associated with the acquisition of a new product or service,[39] they may look at secondary data sources such as a firm's rating by Dun & Bradstreet (D & B) as a step toward minimizing risk. Firms not listed in D & B may be considered too risky financially to be viable suppliers. Generally the more risk involved in the decision, the more a purchasing agent pursues risk-reduction strategies.[40]

Social factors may reduce risk when even more objective criteria give unfavorable results. Trusting or liking the seller and hearing good reports about the salesperson both reduce risk. Experience and expertise are more important when risk is high. Size and length of time in business of the supplying firms often translate into the reliability of a supplier.[41] A buyer may prefer a smaller supplier but may not be able to afford the risk of possible contract noncompliance.

**Type and Quality of Communications.**   Communication ability affects a buyer's efficiency. The purchasing agent's face-to-face and written communications are vital to the purchasing decision. Purchasing agents gather and interpret information, assimilate technical data, and relate it accurately and completely in technical terms for some personnel and, in "layperson's" terms, for nontechnical personnel.

In two-way communication, data come from inside a firm (technical and nontechnical personnel) and outside the firm (consultants, trade shows, salespeople, and journals). Most purchasing agents feel that they should see several salespeople for help in information gathering, even though only one of them will be making a sale.[42]

Salespeople who are unable to communicate effectively with consumers often realize little satisfaction when attempting to meet the needs of the household. Some consumers come into the marketplace disgruntled and ill informed. A seller with good communication skills can help the buyers solidify perceptions of their needs as a person as well as the needs of their buying household.[43]

Each of these factors is of interest to the decision maker. Only through listening to and observing the verbal and nonverbal behavior can the salesperson learn what factors are important to the decision maker. Bob Skidmore discusses the importance of good communication (see *Partnerships,* p. 150).

# The Decision Maker

Central to any buying center is the person who executes the order. Although the decision maker is part of the buying center, his or her frequent interactions with salespeople warrant more attention. Therefore we discuss the decision maker as a separate but interacting part of the buying

## PARTNERSHIPS

*"Distributors control only 45 percent of their top 20 major accounts."* **Morgan Business Associates (management consulting firm), Santa Barbara, CA.**

This quote means that 55 percent of the available business is being sold by the competition. To better this record, Morgan suggests a three-pronged approach to pinpoint business that is being lost to competitors: 1. Salespeople should make a deliberate effort to talk about the products key clients are not buying from your firm; 2. Arrange for a specific appointment time to do more business with your clients; 3. Keep an accurate record of what information was obtained during the calls.

Bob Skidmore, President of Cerritos, agrees with Morgan's basic points. "There is no doubt that when the lines of communication have been opened previously, it's easier to sell," Skidmore says. "After all, the customer has already established a credit line and been placed on the computer for billing purposes. Sure, it's easier selling existing customers, but you have to offer them something, either a service or product, that they're not getting from somebody else." Morgan reminds us, "It costs five times as much to find a new account as it does to expand business with an existing account." A key to building business with current customers is to maintain the flow of communication of important information. The best way to get the business is to ask for it.

*Source:* Steve Zurier, "Get More Sales out of Existing Accounts," *Industrial Distribution* 78 (March 1989). Reprinted by permission of Cahners Publishing.

center. In the case of an organization, this person is called a buyer, or purchasing agent. Although many members of the buying center may help determine criteria for evaluating alternative products or services, a part of the joint decision and the placing of the order usually depend on a purchasing agent. More than a mere order writer, the purchasing agent is an integral part of any purchase. He or she acts as a gatekeeper of information for those parties who make the decision and thus is the "hub in the wheel" of organizational purchasing.[44]

**decision maker**

In household purchasing, the individual who makes the decision, male or female, adult, teenager, or child, is referred to as the **decision maker.** Only by asking good questions concerning the purchase decision will the salesperson find clues as to who is responsible for the decision role on this purchase. Through listening, a salesperson can gather needed information about what happens to a decision maker while gathering information, how strong are the environmental influences, and which forces dominate the buyer's decision.

## The Decision Process

During the dialogue process the salesperson can discover much relevant data, such as the buyer's interests and influences on the decision. The activities in the decision process are shown in detail in Figure 6–3.

To discuss the buying process fully, we consider it in the context of a new buying situation. New buys, although infrequent, are important because they set the pattern for future purchases of this type of product. New buys require the use of all the steps in the buying process, whereas modified rebuy and straight rebuy require only a few of the steps.

### Problem Recognition

A problem or need may arise internally, such as a decision to purchase a new carpet for the offices or externally, such as a firm's decision to change production equipment to keep pace with its competition. This phase anticipates or recognizes that a problem exists that may be solved through a purchase.

### Determination and Description of Characteristics and Quantity Needed

Phases 2 and 3 often occur concurrently. For technical products, the "user" department, with possible help from technical users in other departments, may prepare performance specifications or a list of ideal attributes. A salesperson who has good relationships within a firm may even be asked to help write the specifications. Without a doubt, this is an advantageous position for a seller.

### Search for Potential Sources

Search procedures for qualified suppliers vary. For technical goods in the new buying situation, the search mainly involves technical people. The purchasing department may contribute a list of potential suppliers, but an assessment of the technical qualifications of suppliers and products remains the responsibility of technical people. In less complex areas, however, the purchasing agent assumes the search responsibility.[45]

**Flow Diagram of the Organizational Decision Process**

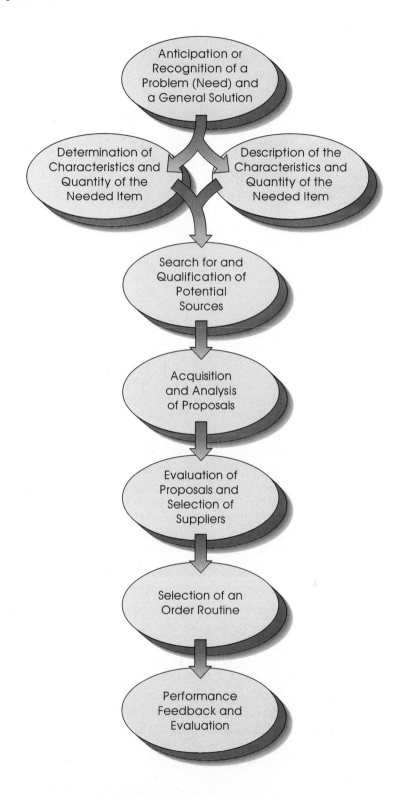

## TECHNOLOGY BULLETIN

### Computer Program

Okonite Co., manufacturer of insulated wire and cable, is on the cutting edge of major changes in its company's relationships with its vendors. This innovative computer program gives them quick, accurate information about all of their vendors, including instant feedback on inventory, supplier delivery dates, dollar amount of purchases from particular vendors, and ready cross-references to other vendors. Vendor salespeople would be wise to make use of this information to better meet the needs of Okonite. By giving a salesperson a better idea of what Okonite is doing, based on ordering and delivering patterns, with a quantity discount involved, the salesperson with this information can develop a program based on these consumption patterns.

*Source:* Richard G. Newman, "Single Sourcing: Short-Term Savings Versus Long-Term Problems," *Journal of Purchasing and Material Management* 25 (Summer 1989): 20–25.

## Acquisition, Analysis of Proposals, and Selection of Supplier

When the basic technical information has been collected and analyzed, economic considerations come into play. Now the buyer begins decision making. Alternatives have been narrowed; and if purchasing agents have a choice between equally acceptable suppliers, they can use such factors as repeat buying, cost, delivery time, customer service, and reputation to negotiate a better price.[46]

## Selection of Order Routine and Feedback Evaluation

The new purchase has been made. If regular repurchases are to be made, the emphasis now shifts from determining what to buy and from whom to purchase and focuses on getting the product at regular intervals to satisfy user demands. It now becomes a straight rebuy. Supplier performance evaluations are made periodically to determine the efficiency of the process and of supplier contract fulfillment.

In modified rebuys and straight rebuys, the buyer dominates the firm's buying center, even when technical changes are involved. Technical people will be consulted, perhaps, in testing; but the buyer will be the decision maker.

These last two phases, order routine and performance evaluation, come after the customer–salesperson dialogues are concluded. A salesperson may have input in the purchase process from the problem recognition stage to the selection stage and beyond. In some cases, however, salespeople may not be involved until the search for potential sources of supply and on through supplier selection.

The process of a household coming to a decision is similar to that of the organization, as shown in Figure 6–4. The buying circumstances, the influencers of the decision, and a less formal purchasing process are all that differ. It is often performed congruently with the introspection of self and the evaluation of the environmental influences.

Households recognize that problems that occur are either routine, because of their expected or planned occurrence, or emergency, because of their unexpected nature. Examples of routine problems are grocery shopping, filling the car with gas, or studying for a test. Emergency problems occur at unexpected times, such as when a cake falls before a birthday party or a six-year-old refrigerator breaks down. Emergency decisions are often based on less than complete information.

After a problem is recognized, assignment of the buying responsibilities occurs before an informal external search and an internal search for possible alternatives. Often the purchase decision process is so extensive that buying responsibilities are assigned to different people in the buying household. In the family, for example, different people may be responsible for purchasing different products. A husband might purchase a riding lawn mower without discussing it with his wife. Likewise, a wife may buy food, clothing—his and/or hers—and small appliances. In both cases, however, the influences of the other family members are felt. She bought food and clothing her family liked. Other times decisions may be made jointly. The salesperson must be observant and listen to the buyer to determine who is involved in the decision.

Internally one searches mentally for stored information related to that particular problem or a similar problem. Recalling experiences plays a large part in an internal search. Questions such as "What did I do last time I had this problem?" and "Was the solution satisfactory?" are asked. The internal search, or memory scan, is not an observable activity. The informal external search process is more evident. This external search, being overt behavior, is observable. When the internally stored information is insufficient to provide worthy alternatives, the person goes to others to search for possible solutions. Prospects search **personal sources of information**, such as family and friends; **professional sources of information,** such as consumer groups and government agencies; and **marketing sources of information,** such as publicity and advertisers.[47]

From these searches of information, possible alternatives to the problem are developed into a **salient need.** It is this salient need that the

**personal sources of information**

**professional sources of information**

**marketing sources of information**

**salient need**

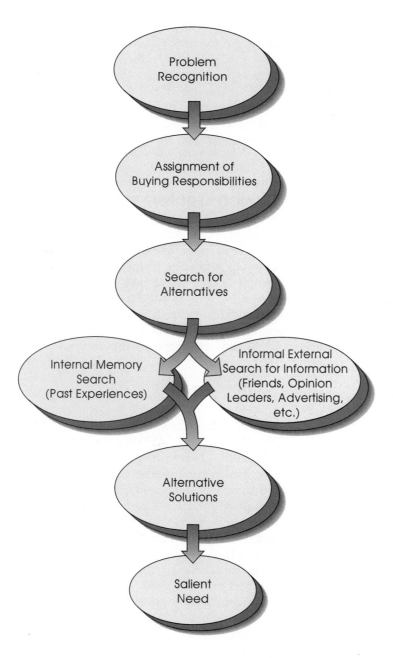

Figure 6–4
**Household's
Decision-Making
Process**

household buyer takes into the marketplace. With this salient need, the customer approaches the marketplace for a formal search and dialogue. Sometimes the salient need is for information for later decision making: "I'm just looking." Sometimes it is for information to confirm and reinforce the decision that has already been made. But most often the salient need is a problem that the customer needs to solve.

Salespeople who accurately and effectively determine the salient need of a customer take a leap toward the solution. In fact, problem definition often accounts for a majority of the time needed in finding a solution. The relationship salesperson maximizes the time devoted to determining salient needs. Within the salient need lies clues to the decision maker's interests and environmental influences. The salient need is the "tip of the iceberg" of the personal and outside influences on the buyer. Like an iceberg, much of the need and its influences are not exposed.

## Differences in Buying Centers ▬▬▬▬▬▬▬

The discussion of the buying centers thus far has shown their similarities. Salespeople also need to know the differences between types of buying centers so they can determine strategies to meet the needs of these two types of buyers. Salespeople do not sell to both markets—organizational and household. However, some salespeople change positions during their career, and knowledge of these differences is helpful in making the transition. Differences between organizational and consumer buying center around the market and the individual buying differences.

### Market Differences

As shown in Table 6–2, these differences are numerous. Market differences center around (1) amount of each purchase; (2) geographical concentration of buyers; (3) type of demand; (4) type of products purchased; and (5) number of buyers. The organizational market makes larger volume purchases per single transaction. The defense department purchases many items, some totaling billions of dollars per item, such as the B-2 bomber.

Geographically the buyers in organizations are consolidated in specific areas. Since organizational opportunities are better in some locations than others, industries tend to concentrate locally. For example, tire manufacturers may locate around Akron, Ohio; and paper manufacturers around areas that have wood pulp supplies.

**derived demand**    The demand for organizational goods is a derived demand. **Derived demand** means that the demand for organizational goods is affected by the demand for consumer goods. If the demand for consumer goods decreases, the demand for organizations that supply goods to the various supporting markets declines also.

Products consumed by organizations are more complete and more technical than those purchased by consumers. For example, buying a fighter plane, computerized tomography (CT) machine, or pollution control equipment may take months.

Table 6–2
**Traits of Organizational Buying Centers Contrasted with Consumer
Buying Centers**

| Market Differences of Organizations | Buyer Differences in Organizations |
|---|---|
| ■ Larger volume of purchases<br>■ Organizational markets are more concentrated geographically than consumer markets<br>■ Demand for organizational goods affected by demand for consumer goods<br>■ Products are more technically complex than in consumer markets<br>■ Organization markets consist of a small number of buying firms | ■ Service after the sale as important as price<br>■ Purchasing agents are trained buyers with technical expertise about the products<br>■ Negotiated price is more common in organization purchasing<br>■ Reciprocal buying exists in organizations<br>■ More group decisions are made in organizations<br>■ Purchasing process is typically longer than for consumers |

Although organizations buy in larger amounts and buy more
often than consumers, there are fewer buyers. For example, there are fewer
than a dozen foreign and domestic automobile manufacturers who have
buyers in the market. Even the number of schools, with their buying
needs, is small compared to the number of households in the United
States.

## Buyer Differences

Differences between organizational buyers and consumer buyers center
also around the buying situation itself. These differences are (1) service
versus price; (2) trained, professional buyers; (3) commonalty of negotiation; (4) reciprocal buying agreements; (5) more group decisions; and (6)
longer purchasing process.

The role of service after the sale is important to all buyers. However, organizational buyers place more emphasis on delivery dates, technical assistance, product quality as well as price. To consumers, price is
important; and many times the necessity for a product can be postponed
to get a better price.

Organizational buyers are professionals trained to buy goods and
services. They are informed buyers who have more technical expertise
than most consumers. Consumers with little training become informed by

necessity as a problem arises rather than buying on a continual basis as organizational buyers do.

The large purchasing power of organizations allows them to negotiate price more often than consumers. Few consumers are able to negotiate the price of staple goods such as paper towels. However, organizations often negotiate a contract a year in advance with suppliers for their towel needs.

This negotiation process often prompts the offer of reciprocal buying arrangements. Businesses that practice reciprocity can be affected by less-than-optimal purchases and restrictions on the normal operation of a competitive market.

Since the purchasing agent is distanced from the users of goods that are purchased by the organization, there are more group-buying decisions in firms than in households. The multiple buying influences impact a firm's buyer more because of the need to get users' inputs. In households, the users are present; thus the decision maker has daily contact with the user. Also, the decider is a user of the product.

Organizations buy products that are more technical and complex, so they take more time to make decisions. They often buy according to a strategic plan calling for increased sales in the future. They must anticipate the short- and long-term demands from their customers. Household buyers often buy for the immediate future rather than for several years in advance of their need.

## Summary

Organizational buying is a complex, multifaceted task that has similarities to household buying. The firm and the household buying processes have been detailed through the buying center concept. This concept takes into account the multiple buying influences on both the organization and the household. The situational environment, or macroenvironment, is examined along with the internal and external environments that affect the buying process. The decision maker must make the purchase after gathering information and being influenced by factors outside and inside the purchase. Because it is an uncontrollable factor, the macroenvironment is monitored in the context of the purchase to be made. Members of the organization, household, and other groups to which the buyer belongs or wishes to belong also exert influence. Conflict can arise in one environment or between environments that can alter the outcome of the purchase decision.

No buyers make decisions in a vacuum. Factors such as needs, wants, and drives motivate one to enter the marketplace. Bargaining power, amount of uncertainty, perceived risk, and ability to communicate influence purchase decisions. The decision process begins as the decider recognizes a problem, internalizes the search, and assigns responsibilities for buying a product or service to solve the problem. Only the activities of solving a problem are exposed in the marketplace. This occurs through the external search to fulfill a salient need.

The salient need a prospect brings into the dialogue is a window into the "inner workings" of the customer. Establishing a trust bond with the customer lets the salesperson know about a client and what influences the decision. Thus the salesperson can more accurately meet the needs of the client.

Also, differences exist between organizational and household buying centers in their markets and in their buyers. Organizational buyers are fewer than household buyers; they buy more complex products that are affected by consumer demand; they buy in larger volumes; and their companies are often concentrated in certain geographical areas.

To the organizational buyer, service after the sale is vital. The purchasing agent differs from his or her household counterpart in the amount of training and in the factors of negotiation and reciprocity. Moreover, the time for making an organizational purchase is longer than that needed to make a household purchase.

## Key Terms

organizational buying
household
nuclear family
buying center
buyers
influencers
deciders
users
gatekeepers
macroenvironments (situational
 influences)
new buy
cultural influences
sfatus groups
social influences
reciprocity
modified rebuy
straight rebuy
needs

want
drive (desire)
functional motives (task related)
psychological motives (nontask
 related)
psychological influences
motivation
expert power
referent power
self-concept
self-perception
risk
decision maker
personal sources of information
professional sources of
 information
marketing sources of information
salient need
derived demand

# Discussion Questions

1. Compare and contrast organizational buyers and household buyers.

2. Who is the buyer for a computer in an organization? In the home?

3. Whom should the salesperson try to influence in the organizational buying center: the decision maker, influencer, gatekeeper, or user? How about in the household?

4. How does the macroenvironment affect the purchase of an office typewriter? A capital good such as production machinery?

5. Which influence, the cultural or social, is more important in a buying center for the purchase of a typewriter to be used in the president's office?

6. What influences do the purchasing agents' interests have on the ultimate purchase of a word processor? On floor wax?

7. Describe in detail the activities a purchasing agent would follow in a new purchase of a corporate airplane?

8. What types of information would a buying center for a corporation need to purchase a word processor? Where would this information be obtained?

9. Who would be included in the buying center of a family-owned furniture store that was purchasing its first computer for its store?

10. Describe decision-making process for the purchasing agent. For a household.

11. How does a family differ from a household?

12. Define salient need.

13. Explain the influence of a decision maker's interests in purchasing a gas stove. A loaf of bread.

14. What impact might other adults in the household have on the selection of an automobile?

# Decision Crossroads: Ethical Issues

Tom Ritter has been selling wholesale for Sherman Tobacco and Candy Company for the past year. He has been very frustrated with his low sales and inability to meet his quotas. He took a day off in his territory to ride with Sally Hunter, a very successful saleswoman for Sherman's. He noticed that she had a practice of giving gifts to entice purchases. In one case Sally called on a female buyer who ran a cafeteria. This rotund lady had a "sweet tooth" and really liked candy. She said, "I play on her emotions and always give her a box of king size Snickers each time I visit. I use the pretense that they would 'melt in the hot sun' in the summertime or 'it overstocks my inventory.' I always get a big order, and it only costs me $3.50. I give her a smaller discount than she really qualifies for to make up for the price of the box of Snickers."

### Discussion:

1. Are Sally's actions ethical? Under what circumstances, if any?
2. Should Tom adopt this emotional appeal in selling?

## Case 6-1   **United Auto Supply**

The United Auto Supply Corporation has been developing a chain of independent, franchised dealers in the auto parts field. When signing up, dealers surrender their identity and become "United" auto supply stores to the public. Each store looks like others in the chain and operates as one unit. However, profits or losses belong to the local dealer. Mr. Knoble, who has operated his own store for the past five years, has been contacted by Mr. Clift of United to win him over to membership in the franchised group. The two men had discussed the program once before.

| | |
|---|---|
| *Clift* | Just ask yourself, Mr. Knoble, who gives you the most trouble—the little independent auto supply dealers or the strong chains? Who does the heavy advertising? Who runs the traffic-building leader promotions? It's the big boys. Right? We want to make you a more profitable, stronger operator. |
| *Knoble* | Sure you do, but at my expense. If I tie in with you, first I have to give up my independence. I become 'Mr. Nobody.' And suppose things don't work out. I practically have to start building my business all over again. |
| *Clift* | It is true you give up your identity but not to become 'Mr. Nobody.' You become a member of a well-known group. Surely you will agree that 'United' is a stronger name in this business than 'Knoble.' |
| *Knoble* | Maybe so. But then you say I must buy all my goods from you—and I can see from your price list that I can do better on many items from other sources. That doesn't make much sense. |

| | |
|---|---|
| *Clift* | Mr. Knoble, I understand what you're saying, but it really does make sense. After all, where does the money come from to run our heavy advertising or to operate the central organization of the chain? We naturally tack on a mark-up to cover these costs. We buy as cheaply as any other distributor, but we must cover the promotional and central organization costs too. |
| *Knoble* | How do I know you aren't charging me too much? After all, once I go with you, I cannot get out easily. I'm not sure. |
| *Clift* | Just look at all the other dealers who have signed up. They know what they are doing. There are some smart men in our group, I'm sure you will admit. Remember, we can only make money if you do. Our organization is only as strong as the individual stores in it. If we didn't think you would work out profitably, we would not invite you in. |
| *Knoble* | The way you say it, it all sounds good. But somehow I've got the feeling that there is a weakness in the proposition somewhere. Let me discuss it with my lawyer. Then I'll let you know my decision. |

**Discussion:**

1. How has the salesman attempted to "clarify need"? Is the picture drawn as sharply as it might be?
2. From the discussion, would you say the benefits to the prospect are quite clear?
3. Do you feel that the salesman has made a strong case for his proposition? Are the doubts of the prospect reasonable? Did he use high pressure?

## Case 6–2   **Franklin Furniture Company**

Often people buy products or services for social-psychological reasons. Words in a sales presentation may elicit sympathetic emotions to develop a common bond between the salesperson and the customer. Analyze the following salesperson's statements and list the social-psychological appeals that were used in the blanks. (Note: Each blank holds a number which represents a word)

*Social-Psychological Buying Motives*

1. Comfort
2. Relaxation
3. Self-esteem
4. Pleasure
5. Emulation
6. Financial gain or loss
7. Romantic desire
8. Physical fitness
9. Fear
10. Creativity
11. Curiosity

"Mr. Jefferies, you are losing money every day with your present set-up (**1, 9, 11**). John Hill over on Pocher Boulevard is outselling you two to one (_____), and his location is no better than yours (_____, _____). Certainly John is no better businessman than you, probably not as experienced (_____). But he is using our merchandising plan to increase his business, and he's making more money than he did with his old set-up (_____, _____). You certainly could use more money, couldn't you Mr. Jefferies (_____, _____)? And you are probably making plans now for the education of your fine daughter (_____). That's going to take more money, isn't it (_____)? Why not make this money you'll need right in your own business? Let me show you how our modern merchandising plan has made extra profits for other dealers in this town (_____, _____, _____, _____)."

## Discussion:

1. Was the dialogue "too pushy" or used properly?
2. In what circumstances would these appeals be appropriate?

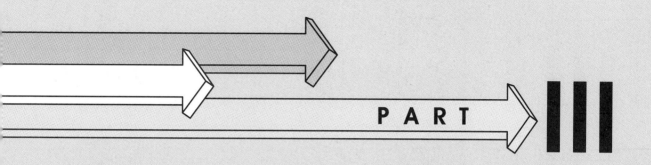

P A R T

III

# Applying Selling Skills

Parts I and II examined *Preparing to Sell* and *Learning Selling Skills* respectively. Skills were presented that, when applied, will help to fulfill the customer's needs. As was shown, the seller reflects the selling skills learned in sales training, while the buyer reflects the influences of the buying environment. Together seller and buyer create a dynamic environment within which to interact.

Part III shows how to apply sales theories to help solve clients' problems. Each of the seven chapters within Part III begins with a diagram (Figure 7–1, Figure 8–1, etc.) illustrating the selling skill that is focused on within the chapter. Together these skills form the customer–salesperson dialogue, the application of the selling skills to the world of selling. In Part III, you are shown how to apply the skills you learned in Parts I and II to find a client (prospect), to analyze the sales situation, to formulate a plan, and to adapt that plan in the customer–salesperson dialogue. You are also shown how to apply sales skills throughout the customer–salesperson dialogue as it progresses stage-by-stage from contact to follow-up.

In the real world, you have a choice: ``to make dust or to eat dust,'' as the trailblazers of the Old West used to say. You can lead the pack and blaze the trail for others to follow (make dust), or you can follow the trailblazers and eat their dust. The choice is yours.

**Chapter Outline**

Prospecting
  Leads from Your Company
  Leads from Current Customers
  Leads Supplied by the Salesperson

Pre-Approach Stage
  Qualifying the Prospects
  Strategic Pre-Approach Information

Information Sources

## CHAPTER 7

# Prospecting for Relationships

**Learning Objectives**

After reading this chapter you will be able to:

- Define prospecting and a qualified prospect
- Recognize and discuss sources within your company that can provide leads for prospective customers
- Explain how satisfied customers can help sellers find prospective customers
- Describe how a center of influence works
- Explain how salespeople supply their own leads
- Discuss the objectives of the preapproach stage
- Understand how a prospect is qualified by the seller
- Recognize the types and sources of information needed to qualify a prospect.

## IN THE FIELD

Many sales leads turn out to be dead-ends. In a single month the DeVilbiss Co. of Toledo, Ohio received 2,700 letters asking about its Norwegian-made Trallfa spray-painting robot. Considering that only 2,000 robots were sold nationwide in a year, the bulk of these leads will obviously turn out to be dead-ends. In fact, "about 85 percent of them fall off after we make an initial phone call," says Timothy Bublick, manager of robot applications engineering at DeVilbiss, a division of Champion Spark Plug. How can a company avoid wasting valuable sales time on these leads? According to Bublick, "We have 62 regional representatives who qualify all leads for us and tell us whether these guys are for real."

*Source:* Al Urbanski, "It's Tough to Find Sales Jobs for Robots," *Sales and Marketing Management* 131 (September 1981). Reprinted by permission, © September 1981.

Finding customers beyond those currently buying from a salesperson requires prospecting. Prospecting for new accounts is important because buyers may begin purchasing from a competitor for various reasons; or there may be a need to increase sales beyond current levels of productivity. As illustrated in Figure 7–1, prospecting begins the Customer–Salesperson dialogue. This prospecting ranges from generating leads to qualifying these prospects and gathering information about them before making a sales call.

> A few people get up bright and early; most of us just get up early.
>
> **Phil Postgret**

## Prospecting

Once a salesperson has had basic sales training, it is time to put these skills to the test. Although most salespeople are assigned a specific territory with an established customer base, they must always be expanding this base to increase sales. **Prospecting** locates and separates prospects from "suspects." The salesperson goes through a qualifying process in the identification of prospects. A list of possible new clients, or **leads** (pronounced leeds), is much different from a list of qualified prospects. Only

**prospecting**

**leads**

Figure 7–1
**Prospecting's Place in the Customer–Salesperson Dialogue**

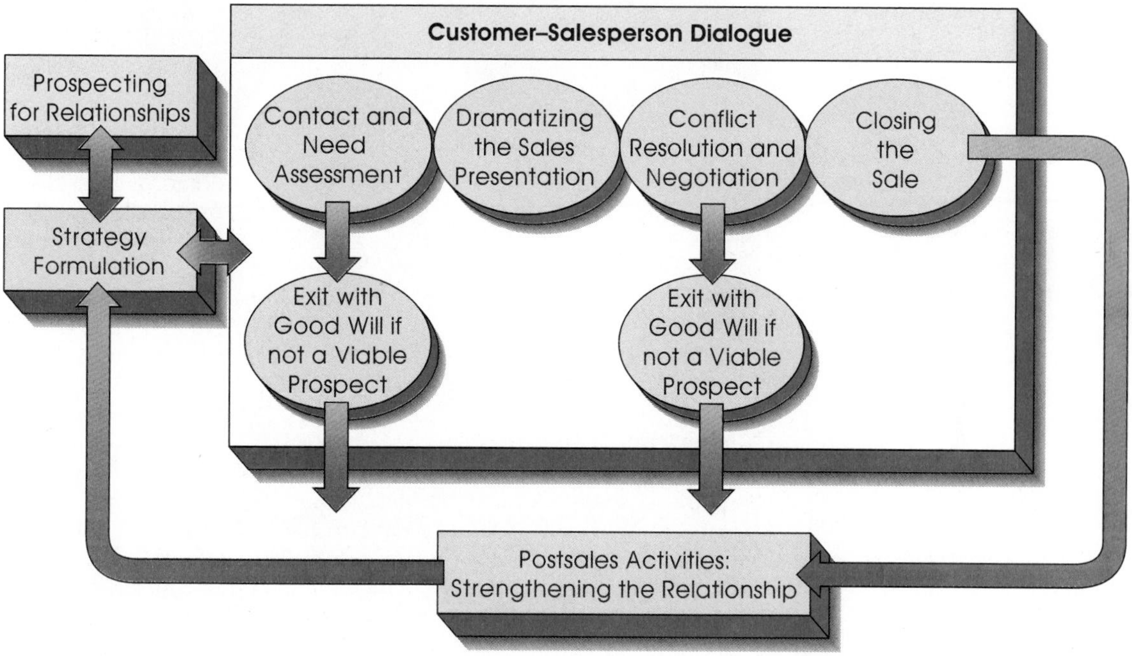

a client who needs, can benefit from, can afford, and has the authority to
buy a product is a **qualified prospect.** Before a salesperson can qualify    **qualified prospect**
people, however, he or she must develop a list of prospective clients. This
list can come from a variety of sources.

## Leads From Your Company

Leads from your company are the easiest leads to obtain; yet many salespeople fail to use them fully. In addition to the sales department, sources
may come from such areas as the credit, service, and promotion
departments.

### Sales Departments

Sales departments have current, active, customer lists, which are the easiest type of lists to obtain. Customers who already buy from a company
are naturally the best prospective customers, since they have already been
qualified and they have experience in dealing with the company. Many

Leads come from many sources. Here, a saleswoman reviews lists of inquiries from prospective customers who have completed and returned coupons seeking additional information.

salespeople concentrate the majority (up to 90 percent) of their time on current customers. Peter Drucker points out that the odds of making a sale with an active customer are 1 in 2 and with an inactive customer 1 in 4. But with a new prospect the odds are 1 in 16.[1] To be most useful, customer lists must constantly be updated or the list will dwindle due to attrition and the failure to add new prospects to an existing list. Huck Manufacturing, a $125 million fastener systems producer, developed a computerized program to handle the 2,600 inquiries it receives annually from its advertising and promotional campaigns. It now has a systematic follow-up program for information requests by qualifying the lead and salesperson contacts.[2]

## Credit Departments

The credit department is a gold mine of information concerning the inactive accounts of past customers. Even though former customers are not now active customers, they are still good prospects. They have experience with the company and are somewhat knowledgeable about its people, policies, and products. Inactive customers can often turn into active customers if the salesperson can learn and overcome their reasons for nonpatronage.

The credit department belongs to credit rating services. The salesperson's use of these services can provide information concerning newly formed companies and their financial status. Usually this department is not sales oriented enough to provide this service without the salesperson requesting such information.

## Service Departments

Service departments maintain equipment for a company's customers. Service records indicate frequency and type of repairs and amounts spent on repairs. Analysis of these records could indicate that replacement equipment may save the customer money, making that customer a good prospect.

Service people may need incentives to bring possible customers to the attention of salespeople. Traditionally service departments have been operated as though they were a separate, independent branch of the company. A service department can be a source of potential customers, either through looking at records or by making personal contact, thereby creating goodwill.

## Promotional Departments

Promotional departments of a company provide different types of leads from a variety of activities. Because advertising plays an important role

## PARTNERSHIPS

"There's many a sale in your serviceman's tool box," says Sherrill Estes, sales trainer for an office supply firm. "One of my customer's systems was old and constantly breaking down, and my service person suggested that I visit them. I did and sold them $100,000 worth of new equipment. I hear sales professionals complain that their service departments don't turn in leads promptly or develop good relationships with their customers. Perhaps that's because the salesperson took them for granted. I've learned that it's important to build a relationship with all the people who deal with my customers. In fact, I gave a $1,000 gift to the serviceman who gave me the $100,000 sales lead," she reported.

*Source:* "Sales Talk," *Sales and Marketing Management* 141 (June 1989). Reprinted by permission, © June 1989.

in promotional plans, leads come from responses to advertising such as direct mailings, coupons, and customer reply cards.[3] Figure 7–2 illustrates ways of gaining customer leads. Another example is Motorola Communications and Electronics, which developed a direct mail campaign to sell Motorola pagers through its direct sales force.[4]

### Exhibits, Conventions, and Trade Shows

Exhibits, conventions, and trade shows—opportunities for a company to provide a booth—can collect excellent leads. Here, potential customers fill out a coupon or an information card indicating an interest in the company or in its product or in both.[5] Such cards provide leads for sellers. Studies show that more than 20 percent of the inquiries generated through advertising, promotions, trade shows, and direct mail will result in sales within six months if handled properly.[6] Trade shows stimulate interest in products and provide leads as in the case of the DeVilbiss Co. (see *In the Field*).

**Figure 7–2**
**Typical Customer Reply Card**

PLEASE
FILL OUT
CARD
AND MAIL
AT ONCE!

## SALES & MARKETING MANAGEMENT MAGAZINE'S
## FIRST ANNUAL SALES EXECUTIVE'S GOLF INVITATIONAL
### *November 1 through November 6, 1990 in Hawaii*

In order to be considered, you must fill out the entire card. Thank you.

Name: _____    Title: _____
Company: _____    Telephone: _____
Street: _____  City: _____  State: _____
Zip: _____  Fax: _____
Type of Business: _____

Number of attendees I'm considering for Hawaii: _____
I have planned meetings in the following regions: _____

☐ Caribbean      ☐ Mexico       ☐ Northeast      ☐ Canada
☐ Midwest        ☐ Northwest    ☐ Texas          ☐ Southeast
☐ Hawaii         ☐ Europe       ☐ Asia           ☐ California

My last 2 functions were held at (hotel, city) 1. _____    2. _____

My job function includes responsibilities for:
☐ Meetings       ☐ Incentives       ☐ Conventions       ☐ Other: _____

The final decision-maker for site selection is: _____

When are you considering Hawaii for a meeting? _____
For how many attendees? _____

My golf handicap is: _____

*Source: Sales and Marketing Management* 142 (July 1990). Reprinted by permission, © July 1990.

## Canvassers

Companies often employ people specifically to develop personal contact with prospective customers. Often called "**spotters**" or "**bird dogs**", these people generally use the telephone to arrange appointments for other salespeople. These canvassers are often paid directly for leads that result in a sale.

      A modification of this system is to ask other people, such as policemen, bankers, bartenders, retail clerks—people who get around and hear information about other people—to be spotters. These people hear a lot of information that can lead to prospective customers. Paying for this information, however, may present a conflict of interest for the provider of information because of ethics violations that make it illegal in some industries as well as in some states.

"**spotters**," or
"**bird dogs**"

## Subscription Services

Monthly newsletters of collected information are available concerning various industry developments, such as the *F. W. Dodge Report* and Herb Ireland's *Sales Prospector* (Figure 7–3). For a subscription fee, businesses receive various types of information from **subscription services** that can prove to be quite helpful to salespeople.

**subscription
services**

# Leads From Current Customers

Current customers are a good source for new customers; as such, they are called **referral leads.** For the relationship salesperson who keeps his or her clients satisfied, the clients readily recommend the salesperson to their friends on a voluntary basis. Many times leads can be obtained merely by asking. Satisfied customers often recommend places to buy products to friends and acquaintances. More often dissatisfied customers recommend where *not* to buy products.

**referral leads**

## Endless Chain Method

The **endless chain** is a system whereby the salesperson asks for names of others who might be interested in seeing a demonstration. If each person interviewed supplies the salesperson with two or three names, an endless chain of prospects is made. This system works best when the customer is sold on the product and is enthusiastic about sharing his or her good fortune with friends.

      By using the endless-chain method, some companies are effective in the development of prospects, especially in the sale of intangibles such as investments or insurance. Still other companies give gifts to customers

**endless chain**

Figure 7-3   **Lead Subscription Service**

---

*August 3, 1990*

# Sales Prospector®

### GEORGIA, FLORIDA and ALABAMA

---

### ALABAMA

ANNISTON, AL & SPRINGFIELD, MO -- Food Ingredients Technology Co., a converter of processed chicken parts into ingredients for pet food and other products and a unit of International Dehydrated Foods, 2003 E. Sunshine, Springfield, MO 65804 (417/881-7820), is building a new $10 million, 57,000 sq. ft. plant in the Anniston Industrial Park at Anniston, AL 36201 with completion set for next April according to Bill Lile, manager of business development and special projects for the Missouri firm. FITCO has developed a new proprietary technology for further processing of chicken parts which involves converting backs, necks, bones, and other parts left over by chicken processors into protein for use in other foods, such as canned soups. About 50 persons will be employed at first, expanding to a 70-person work force.

BIRMINGHAM, AL -- Birmingham-Jefferson Civic Center Authority, Civic Center Plaza, Birmingham, AL 35204 (205/328-8160) has named Dunn Construction Co., Inc., P.O. Box 11546, Birmingham, AL 35202 as general contractor for a previously announced $33.7 million expansion and renovation of the 350,000 sq. ft. Birmingham-Jefferson Civic Center east complex. A new exhibition and sports museum complex will be built, and existing exhibition space will be renovated.

BIRMINGHAM, AL -- Birmingham-Jefferson Civic Center Authority, Civic Center Plaza, Birmingham, AL 35204 (205/328-8160) will enter into an agreement with Sheraton Operating Co., 60 State St., Boston, MA 02109 to operate the expanded Sheraton Hotel at 21st St., North and Ninth Aves., Birmingham. Work begins early next year on a $40 million expansion of the hotel with completion set for November, 1991 as part of the current $130 million expansion of the Civic Center complex. The project will enlarge the hotel from 405 to 771 rooms, the largest in the state, and is expected to attract more and larger conventions according to officials. The new agreement calls for Sheraton to get six percent of the annual total revenues of the hotel up to $20 million, with a one percent increase for revenue beyond $20 million.

BIRMINGHAM, AL & KINGSPORT, TN -- Healthsouth Rehabilitation Corp., Two Perimeter Park S., Birmingham, AL 35243 (205/967-7116) plans early construction of a 50-bed rehabilitation hospital next to Holston Valley Hospital and Medical Center in Kingsport, TN 37662 according to Tom Carmen, vice president of corporate development. Construction of the Rehabilitation Center will take about one year.

BIRMINGHAM, AL & PHOENIX, AZ -- Birmingham Steel Corp., 3000 Riverchase Galleria, Suite 1000, Birmingham, AL 35244 (205/985-9290) announced it has taken an option on 1,000 acres west of Phoenix, AZ where it may build a steel mini-mill. The $100 million-plus mill could, reportedly, begin producing 500,000 tons of steel a year by late 1992. Up to 250 persons could be employed.

© 1990, Westgate Publishing Company, Inc.

---

The SALES PROSPECTOR® will **increase your sales, boost your profits,** and **save your time and energy.** It is a monthly "prospect research" report for sales representatives and other business people interested in industrial, commercial and institutional expansions and relocations in new or existing buildings. Reports are available for regional or national coverage. Subscription rates and coverage are shown on the last page.

---

*Source: The Sales Prospector,* a publication of Westgate Publishing Co., Inc., 751 Main St., Waltham, MA 02254

## PARTNERSHIPS

Ron Betten, a broker at a brokerage firm that caters to the affluent, learned the value of interpersonal relationships as he made cold calls in 120-degree heat in Las Vegas. "The city is dominated by a handful of old families who've lived there a long time," he says. "And I couldn't break in."

He called Hank Greenspan, then the owner of the *Las Vegas Sun,* 15 times. Betten saw Greenspan as the key to the city. "Once you have the credibility of one important client, getting the next is easier." Greenspan was to be honored at a $1,000-a-plate banquet in Los Angeles, a fund raiser for the Hebrew University, one of Greenspan's and Betten's favorite causes. Betten bought himself a ticket. "I went up to him at the dinner, put my arm around him, and said, 'Hank, I've called you 15 times and gotten nowhere.' It was the happiest day of his life—he couldn't say no. He told me to call him in the morning."

*Source:* Eric Olsen, "Breaking the Sales Barrier," *Success* 37 (May 1990). Reprinted with permission of *Success* magazine, Hals Holding Corp., 1990.

who cooperate in relaying names of others who may be interested in the product.

### Referral Lead

The best lead from a specific customer is a referral lead. Like the endless chain, it is a personal recommendation from a satisfied customer to a friend suggesting that the friend look at your product offering. It differs from the endless chain because it is a more formal approach. Preferably the referral lead takes the form of a formal letter of introduction recommending both you and your product. If it is difficult to get the formal letter of introduction, a note briefly dashed off on a business card will suffice. In either case, the necessary personal touch is present.

The referral method is based strongly on successful, relationship selling, so it will be difficult for the nonproductive salespeople to obtain. Sellers appreciate referrals, since they are based on satisfaction and confidence. Few people will refer a salesperson to their friends if they do not like the product or the seller.

### Center of Influence

A method of prospecting that relies on an informal referral is the **center of influence.** In this system salespeople cultivate a community or group

center of influence

of people who recommend clients to them. Often these people are influential citizens such as accountants, doctors, lawyers, teachers, city officials, or others who are active in social and civic organizations and come into daily contact with many people. Salespeople join social and civic organizations such as country clubs, fraternal organizations, and other groups to gain access to centers of influence (see *Partnerships*). Such contacts can be turned into good leads, but often prospecting must be done before or after meetings.

Centers of influence are important to the success of a salesperson, particularly in industries such as insurance and investments. If a center of influence "turns sour" because of a bad experience with a salesperson, the group will spread derogatory remarks as quickly as it trades compliments when things go right. Because the center of influence method of prospecting can be a fragile relationship, it needs to be built on honesty, integrity, and friendship.

Salespeople using this method usually make an attempt to repay the efforts of their contacts. Gifts at Christmas time, cards on special occasions such as anniversaries, and an occasional lunch are all ways a salesperson can use to say "thank you" to contacts for their personal courtesy and help. Even a brief phone call thanking the center of influence can solidify the relationship.

Each of us is in some way a center of influence, since we exert some influence on others. The more contacts we have, the more centers of influence we can use to find new prospects.

## Leads Supplied by the Salesperson

Many times a salesperson must rely on his or her own resources to obtain leads. These resources include observation, telephone, direct mail, and cold canvassing.

### Observation

**observation**

Careful **observation** can reveal the names of potential customers. Insurance salespeople, for example, can read newspaper birth, death, marriage, and graduation announcements for signals to sell. The alert salesperson constantly looks for signs of a need to be filled. Real estate salespeople, for example, frequently drive around looking for "For Sale by Owner" signs. Such a sign indicates a potential customer who might need help in selling a house. Conversations overheard may provide clues to other potential prospects. Salespeople should always keep their eyes and ears open for leads.[7]

Following up on leads using telemarketing provides the opportunity for the salesperson to assess customers' needs and to gather information to make a more effective sales presentation.

## Telephone and Direct Mail

Telephone calls and direct mailings are frequently used methods of prospecting. The telephone, a direct and personal method to secure leads, is a great timesaver.[8] Telephone calls require little time and expense, so they are appropriate when too many leads make personal qualifying visits impossible.[9] With up to 30 percent of the market having answering machines and the overuse and abuse of people making "annoying calls that interrupt personal time," salespeople have to be careful how they use telemarketing.

One vacuum cleaner seller's wife systematically calls people in the telephone directory until she obtains five leads a day. Eventually she will complete the directory and then begin over again. She just asks to be able to give a demonstration of the vacuum cleaner. She provides so many leads for her husband that he has little time to do additional prospecting. Telephone directories as well as city, trade, social, and professional directories are worthwhile lists of potential customers for some types of salespeople. The business-to-business telephone directory should not be overlooked as a source of potential customers.

When salespeople use direct mail (Figure 7–4), it has a more personalized effect than when a company uses it. Using direct mail allows a salesperson to construct a qualified prospective customer list. Its efficiency is dependent on a good list of clients and a compelling offer. Several door-to-door companies have their salespeople pass out material with return postcards allowing prospects to request additional information from the company.

**Figure 7–4**
**Example of a Direct**
**Mail Letter**

THOMAS   J.   WOLFF,   C L U
Chartered Financial Consultant
Wolff-Zackin Building
P. O. Box H
Vernon, Connecticut 06066
Telephone (203) 875-2591

Ms. Carol Baker
123 Davis Street
Vernon, CT 06066

Dear Ms. Baker:

According to government statistics for every 100 people starting their careers only 3 are ultimately financially successful. The others didn't plan to fail, they failed to plan.

Financial Need Analysis is a new planning service which helps people to establish their financial goals and demonstrates tax advantaged methods which help achieve those goals.

Would you like to receive more information?

To do so just drop the enclosed pre-addressed card in the mail. You'll receive a booklet describing Financial Need Analysis.

There is no obligation of any kind.

Sincerely yours,

Thomas J. Wolff, CLU, ChFC

TJW/ds

*Source:* Reprinted by permission of Vernon-Longman Publishing Inc., 1988.

### Cold Canvassing

Making calls without prior contact with the prospect is called **cold canvassing,** or cold calling. Since it involves calling on every person who might have a use for the product, cold canvassing may prove helpful when other methods of prospecting have proved fruitless.

Cold canvassing is more effective in some industries than in others. The investment and insurance industries are not successful in using cold canvassing. These industries need to establish a professional image with the customer, and cold canvassing does not allow this image to develop as easily.

In reality, most salespeople who use cold canvassing qualify their prospects by observation, thereby actually using a modified cold canvass method. Applying cold canvass in the theoretical sense in the marketplace would take an inordinate amount of time, much of which would be wasted on unqualified customers. For example, it would be practically useless for a salesperson selling central air conditioning systems to call on every home in a city, for those homes that already have new central air units would obviously not be prospects.

Handing out business cards may enhance one's cold canvassing. For instance, Joe Girard, a successful car salesman, puts several of his business cards in the glove compartment of every car he sells. He tells the owner to write his own name on the back of the card and to give it to someone who is looking for an auto. In return, Joe promises the customer a money stipend for every signed card returned to him by a prospect. Joe also distributes business cards from his box seat at professional sports games. When the home team scores, he throws handfuls of business cards like confetti into the air. Some sports fans who retrieve them are prospective car buyers.[10] Many salespeople are not as flamboyant at passing out cards but do distribute their business cards personally and through present customers.

## Preapproach Stage

Now that a salesperson has a list of prospective customers, a strategic plan must be formed to make sure that time is used effectively and productively. There are five objectives of the preapproach stage: (1) to qualify prospects, (2) to gain insight into how to approach the prospect, (3) to obtain information that will help to develop a better relationship between the customer and the presentation (information to customize the presentation), (4) to minimize salesperson errors, and (5) to give the salesperson confidence. The first stage of the strategic plan is to qualify the prospects.

## Qualifying The Prospects

Making sales calls costs time and money. Therefore the salesperson must make sure to call on only those people who are thought to be excellent potential customers, that is, qualified customers.[11] Some salespeople are using telemarketing to qualify customers, as shown in the *Technological Bulletin.* Many salespeople appear to spend more time selling to prospects who do not intend to buy than to those who do intend to buy. The old criterion that measured selling effectiveness by the number of calls made is no longer valid. What matters is the quality of the calls.[12] The salesperson should ask himself or herself the following questions:

- Does the prospective buyer really need my product?
- Do top managers recognize that need?
- Can I justify my product's benefits as a response to that need?
- Do they have the authority to buy?
- Can the prospect pay for it?
- Is the prospect accessible?

These questions can be summarized by focusing on two important issues: (1) Can my company be of service to the client? and (2) Can I bring the two of us together? Perhaps a sales representative should prepare a "prospecting presentation"—a mini sales presentation to get attention and to answer these questions.

## TECHNOLOGY BULLETIN

### Computer Software

Since qualifying customers by telemarketing is efficient, Sawtooth Software, Inc. has developed a program, Ci2, that can be used by salespeople to perform this task. This program provides directions on questionnaire construction, a logic editor, questionnaire administration program, and respondent data analysis. Ci2 allows the creation of up to 250 questions with instructions for their completion written by the salesperson. After gathering the data, simple tabulations and preparation of reports are provided. This analysis allows the salesperson to qualify each client's prospective needs and to anticipate the needs of the client before making contact, thus eliminating calls on customers who are not good prospects.

*Source: Ci2 Software,* (Sawtooth Software: Cincinnati, Ohio) 1985.

Only people who meet the above qualifications are good prospects; thus a salesperson may skip gathering or using additional qualifying information. A good example is the Durolite salesman who sold only fluorescent bulbs. In his calls he first determined if the prospect used fluorescent light fixtures before he began a sales presentation. Otherwise the sales presentation was wasted on customers who had no fluorescent fixtures that used his product.

## Approach Strategy

Each prospect type must be approached differently. Gathering adequate preapproach information will allow the salesperson to customize the sales presentation for each type of client. Some customers want a businesslike approach, yet others prefer an informal approach. Some prefer a rapid tempo, while a rapid sales presentation tempo discourages others from buying. A sound preapproach investigation should disclose a customer's characteristics and preferences. Specific approach strategies are discussed in detail in Chapter 8.

## Strategic Planning

A sales presentation can take many forms. A good sales presentation is built around the customer information discovered during the preapproach stage. Some presentations can be built around low price; however, stress-

Analyzing the lead information helps develop an approach strategy for a qualified prospect.

ing the economic factors of a product would be fruitless if the buyer wants a luxury model. It is the preapproach information that allows the sales presentation to be tailored for a particular customer's needs. Presentation methods are specifically discussed in Chapter 10.

### Error Avoidance

Each customer's peculiarities must be taken into account if a sales presentation is to be successful. Therefore use of the preapproach information concerning a prospect's habits, protocol, likes, and dislikes prevents potential errors from occurring. For example, a candy and tobacco wholesale seller called on a fruit market. His preapproach information told him that the owner's religious beliefs precluded the selling of tobacco products. Therefore the salesman, a smoker, removed his cigarettes before entering the fruit market, thus eliminating the chance that he would inadvertently pull out a cigarette in the owner's office and perhaps squelch a sale. This is adaptive behavior rather than manipulative behavior because there was no attempt made to convince the owner that he did not smoke. He merely adapted his habits to comply with the wishes of the client.

### Confidence

Salespeople are their own worst enemies when it comes to fear. Fear becomes less significant when people realize that the only way to overcome their fear of the unknown is to prepare for events that are likely to happen. Using the preapproach provides salespeople with the information needed to reduce uncertainty in a sales presentation, thus reducing fear. Having knowledge about a situation gives the salesperson confidence, which experienced salespeople point out is an asset. After all, how can customers buy from a salesperson in whom they do not have confidence, and how can they have confidence in the salesperson when the salesperson lacks self-confidence? Being prepared definitely builds self-confidence and lessens fear.

A sound preapproach investigation better prepares a salesperson and makes him or her more able to anticipate and handle objections. Customer objections, such as lack of business, not making a profit, or not needing the product, can often be overcome through good preapproach fact finding. A business may have been given coverage in the local newspaper's business section because of its "up-and-coming" status. In the article the owner may have proclaimed "how profitable her business had become since its inception." To overcome the objection to need, a salesperson can use information cited in a newspaper article to support the "need" because of the growth of the business.

## Strategic Preapproach Information

The type of preapproach information will vary according to the customer and the type of product. If a product is sold for personal use, the preapproach information will be different from that for a product that is being sold to a business. Preapproach information should be gathered from various areas.

### Personally Gathered Information

Key information is sought about each prospect to develop a customer profile. This information is the basic foundation for establishing a relationship with clients according to the owner of Mackay Envelope Corporation. He feels the following information is essential[13]:

- *Names.* People like to be called by their names. Since sellers must spell and pronounce prospects' names correctly, they should ask a secretary or other knowledgeable individual how to spell and pronounce the name before the interview. To remember the name, make an association of the name and face. Use any method, but do remember the name. Also, call a client "Mr." or "Ms." until you are advised otherwise.
- *Age.* People who are older than the salesperson appreciate being treated with an air of respect for their seniority. People who are younger than the salesperson appreciate being recognized for their achievements at their age. Age itself, though, is a sensitive subject, so do not ask a client's age, however, since few people like being reminded of it.
- *Education.* Most people are extremely proud of their accomplishments. The college graduate is proud of his or her degree; the self-made person feels pride in having professional attainment without the degree. Be it formal or informal, education often builds feelings of mutual compatibility between customer and salesperson.
- *Family.* In most instances, people are delighted to talk about their families. What father would not be proud to talk about the most valuable football player award that his son received last week?
- *Place of residence.* Knowing where and how a customer lives provides the salesperson with information concerning the customer's values, since people surround themselves with objects that denote their values.
- *Reference groups.* The values of groups to which a person belongs also give evidence of that person's values. Therefore

knowing that a client has group memberships in organizations such as church, fraternal organizations, and civic groups provides a salesperson with very helpful information.

- *Personal idiosyncrasies.* Everyone has peculiarities, and salespeople must cater to them if they can be discovered. For example, Eddie abhors loud colors. Joanne, knowing this preference, wears only muted or plain earth-tone colors when she has an appointment with Eddie.

  Buyers often disclose their personal idiosyncrasies by their surroundings. Their clothing, habits, and environments disclose the way they feel about themselves. Therefore sellers should make note of clothes, pictures on the wall, jewelry, etc. to become aware of the client's personality.

- *Hobbies.* Sharing a hobby can create a bond of camaraderie and can increase trust. It is important to be honest, however. A seller's attempts to discuss a hobby that he or she followed only briefly several years ago or one about which he or she is not informed can only damage the seller's credibility, unless the seller honestly admits having little or no knowledge of the hobby.

## Company Gathered Information

The more a salesperson knows about a company and the industry in which it is involved, the better he or she can tailor the sales presentation. Listed below are a few questions that a salesperson should try to answer before the interview.

*Overall Company Operations*
- What kind of company is it—public or private?
- What does it produce or offer for sale?
- Who owns it, and who manages it?
- What is the quality of its products and services?
- What is its history and current standing in the industry?
- What are its annual net sales, assets, liabilities, worth?
- Is its management considered conservative or progressive?
- What is its size? How many employees does it have?
- What is the extent of its operations—local, national, international?
- Is it considered a growth company? Why?
- How has its stock fared in recent years?
- What is the current market price of its stock?
- Do you know of any pending mergers or acquisitions for this company at present or in the future?
- Is its credit good?

- What is its plant capacity?
- What manufacturing processes are employed, if any?
- What kind of materials and what kind of machines and equipment are used?
- What seasonal factors, if any, are involved in both production and maintenance schedules? In buying decisions?
- What are the company's purchasing practices?
- What purchasing systems and procedures are followed?
- Does the company buy from single or multiple sources?
- What lead time is involved in purchasing decisions?
- What are the credit factors involved in doing business with this company?

*Company Personnel Factors*
- Is buying done by individuals or on a committee basis?
- Who are the heads of individual purchasing departments?
- What is the specific name, job title, and buying authority of the actual purchase decision maker(s)?
- What people within the purchase department(s) may influence the buying decision?

Knowing answers to the above questions will help the salesperson adapt a presentation to the buyer's needs.

## Information Sources

The same sources that provide a lead can often provide preapproach information. Additionally, other sales representatives selling noncompeting lines will be willing to exchange information concerning buyers. Even competitors may divulge information, particularly if they have been unable to sell to a prospect.

The importance, however, is not in where the information is obtained but in the fact that it is obtained and then used to culminate in efficient selling. Another important point to remember is that confidential information must remain confidential. A salesperson should always try to maintain a reputation of being discreet and closed mouthed to be able to obtain the maximum amount of information.

## Summary

Knowing how to prepare for a good sales presentation is important. But knowing to whom that presentation is to be directed is equally important.

Determining who prospective customers are is called prospecting. Prospecting shows a salesperson where to obtain names of people who may be potential clients.

Qualifying potential buyers changes them from suspects into prospects. Qualifying permits a seller to concentrate on those who need or want to buy, thus saving time, energy, and money.

After possible customers have been identified and evaluated, the salesperson develops a preplanned strategy to help the customer. Using all of the information available, the salesperson designs a presentation adapted to each particular prospect. Having a preapproach plan adapted to the customer's needs allows the actual customer–salesperson dialogue to proceed beyond the client contact stage.

## Key Terms

prospecting
leads
qualified prospect
"spotters" or "bird dogs"
subscription services

referral leads
endless chain
center of influence
observation
cold canvassing

## Discussion Questions

1. Define prospecting.

2. Who is a qualified prospect?

3. List departments in a company that could supply leads to that firm's salespeople. Give examples of the types of leads one might get from each department.

4. Who are called "bird dogs?" What is their function?

5. Describe how the endless chain works.

6. Why is the referral method of getting leads especially good for relationship sellers?

7. What are centers of influence? How do salespeople develop and use them?

8. List some ways salespersons may develop their own leads.

9. What is "cold canvassing"? Discuss its effectiveness as a method of getting leads.

10. What is the preapproach, and what are its five objectives?

11. Describe some preapproach information the seller should know about the client. Why is it important that sellers, especially relationship sellers, have basic information about customers?

## Decision Crossroads: Ethical Issues

Jon Hays, sales trainee, was given notice that if he did well while traveling with his mentor, Phil, he would get his own territory soon. Phil allowed Jon to make several presentations in his own style to some of his established customers. Jon's selling style was much more aggressive than was Phil's, even verging on the unethical. Phil was ill for two days and told Jon to "sit tight" until they could resume the "route." Jon knew Phil's plans for the next two days. Anxious to prove himself, Jon contemplated working the route by himself until Phil could resume his duties; after all, he had all the necessary information concerning these clients, since Phil had given him their files to study.

**Discussion:**

1. In this situation, would Jon be acting unethically if he goes out on his own?
2. What are the possible consequences of this behavior? Are they all bad?
3. What would you do? Why?

## Case 7-1  **PDQ Printing Co.**

Mary Williams sells printing for PDQ Printing. She believes that everyone is a prospect until proven otherwise. One day she rushed into a local restaurant. A rather well-dressed man was standing at the counter buying some drinks to take out. She stood beside him and said, "I don't know how successful you are in your business, but I do rather well in mine. One thing I have noticed is that most successful people have very little time to sit down for lunch." The man laughed. "You're right," he said. "I'm pressed for time and seldom have time even for lunch. Today I'm busy because I've just wrapped up a big deal and have to be at the contract signing in 20 minutes." He looked at Mary and said, "You look like you are in a hurry, too. I like to see enthusiasm in others; I guess I feel that it is an important quality for success." As the man departed with his order, he asked Mary, "What business did you say you were in?" "Printing," she replied. "Well, here's my card. Give me a call sometime soon. I might need some printing done," he said, rushing out the door.

**Discussion:**

1. Evaluate Mary's approach. Do you feel this is an adequate method of cold calling?
2. What should Mary do before she makes an appointment with him?
3. Suggest other ways that Mary could get prospects.

## Case 7–2   Hinkle Metals and Supply

Hinkle Metals and Supply provides custom steel fabrication services to companies that use fabricated steel products. Since 1927 Hinkle has provided slitting, blanking, and leveling of metal products. They offer custom-made metal products and services to industrial manufacturers and sheet metal users throughout the Southeast. By using the latest in technology, Hinkle can produce metal products to a customer's specification at a lower cost than 75 percent of the users could produce in their own plants. Although they provide the best quality fabrication and the best service staff in the industry, Bill Bradbury was having trouble getting new contacts for Hinkle's services in the Texas territory to which he was assigned.

**Discussion:**

1. If you were Bradbury, how would you find prospects in Texas?
2. What approach would you take in appealing to these customers?
3. Go to the library and get a list of potential customers for Bradbury from four different sources.

## Chapter Outline

Planning for Building a Relationship
- Psychological Contract
- Need for Trust
- Need for Interdependence
- Customer Motives

Customer Types
- Silent
- Slow, Methodical/Hesitant
- Overcautious/Think It Over
- Procrastinator/Look Around
- Ego Involved/Decisive
- "Glad Hander"/Fact Finder
- The Skeptic/Chip on Shoulder/Arguer
- Impulsive/Changeable
- Grouch/Pessimist
- Harasser

Sales Plans
- Salesperson-Oriented Approaches
- Customer-Oriented Approaches

## CHAPTER 8

# Strategy Formulation

**Learning Objectives**

After reading this chapter, the student will be able to:

- Discuss the basic elements of strategic planning
- Explain the importance of the trust link
- Recognize customer motives for purchasing
- Discuss the different types of customers and the seller's adaptive behavior for each type
- Compare and contrast sales plan approaches.

## IN THE FIELD

*We took our eye off the ball.*    **John Akers**

John Akers, president of IBM Corporation, determined that customers were flocking to competitors such as Digital Equipment Corp. because of their inexpensive "open systems" that run on industry-standard (IBM compatible) software. The problem was an antiquated strategy. "We pushed for sales of IBM's giant mainframe computers when the customers were turning toward smaller super computers," explained Akers. "Reversing strategy, IBM adapted to its customers' needs by developing a line of open-system (systems that can network) workstations," he continued. However that is not all that is needed. What is making the strategy "fly" is timely delivery of the total package. IBM is back to doing what IBM managers know best: pumping out products and competing hard. Only now they are doing it with a different strategy.

*Source:* Peter Finch, and Andrea Rothman, "25 Executives to Watch," *The 1990 Business Week 1,000* (April 13, 1990): 126.

**strategy**

In earlier chapters, you became acquainted with the inputs of selling and with some ways salespeople get prospects. Strategy formulation enables salespeople to organize these inputs effectively to help prospects solve their problems. A **strategy,** in this case, is a plan designed from precall information to best meet the needs of the client. As illustrated in Figure 8–1, Chapter 8 discusses the components of strategy formulation. Strategy formulation ranges from the planning stage to the presentation of the sales plan.

Planning is essential to efficiency in any field but is especially so to salespeople. Having a strategy minimizes the chances that haphazard diversions could arise to hamper efficiency.[1] In addition, planning requires organization and leads to efficiency. Progress toward a more efficient and therefore a more profitable career comes only when one plans, measures results, and corrects future plans.[2] Emerson speaks of planning when he says, "Thought is the seed of action."

The skills that beginners in sales learn in school, in sales training classes, and on the job help to implement a career plan and to enhance chances for success. Having a complete set of "tools" or skills is not enough for successful selling, however; salespeople must also have a strategy, or plan of action. The most successful sales careers, though, are built upon yearly plans based on successful selling each day—*one day at a time.* Meeting each day's goals brings salespeople one step closer to the fulfillment of plans for that year and beyond.

**Figure 8-1**
**The Place of *Strategy Formulation* in the Customer-Salesperson Dialogue**

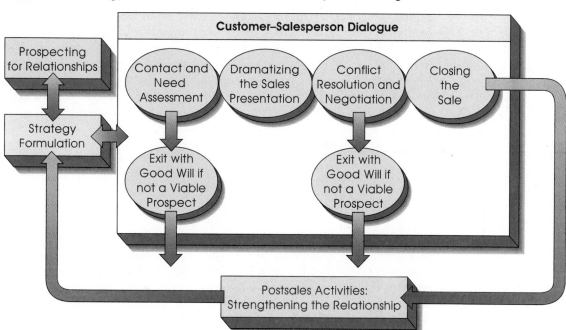

To reach sales goals, customers must be motivated by salespeople to act. Having a *strategy* allows salespeople to *prethink* and analyze situations and then to plan a tentative, tactful course of action that suffices for most commonly encountered situations. Of course, having a strategy for every situation is impossible. Typically one of Murphy's laws, "Anything that can go wrong will go wrong," prevails. Usually Clabaugh's corollary, "If it's going to go wrong, it will happen to me," is also true. However, salespeople come prepared with **contingency plans**—"what if" plans—so they can adapt to unexpected occurrences and react favorably to uncertainty.[3]

**contingency plans**

The **strategy formulation** phase of selling consists of systematically analyzing and classifying buyer input data into contingency plans of action. The seller examines clients by their need category (i.e., type of client) and develops alternative plans of action (sales plans) to minimize uncertainty in new selling situations. Having some strategy already planned enables one to allay fears or the "perceived uncertainty" that is induced by the cognitive process as customers wonder, "What is out there?" and "What can satisfy my needs?" Uncertainty also may relate to "what to do" about a problem or "Whom do I trust for advice?"

**strategy formulation**

## Planning for Building A Relationship ▬▬▬▬▬

Establishing a relationship is an essential goal in every strategy for relationship-building encounters. A *relationship* is established by developing *mutual*, *beneficial*, *empathetic* *rapport* built on trust (*EMBER*).[4] The trust link between customer and salesperson helps to decrease interpersonal tension and to increase communication effectiveness. It builds **source credibility** (believability and trustworthiness in the salesperson). A relationship depends on:

**source credibility**

- Establishing a foundation of shared values
- Aligning both parties on the purpose of the relationship and a commitment to its goals
- One hundred percent support from all personnel involved in the companies of both parties.

In this selling mode, the salesperson moves from selling products and services to supporting the buyer's purchasing decision—a helping relationship. *EMBER* is not only a "glowing" relationship but a growing one that builds over the long-term, not overnight. It establishes a lasting relationship. In new accounts, the relationship must overcome predispositions or biases of the customer, as shown by Stew Leonard's Dairy, Norwalk, Connecticut. He welcomed 2.5 million customers in his 100,000-

Maximizing their time, salespeople can fine-tune their strategies with the latest information from the home office. This may happen while they are performing other activities.

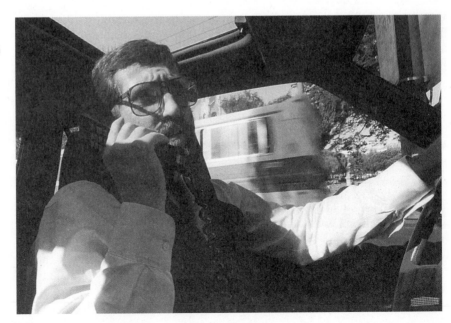

square-foot store ringing up $100 million annually. When he sought to open a second store in Danbury, Connecticut, he set up a circus tent in a parking lot in that town to get preferences of customers before he opened the store.[5]

## Psychological Contract

The mental image (predisposition) of how others should behave before and during the sales presentation is considered a psychological contract. This image is classified through the salesperson's declarative knowledge. **Declarative knowledge** is the database used to interpret and to identify clients' needs gained through experience (knowledge) according to the client's past behavior or clues from similar clients in like situations;[6] that is, before actually meeting the customer, the salesperson develops an image of how the customer will look, respond, communicate, and dress, as well as the product and sales needs. The client is classified according to this image in determining the best strategy to help this type of customer. This process is called "reading the client" and continues during all stages of the sales dialogue beginning with prospecting and ending in the close. The ability to classify clients accurately is a function of the salesperson's experience and motivation to please the client.[7] The more "homework" a sales representative does on the sales account, the more likely it is that his or her knowledge of the client's image will be correct. The end goal of the classification process is to assign clients to the customer type they most closely resemble. Then the strategy and product assortment that worked best for past clients of this type can be used.

**declarative knowledge**

The experienced salesperson knows how to read buyer behavior and how to manage signals to maintain a positive attitude with the buyer. For example, when a buyer appears suspicious or uncomfortable, John Franklin of Hallmark Cards reacts by leaning forward slightly, assuming a relaxed but interested posture, and asking open-ended questions that entice the client out of his or her shell.[8] Since the development of classification clues is experience based, the novice salesperson must obtain this knowledge from sales training sessions and on-the-job training.[9]

The better the seller can identify and adapt to the client's behavior, the stronger the link between seller and buyer. In planning to adapt to the customer's image, the wise seller develops a contingency plan.

Suppose a salesperson has 200 customers. Does it follow that the salesperson formulates 200 strategic plans for dealing with them? No! Implementing this many plans proves too difficult for anyone. Instead the salesperson develops a systematic way of reducing the necessary amount of planning (a *strategy;* see *Partnerships*).

Similarly, customers form their own set of expectations of the sales representative and of the sales process (how they prefer to buy). The more

## PARTNERSHIPS

Peak performing salespeople like Dennis Renter, a million-dollar producer of investment to consumers in Newport Beach, California knows that rapport is crucial to sales. Renter matches and mirrors the prospect's body language until he feels he has established rapport. He then increases interest by leaning forward toward the prospects. If his client does not mirror his physical body language, he knows that he has not established enough rapport with the client and goes back to mirroring. He builds lasting rapport by gaining the prospect's confidence. Dennis is not aware of his nonverbal behavior. After twenty years of selling, he has become unconsciously competent. He is able to generate trust quickly but has no conscious idea how he is doing it. It is part of his natural behavior.

*Source:* ''Prospects Trust People, Not Products,'' *Personal Selling Power* 10 (May-June 1990). Reprinted by permission of Kerry Johnson. Dr. Johnson of Tustin, CA is a speaker, and author of four books including *Mastering the Game: The Human Edge in Sales and Marketing.*

similar each party is to the other party's psychological contract, the more harmonious and trusting their relationship tends to be. Best rapport is built when the salesperson exhibits honest and sincere behavior in a manner expected by the client. Trust is established, and the relationship is strengthened. Thus sellers plan the dialogue based on how they portray the buyer's expectations.[10]

## Need For Trust

Any strategy of selling should be based on obtaining the customer's trust.[11] The need for trust is clear. High levels of fear and distrust cause the customer to be defensive, nonproductive, noncommunicative, and to play counterproductive games. Complete trust is needed; everyone must understand and trust everyone else's intentions. The mutually beneficial relationship establishes the maximum level of trust, thereby allowing a strong relationship.

## Need For Interdependence

Strong trust links demonstrate interdependence and are synonymous with customer loyalty. The stronger the trust link, the more loyal a customer is to a particular salesperson. The most desirable trust links are those that are called *salesperson franchise;* that is, the customer will buy from that salesperson regardless of what company he or she represents. Salesperson franchises are possible in relationships in which there is total accountability and support. J. L. Case looks for what they call "technology infusion." A salesperson who had done his strategic planning correctly knew who the company was doing business with, different ways to get the products they needed, how prices were set up, and how to lease equipment with corresponding tax advantages. He said, "I'm not sure what your current relationship is, but I think there's an opportunity for you to [carve out] a niche in truck leasing." He was asked for a proposal and got the job because he made a contribution to the Case business mission (technology infusion). They said they will continue to buy from this type of salesperson regardless of who he works for. He has developed a salesperson franchise.[12] Everyone takes personal responsibility for the successes and setbacks of the relationship, and everyone commits 100 percent to giving and receiving support until the goal is accomplished.[13] Competing representatives find it difficult to sell to a customer who has a strong trust relationship with another salesperson.[14]

Every dialogue has two input sources of information: the customer and the salesperson. A useful strategy formulates plans that analyze customers' buying motives, types of customers, and sales approaches. The balance of this chapter will therefore be devoted to these topics.

## Customer Motives

A key to successful selling is adapting product knowledge in a logical, meaningful manner to fit the needs of the customer. Fortunately customers exhibit similar types of behavior that allows them to be classified, and presentations can be adapted to different behavior types, reducing the seller's time and energy to a practical, workable level. By studying customer buying habits, a salesperson is better equipped to help the customer purchase.

All customers bring to the customer–salesperson dialogue certain buying motives that cause them to buy goods or services. **Buying motives** may be **functional/rational** or **psychological/emotional,** as shown in Table 8–1.

**buying motives: functional/rational psychological/ emotional**

Motives, whether psychological or functional, are what salespeople seek to tap in finding the needs and wants of the customer. A salesperson "reads" the buying motives through the customer's verbal and nonverbal behavior during the dialogue. Motives form the basis of a customer's buying decision. When selecting a product or a service, some buy-

**Table 8–1**
**Buying Motives**

| Functional/Rational | Psychological/Emotional |
|---|---|
| Cost | Ease and convenience |
| Durability | Safety and protection |
| Depreciation | Play and relaxation |
| Efficiency | Pride and prestige |
| Economy | Love and affection |
| Degree of labor necessary | Adventure and excitement |
| Saving of time and space | Aesthetic pleasure |
| Length of usage | Urge to create |
| Profit and thrift | |

**need**
**product**
**source**
**price**
**time**

ers make "yes" or "no" decisions in five basic areas.[15] These decision areas are **need, product, source, price,** and **time.**

Figure 8–2 is a flow diagram illustrating how a customer makes a decision. Notice that the customer needs to say "yes" to all five buying decision areas or to compensate for a lack in one of the areas before a product is purchased. A person who wanted automobile economy and style might compensate for less styling to gain more gas mileage and a lower price. Therefore the buying decision model provides a good basic structure for the plan of a sales presentation.

Each motive is the basis for a "yes" or "no" in the five buying decision areas. When a customer affirms all five buying decision areas, the product or service is sold. Although a buyer's needs are not fully met in answering one question, the seller's offering may compensate for the deficiency in other areas, thereby causing more of a "yes" answer than a definite "no" answer. For example, a product that has a higher price than a competitive product may be offset by the fact that it can be delivered before the competition. Or one might put more emphasis on one buying area than another, causing the person to buy a product because it is a better offer than other alternatives. In any case, all of these variables determine a purchase/no-purchase decision. In reading the client, the salesperson should determine if the buyer is weighting one buying decision area higher than others and should adapt accordingly.

## Customer Types

Besides basic buying motives and decision areas, a salesperson should have knowledge of basic types of customers. Table 8–2 illustrates basic

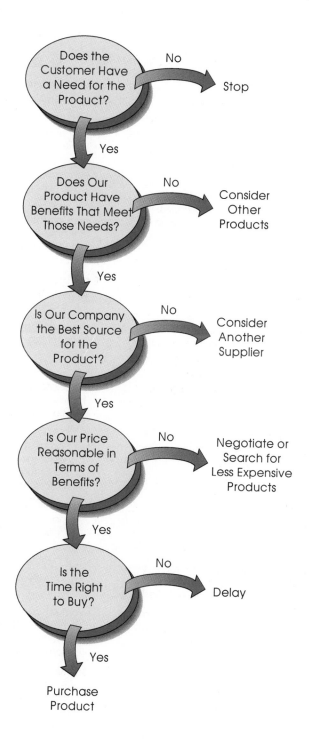

**Figure 8–2**
**The Five Buying Decisions**
*Note:* This structure does not imply that customers always follow steps in this order. Rather it depicts how decisions are made.

Reprinted by permission of Vernon Publishing Inc., Vernon CT

**Table 8–2**
**Identifying Customer Types**

| Basic Customer | Characteristics | What Salesperson Should Say or Do |
| --- | --- | --- |
| Silent | Nontalking, might look for other's advice: may be unsure of own self | Get agreement on small points. "Draw-out" opinions. Ask open-ended questions; wait for answers. Listen! |
| Slow, methodical/ hesitant | Ill at ease/sensitive; may be unsure of own judgment | Make customer comfortable. Use friendliness and respect. Give time to mull over attributes. Don't rush! |
| Overcautious/ think it over | Interested in facts, detailed information | Emphasize manufacturer's facts. Volunteer information. |
| Procrastinator/ look around | "I'll wait, until . . . ." Lacks confidence; insecure | Reinforce judgments. Use testimonials. Help to decide. |
| Ego-involved/ decisive | Alert to salesperson's errors; hates to be managed | Back up statements. Stimulate client's ego honestly. Lead cautiously. Get client's inputs. |
| "Glad-hander"/ fact finder | Knows what is wanted; confident choice is right; enthusiastic | Don't argue. Offer product benefits. Look to close. Don't try to compete with more enthusiasm. |
| Skeptic/ chip on shoulder/ arguer | Takes issue with statements; disbelieves claims; tries to catch salesperson | Support with facts. Demonstrate knowledge. Use indirect denial. |
| Impulsive/ changeable | Quick to decide or select; impatient; talks quickly. Often doesn't finish idea | Close rapidly. Avoid oversell or over talk. |
| Grouch | Definitely in a bad mood; indignant; angry at slightest provocation | Avoid an argument. Stick to basic facts. Show a good assortment. Don't absorb pessimism. |
| Harasser | Wants special "deal" or treatment | Give the client the best offer. Be careful not to compromise. Customer may always want favors or special treatment. Don't "buy" the order. |

customer types classified according to their behavioral characteristics as revealed to salespeople during the dialogue.[16] How a salesperson should deal with each type of customer is also briefly explained in Table 8–2. Any customer may be one of these types.

Further explanation of how to interact with each type during a presentation will become clear as later chapters discuss the sales process. "What a salesperson should say" is the role adaptation by the seller that challenges incorrect statements, reinforces customer's decision-making capability, and provides factual information for support.

The salesperson reads the customer's characteristics and reacts by adapting the presentation to these client characteristics. Complications can arise when a buying center has more than one type of customer influence, particularly if the decider is one type and the influencer is another type; or when salespeople's knowledge is lacking in a given situation and they have little ability to think on their feet (i.e., ability to abstract from previous situations)[17]; or when there is a procedural problem with the presentation. Several types of customers are analyzed, and the adaptive behavior of the salesperson for each type is suggested in the section following.

## Silent

**Silent** customers are reluctant to discuss their situations and the points the salesperson is making. Since the silent customer's oral responses are few, selling to this customer is especially difficult because most communication is one way. It is extremely difficult to know how silent types feel about the product because they are more "thinkers" than "talkers." Perhaps the reticence stems from lack of confidence. Whatever the cause, this noncommunicative nature frustrates many salespeople.

silent

### Adaptive Behavior

Since the silent customer rarely talks, the salesperson is relegated to the interpretation of nonverbal signs. The salesperson should use **open-ended questions** to draw the silent customer into a dialogue. State the questions to require more than a "yes" or "no" answer. Once an answer is given, ask for amplification of the answer to establish two-way communication. Be patient in waiting for an answer. The silence between question and answer might cause tension, but this may be what it takes to encourage the silent customer to speak. Ask a question and pause. If the answer is not forthcoming, look at the customer, establish eye contact, and wait for an answer.

**open-ended questions**

*Examples of Open-ended Questions*
- What options would you want in a computer?

- How do you think the new tax laws affect your estate planning?
- What qualities are you looking for in a supplier of plastic materials?
- How do you feel about our wholesaler benefit program?

Patience is the key to handling the silent customer. Be patient in your attempts to establish communication between the customer and you. Realize that it is almost impossible to satisfy customer needs when they are not verbalized. A straightforward approach is best.

## Slow, Methodical/Hesitant

**slow, methodical/**

**hesitant**

The hesitant customer is **slow** to react. An observer might misinterpret this behavior as an inability to think, but there is no relationship between an individual's being **methodical** and being able to think and communicate. The customer may be buying a product for the first time, and uncertainty is natural. Some needs common to these customers are those of orderliness and autonomy. **Hesitant** clients may need to resist coercion or to satisfy their inquiring minds and may desire to explore, look, listen, and inspect.

**Adaptive behavior.** A salesperson might tend to snub these customers and to consider them to be time wasters. Don't. When you recognize a hesitant customer, adjust the delivery of your presentation. Too rapid a speed will make this customer feel pushed into buying; so slow down. Be sure to pay attention to details. After asking a question, wait patiently for a reply. The customer may mentally juggle several variables before answering. Make use of the art of listening, respect the client, and be friendly and patient. In other words, let the customer set the pace of your presentation.

## Overcautious/Think It Over

**overcautious/think it over**

The customer who appears unsure and consistently seeks advice from others is called a "**think it over.**" Many people feel "two heads are better than one" when it comes time to make a decision. Some of these people may be insecure or have a strong affiliation need. This combination of needs often causes such a person to be unsure even about the reasons for the uncertainty. They often seek to spread the responsibility for a decision among others and may need to avoid failure, shame, humiliation, or ridicule. However, their timidity may be caused by the need to cooperate with a leader, to follow a superior, or to play politics.

**Adaptive behavior.**    You must bolster the "think it over's" self-confidence. Help this customer realize the facts. Be a facilitator. Let them use your phone; provide information that they can take with them, such as testimonials, visual materials, test results; set up a subsequent appointment, etc. Be sure to read the client correctly, and do not make casual remarks about how "easy the decision is to make."

## Procrastinator/Look Around

Many customers put off making decisions. Decision making is difficult because it necessitates foregoing all other possible choices. **Procrastinators** are extremely cautious and would rather postpone a decision than make a poor decision. They want to look at all alternatives before deciding and even then find it difficult to make a choice. The customer's anxiety is high; this person must choose but feels unsure. The natural reaction is to look to others, especially the salesperson, for advice. The procrastinator may suffer from lack of confidence and insecurity.

procrastinator/look around

**Adaptive behavior.**    As a seller, you must be positive, self-assured, and dramatic but not overpowering. Subtly suggest that the procrastinator does have the ability to make the decision. Be dramatic. Use visual aids to help illustrate important points. Since insecurity is a problem, you can reinforce the customer's judgments by summarizing the benefits of a product several times. Repetition also reinforces the confidence that the procrastinator needs. The customer often views the salesperson as an advisor. When placed in this mentor position, you must continue to give your opinion in a sincere and honest manner. Emphasis of features and benefits of your product helps build the look-around customer's confidence in making a decision.

## Ego Involved/Decisive

Decisive customers know what they want and typically have investigated product alternatives in the marketplace before talking to salespeople. Confident of self-formed judgments, opinions, and choices, the **ego-involved** prospect reacts negatively to suggestions and advice. Making decisions seems to feed this person's ego. The client will often show a strong need to dominate, to influence, or to control others.

ego involved/ decisive

**Adaptive behavior.**    This customer wants to feel important, so cater to that need rather than competing for dominance. Instead of stating your ideas as being conclusive, seek the customer's advice and counsel. You can guide the sales presentation without appearing to dominate. Guide the presentation by presenting only the facts the customer wants to hear. Be brief but tactful. Above all, you must sell yourself by impressing the decisive customer with your professionalism and adaptability to his or her needs.

## "Glad Hander"/Fact Finder

**"glad hander"/fact finder**

The basic characteristic of **"glad handers"** is their information-seeking approach and their enthusiasm: they are **fact finders.** This person may be so preoccupied with details that reaching a decision becomes difficult. "Glad-hander"–type people talk about everything and frequently get "off the track." Generally they exhibit high degrees of enthusiasm and seem to have an uncanny ability to understand the benefits received from the product. In a process called networking, these customers readily convert product features into customer benefits rather than needing the salesperson to verbalize the advantages. As the name implies, the fact finder wants information and can readily perceive the benefits derived from facts about the product.

**Adaptive behavior.** Plan to have as much information as possible. Remember one thing, however: keep this customer on the subject. Fact finders can take up an inordinate amount of time to make a decision and may talk about all kinds of irrelevant topics.

Do not compete with the fact finder's enthusiasm. This customer is already so enthusiastic that any more exuberance could turn the sales presentation into a "high-school pep rally!" Just remain positive, factual, and supportive. Often the fact finder will independently arrive at the decision to buy.

## The Skeptic/Chip On Shoulder/Arguer

**skeptic/chip on shoulder/arguer**

The **skeptic/chip on shoulder/arguer** has a doubt about everything you discuss. It is difficult to communicate with someone who is so negative. This individual takes issue with everything, making cutting and sarcastic remarks about selling in general, your company, your products, and even you.

Who knows why customers act in this manner? Often this type of person seems to look down on salespeople, regarding them as "peddlers." They may also be insecure and may feel a need to dominate.

**Adaptive behavior.** Do not argue with the pugilistic customer. Even if you win the battle, you will lose the war. Argumentative customers do not like to be proven wrong in arguments. Therefore the best strategy is to take a firm stance, to display strong product knowledge, to give plenty of factual support for your position, and to show results through demonstration. You can be supportive and indicate that you understand without succumbing to arguing or accepting the customer's viewpoint. Buyers may want the salesperson to argue or haggle over price, and the salesperson must be aware that this is what the buyer needs. There is a distinct difference between negotiation and argument.

Since this person will probe relentlessly to find a flaw in the product, it is often best to hide nothing. No product is perfect. Admitting a product's limitations before the arguer can voice them may reduce the level of skepticism. When trying to overcome this customer's tendency to argue, use facts backed by company and independent research. Also, illustrating the benefits of the product and inviting customer participation in the product demonstration can be effective. Above all, do not allow this type of customer to lower your own self-esteem or to alter your positive attitude.

## Impulsive/Changeable

The **impulsive/changeable** customer speaks rapidly and abruptly and in clipped or incomplete sentences. Often very changeable and impatient, this individual may have a strong need to act differently from other people. The impulsive customer seeks achievement, recognition, or contrivance and may decide quickly or make a selection, then have a "change of heart" before accepting delivery of the product. **impulsive/ changeable**

**Adaptive behavior.**   You must speed up your sales talk if you are going to sell to the impulsive customer. Like the fact finder, the impulsive individual wants to hear only the facts that are necessary and pertinent to his or her decision. Maintain a rapid tempo and provide enough facts to keep the customer sold on the product, but be careful not to risk boring the customer with too many facts. Stay alert for signals to close. Emphasize only key points unless the customer shows a special interest in obtaining more information. Above all, avoid overtalking and overselling.

## Grouch/Pessimist

**Grouch** customers have a **pessimistic** outlook on everything. If you ask, "How are things going?," such individuals might begin a tirade against their health, friends, job, the country, the weather, business—everything. The bad mood will be evident, both verbally and nonverbally. Nonverbally they are always frowning, scowling, and slouching. **grouch/pessimist**

**Adaptive behavior.**    As with the argumentative type, avoid confrontation. Have patience and hear the grouch out. You must remain optimistic, give constructive ideas, and not let the prospect's pessimism rub off on you. Try to demonstrate ways your products will solve this person's problems. If possible, schedule the grouch as the last customer of the day, just in case that bad attitude affects your own; or meet with the grouch when you feel at your best. Carrying over a pessimistic attitude to other customers can drastically reduce your sales. Who wants to buy from a salesperson with a negative attitude?

## Harasser

**harasser**

People who want special treatment are called "**harassers.**" They either want special price concessions, gifts, favors (perhaps personal, monetary, or sexual), or are just hostile customers who take out their frustrations on salespeople. At any rate, they want to be treated differently from other customers for little reason. This prospect makes you think that you must "do something special" to "sell" the account. This is a difficult client to work with because the desired treatment is sometimes implied rather than stated verbally. Moreover, many different kinds of harassment can take place.

**Adaptive behavior.**    For the hostile customer, hear the client out so that feelings get expressed. Verify the problem. Empathize with, "I certainly can understand how this would upset you." Ask what you can do to rectify the problem; then offer a solution if you can. Otherwise, ask for time. Don't "pass the buck" or antagonize hostile clients. If they are angry now, just realize how angry they will be if you don't handle the dialogue correctly.[18]

For the clients who want special favors, company policies instruct you on the latitude you have in giving special concessions. Don't misinterpret the tough negotiator as harasser; it is acceptable to "drive a hard bargain." You need to read the client very carefully to determine his or her intentions. Be cautious. Treating a customer as a harasser when it is not true is offensive to the client. More will be said about this subject in Chapter 15 on ethics.

## Sales Plans ▬▬▬▬

**sales plan**

When salespeople call on customers, they have a purpose for going and a sales plan. A **sales plan** is the strategy a salesperson follows to meet the client's anticipated needs. The sales plan is established from the salesperson's knowledge before meeting the client. When contact with the client

No matter the type of sales plan, practicing the sales presentation, especially with the use of video tapes, provides salespeople the opportunity to see themselves as the client sees them. (The video tape also allows the salespeople instant replay of the presentation.)

is made, the salesperson adapts the strategy to fit the client's needs. If the adaptation is correct, it meets customer expectations in respect to how he or she wants to interact in the sales dialogue, and it solves the problem. In other words, it meets the client's wants and desires in the sales process itself, thereby increasing/decreasing the probability of a sale. Failure to match the approach to the customer brings incongruity, weakens the trust, and decreases probable sales.[19] Adapting the sales plan to the customer type enables the salesperson to maximize the trust with that customer.

Sales plans can be viewed on a continuum by the degree of pre-planned structure, as seen in Table 8–3. The degree of structure, as defined here, is dependent on the amount of time the salesperson spends talking. The most structured is the canned presentation, and the other approaches are adaptive, with relationship selling being most customized.

## Salesperson-Oriented Approaches

Some approaches oriented from the seller's point of view are the canned presentation and the persuasive presentation. In these approaches sales-people concentrate most of their time on talking.

Table 8–3
**Sales Plans**

| Type of Presentation | Structure | Salesperson's Time Spent (Percent) |
|---|---|---|
| Canned presentation | Structured | Talking: 80–90% |
| Formula presentation | Semistructured | Talking: 60–75 |
| Need satisfaction | Unstructured | Listening: 50 |
| Barrier selling | Semistructured | Listening: 60–75 |
| Relationship selling | Customized | Listening: 80–90 |

### Canned Presentation Approach

**canned presentation**

A presentation that is carefully planned to include all the key selling points arranged in the most effective order is called a **canned presentation** (Table 8–4). By analyzing the sales presentations of the best salespeople in that company, a sales presentation is established that can be memorized by company sellers. In this approach the salesperson memorizes what to say to the prospect to evoke favorable comments. The salesperson spends 80 to 90 percent of the dialogue time talking. Customer responses seem so predictable that they are anticipated before the presentation, so that the salesperson has a response. This approach (often known as a stimulus–response approach) is often used in situations requiring presentations that have sales points arranged in logical order, that provide effective answers to the most expected objections, and that allow minimum time for sales training.

Novice salespeople tend to rely on "flip charts" to lead the customer and the salesperson through the sale. However, if a customer raises an unanticipated objection, the tempo of the flip chart and memorized presentation may be upset. Companies that effectively use the canned presentation require the salesperson to be very perceptive in accurately qualifying the customer's needs.

For example, a chartered financial consultant firm provides its salespeople with a standardized outline for a sales presentation. Its salespeople are required to memorize their presentation. Although it is referred to as an organized talk, the salespeople are encouraged to stick as closely as possible to a verbatim presentation of it.

The canned sales talk has several advantages. It is constructed to "ring bells" with the customer. The canned approach ensures that the salesperson provides complete and accurate information concerning the

**Table 8–4**

**Example of a Basic "Canned" Sales Presentation**  The following example sales talk (Financial Need Analysis II Interview Sales Talk) gives you a track to use during the interview with your prospect. The "Comments" column gives suggestions for conducting the interview smoothly; the "Sales Talk" column presents the actual words to use.

| Comment | Sales Talk |
|---|---|
| ***Step 1.  Establish the General Problem*** | |
| *After a normal exchange of pleasantries open the FNA II Salesmaker to the cover page entitled "Financial Need Analysis II" and say ⟶* | John (as I mentioned over the phone), my purpose in seeing you today is to show you a creative new approach to financial planning. |
| *Turn to the page in the Salesmaker that starts with "The purpose of Financial Need Analysis is," and say ⟶* | The purpose of Financial Need Analysis is to help people plan for their future financial security. |
| *Turn to the Salesmaker page entitled "Financial Security is usually built on four types of assets" (see Figure 8–3) and, as you point to each appropriate box at the top of the funnel, say ⟶* | Financial security is usually built on four types of assets. The first of these is **Personal Assets** such as a home, auto, savings, investments and so forth. |
| *Sound sales techniques to create interest are:* | The second is **Business Assets**, such as company sponsored insurance programs, a retirement plan and sometimes ownership in a business. |
| *1. Show prospects somethiing (visual)* *2. Use of "specific number" ("4 types").* *3. Emphasize the problem as a general problem "all of us have." ("Pointing a finger" at prospects may be threatening to them.)* | Next comes **Life Insurance**. This can include not only cash funds that may be part of the insurance during life, but also the proceeds payable at death. |
| | And finally, there are **Government Programs**, such as Social Security, which can provide benefits at retirement, disability, or to the survivors of those who die. Let's use this funnel to illustrate what we own. |
| *Point to the funnel ⟶* | |
| *Point to arrows and funnel underneath boxes and say ⟶* | Each of these assets are part of the funnel. But before they get there, they have to come into being. So we might ask ourselves, how full will the funnel be? |

Reprinted by permission of Vernon Publishing, Inc., Vernon, CT 06066.

**Figure 8–3**
**Example Sales Prop Used in "Canned" Sales Presentation in Table 8–4**
*Reprinted by permission of Vernon Publishing, Inc., Vernon, CT 06006.*

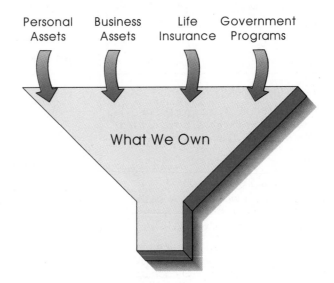

## Financial Security Is Usually Built on Four Types of Assets:

Personal Assets    Business Assets    Life Insurance    Government Programs

What We Own

How full will the funnel be?

company's offerings. Generally users are novices or people selling simple items or intangibles. The canned presentation is easy to learn, cuts training time, and cuts costs for the salesperson's development.[20] It is standardized on the "one best way" to sell the company's products.

Disadvantages of this type of presentation center around the lack of flexibility and its artificial tone. Many novice salespeople lack enthusiasm when giving this presentation, and it tends to make them seem "robotic." Another disadvantage is that it is not applicable to all types of products. It discourages participation by the customer. Since it is memorized, the seller often has trouble restarting the presentation after an interruption.

Success or failure of this controversial approach depends greatly on the ability of the person delivering it. A competent, experienced salesperson can use it so skillfully that clients do not realize it is canned. Novice salespeople, however, often sound less than sincere in using it. The chief weakness of this presentation is that it encourages salespeople to talk too much about their product and to listen too little to the needs of the client, as seen in Table 8–3. All clients are treated the same, without regard for the individual customer's needs. Responses of customers are limited to a few words, resulting mainly in one-way communication.

This approach can be used for any type of buyer, but it can be especially workable with the skeptic and grouch buyers to overcome their negative attitudes. Since these types of customers have a predictable attitude, a canned presentation can fit their needs well. The canned approach maximizes the "logic" used through a memorized presentation of facts to help the client buy. Fewer companies are using this method today than in the past because of its impersonal approach.[21]

## Formula Selling Approach                              formula selling

Salespeople making presentations can be trained to guide the customer through a formula of five mental states: AIDCA—Attention (At), Interest (I), Desire (D), Conviction (C), and Action (Ac). This is a logical, semistructured approach, since each customer must be motivated to travel from one mental state to another to take action. It assumes that similar presentations can be made to similar prospects. You might argue that the salesperson may not be responsible for all five stages, since advertising/promotion or even word of mouth may have created some of them earlier. The salesperson's function is to adapt the presentation to the mental state the client is in before attempting to close the sale. Figure 8–4 shows how the salesperson can use the mental states theory to guide the customer–salesperson dialogue.

In the attention (prospect and need assessment) stage the salesperson gets the customer's attention and begins to develop interest. The salesperson directs the conversation by developing this interest further when moving into the presentation, at which stage customer desire begins to form. Desire is solidified in the need fulfillment stage. The salesperson develops the customer's conviction at this stage as well. Finally, the salesperson calls for action in the close. The progression of the sales dialogue through the mental states leading to the close (action) is easy to see. Simtec, a computer store in Dallas, uses the patterned sales scripts for the   **Mental States Theory**

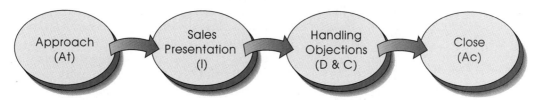

Mental States Key

At = Attention      C  = Conviction
I   = Interest       Ac = Action
D = Desire

Figure 8–5
**Excerpt from the
Compaq Portable
Computer Script**
*Reprinted with per-
mission of Internet
Inc., 1987.*

| Activity | Sales Script |
| --- | --- |
| Hold up the COMPAQ DEMO Disk | Information is stored on flexible diskettes like this one. Diskettes provide an inexpensive means of permanent storage for both programs and data. Information recorded on diskettes remains there even after the diskette is removed from the system. Better yet, information can be protected by simply copying diskettes to produce a backup for security. This can be done in only a few seconds. That is something you can't do very well with a set of manual accounting records or paper documents in a file cabinet. |
| Insert the COMPAQ DEMO Disk, close the disk drive door, and depress the space bar. | To use the information on this diskette, you simply insert it into the disk drive on the system and touch any key on the keyboard. This computer automatically loads this program from the diskette and begins to execute it. |

Compaq portable computer, as excerpted in Figure 8–5. It shows the sales-person what to do and what to say during the presentation to move the buyer through the mental states. The salesperson interacts more with the client during the presentation (talking only 60 to 75 percent of the time) than in the canned approach (talking 80 to 90 percent of the time).

Formula selling encourages making a patterned sales presentation to all types of buyers. The skeptic and the fact finder require logic in negotiating their objections as one requirement of the sales process. For-mula selling is built on the logic of mental states as the foundation of the presentation and therefore is a logical approach to use for such customers.

## Customer-Oriented Approaches

Approaches that are customer oriented include need satisfaction, barrier selling, and relationship selling.

## TECHNOLOGY BULLETIN

### Computer Systems

Two years after testing, Ciba-Geigy's Pharmaceutical Division rolled out its laptops for its 800 salespeople as part of its Electronic Planning and Electronic Communication (EPIC) program. Tests showed computer-equipped salespeople increased their calls 21 percent versus a 6 percent gain by a control group, and they increased their revenues 5.5 percent versus 3.6 percent by the control group. Equally impressive is the sales force's enthusiasm for computerization, indicated by a 90 percent response from participants to continue the system after the test. The system gave them better decision-making capabilities in handling huge volumes of data and better communication to meet customers' needs. Thus the result was better strategic planning.

*Source:* Thayer C. Taylor, ''Improving Sales Force Automation,'' *Sales and Marketing Management* 140 (August 1988): 74.

## Need Satisfaction Approach

In this approach the salesperson asks questions to learn a customer's **needs,** then relates product benefits to those needs. It is an unstructured approach, with the salesperson using probing questions to determine need.[22] Seasoned salespeople eventually find certain needs prevalent in similar situations. For instance, office equipment salespeople are trained to stress the fatigue-reduction benefits of their products because this need is assumed.

The **need-satisfaction approach** allows the salesperson to use the marketing concept, emphasizing the client's needs, not the goods being offered. The presentation is preplanned only to answer frequently raised questions, such as What are the prospect's real needs? and How will my product or service benefit the customer? Additional client needs are met as they are discovered.

**need-satisfaction approach**

The need-satisfaction approach is best used by experienced representatives selling sophisticated or intangible products such as consumer goods, stocks and bonds, machinery, or computers.[23] This approach requires time and effort to determine a client's need and to demonstrate a product's benefits in a way that the client will understand.

Slow, methodical and procrastinator customers need respect and self-confidence, and the need-satisfaction approach allows salespeople to pattern presentations to fulfill these needs. At the same time, salespeople can communicate product or service benefits. Adapting presentations to individual needs makes the need-satisfaction approach more effective with most types of buyers.

## Barrier Selling Approach

**barrier selling**

Visualizing the sale as a steeplechase in which each hurdle represents a barrier to the sale is a good description of **barrier selling.** If the salesperson overcomes the barriers the customer places in the way, the sale is made. This approach is planned much like formula selling to elicit favorable responses during the presentation through two-way interaction. At the conclusion of the presentation, the customer, having agreed favorably at each "barrier," is ready to buy.

Barriers can be described as the five buying decision areas: need, source, product, price, and time. Each area is a barrier that must be satisfied before the next barrier can be overcome. When all five barriers are hurdled, the sale can be closed. Reynolds Machine and Tool sales staff uses the sales barrier approach called *AIDINC*. The six barriers to overcome are *A*pproach (gain rapport); *I*nterview (identify needs); *D*emonstrate (explain features and benefits); Val*i*date (prove your claims); *N*egotiate (work out problems); and *C*lose (ask for a decision).[24]

Barrier selling is also a customized approach, since its content varies according to the customer's needs. It is useful for most types of buyers because it adapts presentations to their particular objections in all five buying areas. This approach is most helpful for dealing with the silent and overcautious types of customers who need more self-confidence.

## Relationship Selling Approach

**relationship selling**

**Relationship selling** (as discussed in detail in Chapter 2) is an interdisciplinary approach concerned with understanding buyer and seller interactions using principles learned from education, psychology, social psychology, sociology, and communication. It integrates all adaptive approaches into one.

The overlapping circles in Figure 8–6 illustrate that a sales presentation is more than a series of steps, as in barrier selling; rather it is a continuous flow of thoughts expressed in a dialogue. In relationship selling, stages are named for conditions occurring in that phase, much like the phases of AIDCA in formula selling but more consumer oriented. For example, presentations are *dramatizations,* obstacles are termed *negotiations,* and the term *closing* is used to express closes which bring the consumer satisfaction rather than closes that merely end the dialogue with a sale. Importantly, beyond the formal term that is used, the relationship seller sees the phases as positive, consumer-oriented interactions with the customer.

In relationship selling, the salesperson tailors all phases of the sales process to meet the customer's needs, much like need satisfaction

**Figure 8–6**
**Relationship Selling Approach**

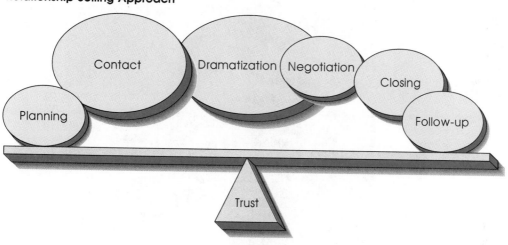

selling but more structured to listening. The personal, emotional, social, and status needs of the customer are all addressed in this approach. This method allows the salesperson to develop a plan for listening to the client and to solve the customer's individual problems by providing complete information in a systematic way. Not the prestructured approach of the canned presentation, nor the semistructure of the formula approach, the relationship approach takes the best of each adaptive approach and weaves into one fabric the most usable portions of each.

This is not to say that relationship selling is unstructured. Most selling situations require structure as opposed to free association. But relationship selling permits more flexibility than any other type of approach for customizing to satisfy particular customers.

For example, a Lazyboy saleswoman selling Lazyboy recliners to a furniture store might develop a plan both to highlight the benefits of her product and to meet the problems of most furniture stores in her territory. She might wear a badge saying "Ask me about C.A.S.H.". C.A.S.H. is a sales acronym standing for benefits of the Lazyboy recliner line listed below:

- *C*omfort of the recliners. Details concerning the construction and its relationship to comfort
- *A*ssortment of styles and fabrics. Selection alternatives
- *S*torage minimums. Regional warehousing programs in 12 areas
- *H*elp. Forms of financing the Lazyboy line

Relationship selling offers flexibility for customizing sales strategy to satisfy particular customers. Here a salesman uses computer technology to develop a particular sales strategy.

Each of these areas is a problem spot for furniture stores. The question the saleswoman would pose—"Mr. Johnson, could you give me 30 minutes to discuss four points that will assure you of more C.A.S.H.?"—should get a "yes" response from the furniture store owner or buyer. During the presentation of C.A.S.H., she may cover *any of the four areas as necessary* to overcome any doubts expressed by the client; that is, she might first cover "S" if the buyer asked about warehousing or storage early in the presentation or "H" if the doubt was about financing. The areas need not be covered in order (C.A.S.H.). Unlike the canned approach, her comments are not memorized to such an extent that she would have to return to the beginning after answering an "early" objection. She has a formalized plan that is completely adaptable to clients' responses yet planned in such a way as to be easily remembered.

Relationship selling provides insight into customers' problems and totally integrates a salesperson's knowledge in solving the customers' problems. It is particularly useful for the glad hander, impulsive, and procrastinator types of buyers because it causes the salesperson to make an individualized presentation to fit the needs of this specific customer, whether those needs are for explicit facts or reinforced judgments.

## Summary

This chapter has laid the foundation for the customer–salesperson dialogue by discussing strategy formulation. Strategies are formed as a salesperson uses fundamental knowledge of selling approaches, along with types and motives of customers, to plan for the dialogue.

Customers' buying motives include such logical ones as the functional motives of cost, durability, efficiency, economy, and profit. Emotional motives include such motives as ease and comfort, play and relaxation, and pride and prestige.

Salespeople need to plan adaptive behaviors for the customer types of silent; slow/methodical; overcautious; procrastinator; ego involved; glad hander; skeptic; impulsive; grouch; and harasser.

The sales plans may be such salesperson-oriented approaches as the canned or persuasive presentations. Or those plans may be customer-oriented approaches such as the need satisfaction, barrier selling, or relationship selling approaches.

## Key Terms

strategy
contingency plans
strategy formulation
source credibility
declarative knowledge
buying motives
   *functional/rational*
   *psychological/emotional*
need
product
source
price
time
silent
open-ended questions

slow, methodical/hesitant
over cautious/think it over
procrastinator/look around
ego involved/decisive
"glad hander"/fact finder
skeptic/chip on shoulder/arguer
impulsive/changeable
grouch/pessimist
harasser
sales plan
canned presentation
formula selling
need-satisfaction approach
barrier selling
relationship selling

## Discussion Questions

1. What is the main purpose of strategic planning?
2. Briefly describe the importance of trust links.
3. How would you sell the silent customer a television set?

4. List some customer buying motives that would be classified as functional motives. As psychological motives.

5. What are the five buying decision areas? How do they relate to the sale?

6. Compare the seller's adaptive behavior in dealing with the arguer customer.

7. What are some suggestions for dealing with decisive, fact finder, and impulsive customers?

8. Discuss the salesperson's adaptive behavior for customers who are hesitant, look around, or think-it-over types.

9. What can sellers do to help the skeptic and procrastinator types make a decision?

10. Contrast the canned sales approach, the formula approach, and the need-satisfaction approach.

11. Compare barrier selling and relationship selling. How are they different?

## Decision Crossroads: Ethical Issues

1. How could the knowledge a salesperson has about how a client buys be used to "push" the sale? Is it ethical to sell in this manner? Discuss.
2. If you were encouraged to use a canned presentation by management of your company as the way to increase sales and you found that this method did not work for you, would you use another technique to sell your clients?

## Case 8–1   Casual Corner

Casual Corner is a clothing store specializing in garments for the "younger generation" of women between ages 15 and 30 years. Patrons can choose from a large variety of skirts, dresses, pants, blouses, coats, and accessories such as costume jewelry and belts. These stores are located all over the country, often in shopping malls. This store gears its sales toward the middle/upper-class woman who is willing to pay slightly higher prices for good, quality clothing.

**Sales Training Program**   Casual Corner's initial training program lasts approximately three weeks. During this time the salesperson is trained to sell clothing to the customer and work the cash register. The store uses three major factors to prepare the novice salesperson for selling:

1. *Role modeling.* The salesperson is assigned to a certain section with someone who has worked in the store for over one year. The experienced salesperson watches how the trainee interacts with customers.
2. *Information.* The salesperson receives a pamphlet that describes the various types of fabrics available in the store and the latest styles. Past issues of the monthly publication are given to the new salesperson to study.
3. *Audiovisual instruction.* The salesperson watches a videotape showing good and bad sales presentations. Approaches, objections, and closes are stressed heavily.

Jill Mason has completed the sales training course and has been assigned to Riverside Mall. Jill works in the front part of the store, where most of the new summer styles have been put out. It is midafternoon and business is rather slow. A woman who looks to be about 25 years of age comes into the store and begins to browse through some of the clothes on the racks.

Jill watches the young woman for a couple of minutes to see what type of clothing interests her. Jill notices her facial expressions when she picks up a certain item of clothing, the style or type of clothing she tends to favor, and whether or not she looks at price tags, which would indicate that she is price conscious. The clothing the customer is presently wearing tells Jill something about her tastes and personality.

As the woman stops going around from rack to rack, a particular pair of sailor's pants seems to be holding her attention. The fact that this customer is looking at a new, trendy style tells Jill that the customer needs a change—something entirely different.

### Discussion:

1. Using the information Jill has, how should she prepare to show this young woman the sailor look?
2. Prepare a brief outline of important ideas to stress during the presentation.
3. Should Jill gather additional information about the customer before presenting the sailor look? If so, what kind of information?

## Case 8-2   **IBM Computers**

Doug Marx has been with IBM for two years since graduating from college. He could be characterized as intelligent, hard working, and professional. After his one-year sales training program with IBM, Doug was assigned to a territory in the southeastern part of the United States and became responsible for introducing the IBM PC Super-20 to retail computer stores such as Bohman's.

John Bohman is the owner and manager of a soon-to-be-opened hardware/software retail store. He makes all buying decisions and is currently reviewing several competing computer lines. Although not planning on limiting his merchandise selection to one brand line, John operates a highly cost-conscious, conservative enterprise. He is known for being tough, shrewd, but honest in his business dealings.

Doug Marx has an appointment to present the PC-20 line of home computers and software accessories. IBM features the best-known, full-featured computer on the market, the PC-20, which Marx will discuss today.

Discussion:

1. Analyze the situation surrounding the Bohman call. What should Doug be aware of?
2. How would you as Doug Marx prepare for the call?
3. Plan a brief presentation outline (strategy) that Doug could use. What type of approach is it?

## Chapter Outline

Before the Contact
Getting Appointments
    Third Parties
    A Letter
    The Telephone
    The Cold Call
    Other Techniques
Waiting for the Appointment
The Contact
    Introduction
    Types of Approaches
Warm-up
Need Assessment
    Confirming and Increasing Trust
    Assessing Current Situation
    Identifying Goals and Objectives
    Validating the Need/Problem
    Decision-Making Criteria
    Analysis of Competition
Misqualifying Customers

# Contact and Need Assessment

**Learning Objectives**

After completing this chapter, you should be able to:

- Discuss the points the seller covers in precontact planning
- Recognize methods used to obtain the interview
- Understand the types of contact approaches
- Discuss the psychological contract and its importance in the contact stage
- Discuss the value of the trust link to relationship selling
- Recognize some activities that occur during the need assessment stage
- Explain how the criteria for making a decision and the analysis of competition affect the decision to buy, to continue the dialogue, or to end the dialogue
- Discuss the results of misqualifying customers.

## IN THE FIELD

"We help them negotiate," says Tom Moore of Amdahl. Amdahl Corporation makes mainframe computers, yet its salespeople enjoy approaching prospects who are firmly committed to IBM products. They give them a coffee mug with Amdahl's name prominently displayed on the side. "We tell the customer to leave this on the desk. The next time an IBM salesman comes around, it'll be good for a million-dollar discount," says marketing manager Tom Moore. "The psychology is interesting," he notes. "Customers tell us that when they've tried the mug, the guy's eyes get bright—and pretty soon a district manager is cutting prices." How well does that help Amdahl? "Once customers see how well the mug with our name on it works, then they start thinking how much more effective it would be if IBM actually saw one of our products on the floor. And once we've sold one system, even a small one, the next sale is 20 times easier."

*Source:* "Breaking the Sales Barrier," *Success* (May 1990). Reprinted with permission from *Success* magazine, © 1990, Hals Holding Corp.

Strategy formulation is the planning stage of the sales dialogue during which the foundation is laid for the customer–salesperson dialogue (see Figure 9–1). Implementation of this strategy begins with the face-to-face meeting with the client, called the *contact and need assessment* stage. During this phase of the dialogue the salesperson arranges an appointment, meets the client, establishes first impressions and performs a need assessment.

In the crucial first three minutes of a dialogue, both the buyer and the seller begin to form a bond of trust that is the basis of relationship selling. Tom Moore of Amdal, makers of mainframe computers (see *In the Field*), establishes this trust bond by showing potential customers how to negotiate better deals with all suppliers. Activities performed effectively during the contact stage often determine whether further dialogue will occur. This concept is illustrated in the advice that follows from Jon Logue, Executive Vice President of Sales and Marketing, Salem Carpet Mills, Inc.:

> Work hard—parts of our culture need to relearn work
> ethics. Listen—keep your antennae up and find out
> customers' needs. And be honest—it goes a long way.[1]

The contact provides three functions: (1) an introduction, (2) a "warm-up" period to establish communication, and (3) a transition into

**Figure 9-1**
**The Role of *Contact and Need Assessment* in the Customer–Salesperson Dialogue**

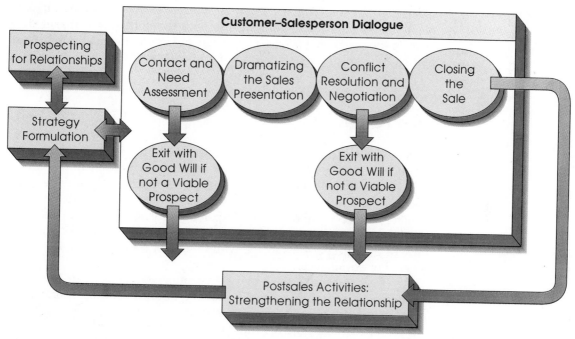

assessing client's needs. After completing these three functions, the dialogue progresses into fulfilling those needs. But additional refining of a strategic plan is needed before the contact with the client.

## Before the Contact

Deciding how to go about getting an appointment with a qualified prospective buyer is a precontact step. Then salespeople determine the best approach to use with this buyer when they actually meet. The chosen approach should get the attention of this particular buyer, stimulate interest, and provide an orderly transition into the sales presentation that precedes it.

## Getting Appointments

It is important to talk to the *right* person. As part of the planning stage for getting an interview with a prospect, salespeople make sure their appointment is with the qualified buyer. Some sellers have had the unpleasant experience of completing an effective sales presentation, only to discover that the person they were talking to was not the person who could make the decision. This error can be minimized when making appointments. Make sure the appointment is with the person who makes decisions in the proper area. Salespeople may get appointments through third parties, by letter, by telephone, and by making cold calls.

## Third Parties

Getting an appointment through a third party involves convincing the person who has the power to grant the interview that the client will benefit from the interview. Often this person is a secretary or receptionist. Undoubtedly the salesperson's attitude is a dominant factor in determining whether a secretary allows the salesperson to meet the buyer. Poise, dignity, appearance—all affect the chances of being admitted. The compatibility of the salesperson's image with the buyer's company image affects the ease of admittance.

Convincing the third party—receptionist, secretary, etc.—is of ultimate importance. Some people treat receptionists and secretaries with little respect. Since they screen out unwanted salespeople, often secretaries and receptionists are the first line of defense (gatekeepers) for the buyer. For example, at Sharma Motor Home Manufacturing, the receptionist is instructed not to admit a salesperson to see the purchasing agent until the salesperson has made the third call. The buyer's thinking is "if a salesperson does not feel we are worth visiting at least three times, without seeing me, we are not important to his or her company." Thus salespeople who never make the third attempt never have a chance to sell to the Sharma buyer.

Secretaries and receptionists are wise to those why try to trick them with bluffing, flattering, and wisecracking. Since they are one of the first barriers to a sale that you must overcome, be honest, sincere, affirming, considerate, and professional. Let them know that you are aware of how important they are to the selling process. Realize that their efforts can make or break you. Thank them for their efforts, and do everything possible to create a positive, professional, long-lasting relationship with these assistants. Facilitate their knowledge of you as a salesperson, of your company, and of your products. Make their work as easy as possible: use business cards and product literature to help them associate names and companies; speak clearly and audibly to help them get the right pronunciation; and be patient when unavoidable delays occur. Also, remember that overfriendliness may inhibit rather than increase your chances of seeing the boss.

## PARTNERSHIPS

Good relationships with clients establish a good track record for future success, as is shown by the following comments from Alan Braslow of Five Technologies.

"When I give people references, I always tell them to find out, when they call the references, how Alan Braslow is serving them after the sale—find out whether I back up what I say, whether I go to their defense, whether we screw up something. The nature of business is that we will make mistakes. But where am I? Am I there if you need me?

I'm going to be there on my client's side of the table talking to our client's service people—and I'm going to be standing up for the client because we're not producing what we should produce. They know that I am their ombudsman.

The point is that you are morally obligated to take care of the guy—and whatever problems or screw-ups the guy has. Remember, that guy is sending your kids to camp and paying your mortgage. Sure, you work for your company, you're an employee and they pay you— but that client is the one you really work for, and too many organizations forget that."

*Source:* Larry Wilson, *Changing the Game: The New Way to Sell* (New York: Fireside Books, 1987), 215. Copyright © 1987 by Larry Wilson. Reprinted by permission of Simon & Schuster, Inc.

In addition to third parties in the buyer's office, other third parties, such as past customers, may be happy to arrange interviews for you if you have satisfied their needs. Many relationships bring about face-to-face introductions or written introductions, as illustrated by Alan Braslow of Five Technologies (see *Partnerships*). He encourages his prospective clients to check out his past record of service after the sale with his current clients.

## A Letter

A carefully written letter to get an appointment gives a salesperson a chance to cover points without the fear of interruption. Attention and interest must be gained immediately, however, to evoke a response from the reader.[2]

The letter should have a *personal* style. The customers are interested in solving a problem, not in buying a product from a salesperson.

They are thinking of themselves; therefore the letter should project the "you" attitude. The "you" attitude is evidence of a sincere interest in the customer's welfare.

For a letter to be effective enough to obtain an appointment, it should have the following characteristics. It should be written with a *positive approach.* An example of the negative approach would be, "You don't want to buy a computer, do you?" Be forceful, interesting, and logical. Tell the buyer what can be done—"You will want to see our new labor-saving computer." The *tone* of the letter must be understandable to be effective. It must be enthusiastic, friendly, natural, and courteous.[3] A letter's *appearance* makes the first impression, and the image a salesperson wishes to portray is exhibited in the letter. Letters with typographical or grammatical errors and erasures portray the "sloppy" salesperson. Before the letters are sent, look at the letters as buyers see them. Every hour of the day, the letters you send out are either creating the right impressions, building goodwill, making friends, stimulating sales—or they are creating wrong impressions.[4] Every letter has a sales job to do, whether it's selling merchandise, service, or you and your firm. Every letter has a chance to make customers say, I *like* to do business with that company! Table 9–1 highlights the characteristics of a good letter.

## The Telephone

Appointments made by telephone provide an opportunity for dialogue between a prospect and the salesperson. Although it is an opportunity for the prospect to say "no," the telephone method saves time and can create a favorable impression while creating interest for both parties. It has been so effective in many industries that some companies have implemented telephone selling, called **telemarketing,** as sales costs have escalated. For instance, in 1987 more than $115 billion worth of industrial products were sold over the phone.[5] More discussion of telemarketing is available in Chapter 16 on Time Management. Telephoning for an appointment, **teleprospecting,** is not haphazard or spur of the moment. It requires good precall planning and excellent delivery. Besides prospecting and qualifying activities, other precall planning activities must be considered if telephoning is to be successful. To begin, *outline* your opening statement. Since the customer's attention is a fragile commodity, the first 10 to 15 seconds of a call must be well planned to gain the customer's attention. If attention and interest are not gained quickly, the customer may say "no" or hang up. To plan an effective opening statement, follow the guidelines listed below:

1. Identify yourself and your affiliation. "Good afternoon, Ms. Wallace. My name is Ann Edwards of Ansom Corp."

**telemarketing**

**teleprospecting**

Table 9–1
**A Letter's "Sell-ability"**

| **Characteristics of a Good Letter** |
|---|
| *Appearance*<br>First impressions last! The letter should be free of erasures, neatly typed on good stationery, with no grammar or spelling errors. It should be balanced and look good to the eye. |
| *Positive Thoughts*<br>Avoid the negatives: "Sorry, but . . . ." Give the good news first. Tell the person what you can do before you state what you can't do. |
| *You-ability*<br>Write sincerely from a "you" perspective. Don't just mechanically spread "you's" around the letter. |
| *Antagonistic Words*<br>Make sure the letter is free of words that could be mistaken (e.g., "You claim," "You say that"). |
| *Tone*<br>Letters should have the right "ring" to them. Sprinkle them with enthusiasm so they sound like you are talking. |

2. Quickly begin to establish trust to overcome negative reactions.
   a. Make a positive remark: "The national publicity on your company's receipt of a Navy contract for the F-16s should increase your company's sales."
   b. Mention something to establish a common bond. "I understand you are an alumnus of Ohio State University, as I am. That makes us fellow Buckeyes."
   c. Tactfully acknowledge the time. "Did I call at a convenient time, or should I call back tomorrow at 10:00 A.M.?"
   d. Use an "interest-gathering" statement to build interest. "Would you like to gain a 30 percent return on your capital investments?"
3. State the purpose for the call, and ask for the appointment. "With our new leasing program, we have secured this type of return for several companies like yours in this area. The Dollars Plus plan requires only 30 minutes. Could you put me on your calendar for 30 minutes next Monday, or would Tuesday be better?"

4. Restate the appointment time. "I appreciate your time, Ms. Wallace. I'll be at your office on Tuesday, March 19th, at 9:30." Then say, "Is that what you have?" to be sure Ms. Wallace has written it down.

Next, *implement* precall plan. Delivery techniques can enhance or destroy a telephone presentation. Some hints to effective delivery are as follows:

1. Since visual communication is not possible, compensate by using good listening and speaking habits.
2. Your voice reflects your personality, so be positive and confident. Your voice should say, "I am friendly, courteous, tactful, understanding, competent, and want to help you solve your problem."
3. Be aware of your rate of speech. No one likes a "fast talking" salesperson with a "canned pitch." Slow down your pace, and personalize your speech by using the customer's name often.
4. Avoid monotony by using variation in your voice. What image do you see when you hear the playback?
5. Let the customer know you are listening. Listen for overtones that indicate the prospect's emotions. Reinforce the prospect's conversation with affirmative interjections such as "Yes," "I see," "uh huh."[6]

## TECHNOLOGY BULLETIN

### Call Enhancer

"Good afternoon. Mr. Smith's office. May I help you?" Sounds correct, right? Wrong. It is the latest hurdle for salespeople. Tele-Receptionist, sold by a Los Angeles firm, creates the illusion that the office you have called is a big office with a receptionist. However, it is Mr. Smith screening his calls through this new device that gives him several choices of response. After you make your request, he may select, at the push of a button, "Just a moment, I will connect you" (after which an intercom rings) or "I'm sorry he is in a meeting; I'll have him call you back." Or Mr. Smith's conversation with you can be interrupted via another button that brings the receptionist back with, "I'm sorry, Mr. Smith, but your Paris call is on the line." This machine can make prospecting by telephone much more complicated.

*Source:* "Sales Talk," *Sales and Marketing Management* 142 (January 1990): 84.

## The Cold Call

The technique of obtaining an interview without a prescheduled appointment is known as the **cold call.** Some companies, such as NCR, IBM, and Sharp, use cold calls on potential buyers as a source of initial contact.[7] It is most effectively used with products that have a multitude of buyers in a concentrated area. A wholesale candy distributor who sells tobacco and candy products might call on all retail outlets that sell candy or tobacco that were not previous customers.

**cold call**

Buyers who accept cold calls from salespeople suggest the following:

1. Accept a firm turndown as just that and move on to the next office.
2. Know the company you are calling on—its reputation in the industry, production capabilities, from whom it is now buying, and what it is getting for its dollar.
3. Know the name of the buyer, and ask for the buyer personally.
4. Be polite, neat, and professional.
5. Be truthful. Promise only what you can deliver.
6. Leave your card, samples, and any other promotional material.
7. Follow up a call—even a negative one—by sending a letter thanking the agent for his or her time and cooperation.
8. And—try again.[8]

Problems that may occur in cold calling depend on the type of prospect. Salespeople calling on the purchasing agent are normally seen, since the purchasing agent's job involves seeing salespeople. However, salespeople may call at the wrong time or find that they are not talking to the decision maker when they call.

Sales managers feel success in cold calls is based on mathematics. The more cold calls a salesperson makes, the more prospects there will be to call back for appointments.[9] Having as much knowledge as possible about the buyer and the company can also aid in making effective calls on prospects. Clients do not want to be called on just because they are potential buyers of some product. Responses are frequently quite negative since the seller did not have an appointment, so the salesperson should not feel personally rejected if a "no" is received. Instead the salesperson must look upon each appointment made as a possible new client.

## Other Techniques

In addition to the methods described above, a variety of other methods can be used to gain an appointment. Some of these techniques—fax, telegram, cablegram, or mailgram—are instant attention getters. For example:

*UNITED TELEGRAM*

GEORGE JONES: Arriving Saint Louis, Monday, July 10 Stop. May I see you at 10:00 A.M. or 2:15 P.M. regarding your line of golf carts Stop. Cable appointment time collect Stop. H. Arnold Palmer, Palmer Golf Carts.

However, since many people associate bad news or immediacy with these type of media, you must use them with care.

For routine calls, some sellers send an announcement card. A postcard may be used for this purpose with the information concerning the upcoming visit.

If possible, it is helpful to determine the approach most preferred by the client to obtain an appointment and to increase the possibility of success. This is not always possible. But information sources that might have that information should be consulted.

## Waiting for the Appointment

Regardless of how the appointment is made or whether one has an appointment, waiting to see the buyer is a part of selling. Successful salespeople use this time to their advantage, preparing reports, studying new

Time waiting to see a client can be put to good use rather than squandered. Reading new sales literature, arranging appointments, contacting the home office, and establishing rapport with clients' personnel are all beneficial activities.

product information, planning calls, or collecting information about the prospect. Knowledge of good time management techniques enhances a salesperson's time usage. If the secretary or receptionist indicates that the waiting period is going to be excessively long, it might be wise to re-schedule the appointment at a different time rather than waste time in a waiting room.

# The Contact

Keeping the appointment, the seller comes face to face with a buyer or purchasing agent, and the actual contact begins. The **contact** starts with an introduction followed by a warm-up period in which the salesperson gets the buyers to talk about their buying motives; then the seller gains the buyer's attention and begins a need analysis.

    This contact stage generally lasts less than five minutes, but they are extremely important minutes. Making first impressions and getting clients to express their views and opinions sets the stage for participation in the sales presentation. In the first thirty seconds of the interview, the customer makes an affirmative or negative decision about seeing the sales-person and listening to the presentation. During the balance of the contact stage, the salesperson obtains brief introductions, establishes rapport, and asks questions concerning the customer's problems or needs.

    Also during this first thirty seconds, the customer's first impres-sions are verified by reading the salesperson. What can a customer verify in thirty seconds? A **salesperson's appearance** is a reflection of that sales-person's self-image. Since credibility is influenced by compatibility be-tween a salesperson and a client, dressing like the customer can increase credibility.

    Appropriate dress reflects a prospect's expectations. Saleswomen should dress conservatively in dresses, suits, or slacks, unless the industry, such as the high-fashion industry, dictates differently. Both men and women should keep their clothing flattering, comfortable, and within fash-ion limits. Also, it is imperative that all sellers adhere strictly to good grooming and personal hygiene habits.[10]

    A **salesperson's manner** should be enthusiastic, confident, and friendly yet relaxed, poised, and at ease. Body carriage is important, since confidence shows when walking at a brisk pace with erect posture and taking lengthy strides.[11]

    Verbal and nonverbal expressions, such as the handshake, can show these characteristics. Sellers should have a firm but not over-powering handshake. Extending the hand first and simultaneously speak-ing your name is accepted practice.

    Experienced salespeople develop the habit of repeating the pros-pect's name often in the dialogue.[12] They use other nonverbal and verbal

**contact**

**salesperson's appearance**
**salesperson's manner**

You never have a second chance to make a first impression. Salespeople, knowing the importance of the first impression, are careful to display favorable verbal and nonverbal behavior.

*mannerisms* to show an appreciation for the prospect's time. Smoking without permission and chewing gum are the two biggest distractions. Finally, salespeople must avoid irritating mannerisms such as slouching when seated, failing to look the prospect in the eye, nodding continuously, pulling at the ear, or rubbing the chin due to nervousness.

## Introduction

During the contact, ten variables can be incorporated into the introduction and warm-up. They are known as the *Ten Points Of Contact:*

1. State the customer's name. Only with permission may you call the customer by his or her first name.
2. Mention your own name to a new customer, and keep mentioning it in future calls, perhaps as a reminder, until names are well established.
3. Mention the represented company's name often when talking with new customers.
4. Express appreciation for having been given an interview.
5. State the purpose of the appointment. Your actions and statements will show the degree of purposefulness.
6. Have questions in mind to obtain information.
7. Use verifying questions to confirm precall information or assumptions made about the prospect.
8. Use exploratory comments in lieu of an all-question format.
9. Establish a climate of mutual compatibility.
10. Make relevant statements that exhibit and establish a degree of empathy and credibility.[13] For example, "I know how it feels to not know what to buy. I was a retail buyer for ten years before I started working for White Stag."

Each salesperson's approach should incorporate as many of the ten variables as possible. But just how do you approach a customer?

## Types of Approaches

Some types of approaches that can be used in the early part of the contact stage will now be examined briefly. Many times a sales representative uses a combination of approaches, starting with one approach, then perhaps switching to another approach during the warm-up to facilitate the transition to the presentation.

## The Introductory Approach

The introductory approach is the most frequently used technique; unfortunately, used alone, it is one of the weakest. The **introductory approach** uses a simple introduction. For example, the salesperson walks into the buyer's office and says, "Hello, I am Jack Morgan from Ball Corporation." This approach gains only minimal attention; interest and transition are quite awkward, since the customer is not at that instant listening attentively. Prospects often miss the name of the salesperson and have to ask for it again. Therefore the introductory approach is used with other approaches so that it can be made more efficient. A better way to use an introductory approach would be: "Hello, I am Jack Morgan from Ball Corporation. In listening to people in the space technology industry, I have heard that inventory control is a big problem. Is that true for your company?" This statement gathers attention, promotes interest, and provides a transition to the sales presentation.

*introductory approach*

## The Product Approach

By placing the product into the hands of the consumer, a salesperson uses the **product approach.** Many small or eye-catching products sell themselves. The product approach maximizes the use of a prospect's senses—seeing, feeling, hearing, tasting, smelling. For example, handing an alarm wristwatch to a prospect, the salesperson says, "Did you ever see such a beautiful watch? Push both buttons and hear its melodious alarm." People like to handle products, and the product approach capitalizes on this liking. However, a salesperson runs the risk of losing buyers' attention (they play with the product rather than listen). Be sure not to play "tug of war" with the client handling the product when making a point. Points can be made about the product while it is still in the client's hands.

*product approach*

## Problem-Solving Approach

Prospects are interested in ideas that help solve their problems, which is the core of the **problem-solving approach.** The more salespeople know about a problem, the better they can help solve it. Novice salespeople often fear this approach will get them a "no" answer to the questions they ask, leaving them with nothing to say.

*problem-solving approach*

For example, handing a facsimile check for $10,000 to a prospective Canon salesperson, the Canon recruiter asks, "How would you like to receive a check like this each month?" Few prospects would immediately respond "no" to this question. Most prospective Canon salespeople would be motivated to work toward a $10,000-a-month income.

## Curiosity Approach

curiosity approach

A **curiosity approach** immediately arouses the customer's interest. Often this approach uses a question designed to tease a prospect's curiosity. This question, asked honestly and not as a trick, may elicit a warm response.

A vending machine operator might say to a doughnut shop owner, "Mr. Archer, you can double your profit from that (pointing to a remote corner) three-square-foot area."

## Question Approach

question approach

The **question approach** normally consists of giving an interesting fact about the product offering, then following up with a question. To stimulate a prospect's participation, the question should be simple and noncontroversial.

The vending machine operator could use this approach by placing a 3 × 3-foot-square piece of paper on the floor of the doughnut shop and saying to the owner, "The model 361 vending machine can increase your traffic and make $100 a week from that space. Are you interested?"

## Statement Approach

statement approach

A **statement approach** uses a product-benefit statement to make contact. However, it is important to have proof of such statements. Statements should be concluded so that they evoke responses from the prospect. For example, "Gloria Murphy of Olson, Inc. was able to help her company save $300 on its cartons by using this new plastic container. Let me see if I can save money for you."

## Premium Approach

premium approach

Everyone likes receiving gifts. The **premium approach** uses gifts to open doors. Few prospects will turn down something for nothing. And in accepting a free gift, some people feel obligated to hear the salesperson's presentation. Unique gifts are attention getters. The gift should, however, be related to the product being sold. Electronic Liquid Fillers Inc. (ELF) encourages prospects by offering to subtract the cost of one round-trip airline fare to their LaPorte, Indiana plant from the purchase if they order an ELF bottling machine. "If we can convince a customer to visit our place, we'll make the sale about 90 percent of the time," says Jim Ake, ELF's CEO.[14] A Portland Forge salesperson says, "Mr. Edwards, I would like you to accept this forged money clip as a goodwill gesture to say thank you for your time."

## Praise Approach

Honest praise or heartfelt compliments are well received. The **praise approach** uses affirmation to compliment the client. False praise or compliments that come only from the head are called flattery and are not well received, since the prospect can easily tell the difference between flattery and sincerity. It is wisest to avoid commenting on the obvious. Often the seller sees something in the prospect's office that is a source of pride to its owner. Sometimes, however, that plaque on the wall or that memento on the desk is overused as a topic of conversation. The story that follows exemplifies just how comical (but annoying) frequent comments on a prospect's possession might be. A buyer, who had never fished in his life, received a mounted fish from a friend; he made the mistake of hanging it on his office wall. After one week he removed it. Every salesperson who called on him that week saw the fish and plunged into a lengthy discussion on fishing.

**praise approach**

## Survey Approach

The **survey approach** uses gathering information as a means of making an initial contact and should be used sparingly. Approaching clients with an offer to survey their business before a problem is well established is insincere. Some unscrupulous salespeople have used this approach in direct selling as a pretext for getting in to see prospects. For example, a pest control company might offer a free termite inspection, or an auto brake company might offer to inspect the safety features of your car. Once they are given permission, they use their "survey" to qualify the customer on their products or services.

**survey approach**

This approach is successfully used in industrial and business settings to sell complex internal systems that require an in-depth analysis of problems before a solution can be discussed. The salesperson makes observations and hears an explanation of a situation before making an intelligent sales proposal on a second call. Gathering necessary information in this manner is problem solving at its best because it is used to determine the need, not just as a way to get a foot in the door.

# Warm-up ■■■■■■■■■■■■■■■■■■■■

As the meeting progresses after the formalities of a handshake and introduction, the salesperson uses the warm-up to capture the attention of the customer. After the initial interaction, a short period of discussion occurs, called the **warm-up,** the object of which is to establish rapport and to

**warm-up**

develop a two-way discussion. Industrial psychologists report that a typical person's effective attention span lasts from several seconds to a few minutes. Therefore it is safe to say that a salesperson cannot hold another person's attention for a long period of time. Often the customer is in the midst of other duties—perhaps signing papers or, in the case of a physician, filling out patients' charts. Thinking that it is possible to do two things at one time, the prospect will say, "Go ahead! I can listen while I do this paperwork." The wise salesperson knows better than to believe this. Attention span is very delicate and precise. For example, Mike Sherer of Upjohn gets a pediatrician's attention by showing the doctor a poster of a child, who definitely needs attention, in a humorous pose. If the buyer's attention is not gathered, further attempts to discuss problems are screened out as irrelevant information through the selective perception process illustrated earlier in Figure 5–2. Because people selectively pay attention to only those items that are deemed relevant, the rest are screened out. Therefore salespeople plan ways to get attention and to keep the customer's interest—preferably, the customer's undivided attention—as they attempt to determine the problem.

## Need Assessment ▰▰▰▰▰▰▰▰▰▰▰

Having a customer's attention from the warm-up, the seller plans to keep this interest. During the assessment, the clients silently evaluate the trade-off between their time and the value of the information they are receiving. It is important to provide the customer with reasons to listen, and a need analysis provides this function. The process of asking questions and lis-

**need assessment**

tening to the answers is called a **need assessment.** The benefits to the client are clear if they understand how they will benefit; what problems can be solved with help; that they will be in a better position; and that they will make more money by investing their time to listen. For instance, if the Upjohn salesperson, Mike Sherer, does not show these benefits to the pediatrician early in the dialogue, the doctor will either lose interest and go back to the paperwork or tell Mike that she's not interested. When customers see few benefits from the discussion, they lose interest and attention, and the transition from need analysis into the sales presentation is hindered.

Relationship selling is distinguished by the need analysis segment. Without asking customers about their needs, a salesperson can only assume that a need exists. This assumption stereotypes customers and shows indifference to the individual's needs.

**qualifying**

Need analysis is often called **qualifying** a customer and is the beginning of the "on-site" information-gathering stage of relationship selling. Effort blocks in Figure 9–2 depict the amount of time and attention

**Figure 9–2**
**Effort Blocks of the Selling Process**   *Note:* The different sizes of the effort blocks indicate the amount of effort expended in each activity.

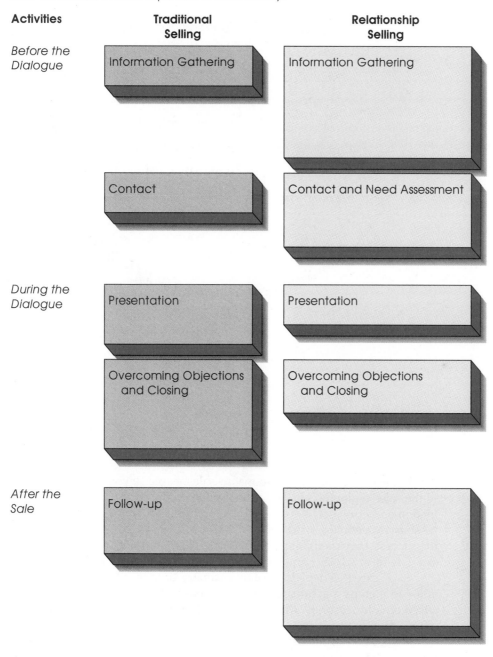

| Activities | Traditional Selling | Relationship Selling |
|---|---|---|
| *Before the Dialogue* | Information Gathering | Information Gathering |
| | Contact | Contact and Need Assessment |
| *During the Dialogue* | Presentation | Presentation |
| | Overcoming Objections and Closing | Overcoming Objections and Closing |
| *After the Sale* | Follow-up | Follow-up |

**Figure 9–3
Flow Diagram of the
Need Assessment
Process**

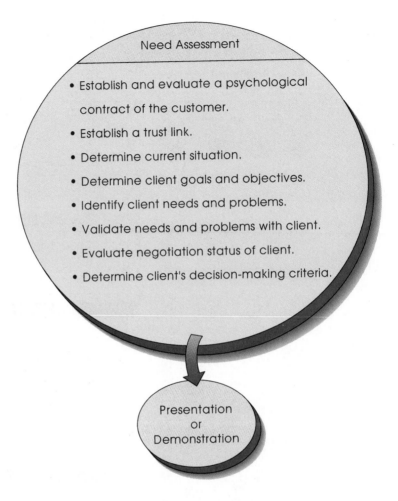

Need Assessment

- Establish and evaluate a psychological contract of the customer.
- Establish a trust link.
- Determine current situation.
- Determine client goals and objectives.
- Identify client needs and problems.
- Validate needs and problems with client.
- Evaluate negotiation status of client.
- Determine client's decision-making criteria.

Presentation
or
Demonstration

that both traditional and relationship salespeople devote to each portion of the sales dialogue. The traditional salesperson's efforts minimize information gathering and maximize overcoming objections and closing using persuasive techniques. In contrast, the professional salesperson reverses the process by maximizing the need assessment stage and the follow-up stage, with much less time spent in overcoming objections.

Figure 9–2 depicts the extraordinary time the "helping" seller devotes to ensuring a satisfied customer base. Relationship selling is balanced on a broad base of follow-up activities illustrated by the amount of effort—almost three times—given the customer following the sale.

Because of its importance to relationship selling, need assessment must be thoroughly examined. Figure 9–3 illustrates the functions that occur during the need analysis. Just as the customer–salesperson dialogue is a process, contact and need analysis continue with one flowing into the next smoothly, just as segments of the need analysis stage flow together. Often in implementation it is difficult to determine where one phase of the process ends and another phase begins.

## Confirming and Increasing Trust

Each contact the salesperson has with a prospect strengthens or weakens the trust between them. Upon meeting a person, first impressions are formed. Regardless of the correctness of the first impression, each person in a dialogue treats others as though the impression is correct. Even before their meeting, the customer and the sales representative each have formed preconceived mental pictures of each other. When they do meet, the preconceived ideas are either confirmed or refuted. If the perception was correct ("He's just as I thought he would be"), the person's preconceptions are reinforced, and a bond is established between the two people. The more buyers and sellers are like their expectations of each other, the more reinforced a person feels. Reinforcement builds trust.

A crucial skill in developing a strong bond of trust is the ability to form accurate impressions. Salespeople must not only be able to read the client's behavioral style but also be able to present the correct image.

During their meeting both the customer and the salesperson evaluate their expectations against the reality. Disharmony occurs when persons are perceived differently from their image. It takes time to adjust to this new perception. If an incorrect image has been formed earlier, the new image must be incorporated into the planned strategy. Failure to adapt to changes after meeting a customer causes the salesperson to become less effective.

Maintaining the trust consists of many steps of "reading" a customer's verbal and nonverbal behavior to gather information. Salespeople should identify the customer's communication style, confirm it, and modify their own style to be as compatible as possible to the client's. That is not to say that the salesperson must put on a "mask" to influence the customer. Salespeople must merely be flexible enough to adapt their own style. The use of this information allows the salesperson to increase the client's trust. A salesperson in an initial call to a new account has relatively weak trust. The more credibility the salesperson establishes over a period of time with a customer, the stronger the trust bond grows.

Building and maintaining a strong trust bond generally increases sales volume. Often a buyer who trusts the salesperson will ask the salesperson's advice before ordering goods. Some trust is so strong between salespeople and their clients that clients turn some of the buying function over to the salesperson. For example, if a wholesale salesperson selling routine items such as cigarettes, tobacco, cigars, and candy has strong trust from a retail store owner, the wholesale salesperson may be given the authority by the retail buyer "to send what we need" without seeking the buyer's explicit permission on each item. In this case the salesperson manages the account because of the trust.

Trust is established, maintained, and strengthened by meeting clients' needs and by efficiently solving their problems with sincere concern and honesty. As evidence of sincere concern, the relationship salesperson carries through on extensive follow-up activities after the sale to ensure customer satisfaction, which in turn solidifies the customer/seller trust. What customer could doubt a salesperson's sincerity when the salesperson shows concern by checking the customer's satisfaction level several times during the use of the product?

## Assessing Current Situation

Before a salesperson can recommend a solution to a customer's problems, the salesperson must gather information concerning the client's situation, goals, and objectives. This information provides a determination of whether a need exists, and its extent and depth. Therefore, it is necessary for one to focus on the current situation by using well-planned questions, which are two of the ten points of a contact, as discussed earlier.

Questions encourage two-way communication between buyer and seller. "Who," "what," "where," "when," "why," and "how" questions open discussion, create interest, reveal problems, provoke thought, discover buying motives, and uncover hidden objectives.[15] Table 9–2 illustrates some guidelines for asking questions.

At this stage of the selling process, sellers can either use: verification questions to establish the accuracy of strategy formulation information; clarification questions to search for a better understanding of the client's feelings; exploratory questions to initiate two-way communication; or the multiple question technique SPIN to accomplish the same purpose but in a more direct way.

**exploratory questions**

The questions which are exploratory are reflective, encouraging, and amplifying. **Exploratory questions** are phrased with a pause that provides the respondent with the opportunity to communicate. The comments may project empathy to the customer. For example, the salesperson might say, "What I'm hearing you say, Mr. Thompson, is that you don't like our service (pause)." The client should feel the need to respond. These questions give the salesperson a better understanding of the client's feelings. Ask for factual information that is publicly available, and then rely on asking for personal information only after the client has shown respect for and trust in the salesperson. Attempting to get personal information too soon in a relationship will make the prospect uncomfortable.

Reflective questions are statements which allow the salesperson to probe deeper into the client's thought patterns. They attempt to expand

Table 9-2
**Guides for Asking Questions**

| Keep Them |
|---|
| Simple—Each should contain only one idea. |
| Complimentary—Show approval in a sincere way. |
| Open ended—Do not compel the prospect to set a price limit. For example, do not ask, "What dollar limit have you set on this purchase?" |
| Direct—Questions are not slanted. |
| Not persuasive—That comes later. |
| Customer centered—A prospect buys to fill needs, not just to buy a product. |
| Impersonal—Ask objective questions. |

on information concerning the client's problems, such as: "Do you hear personnel complaining about their current photocopying situations?" "What are your feelings on your future energy needs?" Each reflective question stimulates additional discussion and can be used without the salesperson agreeing or disagreeing with the client. Reflective questions show understanding.

Questions that are more open ended are called encouragement probes. Words like "Really?" "Uh-huh," "I see," "That's interesting," as well as the nonverbal expression of head nodding encourage clients to expand on their comments. Direct expressions—for example, "Can you tell me more about your computer needs?"—require the client to amplify thoughts in a particular subject area.

The questioning mode searches for information but should not be so obvious or obnoxious as to seem like a game of *twenty questions*. Questions should have a purpose beyond that of idle conversation. They should be used throughout the dialogue as long as they provide pertinent information.

## SPIN Technique

A tailored approach to asking questions involves using multiple questions which provide a framework to confirm precall strategies. The multiple-question technique is called **SPIN**.[16] SPIN stands for (1) *S*ituation, (2) *P*roblem, (3) *I*mplication, and (4) *N*eed-payoff questions. This technique relies on these four types of questions asked in a specific sequence.    **SPIN**

The SPIN technique is important to the consultative, relationship seller. To truly build a relationship with clients, the salesperson must have a thorough understanding of those clients' businesses. Good questioning and listening techniques are vital to gaining this understanding, and the SPIN technique provides a systematic approach to questioning, and results in a depth of knowledge on which the salesperson can build a relationship.

Salespeople who use the SPIN technique, such as those who sell for Xerox, ask questions to determine the client's perception of the situation, followed by problem, implication and need-payoff questions. Since it does require a proper sequential order for questioning, the SPIN technique is described in four stages.

- *Stage 1.* Situation questions. With opening questions in a SPIN technique the salesperson tries to learn about the client's situation as it relates to the product. The product is not mentioned, however. Situation questions involve the client's general situation, like, "How do you see your plant expanding in the next few years?" Or, "how many copies do you make in a month in this office?" Questions such as these result in a broad general statement of the prospect's needs, and they allow transition into questions concerning specific problem areas. Asking specific questions before establishing common generalized information may make the client uncomfortable and uncooperative. Using warm-up questions establishes two-way communication in a non-threatening manner. This shows the general understanding of the prospect's needs.
- *Stage 2.* Problem questions. In stage two, questions that identify specific problems prospects regularly encounter with their present products establishes source credibility. Source credibility shows the prospects that their problems are similar to problems previously faced by the salesperson. Problem questions ask about specific difficulties or problems perceived by the client relative to the situation question, such as, "Do you find that planning for contingencies in plant expansion is difficult?" Or, "Do you find that your present copier is so complex that only a few people can use it efficiently?" These questions, asked early in the presentation, bring out customer problems and demonstrate the salesperson's understanding of these problems.

  Problem questions lead to an admission of a problem (need). However, the salesperson must be able to discriminate between the important and unimportant problems and needs of clients. The more explicit the need is, the more vividly the product benefits can be described to fit the customer's problem.

  An explicit need is recognized as such by clients who then have a desire to fulfill the need and solve their problems.

Questions asked of the client provide input into the need assessment process. The validation of a client's need keeps the salesperson from making the wrong assumptions about the client's problem.

Problem questions are useful in establishing this commonality between the clients, their needs, and the salesperson's understanding of the clients' needs. Continuing the dialogue by using implication questions and need-payoff questions increases the chance of helping the client select the correct product, because the problem has been mutually identified.

- *Stage 3.* Implication questions. Asking about the implications of customers' problems helps the customers realize the dimensions of the problem. Implication questions center around how the problem affects various related operational aspects of the business. For instance: "It seems to me that you would like to find a way to reduce your planning uncertainties in such a way as not to limit your ability to satisfy your customers. Is that correct?" Or; "Do you have to go to the trouble of changing the copier setting, or do you have to do the messy job of changing the copier's ink supply in order to copy red ink?" To get the customer to discuss the problems, the phrasing of the implication questions is very important. Once the customer realizes the true dimensions of the problem, discussion of the problem sets it in their minds. Implication questions motivate clients to solve their problems. Particularly motivating are implication questions that have "bottom line" figures attached. Using prospect's data later in the presentation can show how the product choice can influence the client's cost, productivity, or sales.

The sequences of *S,P,* and *I* questions do not have to be asked in this particular order, and each stage can have more than one question asked. However, situational questions are usually first, followed by problem questions, then implication questions. If you wanted to change the *S,P,I* order for some reason, you could, for example, ask a situation question, a problem question, a situation question, a situation question and a problem question. Importantly, however, Need-payoff questions are always asked last.

- *Stage 4.* Need-payoff questions. Need-payoff questions ask the client if the salesperson has correctly identified his or her salient (explicit) needs. Example need-payoff questions are: "If I can show you how to save 15 percent of your planning cost without diminishing your customer satisfaction, would you be interested?"; or "If I could get a copier for you that would copy red ink, and find a way to exchange your present copier without loss to you, would you be interested?" These questions begin the presentation with a benefit statement (saving money/copying red ink), and show the payoff (savings plus customer satisfaction/copying red ink with no loss on the old copier). Positive response to a need-payoff question indicates the client's explicit need. More *P, I,* and *N* questions may have to be asked to establish all the customer's needs.

  If the client gives a "no" answer to a need-payoff question ("It's not important."), the salesperson starts over by asking *Problem, Implication,* and *Need-payoff* questions to determine an explicit need.

Notice that the SPIN method of questioning does not mention the product, but, rather, leaves it for the presentation. Not mentioning the product allows the salesperson to elicit the need from the customer without the skepticism of knowing what is being sold. Ultimately, the effectiveness of the questioning technique is determined by the salesperson's effectiveness in listening to the need analysis.

Listening to clients' answers to SPIN questions gives the salesperson insight into the customer's perceptions of the need. Because a client often expresses psychological needs in subtle ways, the salesperson who knows how to listen can often become aware of these feelings. For this reason, sellers must listen to all that is said.

## Identifying Goals and Objectives

A salesperson must analyze not only the current client situation but also the client's goals and objectives. Just as knowledge of the current client situation gives the salesperson generalized environmental information, having information concerning a client's goals and objectives allows the salesperson to put a problem into the proper perspective.

Questions in this area should be designed to obtain information concerning the customer's ideals. It will do little good to solve a customer's problem if the customer's long-term goals or objectives are not reached. The customer must be satisfied in both the short and long run. As salespeople ask questions, they gather information about the customer's actual situation (current) and the customer's desired situation (goals and objectives). The distance between these two situations should help to determine whether the decision will be to buy or not to buy.

## Validating the Need/Problem

At some time in the dialogue before making a sales presentation, a salesperson should validate the customer's problem. This vocal statement of the need or problem makes both parties aware of a clearly stated need/problem. Once it has been clearly defined and mutually agreed upon, the salesperson uses information obtained through prior need analysis to help solve the problem. Vocalizing the need/problem statement early in the dialogue prevents the misfocusing of efforts.

## Decision-Making Criteria

Each customer enters the marketplace to solve a problem. Also, each buying center has, or develops, certain criteria to be met before a potential solution is considered acceptable. Each member of the buying center can have a different decision criterion that can cause conflict in the buying center. And some solutions are not acceptable because they violate the criteria of the decision. For example, an individual might decide that he or she wants to gain from college only a college degree. One of the possible solutions would be buying a diploma from a "mail order college." But this alternative is eliminated because the person's decision criteria also include effort, honesty, and credibility.

Decision criteria serve to reduce a multitude of information into a workable form. By passing each stage of the decision criteria, a solution moves closer to becoming an acceptable reality. On the contrary, an alternative solution is rejected in the decision process when a restriction—a criterion variable—is not met. The product is then eliminated as a possible solution.

One of the salesperson's jobs in the need assessment stage is to determine the customer's decision criteria so that nonviable alternatives are eliminated. The more a salesperson knows about a customer's decision standards, the more effective the salesperson is in helping the customer ferret out alternative solutions.

For a solution to be viable, it must have specific, measurable, attainable, compatible criteria. When a decision is being made, the salesperson defines a customer's objectives in specific terms rather than in generalized terms. For example, it means knowing that Mrs. Smith wants "thirty miles per gallon from an auto I buy" rather than "good gas mileage."

Just as specificity is important, so is measurability. Any alternative that is not measurable has difficulty in meeting a customer's criterion of being specific. Wanting to get 30 miles per gallon, for example, would be meaningless if there were no way to measure miles per gallon of each auto.

The third criterion characteristic, attainability, is also a necessary factor. It does a customer little good to establish criteria for a solution to a problem if that solution is unreasonable. Looking again at the gas mileage subject, for example, we know that 100 miles per gallon from an "assembly-line" station wagon is an unrealistic and unattainable goal at this time. Unrealistic ideas of what a client expects of a product are carefully corrected by the salesperson.

Lastly, decision criteria should complement past decisions. If a solution negates past achievements, logic and rationality have been ignored. Once salespeople have discovered a client's decision-making criteria, they are better equipped to help find an acceptable solution.

## Analysis of Competition

To find the best solution to the prospect's problem, the salesperson analyzes the competitor's offerings. The analysis of the competition's offerings allows the seller to evaluate all possible solutions to the client's problem. The Competitive Analysis Worksheet (Fig. 9–4) developed in the sales training, or preapproach, stage provides input into other companies' viable solutions to a customer's problems. Use of this information, when applied against the criteria and needs of the customer, allows the salesperson to be a comprehensive source of information and thus to build expert power with the customer.

After making a need assessment, the salesperson begins a sales presentation. During the presentation the client evaluates all the alternatives to solve the problem(s). To give a presentation on a product that is incompatible with the client's needs is completely fruitless, and is called misqualification.

## Misqualifying Customers

Not all customers whom a salesperson contacts are "qualified" customers. For some reason during prospecting, the salesperson may have picked a

**Figure 9–4**
**Competitive Analysis Worksheet**
*Source:* Reprinted with permission of MGC Distributors, Champaign, Illinois, 1989.

| Key Competitive Factors | | Strengths | Your Competitor's Strengths | | | | | | | | | |
|---|---|---|---|---|---|---|---|---|---|---|---|---|
| Factors | Weights | | | | | | | | | | | |
| 1. | | | | | | | | | | | | |
| 2. | | | | | | | | | | | | |
| 3. | | | | | | | | | | | | |
| 4. | | | | | | | | | | | | |
| 5. | | | | | | | | | | | | |
| 6. | | | | | | | | | | | | |
| 7. | | | | | | | | | | | | |
| Total Strategic Muscle | | | | | | | | | | | | |
| Current Market Share | | | | | | | | | | | | |

prospect who is not a viable customer. Although the salesperson has assumed that the prospect is a qualified buyer, an error in prospecting has been made and the customer in reality does not meet the requirements of a qualified buyer (such as having a recognized need, authority to buy, accessibility, or ability to afford). For example, it is fruitless for a salesperson to try to sell a manufacturing plant to a buyer who does not have the financial clout to obtain a mortgage.

Attempting to make a presentation to a misqualified buyer is senseless. Time is invested in an effort that is doomed at the outset. A salesperson who discovers that the customer has been misqualified should thank the prospect for his or her time and exit with goodwill rather than attempt to proceed with a presentation. Further discussion may agitate and anger the customer. Therefore it is best to exit the discussion as soon as the misqualification error becomes apparent.

Be sure that the customer is misqualified before exiting with goodwill. The fact that a customer is purchasing from a competitor or is happy with a current supplier, for example, is not misqualification. Some customers are not fully aware of all that is being offered in the market. Although they make decisions on the best knowledge available to them at the time, changes in the marketplace mean that you can supply new information through a presentation and perhaps change their purchasing behavior. You should exit the need analysis with goodwill only after learning that you cannot be of any service to the customer.

Any exit with goodwill becomes feedback information. This information (experience) is used to perfect strategy formulation. Exits from misqualified contacts are used to correct prospecting techniques. Customers of this type will not be considered prospects, and time will not be spent on gathering preapproach information.

Most customers are not misqualified if the strategy formulation is sound. Therefore the need assessment stage provides ample background for customizing a sales presentation. Moving from the contact/need assessment into the sales presentation is called **transition.** The professional salesperson makes the transition between the attention and warm-up phase of the contact stage to the need assessment and on into the sales presentation phase so smoothly that they follow naturally. On the contrary, the less-polished salesperson often begins the sales presentation abruptly, making for a rough transition.

**transition**

## Summary

The contact stage of a customer–salesperson dialogue has been called the vital thirty seconds because of the importance of first impressions. Prospect contact and the assessment of needs make up the first stage of the client-salesperson dialogue. Relationship selling builds the sales presentation on the foundation laid in this initial stage of the dialogue.

Following precontact planning, the seller works through third parties, letters, telephone calls, cold calls, or other methods to gain an appointment. Whatever method used, it must make a pleasant first impression, since salespeople who make poor first impressions rarely get an interview with the prospective client. During the contact stage, the tempo of the dialogue is set. The salesperson makes the customer feel at ease, develops rapport, and establishes two-way communication, usually through a combination of approaches.

With the establishment of good two-way dialogue, the salesperson can perform a need analysis for the customer. Through questioning and effective listening, the salesperson gathers and evaluates information about the customer, the decision environment, and the customer's perceptions. This interchange of conversation provides such valuable insights for the salesperson as the client's current situation, goals, and objectives and confirmation of the client's needs.

Once the salespeople have developed a trust bond and have gathered and analyzed need analysis information, they are ready to make a sales presentation built on the customer's information.

## Key Terms

telemarketing
teleprospecting
cold call
contact
salesperson's appearance
salesperson's manner
introductory approach
product approach
problem-solving approach
curiosity approach
question approach

statement approach
premium approach
praise approach
survey approach
warm-up
need assessment
qualifying
exploratory questions
SPIN
transition

## Discussion Questions

1.  What are the three functions of the contact phase?

2.  Explain the selective perception process.

3.  Compare and contrast the methods for seeking a personal interview.

4.  Prepare a telephone dialogue to obtain an appointment at the Campus Bike Shop as sales representative for Schwinn Bike Company.

5.  Illustrate the ten points of a contact by preparing a dialogue for a Cross pen salesperson.

6.  Explain how you would best prepare for the first few minutes of a sales contact if you were employed by Moore Business forms? Fuller Brush Company?

7.  What are the important factors to the need assessment?

8.  List some decision-making criteria for a purchasing agent buying bottles for ketchup. For a homeowner buying a refrigerator. For you buying a car.

9.  Why do sellers and buyers concern themselves with analyzing the competition's offerings in a similar market?

10. What is the SPIN technique?

11. How is the SPIN technique advantageous to relationship sellers?

12. Assume that you are an Eastman Kodak salesperson calling on your clients to tell them about your facsimile equipment. You are a relationship seller who uses the SPIN technique. Write a question for each of the four stages of SPIN questioning, which you could use to elicit your client's perceptions of their needs.

13. What specific communication skills are required of sellers who use the SPIN technique?

## Decision Crossroads: Ethical Issues

1. How could the survey approach be used unethically?
2. Discuss a company's social responsibility to give their sales force all the facts concerning the effects of their products on the environment and personal safety of their customers?

## Case 9–1   U.S. Diver Corporation

Randy is sitting in the office of Mr. Whealton, the equipment purchaser for a new company known as Hydro-Space Commercial Diving company. Looking around the room, Randy notices that his only choice of seating is next to Mr. Whealton. There are few pictures in the room, those being of Mr. Whealton's family. Mr. Whealton's desk is neat, clean, and uncluttered. Since this is their first meeting, Mr. Whealton doesn't feel completely comfortable with Randy and doesn't look him in the eyes at all. Mr. Whealton is aware that Randy is selling the Royal Supreme diving regulator and wants to know what long-range effects it will have on the company. Despite his eagerness to find out what Randy can do, he is uninterested in details.

Randy has his notes and briefcase neatly arranged and in order. He is prepared to inform Mr. Whealton in great detail about the Royal Supreme regulator, so he is confused when Mr. Whealton isn't interested in details. Randy uses precise terms to let Mr. Whealton know what can be expected in the future. Also, Randy is trying to move his chair away from Mr. Whealton and doesn't look him in the eye too much. Randy makes the hypothesis that the regulator will keep repair costs down and shorten down-time servicing, which will result in more working hours for Hydro-Space.

**Discussion:**

1. What type of contact approach would you use for Mr. Whealton if you were Randy?
2. Considering the type of client Mr. Whealton is, develop a contact and need assessment plan for him. Why would you use your plan?
3. What types of questions would you ask Mr. Whealton, and what would you expect his answers to be?

## Case 9-2   Artists Anonymous Company

Marion Kay is the originator and partner in the Artists Anonymous Company. Artists Anonymous carries unique and different products that cater to the needs of specialty and variety stores. Since the company is only a year old, Marion has devised a marketing concept that she hopes will open up new and bigger accounts. The marketing concept that Marion is going to use is the gift approach. When Marion has a meeting with a client, she carries a small but well-organized presentation of her product line. The fifteen-minute presentation of her most popular samples offers specials on large bulk orders. If the prospect wants a larger selection to choose from, Marion schedules an appointment at the home office where all the products are on display.

Because the company is new, Marion knows she has little time to present her wares. She gets the client's attention by giving a gift at the beginning of her approach and has learned to be organized to keep that attention level. She has had no problem in meeting new people because she has always been a friendly person. Like most new entrepreneurs, Marion has realized that the key to success is hard work and dedication, but sometimes she gets discouraged when things don't go well.

Marion meets with Mr. Robinson at 10:00 on Tuesday morning at his office in the specialty shop he owns called Over the Rainbow. The shop is located in downtown Bloomington near the University of Minnesota campus. It is not a very large store, since it is a specialty shop and only deals in unique objects. It is very prosperous, and most of the customers come in out of curiosity.

Mr. Robinson has been difficult to reach and on more than one occasion had canceled his meeting with Marion. Whenever Marion has called to reschedule the meeting, he has always been in a hurry to get to another appointment and has deferred the decision about the order to someone else. Marion expects that Mr. Robinson will be a very hard person to sell since he seems to have little interest in what her company has to offer. Yet she is fairly confident that she has the type of product that would make his store even more interesting to his customers. Marion decides to go into the meeting with the confidence that she will be able to make Mr. Robinson see her point.

**Discussion:**

1. What do you think of Marion's contact plan?
2. If you were the client, what would you expect of Marion? Would she disappoint you? Why or why not?
3. List three other ways Marion could be successful in her contact and need assessment.

## Chapter Outline

Prepresentation Information
    Precall Planning

Presentation Organization
    Two-Way Communication
    Salesperson as a Teacher
    Presentation as a Road Map
    Transfer of Product Knowledge

Presentation Delivery: Dramatization
    Get and Maintain Attention    Improve Understanding
    Present Information    Create Lasting Impressions
      Interestingly    Aid the Salesperson

Methods of Dramatization
    Charts and Graphs    Videotapes, Films, and Slides
    Pictures and Photographs    Models, Samples, and Gifts
    Manuals and Portfolios    Product Demonstrations

Using Sales Aids Effectively
    Improving Presentation Delivery

Prepare for the Presentation
Directing the Presentation

## CHAPTER 10

# Dramatizing the Sales Presentation

**Learning Objectives**

After studying this chapter, you should be able to:

- Recognize the precontact and contact preparations of a sales presentation
- Explain why dramatizing a sales presentation is important
- Contrast modes of dramatizing a presentation
- Discuss how sellers may improve their presentation delivery
- Recognize the importance of effective presentations using sales aids, listening and questioning, preparing for the presentation, and controlling the presentation.

## IN THE FIELD

Car dealers have used personal computer (PC) promotions for years because of the expanding legions of upscale people who are PC users. Buick presells prospects with computer disks and equips displays in shopping malls with PCs that salespeople use to answer questions, reports Paul Harrison of Buick. ``We found that they overwhelmingly liked animation and the ease of obtaining the information they wanted in a no-pressure way, at their own pace,'' says Harrison. Edward Mertz, General Manager for Buick adds, ``Consumers expect the latest technology in the cars they buy, so we want to give them the opportunity to use the same levels of advanced technology to help in their buying decision. The salespeople even use a computer in the showroom to help the customer determine what to buy. The salesperson operates the PC because it is still a business that requires a high degree of personal selling. Customers get used to having the computer help them in both places, and we even write the order on a PC. It helps the presentation in the showroom to have them presold,'' says Harrison.

*Source:* ``How Buick Helps Dealers with Hi-Tech Tools that Pre-Sell,'' *Sales and Marketing Management* 137 (August 1987). Reprinted with permission from *Sales and Marketing Management,* © August 1987.

The contact stage of the dialogue is designed to prepare the customer for the problem-solving mode needed in the sales presentation (see Figure 10–1). A *sales presentation* is the formal delivery of information about products or services that satisfy a customer's needs. Dramatization refers to the words a salesperson uses to make a sales strategy really come alive, enabling consumers to visualize more effectively their need for a product.

**dramatization**

To be effective in communicating the sales message, salespeople need to dramatize the sales message, as the Buick dealers do (see *In the Field).* **Dramatization** is a dynamic process of converting words into action—converting product features into customer benefits. It allows the customer to participate actively rather than merely being a passive object in a static process. Salespeople who do not dramatize the presentation talk *at* and *to* the customer, not *with* the customer.

To dramatize a sales strategy effectively, a salesperson must plan a presentation in a precontact (strategy formulation) stage, then adapt the strategy dramatization during the sales presentation to meet contingencies that develop. This requires talking and thinking at the same time. Al-

**Figure 10–1**
*Dramatizing the Sales Presentation* in the Customer–Salesperson Dialogue

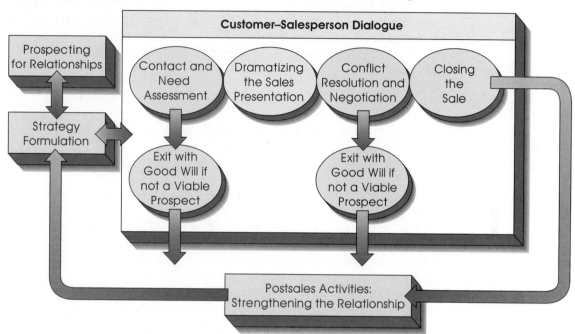

though admittedly a difficult feat, this may be accomplished through practice and careful preparation.

> The salesman was halfway home when the idea struck him: Why, he'd left two important features out of the presentation he'd just given! A few minutes later, as he turned his car into the driveway, the salesman had another flash! He'd missed answering one of his prospect's objections! It'd come along early in the presentation, and the salesman said that, "We'll get back to that shortly— and then promptly forgot about it. Although he made a presentation, he did not adapt his plan to the customer and certainly was not concentrating."[1]

Such inefficiency proves that the salesperson in the excerpt above did not deliver the presentation in a relationship mode, even though he may have begun in this mode. Mistakes like this are costly to a salesperson and to his or her company.

When a salesperson realizes his or her sales presentation to a purchasing agent is only one of over fifty the agent sees and hears in a week, the importance of efficiency becomes clear. A salesperson can, with a good presentation, overcome disadvantages such as being from a little-known company or selling a new product. This was illustrated by an experiment conducted by Theodore Levitt of Harvard. Dr. Levitt compared these selling situations:

- A good presentation by a salesperson from a well-known company
- A good presentation made by a seller from a little-known company
- A poor presentation made by a salesperson from a well-known company
- A poor presentation made by a seller from a little-known company.

As was expected, the best results were produced by the salesperson from the well-known company making a good sales presentation. But more importantly, Levitt found that the salesperson representing a little-known company but making a good presentation can outsell the person from a well-known company who gives a weak presentation.

Dr. Levitt puts it this way: "A well-known company loses the advantage of its reputation if its direct sales presentation is clearly inferior to that of an unknown or little-known company." He then adds: "A little-known company, by concentrating strongly on training its salesmen to make good presentations, may be able to make considerable progress toward overcoming the liability of its relative anonymity. . . . A good sales presentation has greater durability than a good company reputation."[2]

The evidence is clear. Because the sales presentation is the message delivered to the client, it should be memorable.

## Prepresentation Information

A formal delivery of information about products or services that satisfy a customer's needs is called a presentation. It is illustrated through dramatizing the benefits that the customer receives from such a product. Demonstrations are less likely in industrial sales because of the nature of the products. However, materials that highlight the product, if not the product itself, are used in all sales areas.

During sales training in the classroom and on the job, salespeople learn to give sales presentations and demonstrations. In fact, a large percentage of sales training time is spent constructing, delivering, and perfecting the sales presentation. As we have seen in the sales training portion of this book, a salesperson garners extensive information concerning basic product knowledge and sales techniques. Sellers practice adapting this information to various selling situations. With practice, not only does the salesperson learn to customize a presentation but also learns to talk, listen, and modify a presentation simultaneously.

## Precall Planning

While preparing a sales strategy, salespeople organize product information and sales techniques into a plan for the buyer/seller dialogue. In making this plan, they have analyzed their companies' products according to each product's features and its resultant benefits to a consumer.

Features (physical characteristics) of a product exist regardless of who buys the product. However, the benefits of a feature may vary according to the customer and a product's intended use. A **benefit** is the satisfactory fit between a product's features and a customer's needs or problems. Customers buy benefits, not product features; that is, they buy what the product does for them, not just the product. As a world-renowned sales trainer, Dale Carnegie advised that salespeople must ''sell the sizzle, not the steak.''

**benefit**

To sell the benefits of a product, the salesperson converts features of that product into benefit statements. This is done through a features/benefit worksheet such as that shown in Figure 10–2.

The conversion of features into benefits puts them into the customer's language, using their communication style—thinker/feeler, sensor/intuitor. By personalizing them in this way the salesperson builds self-confidence, strengthens trust, and increases two-way communication with the buyer. For example: ''Mr. Tracy, Data Control's new inventory control system, improved order processing procedures, and increased production capacity (features) will ensure that we can maintain prompt and accurate deliveries constantly, year after year'' (benefits). This statement, when made to a customer who has had irregular service from the current supplier, would be an effective benefit, particularly when it is supported through facts and testimonies.

Preparing a formal feature/benefit worksheet in the strategy stage helps the salesperson think through the presentation while maintaining a customer-benefit orientation. Of course, different worksheets have to be made for different types of customers. For example, the ego-involved customer looks at products differently from the skeptic. Therefore several worksheets are made for each product or service. Using this preparation material depends upon determining the type of customer and the customer's problem in the need assessment stage.

Pharmaceutical salespeople, like this Pfizer saleswoman, must illustrate a product's benefits in a very short time span. Meeting physicians between the physician's scheduled patients, pharmaceutical salespeople are trained to demonstrate three different products in as little as five minutes. In this situation, precall planning is obviously critical.

Figure 10–2
**Features/Benefit Worksheet for Compact Passenger Car**

| Features | Benefits | | | |
|---|---|---|---|---|
| | Comfort | Economy | Safety | Convenience |
| **Product Features** | | | | |
| 1. Hip room 54″ | ✓ | | | |
| 2. Leg room 44″ | ✓ | | | |
| 3. Length 184″ | ✓ | | ✓ | |
| 4. Trunk 28.8 cu. ft. | ✓ | | | ✓ |
| 5. Welded body | | | ✓ | |
| 6. Engine alum. 110 hp. | | ✓ | | |
| 7. Canted engine | | ✓ | ✓ | |
| 8. Rustproof body | | | | ✓ |
| 9. Finish | | | | ✓ |
| **Company Features** | | | | |
| 1. Complete service dept. | | ✓ | | ✓ |
| 2. Trade-in allowance | | | | ✓ |
| 3. Easy payment plan | | ✓ | | ✓ |

## Presentation Organization

sales presentation

The **sales presentation** is a sequential process whereby the salesperson presents product benefits and gets feedback on each one before proceeding to the next benefit. This fosters two-way interaction.

### Two-Way Communication

During the two-way communication, four basic functions are established. The salesperson:

- Makes the prospects aware of their problem or need
- Proposes a viable solution to the problem
- Supports the proposal with facts
- Motivates the prospect to solve the problem.

The dialogue from one stage to the next should flow smoothly and bring coherence and continuity to the presentation.

Since each buyer makes a decision to buy or not to buy around five buying decision areas—need, product, source, price and time—it is imperative that the salesperson and the customer have a clear and precise understanding of each. Unconvinced of a need, a customer rarely buys a product. Often the customer is well aware of the need, so little must be done to establish the awareness of the need. It is often helpful, however, to make a tactful verbal statement of the need, so that the customer may affirm it. A great deal of time can be wasted when the salesperson tries to solve a problem the customer is unaware of having.

For example, you probably have not made financial plans or burial plans. Yet you know planning is necessary and that you are going to die. Each of these needs, however, is for "unsought goods." The time to think about them is generally later in life. Therefore it is a salesperson's responsibility, through teaching, to make you aware of the need through dramatization or a graphic presentation.

## Salesperson as a Teacher

A salesperson is a teacher, a showperson; and the presentation is a learning experience for the consumer. As teachers, salespeople illustrate and demonstrate consumer benefits through two-way communication with the use of sales aids. This teaching does not occur in the classroom but in the field, nor does it involve the unpleasant aspect of tests, fear, or a threatening atmosphere. Instead, the seller produces a relaxed, nonthreatening atmosphere conducive to learning for the consumer. A salesperson uses dramatic techniques to show how features benefit the consumer. This is called **showmanship.**

showmanship

Once the customer is aware of a need, the salesperson reaches the heart of the presentation, which is to build confidence. Confidence must be built in the product, and **self-confidence** must be stimulated in the customer. The customer's self-confidence grows along with recognizing the ability to make decisions. Confidence is inspired also when the salesperson proposes solutions in such a way that the customer accepts or rejects them one feature or benefit at a time. How the customer reacts to the feature/benefit statements provides the salesperson with direction for the presentation.

self-confidence

## Presentation As A Road Map

The presentation is organized like a road map, with each feature/benefit statement being a "Y" junction. The intersection of the junction is the salesperson asking for affirmation or denial of a benefit statement. If the customer affirms the benefit, one path is taken. If the customer denies or objects to the benefit, the other path is taken. This process continues until the customer makes the buy/no-buy decision. The most efficient presentation is the one that takes the most direct path and that effectively answers the customer's questions and doubts.

## Transfer of Product Knowledge

Effective presentations are not only built around providing enough features/benefits (product knowledge) to enable the salesperson to determine comfortably if the client is ready to make a commitment (to buy, not to buy, to continue to search), but also they are built around comparative information. Product knowledge built upon comparative information about direct and indirect competition is a salesperson's strongest tool. The salesperson with an abundance of this type of information is of invaluable help to a client. Relationship salespeople interpret the unique, positive, and negative features/benefits of their products in relation to competitive products; and thus they supply a client with information that others are unprepared to give. Having complete information, therefore, creates a differential advantage for the salesperson. Comparative knowledge expressed in terms of client benefits builds value in a salesperson's products and service in the mind of the client.

The presentation has a direction; it moves toward a potentially satisfying solution. However, a salesperson should avoid putting pressure on the client by insisting that this is *the* solution. The client should come to the decision before the salesperson has to point it out. And since each client, each problem, each need, each time influence, and each set of priorities is different, each presentation is different. The presentation is individualized for each customer, which means that a presentation that was successful for the last client may fail with the next one because it is too abrupt, seems "pushy," or may be considered too long to sustain the next client's attention. Because of a customer orientation and awareness of customer differences, the relationship salesperson is organized in the preparation stage and works at customizing a presentation that motivates the client to buy.

## Presentation Delivery: Dramatization

Just as the presentation is customized for each client, the delivery method, or dramatization, is uniquely combined for each customer. Therefore it is impossible to discuss the "best" way to dramatize a presentation. The discussion in this area is composed of tools and techniques that have worked and of cautions about practices that have proved ineffective. It should be remembered, however, that salespeople should constantly ask themselves how they can use their own abilities, resources, and imaginations to make a vividly dramatized sales plan. Through the control mechanism in the sales process (feedback), the salesperson constantly seeks to improve not only the sales plan but also its dramatization. The series of activities that facilitate client action, called dramatization, gets and maintains the attention of a client, presents the information in an interesting way, improves understanding, creates a lasting impression, and aids the salesperson.

## Get and Maintain Attention

The effective demonstration of a product requires use of showmanship to win and to maintain the attention of the buyer. The best way to keep buyers attentive is to get them involved in such a way that they use more than one of their senses. Do more than show and tell. Let the buyer move the product, drop it, turn it; let the buyer experience the full benefit of the product feature, if possible.

One such example of a salesperson who successfully achieves this is the Bic pen representative, who produces a board, a hammer, and a Bic pen and asks the client to hammer the pen through the board. Then the salesperson asks the client to remove the pen and to write with it. This demonstration dramatically shows the durability of the pen. If, however, the product fails during the dramatization, there is little chance that the client will buy. So make sure the demonstration works before it is used. Test it out in the home office or at home with friends. Get their reactions and impressions of the dramatization.

By dramatizing the sales points throughout the presentation, a salesperson can better hold a client's interest until the end. However, a word of caution is necessary, since dramatization can be overpowering and poorly done; it can be tactless or gaudy; and it can be detrimental to the salesperson's goal. An effectively organized presentation can be scuttled by a poor delivery. By frequent evaluations of a demonstration's effectiveness, a salesperson learns which tools and techniques work best.

## Present Information Interestingly

Appealing to multiple senses and involving the customer make the presentation interesting. Multiple-sense appeals can reinforce each other, aid learning, increase retention, and maintain interest.[3]

**Multiple-sense appeals** involve more than one of the five senses—hearing, seeing, smelling, touching, and tasting. Having the customer involved in the demonstration can create an unforgettable impression.

**multiple-sense appeals**

showboating

Dramatization "drives a point home" in a convincing manner through illustration rather than through showboating. **Showboating** is dramatizing a feature in such a way that it illustrates the demonstration's effects rather than highlighting the product's feature. It becomes unbelievable and sometimes unethical. Having the customer hit an unbreakable product with a hammer or put a lighted match on a Formica® surface that resists burning all demonstrate some type of proof-of-performance that adds interest to the presentation. However, to demonstrate these same products by showing a videotape of dropping a five-ton wrecking ball on a break-resistant product or putting a welder's torch to the Formica® surface is demonstrating showboating rather than dramatizing the features of the products. Although some products are difficult to dramatize, only a few products cannot be dramatized in some way.

## Improve Understanding

nonvisual people

visually oriented person

If a client perceives predominantly through one particular sense, a salesperson has a difficult time appealing to that client's other senses. In qualifying the customer during the contact phase, therefore, it is important to discover informally whether the client is a visually or verbally oriented person. Studies on gender-based differences suggest that males are better visual processors and that females have superior verbal skills. **Nonvisual people** (verbal) generally are able to imagine or to pretend from a verbal description. They tend to be followers, not leaders, in fashion and need less eye contact than a visual person.

The **visually oriented person** must see things to understand and to appreciate a description. It is fruitless, therefore, to tell visually oriented buyers to close their eyes as the salesperson describes a scene. Working with a client who has limitations of this sort need not be a source of frustration as long as the salesperson knows how to proceed correctly. Whenever possible, it is better to show and tell and to involve the client. Showing the clients how a product works, telling them how it will benefit them, and, if possible, involving them in the demonstration help them understand the product and presentation.

## Create Lasting Impressions

People remember some of what they hear. They remember more of what they see. Even more remembering is done if they see and hear at the same time. They, however, learn most by doing. Involving a customer in a presentation, if only to hold the package while it is being described, is a useful technique in making the customer remember. A vividly dramatized demonstration, if appropriate, will create a lasting impression deep within a

## PARTNERSHIPS

All salespeople know that customers remember far more of what they see and hear than just what they hear. The challenge is to find a way to come up with visual aids that are easy to use but won't get in the way of the selling process. Paul Mason, who covers the Anoka, Minnesota territory for Electrolux, demonstrates his vacuum's abilities by running it over the prospect's bedsheets to collect skin sloughed off during sleep. He announces that the skin breeds mites, then presents a company booklet showing a blown-up photo of a crab-like mite under the headline, ``Tonight you'll be sharing a bed with this guy!'' Mason says the aids work nearly every time. However, the squeamish customer may be very upset. Adapt your demonstration to the customer.

*Source:* ``Sales Talk: Is Your Sales Literature on the Dull Side?,'' *Sales and Marketing Management* 141 (January 1989): 88.

client's memory. For example, let buyers hit the glass of an oven door with a heavy wrench, compare the sound reproduction of two sets of speakers, smell the scent of perfume, see the differences of heavy metal weights on competitive mattress springs, and enjoy the rich chocolate taste of a new candy bar.

Regardless of the method used to dramatize a product's benefits, it should always be done skillfully, tactfully, and at the proper time so that the client will leave with the lasting, positive impression the salesperson intends. Be cautious that the lasting impression is always seen as a positive experience. This may not be the case in the Paul Mason situation (see *Partnerships*). Although the demonstration is true and factual, some prospects might be "turned off" by this demonstration of reality.

## Aid the Salesperson

Good dramatizations build the seller's confidence. Salespeople find that using pictures and actions can help save time and words and that shortening dramatizations also improves efficiency.

Some salespeople, such as pharmaceutical salespeople, are on very restrictive presentation schedules. Pharmaceutical salespeople calling on doctors have found that they only have five minutes in which to tell their story. In five minutes they present three products: a product introduced at the last visit, a new product, and a reminder of a currently used product. A good dramatization helps get the message across while keeping the doctor's eye and mind on the presentation.[4]

## Methods of Dramatization

Many different methods are available for dramatizing a sales presentation. These visual aids come in a wide variety of types and uses. Writers tell us that "visuals are the most potentially useful, yet the most neglected and misused, means of improving person-to-person (or person-to-group) communicating processes."[5]

What are some of the most common visual aids sellers have at their disposal? Two general types of visual sales aids are **illustrators** and **organizers.** The illustrator type uses graphics or motion to depict one or more aspects of the sales presentation. Visuals such as motion pictures, slides, and maps are all potential illustrators. Good illustrators are simple, convenient, and fit the overall presentation.

The second type of visual is the organizer. It provides a story form, which is the salesperson's presentation. Supporters of this type of visual point out that it has several advantages:

**illustrators**
**organizers**

## TECHNOLOGY BULLETIN

### Computer Software

Presentation software plays a strong supporting role in sales calls and follow-up literature. Fol-Med, a company making medical-grade tubing, uses graphic tools internally to depict trends and strategies. They use Harvard Grapics from Software Publishing Corp., which maps colors to patterns when printing presentations on laser printers equipped for color. Its version 2.3 includes 12 preset palettes of color to ensure the correct color matching for laser technology. This latest version is user friendly, using 500 new symbols that program terminology for charts rather than typed commands. Although most salespeople will not be directly involved in developing the visual materials for presentations, the more they know about their construction, the better equipped they will be in selecting the material best suited for their presentation.

*Source:* Michael Antonoff, ''Presentations that Persuade,'' *Personal Computing* 15 (July 27, 1990): 60–68.

- As salespeople get more and more immersed in the technical aspects of their product or service, they tend to talk product features rather than customer benefits. The copier salesperson gets tangled up in the feed-and-speed story; the salesperson for paint gets sidetracked onto its chemical contents. But the organizer visual is built around user benefits. If either the salesperson or the customer gets bogged down in nuts-and-bolts details, the visuals keep them on course to the end benefits.
- While organizer visuals seem to convert the sales presentation into a one-way communication to an overwhelmed prospect, exactly the opposite happens. The visual encourages a two-way exchange of ideas. Without an organizer, the salesperson is so busy thinking about what to say next that he or she may not listen carefully. But when the salesperson uses this visual, the next step is on the next page. The salesperson can concentrate on listening and become more sensitive to the customer's nonverbal reactions
- Well-designed visuals increase the **closing rate**—the percentage of sales calls in which the call objective is achieved.

**closing rate**

Other advantages are:
- The complete story is told in less time.
- It is easier to get back on the track after a telephone call or other interruption.
- Visuals often get sellers to see some behind-the-scenes buying influence they didn't know existed.[6]

Salespeople can choose from numerous types of visual aids and may use one type of a combination of visuals to present the sales story.

## Charts and Graphs

Illustrators in the form of charts and graphs are useful in showing trends and relationships. Often depicting relationships in terms of bars, circles, or squares, charts and graphs allow the salesperson to show significant changes or benefits. Information in Figure 10–3 is better illustrated in chart form than in its list form.

## Pictures and Photographs

These illustrators are generally used as "emphasis pieces" to elicit a particular emotion or to establish emotion. Since instant cameras can imme-

Charts and graphs effectively illustrate trends in support of the salesperson's presentation. They are an excellent way, when properly prepared and used, to keep the attention of buying groups.

**Figure 10–3**
**Illustrative Data**
106 respondents with a
possibility of multiple
answers.

**Example of Typical Data**

*Where do you use AV equipment?*
- Meetings                91.5%
- Training                87.7%
- Sales Presentations    77.3%

**Illustrative (Better) Representation of Data**

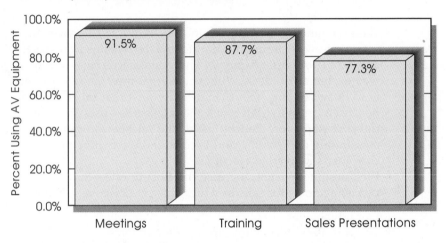

diately make pictures for lasting memories, they provide realistic visuals
at a relatively inexpensive price.

John Chapin, salesperson for B-Dry, a cellar waterproofing company, hands a client a fifty-page three-ring binder while he is inspecting
the foundations. Each page has four Polaroid pictures, each labeled with
a description of water damage. Says Mr. Chapin, "It is a great aid. It gives
potential customers something to look at while the job is being inspected
and measured. In addition, it sends a message that B-Dry has a great deal
of experience in this field."[7] In another application, realtors use facsimile
machines to transmit pictures of homes and to discover available homes
for clients across the nation through their 450 affiliates.[8]

All printed material used for demonstration purposes should be
laminated in plastic. This process not only keeps material fresh, neat, and
clean but also shows that the salesperson values the information enough
to make a permanent record of it. The quality of the visual aid speaks
about how the salesperson and the company feel about the material in the
visual aid. AT&T often leaves blue leather folders, gold embossed with
the customer's name. Customers are impressed when they see the folders
and realize that they are dealing with a top-of-the-line outfit. AT&T took
obvious pains with this presentation and wanted the customer to know.[9]
Poorly produced visual aids exhibit lack of confidence, importance, or
caring on the producer's part.

## Manuals and Portfolios

Many companies produce standardized sales talks that are often illustrated with pictures. These sales manuals are the organizer type of visual aid. As a visual outline, they can be used by novice salespeople to make sure the right aid is used at the right time. Commonly, **sales manuals** contain complete advice on making the sales talk and on the sales job in general. To the contrary, **sales portfolios** contain only material and illustrations on the sales talk itself.

      A sales portfolio is an outline of a sales talk that is designed to be read. Usually it is placed on an easel, spiralbound or bound. Either way, it is designed to guide a customer and the salesperson through the sales talk. Many direct-to-the-customer sales are examples of this type of presentation.

**sales manual**

**sales portfolio**

## Videotapes, Films, and Slides

When salespeople have products too bulky to bring to a customer or when they want to illustrate a production process, they use videotapes, films, or slides. The improvement in the size and portability of projectors and videotape equipment makes these visual aids more prominent. No longer are salespeople required to carry bulky projectors, screens, and cords with them, since many units weigh less than nine pounds and are completely self-contained. The use of visuals, particularly videotaped presentations, is mushrooming. In fact, field sales representatives comprise the largest number of portable video systems users.[10] Now that costs of producing visuals are lower and equipment is no longer bulky, the two greatest disadvantages of audiovisual use have been overcome by technology.[11]

      Films are a good way to educate distributors and their salespeople. Retail and wholesale salespeople can see how a plant is operated and how products are made without the expense of a personal visit.

      Slides or sound-slide films have advantages that films do not have. Modern equipment is self-contained, and slides allow a maximum in flexibility when changes are needed. (A typical slide presentation should be about 12–15 minutes long. Too much of any audiovisual is boring.)[12]

## Models, Samples, and Gifts

Three-dimensional visual aids are a good way to get and to keep customer interest. Many products are too cumbersome to be transported; therefore the salesperson finds it more convenient to use a model or miniature of the product. The more realistic the working model, the more effective a

Cut-away models of the actual product are effective in showing how a product internally operates.

visual aid it makes. Some models are "cut-away" and are designed to show the cross section of the product. This allows the salesperson to illustrate product features that may normally be hidden from the customer.

For example, a shoe salesperson might bring along a cut-away of a running shoe that shows all the features of the shoe's construction. Some products are portable enough to be carried by a salesperson. These are called samples. Having a sample close at hand, a salesperson can readily demonstrate a product's features or benefits. Products such as foods, candies, books, and cigars are often sold through samples.

There are many advantages to using samples. They:

- Maintain interest
- Serve as a reminder to those who receive them
- Reinforce the probability of purchase
- Keep the name in front of the buyer.

Often salespeople carry kits that hold samples. In fact, sample cases have been a traditional symbol of the salesperson.

Gifts are left with a customer as a reminder of what the company has to offer. These gifts may be useful items—paperweights, calendars, pens, watches—or novelty items such as a note pad with cartoon characters on it, posters, or badges.[13]

Both samples and gifts are an extension of the personal salesperson; therefore care needs to be extended to project the correct image.

Models, samples, and gifts should be clean, fresh, and neat. Also, if the item has working parts, it should be checked out to see that it is in working order. There are few things worse than a sample, model, or gift that does not perform (a pen that doesn't write, candy that is stale, a working model that doesn't work properly, etc.). From a behavioral point of view, samples serve a better purpose than gifts (premiums) because they are tied directly to the product, whereas the premium may not be.[14]

## Product Demonstrations

One of the most effective ways to interest customers is by letting them use the product. Most effective product demonstrations, or "demos," enable the customer to see how the product works by using it. Demonstrations are particularly useful for products whose features cannot be assessed in any other manner, for complicated goods, and where trial usage typically precedes purchase. This technique dramatically highlights benefits of the product. In fact, few visual aids can emphasize a fact better than a product demonstration, as discussed in the *Partnerships* box.

Auto salespeople, for example, insist that a prospect take a test drive to "feel the power of the motor," "experience the comfort and handling," and "listen to the quietness." Working on the principle that "seeing is believing," product demonstrations put the customer in a multisense appealing atmosphere in which a sample is actually put to a test.

## PARTNERSHIPS

*Clearly, some products lend themselves to demonstrations so beautifully that the demo itself is the attraction.* **Diane Weintraub, President of Communique**

At a recent medical supplies trade show, one such product was being effectively demonstrated. A defibrillator touted as being small sized and very portable was being demonstrated on an oven-stuffer chicken (dead, of course). "When the chicken was zapped with this device, its little wings and legs would jerk," recalls Weintrab. "What better way to show the portability and small size than on a chicken small enough to fit into a roasting pan?" she exclaimed.

*Source:* Betsy Weisendanger, "Are Your Salespeople Trade Show Duds?" *Sales and Marketing Management* 142 (August 1990).

Product demonstrations that allow the buyer to have hands-on experience with the product illustrate benefits that are hard to describe verbally.

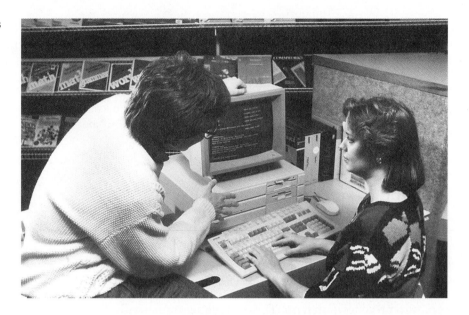

## Using Sales Aids Effectively

Nothing rounds out a presentation better than sincere, complete, convincing sales aids. The good sales aid provides many benefits. It:

- Sets the stage for the customer to listen
- Gets attention and makes the customer see the benefits of listening
- Suggests product benefits and demonstrates why the product has value
- Evokes response from the customer concerning individual needs
- Offers proof to support the salesperson's claims
- Allows for a rapid communication that saves time for the buyer as well as the seller
- Provides a clear, organized format for presenting a message
- Helps overcome sales resistance
- Reminds the customer after the sales call with its lasting impression
- Aids in sales closing.[15]

## Improving Presentation Delivery

The salesperson must be very aware of how the presentation is given. Not only must the presentation be organized and developed in a clear, concise manner, but also it must be delivered in the same manner.

Delivery techniques must be practiced and perfected if the salesperson is to make a sales presentation effective and efficient. Each salesperson must develop his or her own delivery style from the same basic elements.[16]

## Words

Words are tools. They can be nerve grating or smooth, creative or destructive. The English language weighs in as the most complete, flexible, and idiomatic of all modern tongues; therefore a salesperson needs to speculate: Am I tapping its potential? Am I spicing my presentation with words and illustrations that are truly imaginative, arresting, and unforgettable?

Being arresting and unforgettable means choosing words that describe and strengthen benefit statements. It means using words of color—"smooth as glass," "hard as a diamond," "soft as silk,"—words that create moods and that are concise. It also means avoiding words that are vague, such as nice, you know, you see, oh, good, swell, and neat. Words should be *similes* that show the "sizzle" of a steak so well that the customer can taste it.

**The L-O-N-G and the Short of it.**[17]   Don't be a word rambler. Don't try to sound "businesslike" by using involved words and phrases. Use short, natural words whenever possible. You'll cut the length of your presentation, it'll sound better, and the other person will get your ideas quicker.

| The L-o-n-g Way | The Shorter Way |
| --- | --- |
| *All that is necessary for you to do is* . . . | Just . . . |
| *In the normal course of our procedure* . . . | Normally . . . |
| *We have discontinued the policy of* . . . | I no longer . . . |
| *In accordance with your request* . . . | As you wished . . . |
| *In the meantime* . . . | Meantime . . . |
| *Due to the fact that* . . . | Because . . . |
| *In view of the fact that* . . . | Because . . . |
| *At a later date* . . . | Later . . . |
| *Will you be good enough to* . . . | Please . . . |
| *At which time* . . . | When . . . |
| *In regard to* . . . | About . . . |
| *Reduce to a minimum* . . . | Minimize . . . |
| *In the near future* . . . | Soon . . . |
| *In the amount of* . . . | For . . . |

*In order that . . .*              So . . .

*In the event of . . .*           If . . .

Arnold Bennett, the distinguished English novelist, once observed that many of the frictions and problems of daily life—business and social—are caused by abrasive sounds, speech habits, and mannerisms.

### Voice, Tone, and Sound

Our bodies are sound sensitive. They react emotionally to the way a speaker "hits" them. Very often, a customer's yes or no to a proposal is determined by the way the salesperson sounds. Here are a few of the sounds to avoid:

- *Mumbling.* Some so-called "method" actors seem to have built a career out of this irritating mannerism. But it is important for a salesperson to come through clearly and distinctly, to have lively lips, not lazy lips.
- *Monotony.* A salesperson should make a self-analysis to determine whether he or she drones on and on and on. If the answer is yes, that person's presentation may have all the fascination of a dripping faucet. To correct the problem, the salesperson needs to learn to support his or her voice with VEEV (Vigor—Energy—Enthusiasm—Vitality). Practice by using a tape recorder.
- *Nasality,* stridency, too high pitch. Each of these eargraters can set up a fight-or-flight syndrome in the customer. The nose is for breathing, not talking. A salesperson should talk with the sound coming out of the mouth, resonating on the chest bones instead of through the nose. Thinking low pitch helps.
- *Listlessness.* A tired and limp voice can be a better sedative than a sleeping pill. The object of selling is to infect the buyer with the excitement of the salesperson. The energized and vibrant voice can do a lot to spread that infection. Rule for a salesperson: support the voice and project it.
- *Speed.* If the salesperson speaks too slowly, the audience gets fidgety; if he or she speaks too fast, the listeners will have a hard time following and will become jumpy. A good pace to strive for is between 160 and 175 words a minute. Here are helpers a salesperson can use to learn how to regulate the pace when speaking:
  - If one is talking too fast (or too slow), he or she can put a one-eighth-inch square sticker marked "SLO!" (or "FAST!") in the center of his or her watch that will serve as a

reminder to slow down (or speed up). Stickers on the salesperson's telephone, wallet, or appointment book can also help iron out that and other bad speaking habits pronto.

- If the salesperson tends to pad or bridge phrases with expressions such as "y'know," "like," and "uh-huh," the person should write the offending expression on stickers and strike it out with a bold slashing cross. Then the salesperson should paste the stickers where they are certain to be seen readily all day long.

## The Eyes

Our eyes communicate volumes of information. They help us express enthusiasm, sincerity, credibility, interest, confidence, alertness, and approval. They receive messages and transmit them. Salespeople should try to maintain eye contact with customers 90 percent of the time. When they are selling to a group, they should let their eyes sweep from person to person about every five to ten seconds, thereby directing their looks and spoken phrases to each person. However, remember to finish a phrase while looking at one person before directing the eyes toward another. Directing attention to something or someone can be done through using the eyes. If a customer fails to follow the eye movement from one object to another, attention may have been lost.[18]

## The Face

It is the animation, the smile—not the grin—that telegraphs warmth and conviction. Salespeople, put on a happy face! Wear a "good news" expression. Do not let your facial muscles sag any more than you would let your socks fall down. Keep your cheeks up like two firm little apples under your eyes. If you are happy, let your face know it and show it!

## Kinesics

The study of bodily movements (**kinesics**) was discussed more extensively earlier, but use of this information from the salesperson's side is illustrated here. Salespeople's stance tells much about their self-concept and feelings about their presentation. The operative phrase here is "on your toes!" In other words, the salesperson should keep the weight evenly distributed on the balls of the feet, keep the chest up, the solar plexus in, and the head upright. Leaning on the customer's desk or on the lectern when there is a buying committee audience is never an acceptable practice.

**kinesics**

## Proxemics

Not only is the posture of the body important, but the position of the body in relationship to the customer is also important. **Proxemics** is the

**proxemics**

study of space and the movement of people within it. There are four types of proxemics: physical, psychological, territorial, and contact.[19] Where a salesperson stands, sits, and moves can add or distract from a presentation. An awareness of these proxemics and their significance is important for the salesperson.

Personal distance, the socially accepted distance people maintain between themselves and other people, can be depicted as social zones, or bubbles, of space, as shown in Figure 10–4. It is only after one accepts another person that the other person is allowed to move into a closer zone. Only in the most intimate situations are people allowed into the zero to two feet intimate zone in the North American culture. In other cultures the intimate zone is zero to one foot, and the personal zone one to two feet. Other cultures have established closer relationships in terms of speaking distances. However, for our discussion, we will consider only those distances acceptable in the North American culture.

**Figure 10–4**
**Proxemics**

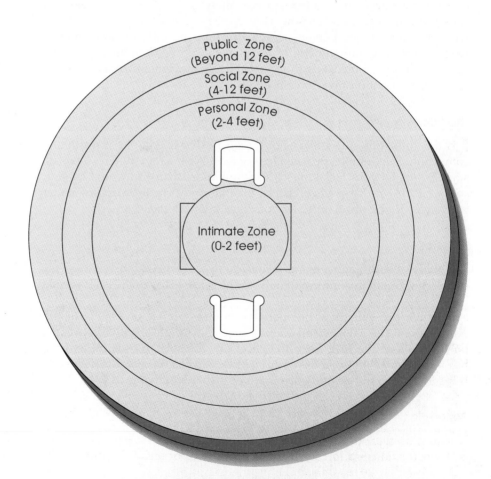

Public Zone
(Beyond 12 feet)

Social Zone
(4–12 feet)

Personal Zone
(2–4 feet)

Intimate Zone
(0–2 feet)

Movement from a social zone to another zone (personal or intimate) without permission causes tension. Therefore the salesperson should attempt to make such a movement only with customer approval. Always salespeople must be conscious of the importance of maintaining the proper distance and be aware of the tension levels in the customer. Tension will rise when one has committed a proxemic violation. Such violations of a customer's proxemic zones without verbal or nonverbal invitation will cause communication breakdown and loss of a customer. Symptoms of such a violation might include the client's rigidness, attention shifts, and body position changes.

In a similar manner, a refusal—verbal or nonverbal—from a salesperson when a client who has verbally or nonverbally invited the salesperson into a closer zone is also a violation that can cause repercussions. Refusing a client's invitation (no sexual connotation intended) can make the salesperson seem "cold," "aloof," and not "persuadable." Either moving without invitation or failing to move with invitation can cause communication "noise" and should therefore be avoided.

Personal space refers specifically to the psychological space as opposed to the physical space discussed above. Violations of psychological proxemics is as disruptive as are violations of physical proxemics. People who have formal personal space (public zone) between them use titles with each other such as Mr., Mrs., Ms., and Dr., whereas in the intimate zone people might address each other by first names or even endearments such as "dear." In the personal zone the salesperson would be given permission to call the client by his or her first name.

In addition, territorial proxemics deals with movement within a space that one defines as his or her personal property. We each develop a sense of having our own "turf." When someone invades another's territory, the tension level is increased. When someone picks up another's personal object without permission or sits in the client's favorite chair, tension is heightened, suspicion is increased, and distrust is created.

The salesperson must be careful of invading a client's territory—of leaning on a client's desk; of using a client's desk for a display table; of moving a personal object, for example. It is also necessary to watch for nonverbal behavior. In such instances a client's attention moves to the object moved and moves away from the conversation. Communication lags, tension goes up, and the trust goes down.

Finally, contact proxemics deal with the sense of touch or closeness. People are categorized as being either contact or noncontact people, that is, as touches or nontouches. Contact people who come into interaction psychologically or physically with noncontact people appear to them (noncontact people) as being overly friendly, clinging, and smothering. The opposite is true of the noncontact people who appear to contact people as being cold, unfriendly, or impolite.

Consequently it is important to be able to "read" a person to find out whether he or she is a contact or a noncontact person. Once the person's category is established, the salesperson can adapt his or her style to build trust.

Having a knowledge of proxemics, therefore, can be an immense help in building rapport between salesperson and client. In fact, the sales process can be viewed initially as a face-to-face interaction that occurs within a social distance. After a period of time this social distance slowly changes into a side-by-side personal distance, with both parties sharing a oneness of direction. Care should be used in not moving too fast or too slowly from one zone to another.

## Gestures

Hands that are always busy with props—pencils, pointers, coins, key chains, paper clips—are distracting. One should gesture only if it comes naturally. Otherwise, hands can be holding notes or just positioned at ease on the sides of the body. If one is sitting, one should not slouch; a lounging figure really does not project that snappy "go-get'em" attitude.

A tight grip (i.e., effective usage) on the five "languages"—words, voice, eyes, face, and kinetics—gives the salesperson a totally positive image and presentation. This image adds up to 13 million-dollar words: "I'm glad I'm here—I'm glad you're here—I know that I know."

## Listen and Question

Elements of good listening were discussed earlier in this text. Why one should be a good listener can be condensed into two very important reasons: (1) listening says "you are important to me" to the customer, and (2) listening provides critical information about the customer.

Knowing that there is a specific time in a presentation to talk and to question and a time to listen is also important; that is, early in the dialogue the salesperson is using good questions; later in the dialogue the salesperson is explaining or pointing out features/benefits of products. The salesperson listens at all times. In other words, as the dialogue continues, the customer talks more and more as the dialogue progresses toward a conclusion.

Listening, however, is only a part of the dialogue. A salesperson also directs the dialogue through questions. Open-ended questions serve to gather data concerning the presentation's points—for example, "Ms. Johnson, how important is gas economy to you?" or "Can you tell me more about the features you want in a home?" They provide information concerning the who, what, where, how, and why of a potential purchase. These questions allow the salesperson to continue to qualify the customer's needs during the presentation. Often presentations begin with questions ("How can I be of service to you?"), end with questions ("When would you like your television delivered?"), and are interspersed with questions that continue to develop two-way communication throughout the presentation.

## Prepare for the Presentation

Salespeople show the product knowledge they possess, and they must show it well. Skill in giving demonstrations and presentations is increased through practice. If a salesperson wants to produce a feeling or mood, everything that might be a barrier to the desired results must be removed. Does the salesperson know where the switches and levers are? Does the equipment work? Has the place been prepared for the demonstration? Bitter experience teaches those who do not prepare or who fail to make a complete check of their equipment. It is hard to make a point on a sales feature when the sales aid does not work properly.

## Directing the Presentation

Encouraging client participation does not mean relinquishing supervision to the client. The salesperson manages the direction of the presentation. For example, it is usually distracting to allow the customer to peruse the sales aids at leisure. Because each visual has a point, a salesperson should use a visual aid to make a point and then move on to the next. The sales talk and the visual aids complement each other, and to be effective, they must be used together. This can only be done if the salesperson is guiding the presentation.

## Summary

The sales presentation is the implementation of all preplanning activities. It is the culmination of the planning effort from a preconceived structured plan to a customized dialogue centered around a customer's individualized needs. When properly dramatized, the sales presentation allows the customer to benefit from the total information presented to him or her.

By actively involving the client in the presentation, the interaction becomes a two-way communication. This is done through dramatizing the presentation by appealing to one or more of the client's five senses. Let the client hear, see, smell, touch, and taste the benefits being illustrated.

Dramatization keeps clients attentive, presents the information in an interesting way, improves understanding, creates memorable impressions, and helps the sellers. Some methods of dramatizing the sales story include charts and graphs; pictures and photographs; manuals and portfolios; videotapes, films, and slides; models, samples, and gifts; and product demonstrations.

The use of feedback helps sales planners improve their presentation delivery by the use of vivid words and images, improved voice qualities, and the use of appropriate nonverbal communication.

Knowing how to use good listening and questioning techniques and how to maintain guidance over the presentation can make sellers' dramatizations more effective.

## Key Terms

dramatization
benefit
sales presentation
showmanship
self-confidence
multiple-sense appeals
showboating
nonvisual people

visually oriented person
illustrators
organizers
closing rate
sales manual
sales portfolio
kinesics
proxemics

## Discussion Questions

1. What prepresentation information does a salesperson need?

2. Devise a dramatization for an automobile that will get a client's attention; one to present the information in an interesting way; one to improve understanding; one to create a lasting impression.

3. Devise a dramatization for a product of your choice that uses charts and graphs; one that uses pictures or photographs or both; one that uses manuals or portfolios or both; one that uses videotapes, films, or slides or a combination thereof; one that uses models, samples, or gifts or a combination thereof; and one that uses a product demonstration.

4. Name several pitfalls sellers can encounter in a dramatization and tell how these may be avoided or overcome.

5. How can salespeople improve their presentations through their use of words and images? Give examples.

6. What voice and speech features should sellers work to improve?

7. Demonstrate some nonverbal communication that might be part of a dramatization.

8. What is the importance of a listening/questioning mode for the relationship salesperson?

9. Why should the salesperson guide the presentation? List some ways the seller can keep the customer "on track."

## Decision Crossroads: Ethical Issues

1. What are the dangers of controlling the sales presentation in such a way as to ensure that the client will buy your product?

2. Do you feel it is ethical to use demonstrations that are specially prepared to illustrate qualities that are going to be experienced in real life?

## Case 10–1 **Bernina**

Lenora Robbins is a regional sales representative of Swiss-Bernina, Incorporated, the manufacturer of Bernina sewing machines. Lenora Robbins has been with the company ten years, while Swiss-Bernina, Incorporated has been in business sixty years. She is well versed on the terminology of her product and has been voted employee of the month several times because of her selling ability.

Swiss-Bernina is based in Switzerland, with sales offices located throughout the world. Metro, the sales office from which Lenora makes her calls, is located in Hinsdale, Illinois.

It is 10:30 A.M. on a cool day in January. Lenora is calling on Mr. Burke Bruster, owner and manager of The Fabric Center, a medium-sized fabric store located across from the Muncie Mall in Muncie, Indiana. Lenora has secured this sales call by making an appointment with Mr. Bruster by telephone the previous week. This is Lenora's first sales call with Mr. Bruster, who is only vaguely familiar with the Bernina brand name.

| | |
|---|---|
| *Bruster* | Come in. |
| *Robbins* | Good morning, Mr. Bruster. I'm Lenora Robbins. I'm here to show you the Bernina sewing machine. |
| *Bruster* | Please have a seat, Lenora. Today has been such a busy day. I really don't have much time to look at a sewing machine. |

| | |
|---|---|
| *Robbins* | If you can spare only twenty minutes, I can show you the main features of the Bernina. If you like it, and I know you will, I'll be glad to come back when you have more time. |
| *Bruster* | Okay. I guess I can spare twenty minutes. |
| *Robbins* | Good. This is the Record Electronic 30, our top-of-the-line model. I understand that you've never seen a Bernina demonstrated. Is that correct? |
| *Bruster* | That's correct. What's so special about this machine? |
| *Robbins* | This machine has many features not found on any other sewing machine, such as an automatically adjusted tension, a knee-lift pressure foot control . . . |
| *Bruster* | The pressure foot control looks like it would be awkward to use. |
| *Robbins* | It is awkward at first; however, once you get used to it, it will become a valuable tool. It saves at least one hour of sewing time out of every eight. |
| *Bruster* | How much does this machine retail for? |
| *Robbins* | This model retails for $1,449. And you get your normal markup of 100 percent. |
| *Bruster* | That's really expensive. No one will be able to afford it. |
| *Robbins* | Actually, more people are starting to make their own clothes. They can justify the purchase of a sewing machine by the savings in clothing costs, and Bernina has several features that cannot be found on any other machine. |
| *Bruster* | Doesn't Muncie already have several sewing machine dealers? |

| | |
|---|---|
| *Robbins* | Yes. But there are no Bernina dealers. If you accept our offer to sell Berninas, you will be the only Bernina dealer in Muncie. |
| *Bruster* | How much do I have to pay for each machine? |
| *Robbins* | We will let you have this model for $750. That will give you a profit of $749 if you wish to sell them at $1,449. And, if I could give you a way to buy the machines now and pay later, would you be interested? |
| *Bruster* | Certainly. |
| *Robbins* | I can take your order today, and you can delay payment for 60 days, at no extra charge. How does that sound? |
| *Bruster* | Well, I'm really not sure. . . . |
| *Robbins* | Mr. Bruster, this is the best machine made. It has automatic thread tension, knee-lift presser foot control, decorative stitches, and a built-in buttonholer. Best of all, you will earn a profit of $749 for each machine sold. When is the best day for Metro to arrange for shipping? |
| *Bruster* | Let me think it over. I'm not ready to take on a new dealership right now. How about coming back April 30? |
| *Robbins* | April 30 can be arranged, and thank you for your time, Mr. Bruster. |
| *Bruster* | Thank you, Lenora. |

### Discussion:

1. What precall information is pertinent in the situational analysis? Did Lenora use this information correctly? How would you use it?
2. What techniques did she use in her presentation? How could she dramatize the presentation?
3. Evaluate her presentation. Rewrite it to be a better presentation.

## Case 10-2   **Billson's Moving and Storage**

Jean Rich sells an intangible service—moving and storage of household goods. To aid her in home sales, she bought a large briefcase with a cutaway side and carefully packed it with miniature furniture. She expected this to increase sales, but it did not.

In selling, Jean preferred to talk to both husband and wife but often could only arrange talking to the wife. The new visual aid to demonstrate the expert packing of furniture did not seem to impress the clients.

To solve her dilemma, she simulated her presentation for her sales manager, Tom Billson.

### Discussion:

1. How could knowledge of the household buying center help Jean Rich make more successful presentations?
2. Develop a presentation that highlights the importance of the visual aids by using descriptive words that would make the presentation come alive.

**Chapter Outline**

Reasons for Objections
Advantages of Objections
Buying Decision Points
    Need
    Product
    Source Approval
    Price Negotiation
    Time

Reasons for Identifying Objections
Identification Problems
    Hidden Objections
    Attitudinal Problems

Techniques for Handling Objections
    Determine Validity of Objections
    Specific Techniques
    Special Techniques

## CHAPTER 11

# Conflict Resolution and Negotiation

**Learning Objectives**

After completing Chapter 11, you should be able to:

- Define an objection
- Discuss the reasons for objections
- List the buying decision points on which an objection might be based
- Classify various objections
- Recognize the different techniques used to handle objections
- State reasons for identifying objections and the problems one may encounter in identifying objections
- Discuss why sellers should welcome objections rather than avoid them.

## IN THE FIELD

*Sales people, both inside and outside, must explain to customers that price is not cost.*

**David Derrow, Ohio Transmission and Pump Co**

Overcoming objections is so important at Ohio Transmission and Pump Co. that Chairman David Derrow developed a 45-minute seminar entitled ``Price vs Value.'' Derrow says, ``There are three reasons why a customer may object to price. First, he thinks the price is too high because you're asking him to pay $125 for an item he paid $75 for five years ago. Second, he has a lower quotation from another source. And third, he is using price as a smoke screen. When he is using price as a smoke screen, he's trying to test you, your selling ability, and your company. This sort of game playing indicates that you have a personal or company-to-company problem.'' Derrow points out that under these circumstances you should reestablish your relationship rather than try to sell a specific product. When trying to overcome price objections, Derrow tells his salespeople to seize the opportunity to sell value, especially when your price is higher than it used to be or competitors have bid lower prices. Derrow suggests that salespeople ask nonconfrontational questions before they start a sales presentation in this case. This is the opportunity to show that price is not cost. ``Price is the up-front payment, while cost is that payment figured over the benefits your product provides during its lifespan.''

*Source:* Steve Zurier, ``How to Overcome Price Objections,'' *Industrial Distribution* (March 1990). Reprinted from *Industrial Distribution*, March 1990, Cahners Publishing Co.

**sales resistance**

A salesperson presents product benefits during a presentation to show prospects how their needs can be fulfilled. As the presentation evolves into more specific discussion, conflicts that impede a customer's buying process can occur. These conflicts will be manifested in prospects' words and body language. Such behavior is called **sales resistance.** Resolution of sales resistance is as important to the client as it is to the salesperson (see *In the Field*). Indeed, conflict resolution and negotiation are critical components of the customer–salesperson dialogue (see Figure 11–1). This chapter discusses ways to resolve conflict, that is, ways to overcome objections in the sales process.

> We are continually faced by great opportunity brilliantly disguised as insolvable problems.
>
> **Anonymous**

Figure 11–1
*Conflict Resolution and Negotiation* in the Customer–Salesperson Dialogue

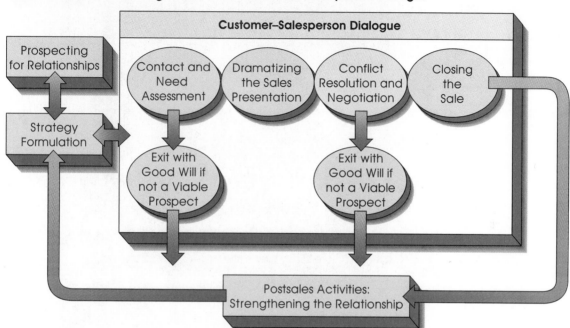

Ideally a sale flows continuously from contact to close. To close a sale, however, all objections must be resolved. The flow diagram illustrated in Figure 11.1 places need fulfillment/conflict resolution as a response portion of the sales process. Some salespeople are apprehensive about encountering sales resistance, but their anxiety is unnecessary; objections create an opportunity to solve a prospect's problem.[1] Few people purchase goods or services without some reservations. Ways salespeople can identify and classify objections and then determine the appropriate technique for answering each of them is examined. Once a salesperson can sufficiently answer a prospect's objection, the path is clear to attempt to close the sale by securing the order.

Most verbal exchanges between the salesperson and the prospect are in the form of statements, questions, or objections. These three forms of dialogue are mixed during the sales process. The salesperson uses questions to involve the prospect in dialogue and to determine the prospect's state of awareness, that is, to uncover the prospect's attention level, interest, desire, conviction, or intended action. Similarly the prospect uses questions to search for information, to clarify information, or to object to information the salesperson has already presented.

Presentations should not be just one-way communication. Clients should become involved and make their opinions known during the presentation. This sales resistance shows the salesperson where the client needs more information.

objection

An **objection** is an expression of doubt or disagreement with the statements or information presented during a sales presentation. Often salespeople view objections as a negative force called "noise" or as sales resistance. Instead of thinking of objections as a negative force, however, the salesperson must recognize objections as a positive sign indicating the prospect's interest. Objections also signal opportunities to close the sale. Professional salespeople, therefore, encourage the prospect to express opinions and objections. When the prospect verbalizes objections, the salesperson has an opportunity to investigate the prospect's decision-making process through probing. A verbal objection indicates which buying decision points stand in the way of a sale. A prospect who says "No" may really mean "Not yet."[2] The objection is a key to what really interests the client.

## Reasons for Objections

Objections represent a variety of reasons. The prospect may:

- Have misconceptions about the potential source of a product or service or of his or her own need

- Want to feel satisfied in his or her own mind (objections may be attempts to clarify unclear points)
- Want to be a part of the conversation, not just a bystander
- Want his or her opinion respected by the salesperson (gaining this respect enhances the prospect's self-worth, so the prospect objects to the salesperson's statements[3])
- Want to be satisfied that he or she, not the salesperson, is the decision maker (making objections allows the prospect to bolster his or her self-image as a decision maker).[4]

This list is not exhaustive, but it does give an indication of what motivates consumers to raise objections. The salesperson must correctly identify and classify the objection and then attempt to answer it. This is true, since the relationship salesperson is interested in a long-term bond with the customer. While the long-run success is composed of many short-run events (individual sales), the successful salesperson builds on a foundation of repeat sales to established customers. Relationship salespeople do not bend under pressure from sales managers to maximize sales "at all costs." They may be tempted to use persuasion to overcome an objection, but this is resorting to the self-oriented approach. Changing orientations destroys the salesperson's trust bond with established customers; and as is known, strong trust between customers and salespeople is essential to long-run success in selling.

## Advantages of Objections ████████████████

Objections have value. Wanting objections—what may seem like seeking obstructions to success—appears contrary to human nature. How many people purposefully make life difficult for themselves? Rather they seek reinforcement for what they do correctly instead of trying to find contrary opinions that serve as obstacles. Without objections, however, the presentation is a one-way conversation between two people.[5]

Exactly how do objections encourage sales? During the sales presentation, the salesperson facilitates dialogue with the prospect by asking questions. These questions, as you remember, should be open ended, requiring more than a yes or no answer. These questions must uncover the prospect's doubts and indecisions. They provide a "door" into the prospect's thought process. An objection, therefore:

- Indicates a prospect's interest
- Indicates that a prospect is listening to the presentation
- Indicates that a prospect is considering buying
- Provides the salesperson with an opportunity to "modify" or "custom tailor" the presentation to the prospect's needs

## PARTNERSHIPS

Duane E. Mason, an independent manufacturer's representative, sells boats for several manufacturers to retailers. Mason began his business after failing as a boat retailer in Taylorville, Illinois. In 1986 he grossed $400,000 on sales of $8 million in sales, after paying overhead that included $100,000 for customer entertainment. Mason cleared $200,000, more than many Miami yacht salesmen make. In May 1987 Duane was named Manufacturer's Representative of the Year.

Like most salesmen, Mason is imaginative at remembering buyer's objections. He remembers walking into one boat dealer to sell pontoon boats. The dealer wasn't buying. According to Mason, ``He said that in two years no one had ever come in and asked for a pontoon boat.'' I said, ``Well I bet no one has come in for a haircut either. But I've got a barber pole in my trunk, and I bet if you put it out, within two weeks someone will come in here and ask for a trim.'' Mason sold him a trailer load of four pontoon boats on the spot and has sold him plenty more since.

*Source:* Monci Jo Williams, ``America's Best Salesmen,'' *Fortune* 116 (October 26, 1987). *Fortune.* © 1987, Time, Inc. All rights reserved.

- Provides an opportunity to present more facts and benefits
- Provides an opportunity to close the sale.

Duane Mason illustrates how questioning past decisions (see *Partnerships*) gives the salesperson insight into factors that are important to each prospect's buying decision process. This interaction allows the salesperson to personalize problem solving for each individual customer.[6] Without the salesperson's questions, some prospects, such as the silent customer, would never make a decision.

> The sale doesn't begin until the customer says "No."
>
> **Sales Adage**

Although the first sale is a short-term goal, the successful, professional salesperson who uses his or her skills correctly and efficiently will realize success beyond the initial sale because the prospect will use the salesperson as a source of information for future decisions. When this occurs, the consumer sees the salesperson as an expert in the field. This transference of power—expert power—will allow the salesperson to have more input into future decisions. Such a salesperson may seem like a limited partner in the prospect's business. Ideally the salesperson seeks to maximize the prospect's confidence in their partnership. Often the prospect will express this ideal level of confidence by telling the salesperson, "Determine what we need and send it to us." In such a case the prospect relinquishes the power of decision making to the salesperson and has created a friendship as well.[7]

## Buying-Decision Points

Before buying a product or a service, a prospect seeks information about various aspects of the buying decision. The prospect can seek information from mass communication sources such as advertising, sales promotion, and publicity or from personal contacts, such as family members, friends, acquaintances, or salespeople. Sellers, because of their in-depth product knowledge and ability to interact with other people, are a very important source of information in the prospect's buying-decision process.

When preparing to buy goods or services, a prospect obtains information in five areas: need, product, source, price, and time. Naturally the prospect could have questions or objections in each area, as shown in Table 11–1.

### Need

Without a salient **need,** prospects do not enter the marketplace. While a **need** consumer with a strong brand preference enters the marketplace looking for a specific product, most of the time consumers enter the marketplace with only the knowledge that they have a problem (need). In the latter case, determining the prospect's specific need will enable the salesperson

Table 11–1
**Buying-Decision Areas**

| Buying-Decision Areas | Typical Objection |
|---|---|
| The Need | "The equipment I have is still good." |
| The Product | "Texide? I've never heard of it!" |
| The Source (the company, the salesperson) | "I'm not familiar with Xerox's policy on rebates." |
| The Price | "That's 20 percent higher than a comparable Xerox model." |
| The Time | "I'm just looking around." |

to develop a sales presentation. In the presentation the salesperson demonstrates how the product's features will benefit this customer and satisfy the need.

Often a need is of a general nature and can be satisfied by many products. For example, if a homeowner needs to drive a nail into a wall to hang a picture, the person can use any object suitable for pounding the nail, such as a hammer, a rock, or the heel of a shoe. A prospect's saying "no" to a need can actually say, "I'm happy with the brand I'm now using" or "I'm just seeking information" or "I don't really need it."

Many clients do not know that they have a specific need for a product until a situation occurs that makes them aware of it. Therefore objections to the need may require the salesperson to stimulate the need awareness of the client.

## Product

**products**

Objections toward the product concentrate around understanding the fit between the product and the customer's need. **Products** are bundles of benefits that customers seek to fit their needs. Showing how a specific product would meet the customer's need better than other available options would require a distinct presentation. In the illustration, many of the products are inappropriate for complete satisfaction of the homeowner's need to drive a nail: This consumer will therefore enter the market-

## TECHNOLOGY BULLETIN

### J-I-T inventory programs

Meeting customers' needs for two-week delivery in a made-to-order business like caskets is unusual. But that's just what Hillenbrand Industries Inc. delivers on about half-a-million orders a year. Hillenbrand, with 300 basic models of caskets, allows customers to choose from a catalog and to simply phone an order to one of the company's 59 U.S. distribution centers that usually deliver in 48 hours. This is all available because of a computerized Just-In-Time inventory program. This Just-In-Time Inventory program's main attraction to funeral directors is the huge savings they gain by keeping their inventories to a minimum.

*Source:* Tom Murray, ''Just In Time Isn't Just for Show—It Sells,'' *Sales and Marketing Management* 142 (May 1990); 64–65. Reprinted by permission of *Sales and Marketing Management,* © June 1990.

place to gather information about potential products that can fulfill the need.

Objections in the product area generally center around the prospect's feeling that the product does not meet the need for quality or fit the particular problem as closely as other products. Illustrative of these presumed incompatibilities of the product are:

- "Your product is too new and doesn't have all the bugs out of it." (quality issue)
- "Your machine only makes 20 copies a minute, and that's too slow for us." (poor product fit)
- "Your trucks are always broken down on the shoulder of the road. I need trucks that are dependable." (quality issue)

These examples show the necessity of demonstrating how a product's features can benefit prospects and overcome their misconceptions. To overcome what a prospect perceives to be incompatibilities of products, the salesperson must convert product features into statements of benefits. The salesperson can then use these statements to show how features provide benefits that can solve the prospect's problems. By presenting facts, the salesperson may correct perceived incompatibilities and get a "Yes" in the product area.

## Source Approval

As the process of searching for information continues, the prospect questions the validity and reliability of both the salespeople contacted, the information they offer, and their company. This is known as **source approval.**

When the need for the product has been firmly established, the salesperson can attempt to get affirmative responses to the source area. Some objections toward source concern negative images from past encounters with the company or the salesperson. The negative image can be based upon the supplying company's policies, its present or past sales personnel, and the impressions people have toward their current suppliers. Other source objections may concern disagreements about services rendered and disagreements on definitions of "fast" service or "completed orders."

Deciding which supplier to patronize generally means the exclusion of all other potential suppliers. Therefore the prospect has given a differential advantage to the current supplier. To overcome the competitor's advantage, a salesperson from another company must introduce facts that cause the prospect to rethink the past buying decision. For example, if a prospect says, "Westinghouse can give me better service because its

**source approval**

A great feeling comes to both the client and the salesperson when they solve a problem in a mutually compatible way. When a salesperson has helped a customer satisfactorily solve a problem, credibility is enhanced. This source approval adds to a long-lasting relationship.

warehouse is closer,'' the salesperson must introduce facts that counteract the decision to buy from Westinghouse.

The proximity of a warehouse to the prospect is no assurance of good service. The professional salesperson would point out features and benefits of his or her company and its policies that surpass those of the Westinghouse Company. For example, the salesperson could explain: "Westinghouse's warehouse is close to you, Mr. Fox, but do you get large numbers of products back ordered? Our warehouse is within 200 miles of you, and past reports (show documented facts) indicate that 99.9 percent of the orders we receive are completely filled at our warehouse without back orders. I think you will agree this is a phenomenal record. Wouldn't you like to be able to have your orders filled this completely?''

Notice that nowhere in this example did the salesperson make detrimental comments about the competition. However, it is permissible to use competitors to emphasize the unique features of the salesperson's product. Salespeople should not attempt to improve their image by criticizing their competitors.

Facts are also needed to overcome negative images. A prospect may have a negative image of a supplier from whom he or she has never purchased merchandise. Only facts will change this prospect's opinion. If the prospect is a consumer, the retailer must produce facts that overcome any negative image the consumer has about this retail establishment.[8] If the prospect is a dealer, the manufacturer must produce facts and evidence to counteract the negative image the dealer has of the manufacturer. A negative image, as mentioned earlier, results from company policies and practices or from company personnel. Since the salesperson is the prospect's personal contact with the company, the salesperson is expected to be responsible for the "faults" perceived by the prospect.

The salesperson must correct the errors that he or she, a past salesperson, or the company, has made that led to the negative image and caused the prospect to say "No" to the source. Attempts to rectify the problem must be made before a prospect will agree to buy from the salesperson. Obtaining a "Yes" answer in the area of source requires the rebuilding of a negative image. Although prospects like the product and company, they want to know the price of the product in comparison to what they planned to pay or in comparison to what they can get from another supplier.

## Price Negotiation

As with objections to products, objections to price center around perceived incompatibilities. The prospect could have **price objections** because of some miscalculations (or misconceptions) of the relationship between value and cost. Some common price objections are:

**price objections**

- "Your price is too high."
- "We have a better offer from IBM."
- "We can't afford to spend $3 million on a new computer at this time."
- "Why is your mower so cheap?"
- "I was looking for a cheaper model."
- "I don't care to invest that much—I'll use it only a short while."
- "I can beat your prices on the copier."
- "Your price is too low."
- "Your price is not different enough to change suppliers."

Generally price objections can be overcome by citing cost–benefit and **price–quality relationships.** Features used to justify prices are quality, guarantees, and warranties. Each product has benefits giving it a differential advantage and allowing it to be competitive in the marketplace. A salesperson should use product knowledge to justify price, whether it is too high, too low, or the same as the competitor's. Build a mental bridge between price and benefits.[9]

**price–quality relationships**

Price objections probably occur more frequently than any other type. Objections to price may be used to cover the real reason for a reluctance to buy. Using "why" questions helps the salesperson to ferret out concealed objections.

## Time

time objections

**Time objections** center around the immediacy of a prospect's need satisfaction. The more pressing needs are fulfilled first.

For example, a prospect whose car no longer works has a need for daily transportation, and this makes the prospect more likely to seek immediate alternatives. A prospect whose car is working may postpone the purchase until the need for a different car is more pressing—when "the time is right to buy."

Some typical time objections are:

- "I'll have to think it over because of the cost." (May be a price or time objection or both.)
- "I'm too busy to decide now."
- "Leave your card; I'd like to wait until next week to decide."

In the case of time objections, the "No" is not "I won't buy"; it may be a procrastination, as shown in the car illustration. Therefore the salesperson must show the prospect the benefits of buying now.[10] Procrastinations are strong buying signals that require strong closing techniques.

As long as an objection is present, the prospect is saying "No" in one or more of the five areas. The salesperson must be perceptive in determining the areas where the customer is objecting. Then, after identifying the objection by area, the salesperson can attempt to overcome the objection before closing the sale. The objection, whether well founded or based on a misperception, is important to the prospect and the prospect's self-image. Regardless of the reason for the objection, it must always be handled with sincerity and honesty.

Before a sale is closed, the customer generally says "Yes" in all five decision-point categories. This "Yes" is not always verbalized; nonverbal responses may imply agreement. If they do not agree on all five areas, sometimes one area compensates for the lack in another area, allowing the person to buy.

## Reasons for Identifying Objections

The reasons for identifying objections are twofold: (1) to determine the importance to the prospect of each variable in the decision, and (2) to be able to meet the objection in a satisfactory manner, one that will lead to a close.

Identifying the objection provides clues that allow the salesperson to concentrate efforts to overcome the prospect's resistance in its correct purchase point area. Correct classification not only provides the opportunity for a salesperson to "fine tune" the presentation to fit the individual prospect; it increases the chances of satisfactorily overcoming the objection. "Fine tuning" the presentation to each prospect's needs follows the relationship selling approach. It allows personalization of the presentation and lets the representative find the prospect's "HOT Button" quickly and close the sale without delay.

## Identification Problems ▰▰▰▰▰▰▰▰

Before discussing techniques for overcoming objections, the reader should be aware of two areas that sometimes cause problems when dealing with objections.

## Hidden Objections

Prospects are not always accurate in expressing their objections, but a salesperson must understand the objection clearly to correctly classify it. Prospects do not always know or say how they feel; instead they mask their "true" sentiments for one reason or another.[11] This is called a **hidden objection.** Therefore the salesperson must understand the buyer well enough to sense if the buyer is expressing his or her true objection. Incorrect classification may prevent the closing of a sale.

**hidden objection**

For example, if a prospect says, "I'm satisfied with the brand I'm now buying," is the prospect indicating that he or she has no need for this particular product at this time? Or is satisfaction the real reason for not wanting to buy a product? Does the stated objection hide some other concern? Is the client objecting to need when the "real" objection concerns resistance to the price or source? Rarely does a buyer say to the salesperson, "I just don't like you." Proper interpretation of an objection is a required skill for professional salespeople.

## Attitudinal Problems

The salesperson's attitude can be one of the largest barriers to identifying and overcoming a prospect's objection. Often the salesperson, so convinced of what he or she is saying, takes offense when the prospect objects. Novice salespeople are usually the most guilty of having this attitude. After being convinced in sales training that their product is the best in all possible areas, novices may become frustrated under the pressure to make a sale. They tend to take a customer's objection as an affront and become defensive. Other guilty parties are the veteran salespeople who have routinized their behavior and become apathetic.

Another problem area stems from salespeople themselves. How can a person stay even tempered and keep a positive attitude when a buyer is stating objections that might be offensive to the salesperson?

The key to maintaining a positive attitude is to remember that clients object to what a salesperson represents, not the actual person. Frustrations can often penetrate a salesperson's normally objective stance and precipitate a defensive attitude. If a prospect objects during a sales presentation, the salesperson with a defensive attitude could verbally attack either the objection or the prospect. This could hurt the prospect's feelings and cost the salesperson a sale. Rather than become defensive, the salesperson must remain objective and analyze the "real" reason for the objection. Classifying an objection's validity helps maintain objectivity. One study shows that presentations that result in sales have 58 percent more objections than those that did not result in a sale.[12]

Professional salespeople should cultivate the ability to anticipate possible repercussions from their remarks. When thinking something negative, they should suppress the attitude or express it only in a positive manner.

## Techniques for Handling Objections

**HAIR approach**

A salesperson's attitude toward an objection is a key variable in a successful salesperson's profile. But equally critical is that person's technique in overcoming an objection. Many salespeople use a four-step **HAIR approach** when a prospect raises an objection. These general guidelines are:

1. *Hear* carefully the prospect's objection. A major pitfall in selling is a failure to listen, as explained in earlier chapters. Failure to listen may result in answering the wrong objection or in a misclassification of the objection. In either case, the failure to listen to the objection is detrimental to the presentation. Practice the art of good listening.
2. *Acknowledge* the objection. By restating the objection in precise terms, you can correctly identify it. This step also allows time to "custom-tailor" the answer.

**"why" questions**

3. *Identify* by asking questions. Questions clarify the real objection. Using **"Why?" questions** can often achieve this. A "why" question from the salesperson focuses on the client's specific objection. The salesperson needs to ask, "Why do you feel that way?" Using the question "why" allows the salesperson to clarify the reasoning behind the objection,

and lets the prospect provide additional information about the buying decision. An objection, such as, "I have to discuss it with my husband, my wife, or my partner . . ." may really be an alibi or procrastination. Different reasons for the objection would require different techniques.[13]

As with all sales techniques, the salesperson must use finesse in determining the reason for the objection. Overusing "why" makes the prospect feel as though he or she were being interrogated. It puts the prospect on the defensive and often promotes hostile feelings toward the salesperson. Used in moderation, however, the "why" concept will yield enough insight into the prospect's buying process to enable the salesperson to classify the objection. It can also give the salesperson a clue as to which technique would best overcome the objection.

4. *Rectify* the objection with a complete and honest answer. Develop credibility.

Together with the *HAIR* technique, you should also obtain agreement regarding the buyer's satisfaction with an answer. You can use this confirmation step to test if you have really answered the prospect's resistance. Using this step saves time and prevents the need to answer the same objection over and over again.

Experience in applying these principles to a prospect's problems will help salespeople cultivate techniques that work quite well. Handling objections, like all other aspects of sales, must be customized for a specific, individual situation, not generalized for a group.

## Determine Validity of Objections

After using the "Why" concept for clarification, the salesperson, as shown in Table 11–2, must classify the objection to determine whether it is valid or invalid. Each type of objection, whether valid or invalid, requires use of different methods to overcome it. A **valid objection** is one that concerns a correct observation of fact that exists from the salesperson's knowledge. A prospect can have valid objections in any or all buying decision areas. An **invalid objection,** on the other hand, is an objection based on perceived facts that are not true or that are a misperception of the client. Like the valid objection, the invalid one can involve any or all buying decision areas. However, the validity of the prospect's objection helps determine which technique the salesperson should use to answer it. The client's objection should never be ignored. The objection is an important point to the client, and neglecting it indicates that the salesperson does not think it worthy of consideration. Most people are offended when they ask a sales representative a question and the representative ignores it.

**valid objection**

**invalid objection**

Table 11–2
Objection Handling Paradigm

| Type of Objection | Time of Occurrence | Objection Handling Technique |
|---|---|---|
| Valid Objections | During the presentation stage | Compensation, boomerang, indirect denial |
| Invalid Objections | During the presentation stage | Direct denial |
| Frequently Used Objections By Most Customers and/or Inappropriately Timed Objections (Valid or Invalid) | Anytime | Use forestalling, delay |
| Particular Price Objections | During the presentation stage | Use various cost-handling techniques |

## Specific Techniques

Different techniques are used according to the classification of the resistance. Using the right technique for an objection that is improperly classified is as ineffective as classifying the objection correctly and using an improper technique to rectify it.

### Valid Objections

When an objection is true, the salesperson should use the compensation, boomerang, or indirect denial method. However, if the objection is not valid, the salesperson's best tactic is to use the **direct denial method.**

There is little use denying a valid objection. The salesperson must admit to the validity of the objection and then deal with it. Agreeing with the validity of the prospect's objection tends to bolster the prospect's self-image and to put this person into a positive frame of mind. It shows that the salesperson has respect for the discriminating opinion of the customer. Agreement alone is insufficient to overcome the objection, but one of three other techniques—compensation, boomerang, or indirect denial—can be effective.

**compensation method**

1. With the **compensation method,** the salesperson uses additional knowledge to counteract the prospect's criticism. After agreeing with

the customer, salespeople draw from their skills (in this case sales training) evidence to offset the criticism. These additional benefits try to compensate for the perceived disadvantage. Examples of the compensation method and the other two techniques are contrasted in Table 11–3 to show their differences.

2. The **boomerang method,** also used to handle the valid objection, begins with the salesperson agreeing to the validity of the objection. The salesperson's next step is to use the prospect's objection as a specific selling point. When appropriate, the skillful salesperson is able to translate the objection into a reason for buying the product. When used effectively, the boomerang technique openly shows the salesperson's ability to direct the situation. It is particularly effective in overcoming objections that consumers support with facts.

   **boomerang method**

   One drawback with the boomerang technique is that the prospect might sense high-pressure sales tactics. Use caution with this technique, since it is only effective in the hands of a skilled seller. In less capable hands it connotes the stereotyped, fast-talking, overpowering, hard-sell sales representative.

Table 11–3
**Contrasting Methods to Overcome Source Objections**

---

*Objection/Classification*

``Owens-Corning Gives Me Fast Service.'' (Valid Objection)

*Rectification:*
- *Compensation Method.* This method would be used because the answer concentrates on completed orders and minimizing freight damage rather than addressing fast service. For example: ``Yes they do have fast service. Do you have problems with freight damage? What about completed orders? We ship 99 percent of all our orders complete within two weeks of notification, and we ship with our own trucks. This helps us minimize the freight damage and give specialized service.

- *Boomerang Method.* This method would be used because it takes the objection and makes it the reason for buying. For example: ``Yes, Mrs. James, that's why you should buy from us. We deliver in our own trucks within two weeks of notification. That's faster service than Owens-Corning, right?

- *Indirect Denial Method.* This method would be used because no additional benefits are supplied except those that support the answer to the service objection. For example: ``Yes, Owens-Corning is known for their service, but we can be here faster since our warehouse is only 55 miles from your store. In fact, we have proven our exceptional service. Here are names of ten clients with whom we do business within this area.

**indirect denial method**

3. The **indirect denial method,** also used to overcome valid objections, is often called the "Yes, but" method. By indirectly denying statements, the salesperson restates the objection in a positive manner. This lets the salesperson create a positive frame of reference between the salesperson and the prospect. The prospect is not directly confronted with the inaccuracies of his or her values. As shown in Table 11–3, the salesperson takes this opportunity to become an educator, adding information to the prospect's perceptions to correct inaccuracies. Proper application of this technique fosters a stronger trust link throughout the prospect–salesperson dialogue. The salesperson must avoid overexplaining or protesting too much, however. Too much protest is detrimental. Above all, this technique should be used honestly and with the complete support of facts.

### Invalid Objections

When a prospect raises an objection that is not based on a valid statement, the salesperson will not be able to agree and must classify it as an invalid objection. Handled improperly, invalid objections can create problems. Any attempt to deny a prospect's misperceptions must always be employed delicately and with great care and finesse. Prospects usually state what they believe to be true. Whether true or false, these expressions are part of that person's attitudes, his or her cognitions. Since attitudes exemplify a person's values in specific situations, to question someone's values is to question the person; and people, even when they are intentionally lying, do not enjoy having their integrity questioned. This underscores the need to deal with invalid objections in a way that will not jeopardize the sale. Arguments with a prospect, even when the prospect's statement is completely false, should be avoided. The salesperson always loses, as illustrated in the sales adage:

> Lose the argument; lose the sale. Win the argument; lose the customer.
>
> **Anonymous**

**direct denial method**

Giving in to argumentative attitudes destroys the relationship approach.

The **direct denial method** is the method for handling the invalid objection. A prospect might raise an untrue objection about the salesperson, the product, or the company. The salesperson, though naturally feeling defensive, must resist the temptation to show feelings of irritability.

Occasionally a prospect will make an inaccurate statement just to double check the salesperson's story. This action is an attempt to verify honesty. Always the salesperson must react in an honest, forthright manner without showing aggressive or defensive tendencies.

Generally the salesperson uses the direct denial method when the prospect disputes the integrity of the company or of the salesperson. By directly saying, "No, Mrs. Fox, you are not correct," the salesperson is challenging the prospect's perceptions. Overcoming this direct attack on the prospect's beliefs requires that the salesperson have accurate and easily obtainable facts. These facts should be visually expressed. They are usually obtained through independent sources, which add to their credibility. Often salespeople carry such facts in their sample bags to use in refuting the most frequently used objections.

For example, if much has been publicized about several firms in the industry conspiring to fix prices, the professional salesperson will have clippings from newspapers of the actual trial results showing that the salesperson's firm was exonerated of such charges. Showing visual proof from outside sources helps the salesperson to overcome the incorrect assumption. It should be kept in mind, however, that if the prospect's statement is valid, denying its truth is only verifying the salesperson's dishonesty.

Situations do occur, however, where the salesperson has either incorrectly prepared his or her "skills tool bag" or has never before heard the objection. Therefore the salesperson may have to postpone comment until after gathering the proper facts. Appropriate statements in such a situation include: "I've never heard of that before. Let me check on it and get back with you" or "We've never been accused of that. If it's important to you, let me call Mr. Grant, the general manager, and see what he has to say about it."

## Special Techniques

Objections occur during almost every sales presentation. The salesperson may choose to build into the presentation answers to these common objections. This technique is called forestalling.

### Forestalling Technique

Using the **forestalling technique** eliminates objections before they occur. Because a salesperson often knows from experience the typical objections a prospect makes at a particular point in the presentation, the salesperson can adapt the presentation to answer the objection before the prospect objects. As soon as a client verbalizes an objection, it immediately takes on importance in the client's mind. Therefore the forestall has psychological alarm supporting it.

**forestalling technique**

Forestalling allows the salesperson to guide the pace of a presentation without being sidetracked by a common objection. The salesperson is not raising the objection but is including the answer in the sales talk.

For example, a salesperson who anticipates the objection, "I don't have any money," could include a forestalling technique in the opening statement, such as, "I am interested in talking with people who have only $5,000 to invest in a unique fast food franchise."

That statement qualifies the buyer in the first five minutes of the sales talk. Once the prospect has acknowledged this qualification, prospects would have more difficulty disclaiming interest because of a "lack of money." Product objections such as "Your typewriter is too complicated for my people to operate" can be handled with a forestalling technique during a demonstration. If possible, the salesperson should have the prospect's personnel operate the machinery and in so doing overcome an objection before it is raised. Again, caution is necessary. Overuse of the forestalling technique will repel skeptics or logical thinking prospects.

### Delay Technique

**delay**

Some objections occur at inopportune moments in the presentation. These must be acknowledged because ignoring an objection provokes antagonism in the prospect. A variation of the forestalling technique, the **delay,** can be used when the objection occurs before the salesperson wants to handle it. After acknowledging the prospect's question, a delay technique can be applied.

The salesperson may say, "You have a good point. Can I wait and cover that a little later?" To a question about price, the salesperson might comment, "We're going to talk about how competitive we are 'pricewise' in a few moments."

If the delay technique pacifies the prospect, the salesperson may continue the presentation as planned. However, if the prospect refuses to postpone the answer to the objection until later, the salesperson must handle the objection immediately. Until an objection is sufficiently handled in the prospect's mind, it is "noise"—a barrier—in the communication system. If not controlled, this "noise" will eventually cause a breakdown in the prospect–salesperson dialogue. The seller should eventually answer the question. As stated earlier, delaying without actually answering the question is inappropriate.

### Price Objections Techniques

Price objections occur frequently enough to warrant special techniques. After classifying the validity of a price objection, the salesperson can follow one of several procedures. They are:

1. Selling *price-quality relationship.* Even the lowest priced product in the market should have quality for the price. If the product is higher priced than the competition's products, the salesperson can promote the de-

sign, craftsmanship, and image of the product's features and their compatiblity with the prospect's self-image. The key to selling higher priced items is emphasizing their value and image.

2. **Breaking price into smaller units.** Although the initial cash price may astound the customer, a professional salesperson can anticipate this objection. Price can be reduced into small units, such as monthly payments or daily usage rate. For example:

> The purchase of a $180 BeautyRest mattress with a twenty-year guarantee may be too difficult for a person to handle mentally. However, the salesperson could break the price down to a daily rate:

$$price\,/\,usage\ \ rate = cost\ \ per\ \ day$$
$$\$180\,/\,7{,}300\ \ days\ \ (20\ \ years \times 365\ \ days) = 2.4\ \ cents\ \ per\ \ day$$

This lets the salesperson justify the price at only 2.4 cents per day rather than allowing the customer's objection to the $180 total price.

3. **Presenting the product as an investment.** High-priced items generally are expected to last a long time; replacement is not a problem that is likely to occur. Emphasizing this point allows the salesperson to compare products with a return on investment philosophy. For example, if an IBM computer has a ninety-day guarantee and costs $5,000, it can be compared with a Zenith computer with a 180-day guarantee costing $8,000. "There is a $3,000 savings, even without your considering the time you would spend purchasing."

4. **Building a mental bridge.** Generally a salesperson has a variety of models of a particular product. These products can be arranged by price line. The salesperson must build a mental bridge between different models and their prices. Each model, a variation from a basic model, adds features to justify an increase in price. Using this technique, the salesperson can "step" people up to a higher quality and higher priced item if it fits their needs.

Most price objections involve incompatibility between value and cost, and the question "Does the product fit the prospect's needs?" Most of these types of problems should be handled when the salesperson qualifies the customer in the approach stage of the presentation. For example, after hearing a couple mention several recent years of unemployment, the salesperson knows that they are not the best prospects for a new car. The astute salesperson, however, knows that they might be a prospect for a used auto.

Anticipated objections for which a salesperson has developed excellent answers may be used later as an opportunity to close the sale. This technique, illustrated below, is called *saving,* or **closing on objections.**

**breaking price into smaller units**

**presenting the product as an investment**

**building a mental bridge**

**closing an objection**

If a person from a lawn care company calls on a prospect to entice them to subscribe to the service, the prospect might say he is selling his house. If the salesperson is an amateur, she might respond by saying "Sorry I bothered you." A pro would say, "Great! I'm sure you'd be interested in attracting more prospects. Let me explain how I might be able to help you give your house more curb appeal." And then the pro would keep on selling.

**Sherrill Estes, Author of *Sell It Like a Pro*[14]**

After acknowledging an objection that the prospect has raised, identifying it according to the prospect's buying decision areas, and fully understanding it (with the salesperson using the "Why" question), the salesperson can attempt to close. To close on an objection, the salesperson:

1. Asks if this is the only reason the buyer is not purchasing
2. Asks the prospect a conditional closing question ("If I can resolve this problem to your satisfaction, will you approve the purchase today?").
3. Gives a complete and logical answer to the objection and asks for the order.

If the salesperson has satisfactorily overcome the objection, the prospect should buy. If additional doubts exist, the prospect will raise further objections. Techniques must be adapted to the prospect; using the wrong approach may only frustrate a potential buyer.

For example, a customer who is skeptical might become agitated if the salesperson were to use excessively the forestalling technique of anticipating an objection and preplanning to include the answer to the objection in the presentation. The skeptical or suspicious prospect is a logical thinker, and therefore a person would expect his or her skepticism to be handled individually rather than as an obvious part of a sales presentation.

Techniques of handling objections must not only be tailored to the prospect's need but also must be customized to achieve successful conclusions to the sales presentation. However, using general rules for handling objections may be quite useful.

Whatever the situation, objections should be handled only from a position of strength. Strength to overcome invalid objections comes from having knowledge of facts and experiences. When the salesperson lacks this necessary strength, the salesperson may use a postponing strategy such as the delay. Realizing how important it is to know a prospect's true feelings, the professional salesperson encourages objections.

## Summary

The buying decision makes a consumer choose between alternatives. Sales resistance is any behavior, verbal or nonverbal, that impedes a consumer's buying process. Therefore it is natural for resistance to occur while making a choice. Before a consumer can make a choice, he or she must take affirmative actions in the five buying decision areas: (1) need, (2) product, (3) source, (4) price, and (5) time. Possible sales resistance can occur in each or all of the five areas. It is necessary to overcome this resistance if the salesperson is to procure an order.

There are two distinct areas of concern when trying to overcome objections: (1) the attitude of the salesperson and (2) the possibility of hidden objectives. The salesperson must have a positive mental attitude toward objections and view them as a guide to the consumer's buying motives. When dealing with the prospect's objection, not only is it necessary for the salesperson to maintain a positive attitude, but also the salesperson must be able to classify correctly the type of objection. Correct classification of the objections minimizes time and frustration and allows the seller to apply the proper handling technique. Some of the techniques one may use include asking "Why" questions, determining if the objections are valid, developing price objections, and using some special techniques.

Salespeople view objections as an advantage. The client is not saying "No" but is saying "Not yet." It facilitates prospect–salesperson dialogue and also bolsters the mental attitude of the professional salespeople while they probe the prospect's buying decision variables. Therefore the professional salesperson should encourage objections and use them as a guide.

## Key Terms

sales resistance
objection
need
products
source approval
price objections
price–quality relationships
time objections
hidden objection
HAIR approach
"why?" questions
valid objection

invalid objection
compensation method
boomerang method
indirect denial method
direct denial method
forestalling technique
delay
breaking price into smaller units
presenting the product as an
  investment
building a mental bridge
closing on objections

## Discussion Questions

1. Cite a typical objection in each of the five buying-decision areas.

2. Identify the five steps that the book suggests for handling objections.

3. Compare and contrast valid and invalid objections.

4. Discuss how the boomerang method of handling objections can be both positive and negative.

5. List and briefly discuss the procedures a salesperson can use to handle price objections.

6. Why should a salesperson view an objection as an advantage?

7. What is the best way to determine if you have qualified the objection correctly?

8. Why do customers sometimes not tell the salesperson exactly how they feel? How could you best overcome this problem?

9. Why is price generally the most decisive issue when buying a product? Is it always better to handle this objection by forestalling?

10. Explain the difference between delaying and forestalling.

11. What are invalid objections? Give an example.

## Decision Crossroads: Ethical Issues

1. How could salespeople use objections to convince a person to buy even if the person was uncertain about the product? Give an example.

2. Would you be tempted to pressure clients to buy products if you were not making your sales goals each month, or would you look for another job? Discuss.

## Case 11-1  Pro-Tour Golf Company

William Tony is the area sales representative for the Pro-Tour Golf Company. He is the top salesperson for the company and has been so for the past three years. He is 29 years old and a determined salesperson. He is calling on Dan Robinson, who is the head pro at the Dallas City Golf Course in Dallas, Texas. The Dallas City Course has carried the Pro-Tour line of golf equipment for five years and has done a good job of moving the product. The majority of the Pro-Tour sales (85%) have been through the sales of golf balls. The remaining sales come from accessory items such as golf gloves and bags.

Today Mr. Tony will attempt to sell Mr. Robinson a new line of Pro-Tour Golf clubs. These new clubs have been designed to provide a more uniform hitting surface that would help learners and intermediate players be more consistent.

It is 1:10 in the afternoon on Friday, and Mr. Tony has an appointment with Mr. Robinson.

*Tony*  Good afternoon Mr. Robinson. By the looks of the course, you are having a busy day.

*Robinson*  Good afternoon, Bill. It's about average.

*Tony*  The Pro-Tour Company has a new club that the good golfer can really appreciate. I've brought with me a set of irons for you to examine. We call them the Pro-Tour Custom.

*Robinson*  They look pretty nice and feel solid.

*Tony*  Like I said, the good golfer can appreciate the quality.

*Robinson*  I really don't need any more clubs right now.

*Tony*  I think if you get these in stock now, by the middle of next summer they will be your biggest selling club.

*Robinson*  I don't like to deal with too many brands of clubs.

*Tony*  You do carry other Pro-Tour equipment, and I assume you are satisfied with our products and our service? I think that you would be happy with these clubs as well. The golfers who already use other Pro-Tour equipment will be glad to see you handling our new clubs.

*Robinson*  Do you have any requirements for buying?

*Tony*  We do require you to buy a minimum of five sets, but this is only because we are sure you will have success in selling these clubs.

*Robinson*  How much would five sets cost me?

*Tony*  The cost to you would be $165 a set, and they retail at $225.

| | |
|---|---|
| *Robinson* | It is a little late in the golf season for selling clubs. |
| *Tony* | That's not necessarily true. Surveys taken over the last five years show that the best time to sell clubs is late in the season. It is when everyone gets tired of their old set. So this would be the most opportune time for you to sell. |
| *Tony* | So can I call in your order right now? |
| *Robinson* | Yes, I guess you can. Order me five sets with regular shafts and standard length, and you can order me a five and a three iron for demonstration models. |
| *Tony* | Thank you very much. I'm sure you will be satisfied with our clubs and my service. I'll check back with you within three or four weeks. Goodbye. |
| *Robinson* | OK, goodbye. |

**Discussion:**

1. What did the salesperson do right?
2. Did he overcome the objections properly?
3. Rewrite the dialogue demonstrating a better use of objection techniques.

## Case 11–2  **Master Air Incorporated**

Ronald Luffer is a sales representative for Master Air, Inc., who manufactures and sells commercial ventilation systems. Mr. Luffer is 24 years old and has been selling ventilation systems for three years. Northern Illinois is his territory and has been the only territory that he has covered for Master Air.

Thomas Harris is the owner of a French restaurant in Rockford, Illinois. He is currently expanding his business enterprises to include two franchises for Burger Castle in Rockford. This is Mr. Harris's first venture into fast food, but he has been in the food service for over ten years with his restaurant called Frontaine's.

Mr. Luffer's objective is to sell Mr. Harris the Master Air Ventilation system for his two new fast-food restaurants. Mr. Luffer obtained information that two new Burger Castles were opening, and through his research and contacts he found that Mr. Harris was the owner. After finding this information, further research found that Mr. Harris was very conservative and did not like to change.

The Master Air Ventilation system is unique in that most ventilation systems for food preparation will vent 100 percent of the air out of the building and subsequently lose heat or cooling for the building. The Master Air System, on the other hand, reclaims 80 percent of the heat or cold and returns it to the building, thus reducing the cost of heating/cooling.

Ronald Luffer's objective is to sell Mr. Harris the Master Air System for his two new fast-food restaurants now under construction. It is 2:00 P.M. on a Wednesday at Mr. Harris's office at Frontaine's.

| | |
|---|---|
| *Luffer* | Hello Mr. Harris. I'm Ronald Luffer with Master Air Inc. How are you doing this afternoon? |
| *Harris* | I'm doing just fine, Mr. Luffer. How are you? |
| *Luffer* | Ron, please, and I'm doing very well. Thanks. May I call you Tom? |
| *Harris* | Yes, please do. Now what can I do for you this afternoon? |
| *Luffer* | Well, like I said, I represent Master Air, and I'm here today to explain our revolutionary ventilation system to you. I understand you're opening two new restaurants. |
| *Harris* | Yes, that's true, one in E. Rockford and one in W. Rockford. |
| *Luffer* | I'm going to show you how, by purchasing a ventilation system from Master Air, you can save on your utility bills. The system will actually pay for itself in about two years. I'm sure you agree that with the economy and the energy situation being like it is, this system would be very beneficial to have. |
| *Harris (skeptically)* | This all sounds wonderful, but how much more am I going to have to pay for this wonderful new invention? |

| | |
|---|---|
| *Luffer* | It is true the Master Air system does cost more than the conventional systems, but as I mentioned, the fan will literally pay for itself in about two years. You will then have a free fan. Let me show you a letter from one of our customers. (Shows letter from MCL Cafeteria) |
| *Harris* | This is only one example; how do I know my savings will be this good? |
| *Luffer* | As you know, when air is removed from a room, air must be returned to the room to keep the air pressure steady. With a conventional system, two fans are used. One fan, the exhaust fan, exhausts 100 percent of the air to the outside, and the other fan returns 100 percent of the air from the atmosphere back into the room. During the winter, a gas-fired or an electric heater must be used to heat the air (shows diagram). With the Master Air system the heated air is filtered through grease filters and is exhausted to the rooftop heat recovery unit. At this point, depending on the season of the year, the hot air is either totally exhausted to the outside, or portions of it are directed through an electronic filtration section. The hot air is now combined with outside air, and 80 percent is returned into the room (shows diagram)—a savings in that you do not need to heat the returned air. |
| *Harris* | What about smoke? Cooks complain a lot about smoke; I need to be sure the fan will clear out all the smoke. |
| *Luffer* | The 20 percent of air supplied by the building system will keep all kitchen smoke and odors moving toward the kitchen hood and then exhausted. |
| *Harris* | How much money is this actually going to save me? |
| *Luffer* | Are you going to have gas or electricity? |

| | |
|---|---|
| *Harris* | Well, the restaurant opening in E. Rockford is gas, and the one opening in W. Rockford is electric. |
| *Luffer* | Okay. It depends on the size of the kitchen and the temperature outside. But according to a study done in 1989, if it costs $833 a year for gas, you will save $620 a year with Master Air; and if you pay $2,222 a year for electricity you will save $1,777 a year (shows study). You can have your system paid for in two years with the amount of money you save on utilities. Doesn't that sound like a smart purchase? |
| *Harris* | Yes. This all sounds very good. I just think I'd feel better dealing with a nationally known company like Jenn-Air. |
| *Luffer* | I understand your feelings, Tom. But the fact that we are a small company means we can get to know our customers better, and therefore we can give you a more personalized service that you would appreciate. |
| *Harris* | What about warranty? What kind of code approval does this thing have? |
| *Luffer* | All of our equipment meets or exceeds the requirements of the National Fire Prevention Association, the National Sanitation Foundation, and the National Electrical Code. Master Air also warrants the hood to be free from defects in material and construction for one year from the installation date. Small parts will be returned to Master Air for repair or replacement, and items that are affixed to the building or are too large for shipment will be repaired or replaced by Master Air at the job site. |
| *Harris* | Is it also U.L approved? |
| *Luffer* | Yes it is. Don't you agree the Master Air system can save you money and therefore is an economical purchase? |

| | |
|---|---|
| *Harris* | Your product is very revolutionary and economical, but I have an appointment with a representative from Jenn-Air next week. |
| *Harris* | One more thing. I'm real worried about grease fires. Is it safe? |
| *Luffer* | That's a very good question. Yes. If there is a fire, the unit contains the fire, and the fan is automatically turned to exhaust only. The grease filters we use are the safest filters available. They are called the Fire Fighter and provide a flame barrier and unsurpassed performance in grease removal (shows paper on the Fire Fighter). |
| *Harris* | How much operating time will I lose if there is a fire? |
| *Luffer* | Char's restaurant in Springfield had a fire and lost relatively no operating time (shows letter). All electronic wiring is located outside of the exhaust hood so it can be rewired immediately after the fire has been extinguished. |
| *Harris* | Very interesting. |
| *Harris* | How long does it take to install one of your systems? |
| *Luffer* | To install both the hood and the roof top unit and do all the wiring takes normally about two to three weeks. So, it's a deal? |
| *Harris* | Yes. |
| *Luffer* | Thank you, and have a good day. I'll be back in touch with you before next week. Goodbye. |

Discussion:

1. Where could the salesperson have offended the client in his use of objection techniques?
2. What objection techniques were used? Should the salesperson have used different ones?
3. Rewrite the dialogue using different objection techniques.

**Chapter Outline**

Closing Opportunities
Verbal Signs
Nonverbal Signs

Trial Close
Customer Says Yes
Customer Says No
Customer Has No Further Interest

Closing Techniques
Composition Closes
Conclusive Closes

Application of Closing Techniques
Dependent Clients
Dominant Clients
Logical-Thinking Clients

Causes of Closing Failures
Improper Attitudes
Improper Preparation

## CHAPTER 12

# Closing the Sale

**Learning Objectives**

After completing this chapter, you should be able to:

- Differentiate between a trial close and a close
- Compare and contrast closing techniques
- Understand the buying signals that tell you when to try to close
- Recognize the reasons why salespeople fail to close

## IN THE FIELD

*"The way to close a sale and pave the way for future sales is to define the customer's biggest problem and solve it. Once the problem has been identified, I entice them with Guaranteed Trial Offer (GTO). I get the correct specifications, so that I have the correct product that's going to work. After 6 months of customer testing, I assume they are going to order it and proceed to sell other compatible products. . . . I am amazed at the number of competitors who don't ask for the order and don't assume they are going to buy. People don't take it (the product) away from them."*

**Andrew Dunbar, Vice President,
Central Engineering A General Line Distributor**

Source: Steve Zurier, "Problem Solving vs. Order Taking," *Industrial Distribution* 76 (November 1987): 99. Reprinted from *Industrial Distribution*, November 1987, Cahners Publishing Company.

The *close* is the culmination of the dialogue that can be a sale, commitment for another meeting, or exit with goodwill (see Figure 12–1). In relationship selling, the salesperson *does not* overpower the customer's desires through persuasion or by pushing a product just to make a sale. Rather the close culminates the examination of customer needs and all possible solutions to those needs concluding with a buy/no-buy decision. This chapter acquaints you with techniques that you can use to help buyers make a good decision.

"You lose 100 percent of the sales you don't ask for."

**Anonymous**

**assumption close technique**

When the sales process is followed properly, closing the sale should be a natural conclusion to the dialogue, as expressed in *In the Field*. Andrew Dunbar, using an **assumption close technique,** assumes they are going to buy after six months' trial period and so begins selling other correlated materials.

Figure 12–1
*Closing the Sale* in the Customer–Salesperson Dialogue

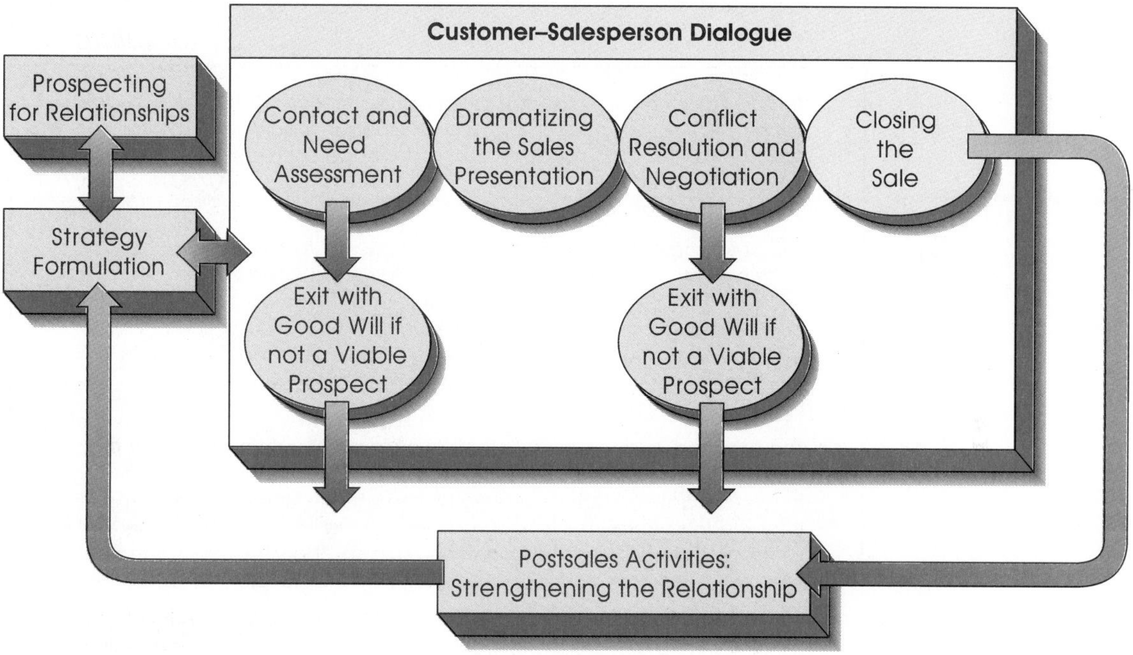

## Closing Opportunities

Closings, like presentations, must be custom-made. Analysis of salespeople's successful presentations show that they unconsciously follow these principles: (1) they really listen; (2) they adjust the close to the prospect's personality; and (3) they close only on recognized buying signals.[1]

The salesperson can spot spontaneous **closing opportunities** that arise or can deliberately plan closing opportunities in the sales presentation as buying signals develop. A **buying signal** refers to any indication, verbal or nonverbal, that the client is ready to buy. When you see a signal, it is time to ask a closing question. A few examples of buying signals are shown in Table 12–1.

**closing
opportunities
buying signal**

### Verbal Signals

Clients want to buy products that satisfy their needs. They want a "solution to their problem" as the reason behind a salesperson's selling mo-

Table 12–1
**Buying Signals**

| You Should Close When |
| --- |
| 1. *The buyer agrees with the salesperson's description of the value of an important benefit.* For example, the salesperson would say: ``Other users have found that Sanatol cuts their maitenance costs by anywhere from 5 percent to 15 percent.''<br>Client: ``That's certainly worth doing.'' Close! |
| 2. *The buyer agrees with the salesperson's answer to the objection.* For example, the client may argue that ``It takes your company too long to deliver,'' and the salesperson could respond: ``Yes, we do take a couple of weeks longer, but that's because we give you your choice of drive-motor sizes, reduction gears, and output housings—and that makes it worth the slight delay, don't you agree?'' Should the client agree: ``Yeah, I guess you're right,'' close! |
| 3. *The buyers give some indirect indication, verbal or nonverbal, that the product would benefit them.* The customer's indication might be a nonverbal action, such as picking up the sample or model and examining it for the third or fourth time, or such as leaning forward in his or her chair. Or it could be a customer's question, such as ``How well does it resist wear,'' or ``You say your people will help train us to use it?'' Close! |
| 4. *There is an ``abnormally'' lengthy pause.* The salesperson has made the total presentation, and the buyer has no further questions. A pause in the dialogue could indicate that it is time to close! |

*Source:* Reprinted with permission from *The American Salesman* ©, The National Research Bureau, Inc., 424 North Third St., Burlington, Iowa 52601-5224.

tives. Prospects want responses to their signals, and they resent the salesperson who does not respond. They may say things voluntarily, like:

- ``I wish I had done something like this ten years ago.''
- ``What was that price again?''
- ``What terms can we arrange?''
- ``How soon can you ship it?''
- Exclamations such as Oh! Ah, Umm, or clearing the throat to speak (involuntary verbal signals).

## Nonverbal Signals

Verbal buying signals are often hard to recognize if you are not listening carefully; nonverbal signals are even more subtle. No nonverbal sign is completely reliable on its own, but here are a few signals that might indicate, together with verbal signals, that a customer is in a ready-to-buy situation:

- Reaching for, touching, glancing at or asking to see the contract
- Stepping back for a better look
- Lifting an item
- Rereading literature
- Raising eyebrows
- Reaching for or playing casually with a pen or pencil
- Look of interest in the eyes
- Leaning forward in chair
- Relaxed muscles and body frame.[2]

Also, changes in body stance often show signs of the customer's wanting to move on with the presentation or to conclude it. Interpreting nonverbal signals gains better insight into the customer's real thoughts and feelings.

Being able to read buying signals makes salespeople better at adapting their closes to their different clients. Most customers tell them, through verbal and nonverbal signals, when and how to close. If you concentrate too intently on making your points clear, you may miss obvious signals, ignore psychological differences between clients, or fail to ask for the order. You might not make the sale if you don't listen properly with your eyes and ears to these buying signals.

Experience has shown that in roughly 60 percent of customer–salesperson dialogues, salespeople have failed to make an effort to close; in 20 percent of all customer contacts, the salesperson has tried to close; and in 20 percent of the contacts, the customer has initiated the close ("that sounds great, I'll take it").[3] With so many possibilities, a salesperson is apt to wonder just when *is* the right time to close?

Recognizing buying signals is a key to know when to close. As shown in Table 12–2, you can close as early as client contact and as late as the next meeting. When to close? Simply put, close when the buyer is ready. Ninety-nine percent of the time, however, the close is made after the presentation of benefits.

The close phase of the dialogue is as much a part of the presentation as is the resolution of conflicts. Attempting a close is used as a test (trial) to determine where customers are in their thinking and as a guide to further dialogue.

Several things may happen during the close stages of the selling process. Figure 12–2 diagrams the activities that may occur during the concluding phase.

Table 12–2
**Ten Times to Close**

| Close Can Be Made: |
| --- |
| 1. Early in the presentation |
| 2. Before completing the presentation |
| 3. After the demonstration |
| 4. Upon agreement with the benefit statements |
| 5. After the presentation |
| 6. After the resolution of each statement of sales resistance |
| 7. After ``reading'' buying signals |
| 8. After each trial close |
| 9. After trying multiple close strategies |
| 10. At another meeting time |
| **When the buyer is ready!** |

## Trial Close

**trial close**

Toward the end of the need fulfillment and objection stage, the salesperson seeks affirmation for the proposed solution to the customer's problem by asking for a commitment. This initial commitment step is called a trial close. A **trial close** solicits additional customer inquiries in an attempt to finalize a sales presentation. It is a barometer to determine the "rightness" of the time to ask for the order. The trial close can receive a "Yes," a "No," or an "I want further information" response.

As shown in Figure 12–2, *trial closes are an integral part of the presentation as well as its conclusion.* A trial close and a close use the same techniques to ask for the order. The difference between a trial close and a close is in the results from the customer.

When a trial close is answered by the client with more concerns, the salesperson meets the objection and tries another trial close. When the trial close is agreed to by the client by saying "Yes," the trial close becomes a close regardless of whether it is the first attempt to close or only the last of many.

## Customer Says Yes

**close**

If the customer says "Yes" to the trial close, it is no longer a trial close but begins the conclusion to the dialogue (*close*). A **close** is a trial close

**Figure 12–2**
**Flow Diagram of Sales Conclusions**

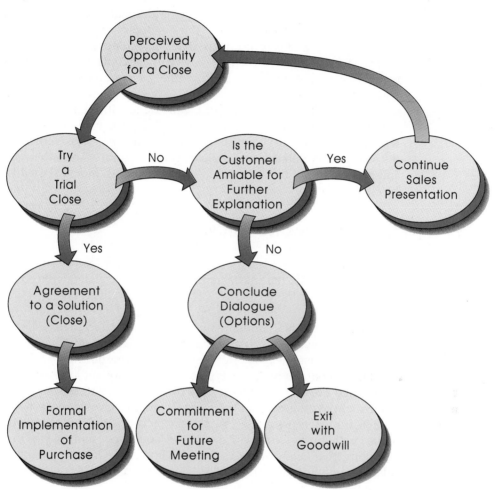

that elicits affirmation, a "Yes," to the proposed solution to the client's needs. A "No" or "I need more information" response becomes another objection requiring resolution and another trial close. Until a "Yes" is received, the salesperson continues to answer objections posed by the consumer. Obviously the close with a sale is the most desired outcome of the customer–salesperson dialogue, if the client's needs can be met. The actual close happens when a formal agreement to the customer's need is implemented, with the salesperson writing up the order and getting a signature of approval when necessary. Remember that salespeople do not always get a "Yes" with the first attempt at a close.

The actual close happens when a formal agreement to the customer's need is implemented, with the salesperson writing up the order and getting a signature of approval when necessary. Remember that salespeople do not always get a "Yes" with the first attempt at a close.

# Customer Says No

When the customer says "No" or raises additional objections or questions, the salesperson must determine if the customer is open to further discussion and explanations or if it is more feasible to discontinue the dialogue. Getting a "No" is often seen by novice salespeople as personal rejection when it actually might mean that the customer merely needs more information.

It is only necessary to exit the dialogue with a customer when you read the client's verbal and nonverbal language as committed not to buy, which under normal circumstances should not happen. Until that time, the salesperson initiates a trial close, gets a neutral or negative response, and proceeds to fulfill the request of the client with more information and another trial close.

# Customer Has No Further Interest

If a customer shows a total lack of further interest (shown by verbal and nonverbal signals), the salesperson concludes the dialogue in one of two manners. First, if the customer was properly qualified and is on friendly terms, the salesperson should ask for another meeting. This gives the salesperson time to accumulate more information and to formulate a new strategy for solving the customer's problem. Second, the disillusioned or misqualified customer may not respond to suggestions for another meeting. Future contacts with this type of customer are apt to be fruitless sales efforts, and the salesperson should exit with goodwill. Exiting with goodwill may allow the seller to get referrals and positive word-of-mouth promotion from the prospect. You should be cautioned not to exit the dialogue prematurely. Your clients will let you know with plenty of verbal and nonverbal language when to exit with grace. Only the nonperceptive salesperson who is not attentive to clients' needs would continue until the customer is hostile.

In the closing stage, salespeople sometimes find it tempting to shift from the relationship to a persuasive orientation, particularly if the customer is "difficult." The salesperson is naturally biased toward his or her company's products, since confidence in one's product is necessary in successful selling. However, the relationship approach requires that the salesperson disclose the facts without distortion, having readily admitted a bias toward his or her product. Remember, too, that the customer, not the salesperson, has the "last word." Pressures, such as needing to meet sales quotas, may tempt the salesperson to persuade a customer to buy a product; but that should not happen, since it will damage the relationship.

Since the salesperson's goal is long-range success, it is important to maintain a cordial relationship with the customer. High pressure tactics may sell a customer the first time, but will the customer continue to buy from such a persuasive salesperson? Most likely the customer will buy from a salesperson who can evaluate alternatives, suggest a solution, and abide by the customer's decision.

## Closing Techniques ▰▰▰▰▰▰▰▰▰▰▰▰

The first step in a good closing is to relax. Both you and the client may feel tension. Customers often feel some tension because they are making an important decision that precludes all other choices at this time. The salesperson may be apprehensive because the customer is initiating behavioral pattern changes in the close. The close can go more smoothly if the salesperson lays some groundwork during the presentation. Trial closes made early during a presentation are one good way to do this. They demonstrate an attempt to evaluate the customer's needs or problems. Posing trial closes only toward the end of a presentation makes the salesperson appear more interested in the sale than in the client's problem. Early trial closes also enable the salesperson to assess more accurately the prospect's feelings, intentions, and attitudes.[4]

Read the client wrong, and lose a sale. The close that works best with one type of client will not work with another. To close successfully the salesperson must:

- Maintain a positive attitude that includes enthusiasm and confidence
- Keep control of the dialogue without pressuring the customer
- Adjust the dialogue speed to the customer's pace
- Give the customer a chance to buy
- Keep some buying points on reserve
- Help the customer buy the right item, the right amount, at the right time and price
- Know when to use silence effectively.

There are ten primary closing techniques, and each varies somewhat. If one method is unsuccessful, the salesperson needs to try another and perhaps another until the customer is satisfied.

Closing techniques are categorized according to their purposes as either composition or conclusive. Each has five variations, giving ten useful closing techniques, as summarized in Table 12–3. Most often it takes a **combination of closes,** both combination and conclusive, to make a sale.

**combination of closes**

Table 12–3

---

**Closes Available to Salespeople**

---

*Composition Closes*

Built of a series of customer–salesperson responses in which the salesperson rephrases key points to influence the buyer's decision.
- *Affirmation*—compliments the buyer on sincere values both buyer and seller have in common; develops a positive image
- *Continuous yes*—gets continuous, affirmative responses to questions during presentation, particularly towards the end.
- *T-account (summary of benefits)*—a balance sheet approach to summarizing the positives and negatives of purchase
- *Review of buying decisions*—takes the client through the steps of the buying decision to obtain a ``yes'' to each
- *Emotional*—appeals to the client's emotional motives of purchase

*Conclusive Closes*

Designed to complete the presentation quickly to urge the client into action
- *Standing-room-only*—used to emphasize the immediacy of making a decision *now*; should be used sparingly
- *Single obstacle*—narrows the nonbuying reasons of the client to a minimum number of obstacles. Each obstacle is handled one at a time, with affirmation sought on each before proceeding to the next obstacle.
- *Assumption*—assumes the client wants the product and begins to suggest accessories or a service contract; builds on the assumption that the client wants to buy
- *Direct appeal*—asks for the order directly: ``How many do you want,'' ``Can I have it delivered Tuesday?''
- *Positive choice*—gives the client a choice of two products and asks which one is preferred

*Combination Closes*

Uses a mixture of conclusive and composition closes to end a sale

---

## Composition Closes

**composition closes**

**Composition closes** are built from a series of customer–salesperson exchanges in which the salesperson rephrases key ideas influencing the client's decision. These closes draw the client toward a conclusion through a series of events rather than through a direct statement, as in a conclusive close. Closes in the composition category are the affirmation, continuous yes, summary of benefits, review of the buying decisions, and emotional closes.

## Affirmation Close

The salesperson using the **affirmation close** states a benefit of purchasing a product as a fact. For example, a Procter & Gamble salesperson might say, "It's obvious that you know a lot about the grocery business. Your store is well supplied with all the fastest selling brands. That's why you need to stock. . . ."

      This close is not a license to stretch the truth. An affirming comment comes sincerely as the term implies. The affirming technique is not for every customer but is very effective when the salesperson and customer have strong trust in each other. The following statement from an NCR representative demonstrates such a relationship:

> It is obvious from our discussion and from the appearance of your store that you are very forward-thinking and use new ideas readily. Tell me, Frank, how do you think your company could benefit from a point-of-sale computerized cash register?

**affirmation close**

## Continuous-Yes Close

Similar to the affirmative close, the **continuous-yes close** asks for a series of "Yes" answers to questions posed throughout the presentation. This technique helps the logical thinking customer who needs to be led step-by-step through the presentation. For this customer, saying "Yes" on each point makes it easier to say "Yes" to the sale.

      An Eli Lilly Pharmaceutical salesperson, for example, might use this technique to assist doctors in arriving at a decision. Convinced that a doctor would be better satisfied with a name-brand drug rather than a generic one, the salesperson includes in the presentation several questions concerning qualities of the drug the doctor desires to prescribe. The salesperson might inquire as follows:

**continuous-yes close**

| | |
|---|---|
| *Salesperson* | I would suspect you want a broad spectrum antibiotic drug that has the fewest side effects? (pause) |
| *Doctor* | Yes. |
| *Salesperson* | Needs few complicated directions for administration? (pause) |
| *Doctor* | Yes. |

| | |
|---|---|
| *Salesperson* | Do you have many hard-to-treat bacterial infection cases? (pause) |
| *Doctor* | Yes. |
| *Salesperson* | (after showing the benefit brochure): Can you see how it is safer to prescribe this broad-based antibiotic than a lesser known one? (pause) |
| *Doctor* | Yes. |
| *Salesperson* | Would you like a drug that has proven dependable year after year? |

A "Yes" answer is probable for each question, and each exchange highlights the advantages of the branded drug over a generic substitution.

The goal of this close technique is to keep the client in a positive frame of mind by eliciting "Yes" responses. The entire presentation should be positive, without questions likely to get "No" answers. A question such as "Have you had good results from our other products?" would not be asked because the customer could say "No." The adept salesperson would ask, "Which do you prefer to prescribe, generic or branded medicine?"

### T-Account Close

**T-account, or summary of benefits technique**

With the **T-account, or summary of benefits technique,** as with the continuous yes, the client and salesperson go over each major point, one by one, getting agreement on each point before moving on to another. The summary may be as informal as counting off each point on the fingers, or the salesperson may formally write each point in a T-account, as shown in Table 12–4. Both the salesperson and the client develop the reason-to-buy list. This technique works best for those customers who compensate some benefits for those that may be lacking in the product. The customer volunteers the reasons-not-to-act list.

The T-account appeals to rational and logical thinking buyers, particularly industrial buyers who are accustomed to balance sheet, profit-and-loss–style thinking. If the list for buying is longer and more important than the reasons for not buying, the customer should buy the product upon seeing such proof.

The T-account technique is easily combined with other types of closes, especially a direct request for the order. For example, a salesperson might approach a customer after summarizing and getting agreement on each point in this way: "Mr. Baird, in view of these impressive facts (pointing to the T-account), don't you feel that your firm needs the electromagnetic generator now?" When presented in a logical, enthusiastic

Summarizing the benefits one at a time is a way to make sure the slow/methodical buyer understands how the product will solve the client's problem.

manner, this *composition*-type close builds up a summary, fact by fact, from lesser to more important facts and ensures final agreement.

## Review of the Buying Decision Close

Instead of summarizing the facts, the **review of the buying decision (RBD) close** reviews the buying decision areas of need, product, source, price, and time. Since the buyer must say "Yes" to each of the five buying-

**review of the buying decision (RBD) close**

Table 12–4
**Example of a T-Account Close**

| Reasons to Act | Reasons Not to Act |
|---|---|
| 1. Save $500 by buying now | 1. Costs too much |
| 2. Saves time and energy | 2. Need to talk with my husband |
| 3. Can take it with me now; don't have to wait for delivery | |
| 4. Really like this one because it saves money | |
| 5. Will save $100 a year in operating cost | |

decision areas before making a purchase, a salesperson can formally review each decision area in the close. A verbal "Yes" to each point is not
necessary; the lack of a "No" is assumed to be a positive response.

In a manner similar to the T-account technique, a RBD highlights
for the customer the reasons for making a decision. Like the continuous-
yes approach, RBD is designed to get a formal, positive response to each
of the five areas. After receiving five affirmatives, the salesperson can use
an additional closing technique, such as the assumption close, which is
discussed later in this chapter. This technique works best for those customers who do not compensate for benefits that do not meet their needs.
Such a combination is illustrated in this example of Gene Kern, a salesman
for Merrill-Lynch, who is talking to Mary Mobly about an investment
plan:

> Well, Mary let's see how the ninety-day Money Market fits
> your needs. You need the highest rate of return with
> minimal risk, right? (Need) You have enough liquid assets
> that the $10,000 minimum investment for 90 days will not
> be a hardship, isn't that so? (Product) You have been a
> customer of ours for a long time, and we're glad you chose
> us to do your financial planning. We hope to maintain that
> precious relationship a long, long time. (Source) Now is
> the best time to invest in money markets. Interest rates are
> the highest they have been in months, and of course we
> don't charge you anything for our service. (Time and
> Price) Will you keep the account under the same names as
> in your savings account? Please sign here.

### Emotional Close

**emotional close**

**impulse buying**

The **emotional close** appeals to the client's desires for thrift, pride, prestige, or freedom from fear. These emotions figure prominently in buying.
**Impulse buying**—when people buy, often for emotional reasons, when
they did not intend to buy—accounts for a substantial portion of sales at
the retail level.

After a carefully prepared presentation, the emotional close can
be a powerful psychological tool, but it should be used with extreme care.
Emphasis must continue to be on clients' needs and not just on their emotions; or they may later return the product.

Normally a salesperson appeals to emotions to help certain types
of prospects make up their minds. The emotional technique works best
with positive appeals to emotions other than fear. For example, a Xerox
representative might ask a customer: "Would you feel better knowing that
you were affiliated with Xerox?" Or a BMW saleswoman asking,

"Wouldn't you feel good to be seen in this machine touring down the road?" knows the customer will usually answer "Yes" because she is appealing to the pride of ownership.

Although powerful tools, emotional appeals have to be stated very delicately or their use verges on manipulation and the unethical. For example, several years ago some door-to-door smoke alarm salespeople would enter a home, make a presentation, and close by showing a picture of a home fire with the headline, "Two Killed in Fire." Then they would make statements such as, "This fire was in your city. City Fire Inspectors say that the two children killed could have been saved if the family had installed smoke alarms in the house. How can you sleep tonight knowing that this might happen to you or your children because you don't have a smoke alarm?"

Being confronted by such graphic evidence would certainly be remembered. But making a sale by exaggerating fear is manipulative and ethically questionable. Emotional closes built around exaggerated fear *should not* be used by a relationship seller. Many products are purchased because of uncertainty, for instance, insurance and IRAs; and salespeople can point out the need for such products without exaggerating the client's fears.

## Conclusive Closes

**Conclusive closes** are designed to conclude the dialogue with a solution, a decision. They nudge the customer into making a decision and typically are combined with composition closes. Conclusive closes are the standing-room-only, overcoming a single obstacle, assumption, choice, and direct appeal techniques.

**conclusive closes**

### Standing-Room-Only Close

Using a close that puts time limits on the client is called **standing-room-only** (SRO). Often a salesperson gives a reason to buy now: "Our big sale ends Friday" and "I only have three left at this remarkable price," illustrate SRO closes. Such a close could be seen as an attempt to hurry the customer into a decision.

**standing-room-only close**

Like the emotional close, the SRO must be used very carefully, if at all. Use SRO only when there is truly a *limited* quantity or time offer. Unfortunately the SRO has been overused and abused by salespeople for years, and buyers are leery of such claims. Here is one such example: A Maytag representative is talking to Macy's appliance buyer about a special purchase offer on limited edition dishwashers. The buyer is hesitant. The representative remarks, "I know you like it, and it's a big investment. There are only a few being made. I will give you this model exclusively if you decide to carry my line. But I have to know today."

This incident shows the time restraints SRO puts on clients. Some buyers even take offense, which hurts the salesperson's credibility. Used often in retail sales, an SRO close makes many retail customers suspicious. Few indecisive clients like increased pressure, particularly when it is close to the decision point. Too often the pressure backfires, and the client does not buy. Under the pressure, the client may buy only to cancel the order later after the pressure subsides.

Industrial and field salespeople can use SRO more efficiently because they can support their claims with evidence, such as news of an impending strike, company brochures with dates, and knowledge of shortages. Any salesperson using this technique must do so only with complete honesty.

## Single Obstacle Close

**single obstacle close**

A salesperson may think a customer has said "Yes" to each buying decision area only to discover a lingering objection at a close. This situation calls for the **single obstacle close (SOC).** Employing the SOC, a salesperson narrows the sales resistance down to a single obstacle, states this resistance to the client for confirmation, and gets a commitment to buy if the obstacle can be explained to the client's satisfaction. Once this statement is made, the salesperson then uses other techniques, such as a review of the buying decision for a T-account close, to overcome the objection, as demonstrated in the following dialogue.

| | |
|---|---|
| *Salesperson* | Mr. Keck, What is your biggest reluctance to buying my Sharp copier? |
| *Mr. Keck* | Price! |
| *Salesperson* | If I can show you how this Sharp #4213 is the best value on the market, will you select it? |
| *Mr. Keck* | Yes, I will. |

The salesperson stated the obstacle, price. The next step would be showing the truth of the claim made in the direct statement and then using another conclusive close, such as "We can deliver it on Monday. Will that be soon enough?"

## Assumption Close

Using the *assumption close,* the salesperson assumes that an agreement to buy has been reached without asking for the order. The idea that the customer wants to make a purchase is basic to every sale. This assumption indicates a marketer's positive attitude and high self-esteem. An assumption at the close becomes a positive suggestion. The salesperson assumes by word and action that the client wants the product. Unless the prospect stops the salesperson, the salesperson assumes that the client agrees, and the sale is closed.

You must be careful not to be manipulative by enticing customers to buy merchandise they don't want. They generally cancel the order before delivery or return the merchandise. Assuming too much is presumptuous and destroys the trust bond.

A submissive client who depends on the advice of others would probably readily accept an assumptive close. Others might feel offended, possibly setting a negative tone for the conclusion of the selling process. Like the single obstacle close, the assumptive close may bring out latent sales resistance. The longevity of the customer–salesperson relationship affects the efficiency of the assumptive close. The stronger the relationship, the more apt the client will be to rely on the salesperson's judgment and therefore to agree with the assumption.

## Direct Appeal Close

The **direct appeal close** is often called "asking for the order." It seems simple enough. Ask for the order. Often the novice salesperson loses a sale simply by not asking the client to buy. This is not a problem for Employee Benefit Plan Administration, Inc. salespeople, reports Pat Hughes, sales director (see *Partnerships*). "We train all our people to present the facts in our proposal and put the decision in the hands of the buyer. They close the sale," Pat says. Professional buyers report that an amazing number of salespeople never ask for the order. These salespeople may fear rejection. But whatever their reasons, they need to realize the error of their ways. The fear of closing is not true at Tracy's (see Tracy, Robinson, & Williams *Partnerships*). They asked for a commitment of one barrel of lubricant per machine and sold sixty barrels. Asking for the order can salvage seemingly hopeless sales. Often a customer's objections for not buying are trivial and only confuse the situation. Directly asking for the order halts the confusion and encourages the customer to make the order. There's nothing wrong with saying:

**direct appeal close**

- "May I get your purchase order number?"
- "We deliver to Pittsburgh on Thursday. Is that all right?"
- "How much money can you put down at this time?"

## Positive Choice Close

Between the direct and assumptive closes, the **positive choice close** presents the client with two alternatives: "Do you want A or B?" This close

**positive choice close**

## PARTNERSHIPS

Salespeople at one of the fastest growing third-party administrators of health plans in the United States are trained to close. According to Pat Hughes, Sales Director of Employee Benefit Plan Administration, Inc., salespeople ``. . . present all the data in their proposal, then close their presentation book, thus physically putting aside the issue of rates and costs. At this point the salesperson simply says 'Now, the decision you have to make is whether you want our organization to administer your health program.' That's it.'' Pat's salespeople close on the company's reputation for service, professionalism, personal trust, and quality product.

*Source:* Jack Falvey, ``For the Best Close, Keep an Open Mind,'' *Sales and Marketing Management* 142 (April 1990): 12. Reprinted by permission of *Sales & Marketing Management,* © April 1990.

makes a direct appeal for a purchase and assumes that the client wants A or B. This technique is the favorite close technique in a survey of salespeople. It was preferred by almost 75 percent of the respondents.[5] Selection in a sale is important, but too many choices are confusing. As the number of options increases, the decision becomes more difficult, if not impossible.

Using a positive choice close, the salesperson should remove those items the client is no longer considering. This saves the client from getting bogged down with the entire selection. Closing on choice enables the client to make a wise decision because conflicting and confusing alternatives are gone; the client's attention is focused on the two most desirable options.

A securities broker, for example, after presenting a client with a plan for investing a fixed sum each month, might ask, "Do you feel your budget restraints would allow you to invest $300 a month, or would $200 a month be better?" The broker has discouraged the client's investing less than $200 a month by mentioning only the two amounts.

## Application of Closing Techniques

Knowing when to close is very important. But knowing which closing techniques to use for each type of buyer is equally needed. Using the wrong techniques can have an adverse influence on the closing opportunity.

## Dependent Clients

**Dependent clients,** for instance, want to relate on a personal level, to talk about themselves and the salesperson. They reflect warmth; their offices are homelike and personalized with pictures of family and friends. A summary of benefits close will seem cold, calculating, and frightening to dependent clients. Instead, a salesperson must be warm, enthusiastic, emphatic, and caring when closing with a dependent customer. Also, the salesperson should minimize the fear of making a decision by trying to make it seem smaller and less frightening to the client. The continuous-yes is effective with the dependent client.

**dependent clients**

## Dominant Clients

The **dominant client** is quite different from the dependent client. The dominant personality type tries to control and to impress the salesperson, preferring respect and deference rather than friendship. Their offices communicate their status consciousness. Since they respect only strength, a salesperson must be tough and ask for the order. Sometimes a salesperson must ask for the order again and again because some dominant people will not buy until salespeople prove their persistence by trying to close several times.

**dominant client**

## Logical-Thinking Clients

**Logical-thinking clients,** often called detached people, dislike warmth and dominance. They keep their distance and are nonpersonal. They tend to study information for facts, ask detailed and technical questions, and dislike emotional appeals. Since detached people need solid evidence of claims and logic, it is best to avoid personality appeals, such as attempting to assume an "I'm-just-like-you" attitude. The T-account close works best with these people. Make customers aware of the cost of indecision. If the clients hedge, remind them that they will lose out on whatever it is that makes the product or service special—attractive price, increased productivity, and the like.

**logical-thinking clients**

## Causes of Closing Failures ▆▆▆▆▆▆

Many personal barriers inhibit the closing of a sale and may affect whether one closes the sale or not. Invariably these barriers center around attitudes and preparation as shown in Table 12–5.

Table 12–5
**Roadblocks to Closing Sales**

| Improper Attitudes | Improper Preparation |
| --- | --- |
| Fear of rejection | Poor or inadequate training |
| Guilt | Misreading clients |
| Lack of self-confidence | Failure to adapt to clients |
| Negative attitude | Lack of developing a relationship |
| | Failure to ask for the order |

# Improper Attitudes

Many people in sales have attitudes that make closing, and therefore sales, difficult if not impossible. Foremost is the fear of failure. Some salespeople, so programmed for success, are devastated or debilitated if they receive a "No" when they ask for a commitment. Salespeople's confidence in themselves, their products, and their companies is contagious to the buyer. Overcoming obstacles of fear and guilt can build that confidence.[6]

### Fear

The fear of hearing "No" should not destroy a salesperson's confidence. Salespeople expect to be turned down several times before making a sale. Confidence means facing fear directly and not taking a negative response as a personal rejection; instead it should be viewed as an opportunity to grow, mature, and improve the presentation.

### Guilt

Guilt creates another obstacle to success. Some salespeople fail to close because they feel guilty about asking a client to buy. They often feel guilty for asking for customers to spend their money or for having to discuss unpleasant topics like death. They may even feel guilty about their profession.[7] Evidence supports this. A study done by the Life Insurance Institute determined that the single greatest cause of failure among life insurance agents was that they felt guilty, which, in turn, led to a lack of confidence.[8]

### Inferiority about Career

Salespeople should not feel as though they are begging for a living. To the contrary, they should remind themselves that sales is an important profession; business depends on it. Not all people would be happy in sales, but the person who wants immediate reinforcement for his or her behavior, likes talking to people, and is motivated can find an exhilarating, challenging career in selling.

### Negative Attitude

A negative attitude, like guilt and a lack of confidence, can cause a failure to close. Who wants to buy from salespeople who are not positive about themselves, their companies, or their products? Negativism is as contagious as enthusiasm; clients catch either easily. Negativism unfortunately stifles the sales dialogue, so the salesperson must find and express the positive in even the most negative situation.

## Improper Preparation

Like an improper attitude, poor preparation can immobilize a close. Not taking the time to train or not realizing the importance of training can be detrimental to one's closing ratio.

### Poor Training

Poor training or a lack of good selling skills accounts for many failures. These problems become apparent in a salesperson's errors in perceiving a customer's needs, feelings, and attitudes, together with an inability to handle objections and use sales tools properly. These imperfections cause the salesperson to lose control of the sale. Without control, the close will not lead to a natural conclusion, and the presentation will become ineffective.[9]

Proper training and determination to improve make a more effective salesperson. Effective salespeople continually think on their feet, adjust the presentation, and are aware of the possibilities of closing to any new situation. In the field, salespeople have little to rely on except training and skills, so they seek continuing opportunities for training and practice good selling habits to realize their highest potential.[10] If the company fails to provide adequate training for effective selling, it is the responsibility of salespeople to see that they get the training needed on their own. You must analyze and learn from each presentation you make, successful or not, and incorporate the success factors into the next closing opportunity.

### Errors in ''Reading'' the Client

Salespeople fail to close a sale when they misread the client. If customers feel that the salesperson is not considering their problems, they often refuse to buy. Most clients like to be ''helped to buy,'' but few like to be ''sold'' products.

Failure to recognize or to acknowledge buying signals causes closing failures. Although there is no magical moment at which to close a sale, there are times better than others. Reading and reacting to the client's buying signals are imperative to effective closing.

### Failure to Adapt to the Client

The relationship salesperson shows clients that he or she cares by adapting to the situation. Giving the same "pitch," or standard, canned presentation, to all clients when a customized presentation is required is impersonal. Impersonal presentations rarely succeed in sales and only then if there is no other alternative choice. Frequently buyers refuse to buy from those people who are so impersonal that they refuse to match their presentation to the client's specific needs.

### Failure to Develop a Relationship

Since clients like continuity of supply, they are dismayed when they feel that the seller is not trying to secure a long-term relationship with them. Most people can sell someone something once. The real challenge is to help clients buy repeatedly. The easiest customers to close are those who are already purchasing from you. They have already said "Yes" to the source, so part of the close is already made. Customer satisfaction builds the relationship on a strong foundation, giving the salesperson an advantage in filling future customer needs, as shown by Chittenden and Smith's relationship with Stanley's Specialty (see *Partnerships*, p. 343). Developing a relationship puts the salesperson at a distinct advantage. Failure to develop this positive relationship puts the "advantage in the competitor's court."

### Failure To Ask For the Order

As ridiculous as it seems, a frequent reason salespeople do not close is that they do not *ask for the order*. It is logical that people would not buy if they did not like the seller, the product, or the price or if the time was not right to buy. But some sellers get so involved in their presentation of features and benefits that they never ask for the order.[11] It goes like this:

| Salesperson | Well, Dr. Cary, do you see all the advantages we have? |
| Dr. Cary | Yes. |
| Salesperson | Do you have any other questions for me to answer? No? Well, I'll see you next time. |

## PARTNERSHIPS

If Tracy, Robinson & Williams (a small specialty distributor of lubricating oils and abrasives) wanted Stanley's (Stanley Specialty and Manufacturing Business, a maker of knife blades, nail sets, and hundreds of different metal parts for Stanley products) lubricant business, Ken Neves, businss manager for Stanley's Specialty Manufacturing Business, told the industrial supply house that it had to meet three goals: (1) eliminate drums on his plant floor; (2) reduce the number of oils used; and (3) become a single-source lubricant supplier. For Alan Chittenden and Tim Smith, salespeople for Tracy, such obstacles are nothing new. After completing a machine lubrication survey, they made a proposal to Ken Naves and several other officers. This proposal met all three goals (obstacles) plus asked for a commitment—one drum of lubricant for each of their sixty machines. With few other objections from the group, the proposal was approved. Smith and Chittenden had opened the doors to Stanley's business and increased their market share. The next trip through, Tracy is trying to get Stanley to buy their Castrol line of cutting fluids, and Stanley seems to be listening.

*Source:* John G. F. Bonnanzio, ``Helping Stanley Do Things Right,'' *Industrial Distribution* 79 (May 1990). Reprinted from *Industrial Distribution,* May 1990, Cahners Publishing Co.

The sale was lost because the salesperson did not ask for the order or ask the right questions. Occasionally buyers insist on having the product delivered without being asked, but that is not standard practice. Fear of hearing "No" is no reason for failing to ask for the order.

Asking for the order puts the sales presentation into perspective. It finds out where the client is in his or her thinking and gives clues to the salesperson concerning where there might be barriers. Asking for the order is the natural conclusion of the presentation stage and is a beginning of the follow-up stage.

The closing process progresses into a follow-up, not just the conclusion of the selling process. And as a former comptroller of a Midwestern wholesale tobacco distributor pointed out to a salesperson, "A sale is not closed until it's paid for."[12] Perhaps a sale is never closed, for if a sale is made, a relationship is started, and if a sale is not made, the learning process is altered. Learning from the successes and the failures in life allows us to be more efficient.

## Summary

The close concludes the dialogue process. In reality, the keys to successful closing are good techniques, preparation, and skill in execution. Closing techniques are classified according to the composition closes of affirmation (continuous yes, summary of benefits, review of buying decision, and emotional) and to the conclusive closes (standing-room-only, single obstacle, assumption, direct appeal, and positive choice). Experienced sellers know that they may attempt a close anytime after the initial contact phase of the dialogue, although it is common to wait until during or following the presentation.

Closing failures can be attributed to an improper attitude or to improper preparation on the part of the salesperson. Fear of failure, fear of hearing "no," inferiority about a sales job, and feelings of guilt all lead to a negative attitude. Adequate preparation comes from thorough training and experience in interacting with all kinds of people.

As shown in the flow diagram at the beginning of the chapter, the seller may close with a sale, exit with goodwill with no sale, or get a commitment for future meetings. The ultimate goal, however, is getting the customer's name on the order blank and at the same time gaining a customer who has been served well.

## Key Terms

assumption close technique
closing opportunities
buying signal
trial close
close
combination of closes
composition closes
affirmation close
continuous-yes close
T-account, or summary of
   benefits technique
review of buying decision (RBD)
   close

emotional close
impulse buying
conclusive closes
standing-room-only close
single obstacle close
direct appeal close
positive choice close
dependent clients
dominant clients
logical-thinking clients

## Discussion Questions

1.  Discuss why, over the long run, a salesperson should use the relationship style of selling.

2.  Distinguish between a trial close and a close.

3.  Define composition closes and conclusive closes.

4. After each of the following types of closing, write a composition closing or a conclusive closing as an illustration of that type of closing.
   - a. Affirmation
   - b. Standing-room-only
   - c. Continuous-yes
   - d. Overcoming a single obstacle
   - e. Assumption
   - f. Summary of benefits/T-account
   - g. Review of buying decision
   - h. Positive choice
   - i. Emotional
   - j. Direct appeal

5. Nonverbal signals are often difficult to notice. List five nonverbal signs that might suggest attempting a trial close to a salesperson.

6. Consider three types of clients: the dependent, the dominant, and the logical–thinker. Briefly define each type of customer and suggest a type of close suitable for that person.

7. What is the difference between improper preparation and improper attitude?

8. During a successful close, a salesperson must remember many things. Name five of these important areas.

## Decision Crossroads: Ethical Issues

Jan Thompson sells for Russo Tools. She usually uses a premium approach to getting in the door by giving potential buyers a crescent wrench for their personal use. When she used this approach with David White, he was noticeably pleased. During the presentation David fondled the wrench. The close was becoming very difficult, with David objecting vigorously about pricing discounts. Jan used a direct close: "What will it take for you to buy your company's tools from us?" David then implied that he was in the process of upgrading his "tool collection" and really liked her company's quality. Jan felt that if she gave David a set of tools, he would sign the order. A set of tools was only $465, and the company's order would be over $46,000. She pondered what to do.

### Discussion:

1. If you were Jan, what would you do?
2. Do you feel it is unethical to buy "business"?

## Case 12–1  **Pioneer Chemical Company**

Brian Culver is the local sales representative in Allentown, Pennsylvania for the Pioneer Chemical Company. Pioneer Chemical has its headquarters and main plant located in Elizabethtown, Kentucky. Mr. Culver began selling chemicals two years ago. At that time he had been unable to close a sale, but since then he has improved his closing average tremendously by working hard and by practicing. In this case he is trying to sell a chemical that will remove rust from steel that has been stored too long. The chemical is called CLEAR 191.

Arthur Silitzer is the purchasing agent for Pennsylvania Power Company, manufacturer of transformers. Mr. Silitzer and Mr. Culver have had business transactions before but not with this product. Mr. Silitzer had contacted Mr. Culver to see if he can provide a chemical to remove the rust from $50,000 worth of steel that his company has stored too long.

Mr. Culver's product, CLEAR 191, is a phosphoric acid-based product that is nonvolatile and is not dangerous for employees to handle. This is not the case with all other competitive products, which are harmful if they come in contact with bare skin.

The process to remove rust is to place the steel to be derusted in a stainless steel tank of CLEAR 191 for two hours.

| | |
|---|---|
| *Culver* | Hello Mr. Silitzer! How are you today? |
| *Silitzer* | I'm fine Brian, and yourself? |
| *Culver* | Oh, I can't complain, except for this weather! |
| *Silitzer* | I know what you mean! It's hot! |
| *Culver* | On my last visit here, you mentioned the fact that you had a lot of rusted steel that could not be used in production. I've got a sample of CLEAR 191, our new rust remover. If you'd like, we can go down to your laboratory and see what it can do. |
| *Silitzer* | OK! Let's go. |
| *Culver* | (after laboratory testing): Well what do you think, Mr. Silitzer? |
| *Silitzer* | It sure looks like it will work. Tell me a little about it. |

| | |
|---|---|
| *Culver* | CLEAR 191 is a little more expensive than the other product, but the expense is worth it. CLEAR 191 is safer for your employees to use— no dangerous fumes, no dangerous gases or erupting bubbles. Plus the phosphoric acid-based product will last longer than the hydrochloric acid-based product. |
| *Silitzer* | Just exactly how much is it? |
| *Culver* | Well, Mr. Silitzer, it is $435/drum including the all-poly drum. If you purchase 4 drums, we will give you a 4% discount, and if you want more than 4 drums, you will receive an additional 4% discount. Can I set you up with 8 drums? |
| *Silitzer* | Eight drums! I don't think I need that much. |
| *Culver* | Well, Mr. Silitzer, if you purchase 8 drums of CLEAR 191, this will be only 440 gallons in your 800-gallon tank. You need to be close to half-way in your tank for proper exposure for the steel. |
| *Silitzer* | Oh, I see. Well I think that I will order 8 drums. When can I expect them? |
| *Culver* | We have a truck coming down this way on Monday. Will that be soon enough? |
| *Silitzer* | Fine. (Phone rings) I'll see you later Brian, thanks a lot. |
| *Culver* | My pleasure. I'll see you in a week to check up on our new product. (Exit) |

### Discussion:

1. What close technique did Culver use? Why was the close so easy?
2. Could Culver have closed sooner? Used a trial close sooner?
3. How would you improve the sales presentation?

## Case 12–2 **Yarsinski Carpets**

The sales call takes place in Jack Yarsinski's office, which is located in the Yarsinski Carpets building in Dunwoody, Georgia. This is the second visit by Velma Starch, who is representing Just Carpets. In the first visit Mr. Yarsinski described the types of carpet he needed for his store. The company that Mr. Yarsinski used to buy from before this meeting had failed to meet the orders Mr. Yarsinski had placed. The orders they did fill were late arriving, causing bad relations with the customers. Mr. Yarsinski needs quality carpet at a reasonable price. He wants an up-to-date catalog to work with and order from. He also wants to work with a company that has a warehouse within a sixty-mile radius and can fulfill the orders on time.

Mr. Yarsinski's competition is Yang's Carpet. The quality of their carpet is not as good as Mr. Yarsinski's, but Yang's can fill their orders on schedule.

Mr. Yarsinski has heard of Just Carpet's excellent reputation. Just Carpets, located in downtown Atlanta, is a small organization that has been in operation only a few years. Mr. Yarsinski has done some background checks on Just Carpets and has heard only good things on the organization.

As the owner of Yarsinski Carpets, Jack has only to satisfy his qualifications for quality and standards. He has been in operation for fifteen years and has built an excellent reputation for himself and the store. Except for the past month's blunders, he hasn't had any major complaints.

The families living in Dunwoody are middle to upper middle class. They expect good service and quality merchandise and are willing to pay extra to receive this.

During their first visit, Mrs. Starch seems knowledgeable about her product and willing to work with Mr. Yarsinski to satisfy his needs. Even though they are still on a formal name basis, the atmosphere between the two is friendly. The second visit is to take place one week after the initial visit, on Wednesday at 9:00 A.M.

| | |
|---|---|
| *Starch* | Good morning, Mr. Yarsinski, how are you today? |
| *Yarsinski* | Hello, Mrs. Starch. I'm pretty good, but things could be better. |
| *Starch* | Yes, things could be better. But they could also be worse. Speaking of things being better, I brought that sample of the Temple Garden Line carpet we were talking last week. Here. Take a look at it (hands the sample to Mr. Yarsinski). You said you needed something in a plush, solid color that would also be durable, correct? |
| *Yarsinski* | It does have a nice color. But are you sure it will be durable? |

| | |
|---|---|
| *Starch* | You have hit on the strongest selling point of the Temple Garden line—durability. Temple Garden carpets are made of Antron III nylon fibers. This is the strongest carpet fiber made today. It is highly abrasion resistant, which means that even in high traffic areas it won't wear down. Do you carry any carpets with the Antron III fibers? |
| *Yarsinski* | No, not at the present time. |
| *Starch* | What are your customers' most common complaints concerning carpets? |
| *Yarsinski* | I would have to say static shock and stains are at the top of the list. |
| *Starch* | As you know, there is nothing so annoying as being shocked everytime you walk across your carpet and touch someone or something or having that first spill ruin your carpet. The Antron III fiber used in the Temple Garden line is double protected against static shock and stains. First, the fibers are processed with Scotchguard® to protect against stains, and this also helps reduce static shock. Next, the fibers are treated against shock via round conductive filaments that also help eliminate static shock. What do you think of our carpet line, Mr. Yarsinski? Do any of your carpet lines offer these features? |
| *Yarsinski* | These are exceptional features, and no, none of my lines have these features. |
| *Starch* | It is truly a superb line of carpet. If you will tell me what colors you prefer, we can get a shipment to you immediately. |
| *Yarsinski* | But won't the lighter colors show dirt and soiling easy? |
| *Starch* | No. The Antron III line is not deeply creviced, which allows it to be easily vacuumed. Plus the shape of the fibers allows light to scatter, thus minimizing the dulling effect of soil. All this adds to the lasting beauty of the carpet. |

| | |
|---|---|
| *Yarsinski* | Yes, and that's what people want, beauty and durability. |
| *Starch* | That's exactly what the Temple Garden line will give them. |
| *Yarsinski* | When is delivery usually made? |
| *Starch* | Our trucks run every Wednesday. But if you ever need a delivery before then, I'm sure a special delivery can be arranged. Now, how much would you like to order the first time? |
| *Yarsinski* | I'm not really sure that now is the time to buy. I'm not sure that I need a new carpet line. |
| *Starch* | On the contrary, I think I noticed some empty floor space up front as I came in. That empty space is costing you money. By placing the Temple Garden line in that space, it will become profitable. |
| *Yarsinski* | Speaking of profit, how much is your carpet? I had completely forgotten about price. You may have wasted a trip. |
| *Starch* | I don't think so. If I didn't think the Temple Garden line was what you needed or was too expensive a line for you, I wouldn't be here. I think that at $15.99 a square yard, the Temple Garden line is exactly what you need. |
| *Yarsinski* | So $15.99 a square yard is my cost, correct? |
| *Starch* | That's right. And if you will just sign right here, I'll arrange for your first shipment to be on the way. (Gets out her order pad) |
| *Yarsinski* | Well, it sounds good to me; hand it here. |
| *Starch* | I'll be back next week to help you set up some store promotions and to brief your sales staff on the selling points of the Temple Garden line of carpets. Thank you, Mr. Yarsinski, and have a good day. |

*Yarsinski*                    Thank you, Mrs. Starch, and I look forward to
                               your visit next week.

**Discussion:**

1. Evaluate Mrs. Starch's objection handling techniques. Could you give
   her some suggestions?
2. How could the client have taken offense from her techniques?
3. Rewrite the dialogue to show how using different sales techniques
   could be effective?

**Chapter Outline**

Customer Partnership
  Building Customer Loyalty

Follow-up Activities
  Dialogue Conclusion
  Preconsumptive Activities
  Postconsumptive Activities

Activities Following A "No Close"

Preclose Conclusions
  Analysis of Closing
  Timing of Close Activities

Using Follow-up Information

Sales Reports
  Quantitative Reports
  Qualitative Reports
  Retail Reports

## CHAPTER 13

# Postsales Activities: Strengthening the Relationship

**Learning Objectives**

After reading this material, you should be able to:

- Discuss the importance of the follow-up to the salesperson
- Understand the importance of providing servicing in the sale
- Differentiate between preconsumptive activities and postconsumptive activities following a sale
- Explain the follow-up when there has been no close and the importance of such follow-up
- Understand the importance of providing services after the sale
- Discuss how follow-up information is used in strategy formulation
- Recognize some quantitative sales reports and their use
- State the importance of qualitative reports
- Understand types of sales reports that may differ from those filed by other marketers.

## IN THE FIELD

*"If you try to scrimp, you end up having to spend more time supporting it. . . . Then they say bad things about you and your product."*

**Barry Fribush, President Bubbling Bath Spa and Tub Works Inc.**

Bubbling Bath placed 304th on the 1989 INC. 500 list of fastest growing private companies. Mr. Fribush, a former road manager for Motown groups such as the Temptations, Supremes, and Marvin Gaye, uses customer service as his competitive edge. Unable to afford splashy spot advertising, he realized the least expensive way to get customers was through word-of-mouth referrals. So from the start he makes sure a faulty spa does not get to the customer. "We test every spa *before* it gets out of here," Barry says. If customers have a complaint, Barry boasts of a four-hour response time without a full-time service staff. He even requires each service person to own a spa. "That way they'll know first hand what is likely to go wrong," says Barry. He estimates that 65 percent of the people who walk through his showroom door do so because he was recommended by a friend or neighbor. Mr. Fribush does relate a downside to service. "It has restricted our growth. We will only sell what we can support. At the moment I can't find enough good people to grow any faster." However his growth rate was 844 percent last year. It seems that service is selling at Bubbling Bath.

*Source:* Paul R. Brown, "For Your Valued Customer," *Inc.* (January 1990). Reprinted with permission from *Inc.* magazine, January 1990. © 1990 by Goldhirsh Group, Inc., 38 Commercial Warf, Boston, MA 02110.

Face-to-face interaction in the dialogue concludes with a sale, a commitment for another meeting, a "No" from a customer declining to buy the product and desiring no further meetings with the salesperson, or an exit with goodwill when a prospect's needs cannot be met. Activities stemming from these buyers' actions are generalized as *postsale*, or *follow-up*, activities. As shown in Figure 13–1, these activities are an important part of the customer–salesperson dialogue.

The importance of customer satisfaction is illustrated (see *In the Field*) by Bubbling Bath. However, not all companies and salespeople feel its importance. Studies in the late 1980s found that at least one third and possibly as many as two thirds of us have felt cheated during recent purchases.[1] One implication of this alarming statistic is that a great percentage of the population does not trust salespeople. Some salespeople are un-

**Figure 13–1**
*Postsales Activities* in the Customer–Salesperson Dialogue.

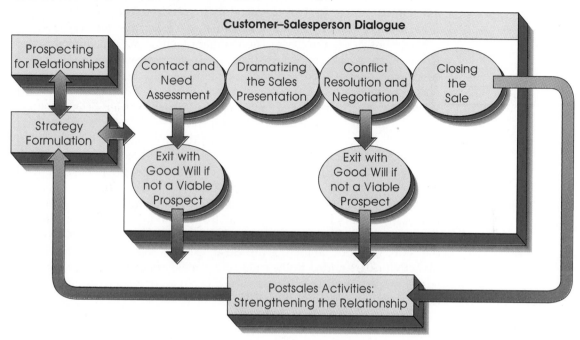

aware of this latent, hostile attitude. They perceive the attitude as "sales resistance" or buyers' remorse. **Buyers' remorse** occurs when a customer becomes dissatisfied after the purchase. With this mistaken view in mind, the salesperson may abandon the relationship approach and try persuasion to convince the customer to buy. The salesperson may or may not sell the product but has a better than average chance to create an even more hostile customer.

**buyers' remorse**

> The key is not the "Will to Win" . . . everybody has that. It is the "Will to *Prepare* to Win" that is important.
> **Bobby Knight, Indiana University Basketball coach**

The follow-up in a sale can provide a "checkpoint" for the salesperson. A **follow-up** is the process of providing services expected or promised after the sale. During the prepurchase evaluative process of determining which products are going to fulfill a customer's needs, the customer develops expectations concerning "the product." All aspects of the sale, including product performance, salesperson's attitude, price, delivery, service, and warranty are evaluated and purchased as a group of benefits

**follow-up**

called "the product." The customer considers "the product" the sum of all the benefits he or she will receive, even though some benefits per se are not a physical part of the product or service. After purchasing and using the product, the customer evaluates the benefits received and the expectations of the purchase. The resultant feelings, satisfaction or dissatisfaction, are a customer's measures of the *effectiveness* of the decision process.[2] Salespeople who provide service in a sale, that is, check on the satisfaction/dissatisfaction of customers, obtain an external evaluation of their own effectiveness. Lee Iacocca talks about Chrysler's customer satisfaction rate in *Partnerships.* A salesperson who looks forward to checking back with the customer is strengthening the relationship. Those who do not check back or who dread checking back with the customer probably sold the product with "arm twisting" or other improper persuasive techniques. "Why call back to get a complaint?" is their motto.

Salespeople who consider a sale to be complete when the customer signs the sales contract are far from reality. In building a relationship, getting a signature on the contract is only the first step in completing the sale. All action following the close becomes follow-up. These follow-up activities are added to the salesperson's experience (declarative knowledge) and are used to improve future evaluations of a customer's needs and the selling scripts that effectively satisfy those needs.

## Customer Partnership

*Follow-up* activities consist of all services necessary to complete the sale and to build goodwill. Making a self-evaluation of sales performance, writing sales reports, and adjusting future strategies are such activities.

## PARTNERSHIPS

*"GM is bigger. Ford is richer. But neither of them beats Chrysler when it comes to satisfying customers. Who says? You do. For three years in a row, Chrysler has had the highest customer satisfaction of any American car company. Not GM. Not Ford. Chrysler."*

**Lee Iacocca, Chairman, Chrysler Corp.**

*Source:* Paul R. Brown, "For You, Our Valued Customer," *Inc.* 11 (January 1990): 108.

As a control device, the follow-up checks customer satisfaction. Since relationship selling's primary goal is to sell "service," follow-up activities provide a twofold purpose: (1) measuring customer satisfaction and (2) providing information to help the salesperson to fulfill the needs of present and future customers. Problems in past presentations can be noted in self-evaluation, enabling the salesperson to correct future efforts.

Salespeople who fail to follow-up neglect the customers' feelings. They deprive themselves of feedback that helps them "fine tune" selling skills, which otherwise will inhibit their success. Successful salespeople develop customer loyalty for themselves rather than just toward their products.

## Building Customer Loyalty

The highest compliment a customer pays a salesperson is to insist on buying from that salesperson first. Such a customer has developed *customer loyalty*, that is, a strong relationship with a salesperson, and buys from others only after talking with the preferred representative. Customer loyalty of this strength plays a significant role in repeat purchasing and is called a **salesperson franchise.**

**salesperson
franchise**

### Salesperson Franchise

A *salesperson franchise* does not mean buyers purchase all they possibly can from one seller. Rather the term is used when a purchasing agent becomes heavily dependent on one seller. Few buying centers, however, rely on a single supplier for a particular good. For obvious reasons, to do so would put the buyer at risk should that supplier have a strike, fire, or other calamity. The supply would be interrupted. The purchasing agent would need to get new suppliers for goods quickly. Lacking experience with these new suppliers, this situation would be inefficient and threatening for the purchasing agent. Research conducted by Morgan Business Associates finds that only 45 percent of industrial distributors are heavily depended upon by their top 20 major accounts.[3] However, it is more efficient for salespeople to increase sales to current accounts instead of trying to increase market share by finding new accounts. As pointed out in *Success* magazine:

> It costs five times as much to attract a new customer as it
> does to maintain an established one.[4]

This salesperson franchise is enhanced by being available to the customers when the customer needs to see or talk with the salesperson, not just when the salesperson calls on the client. New electronic devices such as cellular

## TECHNOLOGY BULLETIN

### Pagers

For those suffering from Dick Tracy envy, Motorola recently announced the new 2-oz. Wrist Watch Pager (WWP). As the result of a joint venture between Motorola and Timex, it looks like a sleek, black, sports watch. It can receive signals in every Standard Metropolitan Statistical Area (SMSA). The WWP can receive and store up to six numeric and two tone messages. Caller's phone numbers are displayed on a LCD screen, and tones are as loud as belt-styled pagers. Also displayed are the time, day, and date of the messages. Like other pagers, there is an on/off feature that can screen out pages at inappropriate times.

*Source:* Bristol Voss, ``Sales Tools,'' *Sales and Marketing Management* 142 (November 1990): 106.

phones, portable fax machines, and pagers are common means of maintaining contact between buyers and sellers. The *Technology Bulletin* in this chapter illustrates a new product in this area.

### Building a Trust Bond

In a salesperson franchise situation, the salesperson remains prominent in the purchasing agent's mind and behavior. Maintaining the sale after a close strengthens the trust between them. Following through with promises made during the sale enhances the relationship. All salespeople need to create strong trust bonds to maintain ongoing relationships. Using follow-up activities helps them work toward this goal.

### Relationship Management

Salespeople who continue to build a trust bond with their clients must maintain the relationship just as they maintain a friendship. One slip or dishonest act can ruin years of a good relationship. When a customer's needs change and the salesperson is unaware of this situation, the account is generally lost to a competitor. More sales are lost from neglect (not maintaining the relationship) than for any other reason.[5]

## Follow-up Activities

Even in the best of circumstances—when there has been a close—the sale is not complete. The sale signals the beginning of a new task—customer service.

## Dialogue Conclusion

Different customers need different levels of service, and it is up to the sales representative to identify what is important to each person. Knowing this, the salesperson must pay adequate attention to these factors and keep the customer satisfied. Customer service includes **preconsumptive activities,** those services that take place before the product is consumed, such as delivery and payment, and **postconsumptive activities,** those services that come after the product is consumed.

**preconsumptive activities**
**postconsumptive activities**

## Preconsumptive Activities

Each sale will have its own *preconsumptive conditions* for delivery date, payment date, and perhaps a display set-up date. These preconsumptive conditions are part of the sale. To be of greatest service, the salesperson must follow an order's progress through processing and shipping until it reaches the customer's work area. This can be done in three steps:

1. Establish three files—an account file, a pending order file, and a follow-up file.
2. Make two copies of the customer's completed order form. File one copy in the account file and the other in the pending order file.
3. File orders by date, so that after a ship date the order copy is moved from the pending order file to the follow-up file.

Information from the follow-up file is used to follow through on all aspects of the sale, such as verifying correct pricing and billing, setting up displays, or perhaps rearranging stock. Following through with a sale demonstrates the salesperson's willingness to support the customer's needs, thereby building the salesperson's credibility. Follow-up mailings should include a business card. Richard Kerndt of Richmark Group, a consulting firm, has conducted polls that show that secretaries often file business cards for future reference.[6] Expediting an order; taking care of returns, allowances, and adjustments; as well as providing additional information are all customer services and are integral parts of the sale.

## Postconsumptive Activities

Representatives' *postconsumptive activities* determine who will be successful and who will stay mediocre. A salesperson using persuasive techniques to close a sale generally is reluctant to voluntarily check customer satisfaction. That type of salesperson usually prefers to sell to more people rather than contact past customers to see if they are happy with their

To the relationship seller, activities after the sale are just as important as the activities before the contract is signed. Making sure that your company delivers what you promised, when you promised it, requires that you track the order. You should be apprised of the order status before making a follow-up call.

purchase. They often express their feelings as: "Why ask for trouble! If they have a complaint, they will contact me. I use that time to sell more merchandise. That's what I get paid for."

The relationship salesperson makes sure the product fits the needs of the customer. Remember that follow-up activities, communications, and customer sensitivity are all highly valued attributes in top sellers, as shown in Table 13–1. Those categories are also the top-ranked attributes by purchasing agents in annual surveys since 1981.[7] However, a recent study by *Training and Development Journal* shows that salespeople did not perform well on any of these activities. Average sellers fail significantly to meet the expectations of their customers on all 10 of these attributes.[8]

**complaints**

The contention that dissatisfied customers will voice **complaints** if they are unhappy is supported by studies on customer satisfaction/dissatisfaction and complaint behavior. In fact, most studies on dissatisfied customers show that a typical dissatisfied customer tells 10 and often up to 20 other people but *does not* complain to the supplier or their salespeople. Of all dissatisfied customers surveyed, the number who actually lodged complaints varied from 10 percent to 70 percent.[9]

Customers who leave you are unhappy with you—and the unhappy customer shares their gripes with other people four or five times as frequently as happy customers share their joys of doing business with you, reports Eric Birch, Vice President of Office Systems Division, Nashua Corp.[10]

Table 13–1
**What Customers See In Ideal Sales Reps**

| Trait | Percentage* of All Respondents | |
|---|---|---|
| | *1988* | *1980–1987* |
| 1. Thoroughness and follow-through | 73 | 73 |
| 2. Willingness to fight for customer | 52 | 53 |
| 3. Willingness to go to bat for the buyer within the supplier firm | 51 | 51 |
| 4. Marketing knowledge and willingness to keep the buyer posted | 47 | 38 |
| 5. Imagination in meeting the buyer's needs | 28 | 25 |
| 6. Preparation for sales call | 17 | 18 |
| 7. Knowledge of buyer's product line | 13 | 15 |
| 8. Regularity of sales calls | 11 | 10 |
| 9. Diplomacy in dealing with operating departments | 5 | 12 |
| 10. Technical education | 3 | 5 |

*Note that percentages total 300 as respondents were asked to check three outstanding characteristics for their nominees.

Adapted from Somerby Dowst, "Buyers Give Top Honors to Quality Salespeople," *Purchasing* 91 (August 20, 1981): 65; and Somerby Dowst, "Good Salespeople Make the Difference," *Purchasing* 106 (February 23, 1989): 21. Reprinted by permission of Cahner Publishing.

Following through minimizes disgruntled customers.

A U.S. Office of Consumer Affairs (OCA) nationwide study of 2,500 households revealed these findings:

- "About one third of those questioned said they had one or more consumer problems in the last year.
- Seventy-five percent of all complaints were about the poor quality of products and services.
- The majority of the problems cited with automobiles and appliances involved poor service or lack of service.
- One sixth of the consumers questioned said they lost time at school or work trying to remedy problems with products or services.
- Respondents' average monetary loss was $142.
- A majority of the consumers said their first course of action in dealing with a poor product is to complain to the retailer who sold them the product.

- About 75 percent of consumers will complain if they have problems with a product costing $6 to $10. Ninety-five percent of consumers will complain if they have problems with a product costing between $500 and $1,000.
- Ten percent of consumers have complaints regarding products or services but do not follow up on them because they feel it is not worth the time or effort, they do not know how or where to complain, or they believe no one will care about the problem or bother to solve it."[11]

**positive word-of-mouth promotion**

Contacting customers after they have used the product allows salespeople to reinforce their advice and to correct any problems that may have occurred. One should not hesitate to follow up the sale. Some problems may be difficult to solve, but an attempt to correct the problem is better than neglecting a customer, who may tell friends what the seller did wrong. **Positive word-of-mouth promotion** is priceless; the testimony of a friend relating how helpful a seller was in solving a problem goes a long way in providing that person with new prospects. Satisfied customers are the best promotion, and losing customers is expensive. Remember it takes five times the effort, time, and money to attract new customers as it takes to hold old ones.[12]

## Activities Following A "No-Close"

**no-close activities**

Follow-up is necessary even when there has been no sale. The customer may want time to think about a purchase or may need additional information before making a decision. These conditions do not inhibit a sale; they merely postpone the decision. Thus, **no-close activities** are extremely important.

## Preclose Conclusions

The follow-up without a sale, like the follow-up after closing, requires action. Since there was no sale, one or more barriers to closing were present. Was the failure in the preclose due to poor client need assessment or were there flaws in the selling process?

## Analysis of Closing

Analyze the dialogue promptly after concluding the contact. What were the resistance signs that you were not able to overcome? Why did the

Follow-up is necessary even when there has been no sale. Indeed, getting complete and accurate follow-up information to a client as quickly as possible helps establish source credibility, and may enhance future sales opportunities.

client not buy? When did the client seem to indicate with nonverbal and verbal signs that a close was not possible? Was there a flaw in the selling procedure or in unsuccessfully addressing the client's needs? Record the positive and negative points about the dialogue in each step of the process. Before the future meeting, use these records to prepare a new, fresh presentation. Do not just "beef up" the old one. Learn from mistakes.[13]

## Timing of Close Activities

Sometimes misqualification of a prospect or inability to resolve conflict causes a salesperson to conclude the dialogue before reaching the closing stage—*preclose dialogue.* Exits in the contact and needs-assessment stage happen because the salesperson's techniques caused the prospect to be misqualified. For example, a doctor who purchases a computerized billing service is not a likely prospect for repurchasing business billing forms.

Exits also occur in the conflict resolution stage. Not all products fulfill the needs of all customers. Through product differentiation, manufacturers design a product to meet the needs of a specific target market. However, many people who fit the target market characteristics for the product do not always buy according to manufacturer predictions.

For example, Ford's Mustang was designed as an inexpensive sports car for recent college graduates and other people in their early 20s. However, professional people purchased the more expensive models as a second car. Although the product was successful, think of auto salespeople's frustration if they prospected only new college graduates!

If a product does not fit the customer's needs, it is better to keep an amiable relationship than to force the sale and have an unfulfilled customer. "The service industry often depends on cross selling and penetration to expand revenues," says Frank Dowd, sales management specialist for Towers Perrin. **Cross selling** occurs when different people in the same organization sell different specialized services, such as one person promotes mortgages, another trust services, and yet another is a loan manager. Effective cross selling depends on all the sellers working as a team to meet the clients' needs and keep them satisfied. Cross selling occurs mostly in the service industry.[14]

**cross selling**

In the preclose stage, it is often tempting to use persuasion to overcome a conflict or an objection. There is a feeling of power in persuading the customer to "your way of thinking." However, power means to dominate, lead, or coerce, rather than be co-equal, share, and reward. Who wants to be forced into a decision? That is how selling received its negative connotation. When need fulfillment is not possible or conflict cannot be resolved, conclude the dialogue! By all means, never make remarks that can be construed as sarcastic or demeaning, such as: "See if you can find a better price." "Ask your spouse? Who wears the pants in your family?" Prospects may not become customers, but they know plenty of other people. Negative word-of-mouth from prospects can hurt salespeople as much as complaints from disgruntled customers.

## Using Follow-up Information ▬▬▬▬▬

All information from either preclose exits or postclose exits becomes input into strategy formulation. This information is commonly called follow-up information.

Most behaviorists would call such input *experience* (declarative knowledge). It is experience, but it involves more than the word experience connotes. The feedback from preclose and postclose experiences becomes more than a flashback to a personal encounter; it becomes a good teacher on which new sales strategies are built.

**self-evaluation**

Follow-up information is composed of **self-evaluation** of all experiential processes. In the selling process, this self-evaluation makes it possible for sellers to correct errors and to reinforce success, thus increasing efficiency by perfecting one's style.

Effective self-evaluation occurs not only after a failure to close but also after a successful sale. Finding out why you were successful is just as important as finding out why you failed. Analyzing success reinforces the positive attributes that make a person successful. Reinforcing good habits is easier than reconstructing bad habits. Without correcting selling habits through self-evaluation, the salesperson would have no way to reformulate strategy for particular customers.

# Sales Reports

The **sales report** is the formal informational tool of the follow-up stage. Reports vary considerably from company to company. Nonretail salespeople have more reports to fill out than their retail counterparts. The main function of these formalized reports is to provide information needed by sales managers to organize, direct, control, and supervise salespeople's efforts. Many salespeople resent spending the time necessary to fill out the reports; they see it as a waste of productive selling time. As seen in Figure 13–2, the amount of time spent on paperwork is no small matter. On average the respondents in a survey of 10,000 sales representatives from 192 companies spent 10 percent of their time on paper work, 16 percent on account/service coordination (which includes reports), and 5 percent on internal meetings.[15] That is almost the equivalent of over two hours a day. It has been said that "the age-old problem of salespeople is that as your business increases, so does your paperwork."

Although most salespeople abhor filling out sales reports, these reports provide management with information concerning your clients and your accomplishments. With this standardized information, management can then facilitate your sales activities and help make you more successful.

## Quantitative Reports

Most companies ask sales representatives to send their supervisors weekly reports. Requirements vary, but **quantitative reports** typically include summaries of daily log sheets containing number of calls made, number of sales closed, number of sales not closed, and expenses incurred. A daily personal planner allows the salesperson to manage time effectively. Daily plans are usually summaried by weekly reports. An example of such a summary is the Activity and Earnings Report shown in Figure 13–3. This report can increase efficiency dramatically. Projected weekly reports allow the salesperson to plan even on a yearly basis. A person can rarely plan too much. The old adage "plan your work, work your plan" is worth remembering.

**sales reports**
**quantitative reports**

## Qualitative Reports

Periodically management will require salespeople to write qualitative reports. **Qualitative reports** help management personnel determine the overall view of what is happening. Such reports requested might concern

**qualitative reports**

## Figure 13–2
## How Salespeople Spend Their Time
*Source:* Reprinted with permission of MGC Distributors, Champaign, Illinois, 1989.

**Goal**

_____    _____
MONTH            DOLLARS

By using this goal sheet you'll be able to determine at the month's end your track record by using the formula shown below.

_____

### END OF MONTH SUMMARY

TOTAL A ÷ B = _____
        # Calls to get one presentation

TOTAL B ÷ C = _____
        # Presentations to sell one distiller

TOTAL A ÷ C = _____
        # Contacts to sell one distiller

TOTAL D – E = _____
              PROFIT (P)

_____

(P) ÷ A = _____
        Average earnings per call

(P) ÷ B = _____
        Average earnings per presentation

(P) ÷ C = _____
        Average earnings per sale

(P) ÷ F = _____
        Average earnings per hour

| | Contacts Made | Presentations Made | Distillers Sold | Dollar Sales | Dollar Cost | Hrs. Worked |
|---|---|---|---|---|---|---|
| 1 | | | | | | |
| 2 | | | | | | |
| 3 | | | | | | |
| 4 | | | | | | |
| 5 | | | | | | |
| 6 | | | | | | |
| 7 | | | | | | |
| 8 | | | | | | |
| 9 | | | | | | |
| 10 | | | | | | |
| 11 | | | | | | |
| 12 | | | | | | |
| 13 | | | | | | |
| 14 | | | | | | |
| 15 | | | | | | |
| 16 | | | | | | |
| 17 | | | | | | |
| 18 | | | | | | |
| 19 | | | | | | |
| 20 | | | | | | |
| 21 | | | | | | |
| 22 | | | | | | |
| 23 | | | | | | |
| 24 | | | | | | |
| 25 | | | | | | |
| 26 | | | | | | |
| 27 | | | | | | |
| 28 | | | | | | |
| 29 | | | | | | |
| 30 | | | | | | |
| 31 | | | | | | |
| TOTAL | | | | | | |
| | A | B | C | D | E | F |

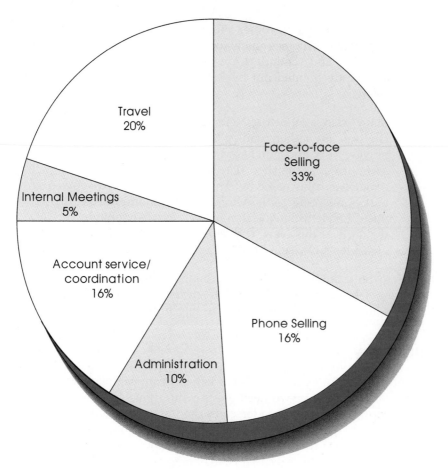

Figure 13–3
**Activities and Earn-
ings Report**
*Source:* Adapted from
William A. O'Connell,
and William Keenen, Jr.,
"The Things to Come,"
*Sales and Marketing
Management* 142 (Jan-
uary 1990): 39.

new product evaluation, new audiovisual presentations, informal credit
reports about an overdue account, or account summaries. Qualitative reports require the salesperson's perception and evaluation.

## Retail Reports

Retail selling, for the most part, requires less paperwork than other parts
of the profession. However, **retail reports** are important as retailers be-        **retail reports**
come more personalized and selective in meeting customers' needs. An
excellent example of personalized retail service comes from Neiman-
Marcus. Neiman-Marcus is internationally known for its quality merchandise and customer service that is based on the store's emphasis on keeping
good client records. Employees not only keep personalized records of past

purchases but also of a customer's future purchase needs. The Neiman-Marcus salesperson becomes an in-store consultant for each client. Letters, thank-you notes, and reminders are all used to satisfy a client's needs. This is most aptly pointed out by Richard Marcus, former chairman of Neiman-Marcus.

> Many years ago, before Neiman-Marcus had a Men's Division, my father, Stanley Marcus, visited a small shop in New York and purchased two suits. Almost a year later he returned to the shop. The salesperson not only remembered his name but knew his size and had some idea of his preferences. My father was so impressed with this clientele technique that he continued shopping regularly at this New York store until we developed our own Men's Division.[16]

By using the techniques outlined in this book and initial sales training, beginning salespeople will be able to develop similar customers—customers who will go out of their way to buy from their consultant.

## Summary

A customer service orientation is the key to relationships selling. Follow-up, coupled with extensive need assessment, transforms the philosophy from theory to reality and underscores the importance of the customer.

Salespeople can differentiate themselves from their persuasive counterparts at the follow-up stage of the selling process by a complete follow through after the sale, that is, making sure the customer is satisfied.

Another aspect of follow-up is analyzing all feedback from the sales dialogue, even when there has been no sale. Feedback permits self-evaluation of personal performance, a step that is equally important when the presentation progresses to a close and when it does not. Self-evaluation after closing a sale reinforces successful sales techniques. When done after an unsuccessful close, self-evaluation can point to bad habits that need correcting.

A third element of follow-up is completion of sales reports. Reports, though time consuming, supply sales managers with essential information and enable salespeople to better plan and evaluate their work.

> *Service.* Everybody talks about it, but not too many people are happy about it. Yet quality service is becoming more and more important in business today. Service is a critical factor for survival—the competitive edge in many organizations.
>
> **Karl Albrect, President Service America Corporation**[17]

# Key Terms

buyers' remorse
follow-up
salesperson franchise
preconsumptive activities
postconsumptive activities
complaints
positive word-of-mouth
   promotion

no-close activities
cross selling
self-evaluation
sales report
quantitative reports
qualitative reports
retail reports

# Discussion Questions

1. Compare and contrast the importance of the follow-up to the relationship and persuasive selling approach.

2. How can a salesperson improve customer service before the sale is made?

3. What is a customer franchise, and why is it important to a salesperson?

4. What activities should a salesperson perform after the sale? Which are quantitative and which are qualitative?

5. Explain the importance of good word-of-mouth promotion for a salesperson.

6. "I don't get paid for handling complaints. I get paid a commission for what I sell. Therefore, I'm not about to initiate a follow-up call." What does this statement tell you about a salesperson?

7. How can follow-up information influence a salesperson's next call on the customer? Illustrate with an example.

8. Why do salespeople have to spend so much time filling out so many reports?

9. The sales manager of your company wants to decrease each salesperson's territory from having the whole state as one's territory to having only half the state. This will add more salespeople and will allow each to call on customers more often. It has drawbacks too. Write a qualitative report objectively setting forth your position.

10. Write a letter that could be used by your company—a large department store—to welcome new customers and to tell them about your facilities, services, hours, policies, etc.

# Decision Crossroads: Ethical Issues

Mike Smartson is a salesman for D. B. Stone Home Improvement Co. He sold a screened room to Tom and Mary Haggard. Because of the expense, they chose the Model 2731 Cool Breeze Room. It was installed three days ago. Mike is making a follow-up visit to see if they are satisfied.

| | |
|---|---|
| *Mike* | Hello, Tom. How are you and Mary getting along? |
| *Tom* | Fine. How are you doing? Come on in. We're glad to see you. |
| *Mike* | Hi, Mrs. Haggard. |
| *Mary* | Hello. Would you care for a cup of coffee? |
| *Mike* | No thank you. But I would like to see your room. |
| *Mary* | We are well pleased. It is so comfortable. |
| *Mike* | Well, that's exactly what I want to hear. Say, looks like the installers did a nice job. |
| *Tom* | We think so, too. They built it just as you said they would, maybe even a bit better. |
| *Mike* | They certainly do good work. We want to be proud of every installation, just like you are of this one. Mrs. Haggard, since you mentioned how comfortable the room was, how would you feel if I could make it just a little nicer for you? |
| *Mary* | That would be great, but how? |
| *Mike* | Since this is the time of year when evenings are beginning to cool, let me show you the windows we install in these rooms. They will add about three months available to you on a yearly basis to spend enjoying the room. Most folks put them in around this time of year. |
| *Tom* | I remember you showing them to us before. How much do they cost? |

| | |
|---|---|
| *Mike* | Not much at all . . . (Salesman pulls out his samples and begins a presentation). |

**Discussion:**

1. Should the salesman sell more merchandise on a follow-up call?
2. Tom and Mary really liked the windows the first time, but felt they were too expensive. Should Mike push to close on the windows? (They will add only $10 a month to their affordable payments of $83.75 for 60 months.)
3. Tom and Mary want to wait until next year to buy the windows, "when we have the balance paid down some," said Tom. What would you say to Tom?

## Case 13–1  **The Stereo Shop**

A college student, Gary Wood, bought a Pioneer 350 SL belt-driven turntable for a sale price of *$116* and began making layaway payments. To date he has made two payments totaling $70. Now, instead of making two or three more payments as planned, Gary wants to pay the balance and get the stereo in time for his graduation party. Since the purchase was made on a standing-room-only close (SRO), Gary assumed his turntable was the last Pioneer 350 left in the store. Unfortunately when he goes into the store to finish the payments and pick up his turntable, he finds out that the turntable has been either lost, stolen, or sold to another customer.

| | |
|---|---|
| *Gary* | (Walks in and looks for the salesman who served him.) Mr. Smith, how are you doing today? |
| *Smith* | (Busy reading some information on new products.) Pretty good. Just going over some of our newest lines of preamps. Would you be interested in looking at a model? |
| *Gary* | (Laughing.) No, no, I'm already spending too much money on this turntable. I just came in to finish the payments and pick it up. |
| *Smith* | (Stutters and hesitates.) Oh, ah, you are, huh? Why all the payments at once? |
| *Gary* | Well, I've been working overtime to get the money for the turntable. I want to have it before graduation so I can throw a big party. |

| | |
|---|---|
| *Smith* | (Looking worried.) A big party, huh. Well, I can understand that. Just a minute, and I'll go get the turntable for you. What's your name again? |
| *Gary* | (Sighing.) Gary Wood. |
| *Smith* | (After several minutes.) Gary, I hate to tell you this, but I can't find your turntable. |
| *Gary* | What do you mean you can't find it? It was here three weeks ago when you had it on sale. |
| *Smith* | I can't understand it. Someone must have misplaced it or something. I'll tell you what. You come back in a week or two and I'm sure we will have it by then. |
| *Gary* | Two weeks! What good is that going to do me? I graduate this Saturday, and I need it for my party. |
| *Smith* | Gary, I'm sorry. But there is no way I can have it by this Saturday. I'll tell you what. I can give you the 450 SL Direct Drive. It costs a little more, but it won't be any problem switching the payments over to this model. |
| *Gary* | Look, I can hardly afford the 350 Belt Drive, and besides, with my equipment I don't need that quality turntable. |
| *Smith* | For an extra $50, it is a much better turntable. And when you break down the payments, it will only take you two or three more weeks. |
| *Gary* | No. That is too much. Besides, I need it this weekend. |
| *Smith* | Well, how about the Pioneer 250? It costs less and you could have it right away. |
| *Gary* | The Pioneer 250 is a cheap model. It would break down in a year or two. |
| *Smith* | I have to disagree, Gary. The Pioneer 250 has a two-year guarantee and is one of our best-selling models. If anything did go wrong, our service department would fix it right away. |

| | |
|---|---|
| *Gary* | Look. The 250 isn't fully automatic, doesn't come with the blue-tip diamond cartridge, and wouldn't look good with my existing equipment. |
| *Smith* | Yes. I agree the 250 doesn't have all of the features of the 350, but you would save money and get it just in time for your graduation party. |
| *Gary* | (Getting angry.) Listen, I want to know what happened to my turntable. All along you have acted as though you knew it wasn't here. |
| *Smith* | I'll find out just as soon as possible. It's probably just misplaced somewhere in back. |
| *Gary* | Misplaced (shaking head). I don't believe it. I bet you sold it to someone for the regular price and hoped you could get a model before I paid it off. |
| *Smith* | Why do you feel this way? |
| *Gary* | First, you acted bothered because I wanted to pay off the turntable all at once; then you tried to sell me a more expensive model; then you tried to sell me a cheaper model. You don't care about what I want; you just want another sale to make your commission. |
| *Smith* | Gary. I do want to see that you get what you want. But I'm limited to what I can do. What would be fair to you? |
| *Gary* | How about giving me the 450 SL Direct Drive for the same price as the 350 SL Belt Drive? |
| *Smith* | I'm afraid that wouldn't be possible. I could take off maybe $20, but not the entire $50. |
| *Gary* | Sorry. An extra $30 is too much for me to pay right now. |
| *Smith* | I could set you up with a cassette recorder for about the same amount. The CL 100 is on sale this week. |
| *Gary* | I don't have any use for a cassette recorder. I don't even have any tapes. And besides, I know I can't get a decent tape recorder for under $200. |
| *Smith* | Gary, would you eventually like to build up your stereo equipment into a total system? |

| | |
|---|---|
| *Gary* | Yeah. |
| *Smith* | And don't you think that the CL 100 cassette recorder or the 450 SL Direct Drive Turntable would add quality and variety to your entire stereo system? |
| *Gary* | Yes, I guess it could. |
| *Smith* | Which one would you prefer, the cassette recorder or the turntable? |
| *Gary* | Neither one. I want my money back. |
| *Smith* | Gary, you don't have to do anything that drastic. Give me a day or two and I'll see if I can't find you another 350 Belt Drive. |
| *Gary* | What if you can't get one before Saturday? |
| *Smith* | If I can't get one before Saturday, then I'll give you the 450 Direct Drive for the same price. |
| *Gary* | No. I don't think so. I have already spent a lot of time coming back and forth and arguing with you. |
| *Smith* | Gary, you can't beat an offer like this. A chance to get our best turntable for the price of the 350 Belt Drive. This is probably the only chance you'll ever have to get such a good deal on a turntable. |
| *Gary* | Why didn't you make me this offer earlier? |
| *Smith* | Well, ah, I didn't realize how difficult it would be for you not to have your turntable by this Saturday. |
| *Gary* | (Shaking his head.) I've been telling you this since I arrived. |
| *Smith* | Gary, I'm sure that the fully automatic direct drive, all-chrome turntable would be to your liking. With the blue-tip diamond cartridge and the slashed price, I know you will be satisfied. |
| *Gary* | (Disgusted.) So now you're offering me the 450 SL Direct Drive without even trying to find the 350 Belt Drive? |
| *Smith* | Ah, yes, I'll go get one for you right now. |

| | |
|---|---|
| *Gary* | Forget it. I don't want any favors from a swindler. Give me my money back. |
| *Smith* | I'm sure we can come to some agreement. |
| *Gary* | Give me my money, now! |

**Discussion:**

1. How could Mr. Smith have gained more control of the situation?
2. How did Mr. Smith handle the objections?
3. How could Mr. Smith have handled the trial closes better?

## Case 13-2  **Street's Outdoor Outlet**

Street's Outdoor Outlet is a backpacking, skiing, and canoeing specialty store located in Indianapolis, Indiana. Megan Carter, a well-known resident of Indianapolis, has bought several items from Street's store but not in the last couple of years because of an unpleasant experience. Carter had purchased a Gore-Tex rain jacket that leaked in the seams, which they are guaranteed not to do. Upon returning it, Chris Becker, the salesman, promised a replacement within two weeks, but Carter didn't receive one for four weeks.

Megan Carter is planning a trip to the North Cascades, Washington, in a couple of weeks and needs to rent a backpack. Megan is hesitant about Street's Outdoor Outlet but goes there anyway. Upon entering the store, Megan intends only to rent a pack and be on her way.

| | |
|---|---|
| *Megan* | (Noticing Chris Becker behind the counter.) Hi, Mr. Becker. How ya' been? |
| *Becker* | (Noticing Megan.) Oh, just fine. Yourself? |
| *Megan* | (Joyfully.) Couldn't be better. I'm going to the North Cascades in a couple of weeks, so I'll need to rent a pack. |
| *Becker* | (Excitedly.) Is that right? I just got back from a trip out there a couple of weeks ago. |
| *Megan* | (Questioning.) Where about did you go? |
| *Becker* | (Laughing.) Well, we started out at the North end, the Waterville entrance, then hiked for a few days until we ran into a lot of snow. So we had to turn around and come back the same way. We |

decided we would wait a day to see if the snow would stop, and it did. So we went back up and stayed for two weeks. (Recalling the jacket experience, Chris thinks of a deal he could give her on a new pack, since he is afraid that Megan has been spreading the word about what happened.)

*Megan*        (Surprised.) We're staying out at Waterville, too!

*Becker*       Sure hope the weather holds out for you.

*Megan*        (Seriously.) So what do you have in rental packs?

*Becker*       When are you going to buy yourself a pack?

*Megan*        (Without hesitation.) I don't have the money for one. Especially when I would only use it a couple of times a year.

*Becker*       (Grabbing a piece of paper and pencil.) Let me show you something. You have been spending $20 each time you rent a pack. And won't you be making more trips in the future?

*Megan*        Oh, yes.

*Becker*       Let's say you make five more trips in the future. That would be $20 × 5; $100 you'll be wasting.

*Megan*        (Knowing what he's getting at.) One hundred dollars is too much money for me to let go at one time.

*Becker*       You can make payments on it over a period of time.

*Megan*        (Negatively.) No, I hate credit.

*Becker*       (Not giving up.) When you're not using it you can rent it out. Then after about five rentals you'll have your $100 back.

*Megan*        (Hesitating.) I don't know. I think it will be hard for me to find people to rent it to.

| | |
|---|---|
| *Becker* | (Walking over and picking up a backpack.) Have you seen the new Coleman Peak I backpack? |
| *Megan* | (Showing interest.) I've heard about their new harness system, but I don't know if it has really been tested. |
| *Becker* | (Pulling out a consumer guide.) Look right here. It was voted the best pack over all. |
| *Megan* | (Questioning.) Do I really need a harness system like that? |
| *Becker* | (Putting the pack on her.) Here. Let me show you the difference. |
| *Megan* | Yeah, it feels real good. I don't know about Coleman. All they make is camping equipment. |
| *Becker* | Exactly. All they do make is camping equipment, so that they can spend all their research dollars and time making the best equipment possible. |
| *Megan* | (Doubting.) But do you really think Coleman makes a good backpack? |
| *Becker* | Do you know Mr. Breiner? (Megan, nodding.) He bought a Coleman pack last year and has used it for several trips and loves it. |
| *Megan* | What about warranties? Does it have one? |
| *Becker* | Oh yes, five years on the frame and one year on everything else. |
| *Megan* | How much do these packs cost? |
| *Becker* | Well, if you purchase it before tomorrow I'll give you a 10 percent discount off the $99 list price. |
| *Megan* | I couldn't have the money until next week. |
| *Becker* | (Thinking it over and realizing that this sale would lead to a good relationship with Megan and in turn would lead to future sales.) OK, Megan. I'll continue the discount until you're ready. How does that sound? |

| | |
|---|---|
| *Megan* | (Reaching out her hand.) Sounds great, Chris. We'll see you next week then. |
| *Becker* | All right. Take care. |

**Discussion:**

1. Since Megan is a former customer who has not been in the store in the last two years, what should Becker have done?
2. After Megan's new purchase, what should Becker do to keep Megan as a customer?
3. Write a plan for Becker's salespeople to follow to ensure customer satisfaction.

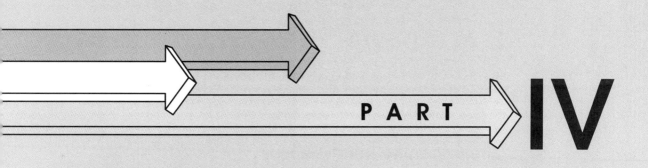

# PART IV

# Strengthening Relationships

Earlier parts of this text examined a historical view of selling, selling skills, and the selling process itself. But what comes next? A career is more than just performing the actual job. The final part of the text examines relationships beyond the customer–salesperson dialogue.

> Every relationship is important because you never know when you're going to meet these people later in your career. You may meet them at the first-line level right now, but in four or five years, they might be middle managers. Another ten years, they might be upper-middle management or higher. They may go from influencer to key decision maker. It's important to treat everybody with equal respect and courtesy. It's also important to have the same needs and problem-solving orientation with every client you meet.
> **Don Walker—Wilson Learning Corporation**[1]

Part IV examines building quality relationships with yourself, with your company, and with society through legal and ethical behavior, time management, and sales management. Looking beyond the dialogue, salespeople should be the best they can be, not just ``another salesperson''. Part IV concludes with a brief examination of sales management for those who may wish to move into management later in their careers.

**Chapter Outline**

Developing Personal Characteristics
External Indicators
Internal Indicators

## CHAPTER 14

# Building Quality Relationships

**Learning Objectives**

After reading this chapter, you should be able to:

- Define the elements of sales motivation
- Compare and contrast the external and internal indicators of a quality relationship with yourself
- Recognize at least five personality traits of salespeople
- Develop a personality profile for a successful salesperson
- Analyze yourself to see where your motivation may be strong or may need to be improved
- Develop a motivational profile of success for yourself.

## IN THE FIELD

*"The key to success in business-to-business selling is maintaining the personal touch."*

**Kathy Serfilippi, sales representative for American Airlines**

By building relationships with some 300 travel agents, Kathy has been able to excel at American. "At first I thought this would be an easy job because I figured everyone likes American as much as I do," she says. "Then I learned that you have to ask for the business. You just don't drop in and say 'Hi, how're you doing?' "

To accomplish her goals, she is in continual training and re-training, which means that every year she attends 10 seminars that last a day or longer and that emphasize motivation and personal growth. Usually you don't get the order by just asking once. "But I'm afraid to go back and ask again," says Kathy. You use your experience and training to pick yourself up when you feel rejected.

*Source:* Martin Everett, "Sellin's New Breed: Smart and Feisty," *Sales and Marketing Management* 141 (October 1989): 61–62.

Managing relationships for our purposes is the planned, goal-oriented interaction between buyers and sellers. Effective relationships are dependent upon developing the personal characteristics of similarity and expertise. These qualities as well as the inherent qualities of relationship selling are discussed in this chapter.

> You have no idea what a tremendous person you can be if you only believe in yourself.
>
> **Robert H. Schuller**

**contact intensity**

**mutual disclosure**

**cooperative intentions**

Relationships are built on selling behaviors that include **contact intensity** (the number of contacts between buyer and seller[2]), an environment of mutual disclosure, and cooperative intentions.[3] An environment of **mutual disclosure** establishes and maintains a climate where buyer and seller share critical business information to solve a mutual, complex problem. **Cooperative intentions** is the behavior that depends on cooperation rather than competition.[4] However, the quality of these relationships is established over a longer term, determined by the trust placed in the salesperson,[5] and depends on satisfaction with the salesperson.[6] Salespeople with one or two years of experience begin to settle in and become established and comfortable in the job. Also they may begin to concentrate on the sales of products rather than on the quality of the relationships. These bad habits often result in nonproductive sales periods called **sales slumps.**[7] When facing intense competitive situations, like Kathy Serifilippi (see *In the Field*), without proper training, relationships can weaken and develop problems. These problems are often cured with a prescription of sales **refresher training** focusing on reinforcing selling skills and improving salespeople's attributes of similarity and expertise.[8]

    *Refresher training* consists of heavy emphasis on improving sales techniques, developing attributes of **similarity** (building empathy, likeability, and perseverance), and **expertise** (building confidence and motivation and learning how to handle rejection). Such attributes enhance quality relationships because they increase trust and satisfaction. Refresher training is meant to correct bad habits and to encourage more "closings" through improved selling techniques. Initial sales training, as you remember, concentrated on developing skills to enhance contact intensity, mutual disclosure, and cooperative intentions. This chapter examines how sellers build quality relationships with themselves.

**sales slumps**

**refresher training**

**similarity**
**expertise**

## Developing Personal Characteristics ▬▬▬▬

Success depends in part upon each individual's attributes and their implementation in a compatible environment. For the most part, you determine your own success. **Success** may be defined as the achievement of one's ultimate goal, which gives to each individual a high level of personal satisfaction. Too often success is equated with wealth or fame. However, many people agree with Schuller's quote. Success is a measurement of your relationships with yourself and with your world. Thus you must set your own success goal. If someone else defines your goals, you may not be satisfied when you reach those goals. For example, if your father wants you to be the sales manager of a large manufacturing firm five years after you graduate from college, you may not be happy even if you reach that goal. Your personal goals may be top sales honors, money, fame, self-worth, personal dignity, or contentment. Only *your* definition of prospective attainments will give you satisfactory personal growth and success.

**success**

    Your criteria for success change over time. When in college, success may have been walking across the stage to get your diploma or getting a job upon graduation. In your first job, success may have been making $30,000 or $35,000 a year. Later in your career, your goals may have been personal satisfaction, work with charities, and feelings of self-worth. Since goals change as you change, the only definitive presumption that can be made is that you are motivated to succeed and that your motivation is apparent to others through external and internal indicators of a quality relationship with yourself. External indicators center around empathy, en-

**personality
handling rejection**

thusiasm, and likeability, while internal indicators are self-confidence, **personality,** and **handling rejection.**[9] These indicators of a quality relationship are highlighted in Figure 14–1.

## External Indicators

**external indicators**

Each of the **external indicators** (empathy, enthusiasm, and likeability) is important to salespeople as they work daily building relationships toward a successful career.

### Empathy

**empathy**

The quality of a relationship has been judged by the amount of empathy shown toward others' problems. **Empathy,** at a general level, is the reac-

Figure 14–1
**Indicators of a Quality Relationship**

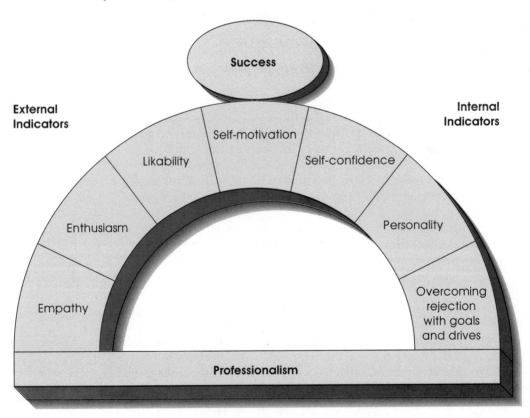

tions of individuals to the observed experiences of other individuals.[10] Davis distinguishes four types of empathy: (1) perspective taking, (2) fantasy, (3) empathetic concerns, and (4) personal distress.[11] Relationship selling relates to perspective taking and empathetic concerns, whereas personal empathy deals with fantasy and personal distress. Focusing on the fantasies of our distress leads to poor relationships with ourselves and with buyers. Therefore when talking about relationships with ourselves, we must be empathetic toward our own condition in the same way that we are empathetic toward buyers' problems with perspective taking and concern. Seeing our problems as outsiders see them provides additional perspective not available in any other way.

### Enthusiasm

Another evidence of a quality relationship is enthusiasm.[12] As we see often on the nightly news, a high degree of apathy exists in modern society. The opposite of apathy is **enthusiasm,** which is intense or eager interest, zeal, or fervor. We say that those people who lack enthusiasm are not really living at all, merely existing. They are unhappy and apathetic, failing rather than succeeding, lacking dynamic motivation—in other words, they are short on enthusiasm.[13] Alfred Krebs, proprietor of a Swiss hotel, once said, "There can be no success without enthusiasm. The secret of a full life is lots of enthusiasm, the kind that keeps you fighting and winning over all obstacles—and enjoying every minute of it."[14]

    You will find that nothing creates interest, stimulates emotions, and promotes action more effectively than the infectious quality of enthusiasm. If you are not excited about yourself and your products, then how can your customer be enthusiastic about them? Frank Bettger, in his book *How I Raised Myself from Failure to Success in Selling,* strongly and clearly makes that point:

> It [enthusiasm] will help you overcome fear, become more
> successful in business, make you more money, enjoy a
> healthier, richer, and happier life. When can you begin?
> Right now. Just say to yourself, "This is one thing I can
> do." How can you begin? There is just one rule: to become
> enthusiastic.[15]

    An unenthusiastic seller is just another salesperson. With the magic ingredient of enthusiasm, you bubble with life and are more likely to become a successful, professional salesperson.[16]

**enthusiasm**

### Likeability

Success is easier for people who are **likeable** (have a positive attitude). People like being associated with others who have a positive attitude. A

**likeable**

**positive attitude**

**positive attitude,** according to Jack Zufelt, sales trainer, is "that frame of mind that allows you to accomplish whatever you want because you know that you can create the opportunity and make it happen."[17] Most often thinking positively inspires dedication to one's job. If you think you can master a particularly hard task, then it may be possible. If you think you can't, it becomes impossible.[18]

A positive attitude for selling is then built on a belief in the product, a belief in the company, and a belief in self. Success attitudes leave no place in the seller's life for excuses that undermine selling effectiveness. Excuses for poor performance or nonperformance are negative traps that unsuspecting salespeople can fall into easily.

> I have been driven many times to my knees by the
> overwhelming conviction that I had nowhere to go. My
> own wisdom, and that of all about me, seemed insufficient
> for the day.
>
> **Abraham Lincoln**

The world can see the quality of our relationship with ourselves by our external signs of empathy, enthusiasm, and likeability. These external evidences, however, are based on internal aspects of motivation that are also discussed in sales training programs.

In a job where the majority of the contacts may say "no," it is necessary to keep a positive attitude. Continual training helps build product knowledge, positive attitude, and self-confidence.

## Internal Indicators

Internal indicators are more nebulous than the external signs, yet they all work together for the achievement of sales goals. **Internal indicators** consist of handling rejection with goals and drives, personality, and self-confidence. Those inner feelings, values, and motives spur the person into action, as shown in Figure 14–1. Since each is a part of the other, it is almost impossible to discuss them separately. For example, **self-confidence** depends on **goals** and **drives,** and goals and drives depend on self-confidence. For clarity's sake only, we will discuss each as a distinct entity of one's internal motivation.

**internal indicators**

**self-confidence**
**goals**
**drives**

### Overcoming Rejection

Most buyers are not overly enthusiastic about a salesperson's visit, and many salespeople take this as a lack of enthusiasm. They feel rejected when buyers say "no." Rejection is best handled with personal goal setting, drives to achieve these goals, and a positive attitude. Goals tell us where we want to go, and *drives* are those desires that force us toward the goals. A *goal* is a specific purpose that guides our actions. After all, we have to know where we are going (goal) before we can know how to get there (**goal achievement**).[19] Once we set realistic and obtainable goals, we will be able to break those goals down into monthly, weekly, and daily

**goal achievement**

## PARTNERSHIPS

Lane Nemeth recently issued herself a challenge, saying that she wants to head a billion-dollar corporation before she dies. The thought probably had not occurred to her when she started a toy distribution company in her garage near San Francisco in 1977.

Acting on a personal need, she discovered that thousands of other people had that same need—retail stores did not carry quality educational toys. That became her mission—to get those well-designed toys into the hands of people who wanted them. Borrowing distribution ideas from Tupperware and Avon, Discovery Toys went to people's homes. There parents could not only examine the products but also, through demonstrations, learn how to use the toy with their children. Starting with three salespeople and no advertising, Discovery Toys went from sales of $273,600 in the first year to more than $34 million in 1984. Lane today is well on her way to meeting her goal.

*Source:* Charles Garfield, Peak Performers: *The New Heroes of American Business* (New York: Avon Publishers, 1986), 85.

objectives. Dennis Waitley, in *Seeds of Greatness*, states that "The reason so many individuals fail to achieve their goals in life is that they never really set them in the first place."[20]

**quotas**

Goals are often imposed upon the salesperson by the company in the form of quotas.[21] **Quotas** are goals expressed as dollars of sales, units of sales, number of customer calls, or number of demonstrations per time unit. These externally applied goals provide a forced direction toward which a salesperson aims.

Other company forces that influence sales goals within the firm are the accountants with collections, production people with deliveries, and research and development with suggestions for new products. External sales goal setting is generally based on a review of past efforts and may be set on such things as (1) cost and profit per call; (2) number of calls each day; (3) new account calls; (4) number of presentations made; (5) number of closes; and (6) last year's goals.

Although externally administered goals are stimulating, having internally precipitated goals is more effective. Goals that you adopt internally as your personal goals are strong motivating forces, since internal goals force a self-appraisal. To make the personal goal more attainable, a salesperson may break the monthly or yearly quota into number of calls per day, the number of demonstrations a day, or the number of hours worked each day. For example, a John Deere Corporation salesperson might set a quota of working eight hours a day or selling ten pieces of equipment a day. If the John Deere salesperson sells ten items in four hours, the incentive goal to work the additional four hours would remain, even though the unit sales goal has been met. Perhaps the hourly working goal would help to motivate the John Deere salesperson to set a new personal sales record rather than to quit working after the successful four hours. Likewise, if the salesperson worked the minimum eight hours and made only one sale, the second goal category might motivate the salesperson to make additional sales calls to accomplish both goals.

**goal achievers**

Salespeople who internally set goals above and beyond the company's goals are generally **goal achievers.** David McClelland describes four insights that determine the intensity of one's achievement motivation. They are as follows:

1. *The level of achievement aspiration* is relative to the actual achievement. The well-motivated person is constantly seeking to do more and to do it better, whereas the less-motivated person either has "pie-in-the-sky" aspirations (unrealistically optimistic goals) or the opposite—goals that fall short of the acceptable level of achievement.[22]
2. *Aspirations are self-generating.* Each goal achieved begets another goal. Thus the well-motivated person becomes a goal achiever and has the initiative to set additional goals.[23]
3. *Goal flexibility is a necessity.* The well-motivated person knows when to quit and when to persist. Moreover, efforts can be redirected toward

reaching obtainable goals rather than at aiming inflexibly at unreachable goals.

4. *Goals are mutually enhancing.* Aspirations form a compatible package free from conflicting goals such as maximizing income along with concern. Personal goals and company goals are congruent.[24]

      People fail because of goal conflict. **Goal conflict** occurs when goals of the individual and others are not compatible. To avoid this conflict, goals must be prioritized. Achieving one's goals requires making sacrifices of time and efforts, and the price (amount of sacrifice of time and effort) required to meet some goals may be too high. Therefore prioritizing and predetermining the price one is willing to pay will help to minimize goal conflict.

      Goal conflict can also occur because of changes in career direction, or **role conflict.** Commonly the new college graduate sets earning money as a goal. After having achieved a comfortable living from a sales career, this same person will often express happiness as the most desired goal.[25] A conflict between the role management wants you to play and how you see the role is called **role ambiguity.**[26] These uncertainties about others' expectations cause role conflict and stress, which nip at sales performance.[27]

      Set realistic goals and objectives to minimize conflict. Do you remember the story of *Alice in Wonderland* by Lewis Carroll? One day Alice came to a fork in the road and spotted the Cheshire Cat sitting in the tree.

**goal conflict**

**role conflict**

**role ambiguity**

Most salespeople have several roles, such as salesperson, spouse, father, or mother. Conflicts between each role's requirements can cause frustration, stress, and negative attitudes.

"Which road do I take, Cat?" was Alice's question. His response was, "Where do you want to go?" "I don't know," Alice replied. "Then," said the cat, "it really doesn't matter!"[28] However, unlike Alice, we *can* determine where we are going by listing specific activities to attain those goals. Figure 14–2 should help you.

Christopher Columbus provides an example of success in goal setting. Five areas in which Columbus excelled brought about his success in life. Columbus (1) set a goal; (2) taught himself what he needed to know to do it right; (3) overcame every obstacle that kept him from attempting to achieve his goals in life; (4) had determination and perseverance to keep going even though nobody believed him; and (5) rose above the discouraging remarks and actions of other people.[29]

## Personality

All the attributes that distinguish you as a person make up your personality. A successful sales personality can be shown by being consistently well above average in appearance, dress, speech and voice, poise, and interests. However, the myth that to be a successful salesperson you have to be a back-slapping, hand-shaking, fast-talking, competitive negotiator is untrue. There is no one "right" personality profile for a successful salesperson. There are, however, certain personality traits that correlate with successful selling.[30] Some positive personality traits for a salesperson are discussed below.

*Social intelligence and tact* are important. Since selling is interacting, it is imperative for a salesperson to have the ability to say or to do the right things in a social situation, thus facilitating communication. Tact is founded on sincerity and is built on a genuine liking of others.

Sellers need the *ability to think fast.* Quick wit is more important than high intelligence in most selling positions. Having the ability to "think on your feet" during a presentation is important if the seller is to adapt effectively to the audience. It does very little good to think of what you should have said an hour after the call has concluded.

Customers expect *dependability and determination.* The seller can be relied upon to do what was promised, since one's credibility is built on dependability. If you promised the product by the 23rd of the month, you must make sure it is there by the 23rd. Determination is often seen as persistence, tenacity, mental toughness, or "bulldoggedness." This trait describes the person who refuses to allow adversity or failure to affect the level of performance. Therefore you must develop determination to persist to a reasonable extent in the selling effort. For example, salespeople who sell large computer systems may need less persistence than those selling small computer systems because of the selling task. Those selling smaller systems may feel a greater need for persistence, since they have less frequent client contact with a greater number of potential customers.[31] Ex-

**Figure 14–2**
**Goal Planning Sheet**

Overall Target Date _____

Desired Goal _____

_____

_____

A.  Obstacles and Road Blocks
    Anticipated

    1.

    2.

    3.

    4.

    5.

B.  Plans for Overcoming Obstacles
    and Road Blocks

    1.

    2.

    3.

    4.

    5.

C.  Expected Benefits to Be
    Achieved

    1.

    2.

    3.

    4.

    5.

D.  Staff, Resources, Procedures
    Necessary to Accomplish the
    Stated Goals

    1.

    2.

    3.

    4.

    5.

E.  Restatement of Goal and, If Necessary, Target Dates _____

    _____

    _____

    _____

perience provides knowledge of when to persist and when to "back off" from a client who says, "No" and those who say "No!" or "Not yet."

You must be *assertive* to be successful in selling.[32] Assertiveness means guiding the sale but not forcing your will on the client. Assertiveness comes from the self-confidence of having knowledge and being able to help others with that knowledge. Do not confuse assertiveness with aggressiveness. Aggressiveness, although important to a degree in selling, is counterproductive when it turns from aggressiveness to abrasiveness.

*Imagination and humor* add to the seller's personality. Imagination is the ability to originate ideas of value to the customer. You use imagination to put yourself mentally in the prospect's place and to anticipate a problem before it becomes a problem. Thereby you will be able to focus on the buying motives and obtain positive results. You deal with problems with a sort of "What if?" approach.

*Humor* must be used with caution. Tactful, clean humor can remove sales tension during a sales dialogue. But humor can be a two-edged sword that can be degrading to others. Laughing at the mistakes, misfortunes, or failure of others causes bad feelings and may lose customers and friends. When you laugh *with* others, their ego is fed and they feel good. Laughing *at* others feeds only your ego while it puts the other person down. Off-color, sacrilegious, or ethnic jokes are offensive. For example, telling a joke about an alcoholic to a prospect may cause ill feelings, especially if the prospect has personal contact with an alcoholic friend or relative. Humor should be spontaneous, yet used carefully.

People like to receive *praise and affirmation* for who they are and what they do.[33] It encourages them and helps them solidify their identity. Although some people have trouble accepting compliments because of how they see themselves, everyone enjoys talking to someone who can honestly praise other people. Affirmation is a sincere compliment, in contrast to flattery, which is insincere and which may be meant to manipulate the receiver. Acknowledging the worth of others will generally bring affirmation back to you. It is like a stone thrown into a pond, the ripples not only hit the opposite shore but also the shore where you are standing. Affirm yourself. You do things right. Reward yourself for the goals you achieve by giving yourself a gift like those in *Technology Bulletin*.

Each personality trait is important to a salesperson, since those who exhibit correct traits generally are successful in sales. However, personality traits are developed, so most bad traits can be removed through a willingness to change.

Scientists are studying how personality changes take place. Cybernetics is a science examining the correlation between the operations of complex electronic computers and the human nervous system. According to the cybernetic model, the mind is like a computer that is programmed to react in certain ways in accordance with your conscious thoughts. Your experiences rewrite your program. You learn from your experiences, but

## TECHNOLOGY BULLETIN

**Motivational Tools**

Can't take a trip? Now you can with VideoTours Inc., a collection of travel-oriented video tapes ($19.95). They take you on behind-the-scenes tours of America's most prestigious museums, historical attractions, theme parks, zoos, and aquariums. Or learn new sports techniques with ''Cross-Country Skiing with Bill Koch,'' ''Golf Fundamentals with Ben Sutton's Golf School,'' and ''Championship Skeet Shooting,'' by DLS Communications. The adventurous can learn Spanish with a hand-held Spanish/English dictionary ($299.95). Nishika's 35-mm 3-D camera ($229.95) by American 3-D takes 3-dimensional pictures with no special film or lens. Film can be developed through normal processing. Either choice you make, you wil have the satisfaction of knowing you have met your goals.

*Source:* Melissa Campanelli, ''What Price Motivation?'' *Sales and Marketing Management* 142 (October 1990): 104–105.

sometimes experience is a bitter teacher. For example, lost sales are expensive. So it is necessary to learn to program ourselves properly and with a minimum of hurt. For that reason, people try to learn and to reprogram (change) without the actual firsthand experiences. Yet you have programmed yourself to be what you consciously think you are. So program yourself with desirable traits.[34]

## Self-Confidence

You show how you feel about yourself, your product, and your company when you communicate with others. These verbal and nonverbal communications indicate your level of self-confidence. **Confidence** is a middle state that lies between the insecure states of self-doubt, characterized by nervousness and fear of people, and ''cockiness,'' characterized by exaggerated conceit and phony exuberance. The self-confident person accepts his or her personality for what it is and constantly tries to correct its faults.[35] Inner confidence comes from being yourself—the acceptance of what you are, the honest acknowledgement of strengths and weaknesses, the maturity and **reality anchoring** (having a realistic view) of your ego. Insecurity results when a person frequently tries to become a new personality or is perpetually, severely self-critical.[36]

     Many people who lack self-confidence often attempt to overcome this inferiority complex by using the defense mechanism of overreacting.

**confidence**

**reality anchoring**

## PARTNERSHIPS

When the great running back Herschel Walker was in junior high school and wanted to play football, he was told by a kindly coach, ``Herschel, you are too small. Go try out for track.'' Walker's response was to undertake a training program—calisthenics, running, stretching, eating carefully—to build himself into an All-American football player and Heisman Trophy winner. He said of his success: ``My God-given talent is my ability to stick with it longer than anyone else.'' Herschel had a mission—the mission of a winner. And mission is bounded by no preconceived limitations. It inspires people to reach for what could be and to rise above their fears and preoccupations with what is. It is that mission that drives success.

*Source:* Charles Garfield, Peak Performers: *The New Heroes of American Business* (New York: Avon Publishers, 1986), 101–102.

In over-asserting themselves they hope to counteract their feelings of inferiority. This type of person is pompous, struts, talks in a loud voice, and tries to give the impression that he or she knows all there is to know. Sounds like a description of the persuasive salesperson! With time, one may overcome fears of being inferior by developing self-confidence.

An integral part of self-confidence is image management skills. **image management**    **Image management** is defined as an attempt made by salespeople to influence the impression they make so that they get a predetermined favorable response on the part of a client.[37] If you are attempting to manage clients' impressions of you by trying to be attentive to their needs, impression management in this context is not manipulative. When used to overpower other selling skills, image management is very manipulative. Therefore it is necessary to put your best foot forward and develop an image that is pleasing to the client and that gives you confidence. Your confidence level may depend on the situation: an expert chef is supremely confident in the kitchen directing l'affaires de gastronome; but if that chef is put on a baseball diamond, the chances are that the chef will appear awkward and bumbling.[38] Inner confidence shows through personality, and outer confidence comes with experience.

To show self-confidence, make both your verbal and nonverbal communications positive. The voice, the content of the message, and personal appearance say a great deal about one's self-confidence.

Your *voice* is important when you are trying to gain acceptance, speaking in clearly delineated sounds. You should tape record your voice while speaking to another person and analyze the recording. Did you enunciate clearly, have good tone and timbre, or did you stutter or stammer? Problems in any of these areas give a clue to a lack of self-confidence. If you lack enthusiasm, it will show in the tone and timbre of your voice and in the pattern of your words. When you use slang and mumble your words, you show lack of sincerity. Using a higher pitched, shrill voice indicates tension. Speaking in an overly loud voice exhibits a lack of self-confidence.

*Message content* can show your self-confidence. First, a salesperson will find that greeting customers with a sincere smile sets the stage for reception of the message. Then, talking in terms of another's interests is always evidence of a salesperson's sense of high self-esteem and self-satisfaction: so the salesperson develops a message that revolves around the prospect's interests rather than around the salesperson's own life history. Messages that sincerely compliment and praise other people are usually acceptable, though many people cannot easily accept compliments.

Your degree of self-confidence is evident in your *appearance*. You should put your best effort into making yourself presentable. First impressions take but a few seconds to make and are often lasting impressions. "You never get a second chance to make a first impression." When you know that your clothes and grooming represent your best efforts, you radiate self-confidence.

Generally when discussing appearance, you think of clothing, since it usually makes the first impression. Dress projects an image that tells of one's self-confidence. There are many books on the subject of business dress, such as John Malloy's *New Dress for Success* (Warner Books,

Appearance generally illustrates a person's self-image. Professional dress, correct for the occasion, gives you confidence. You are saying through your appearance: ``I'm competent and I want to help you solve your problem in a professional manner.''

1988) and William Thourlby's *You Are What You Wear* (Andrews and McNeal, 1987).

If your company has a dress code, it has been established to fit the expectations of your customers. A physician is not too impressed by a pharmaceutical drug salesperson dressed in casual sport clothes. Likewise, a farmer may be suspicious of a salesperson dressed in a three-piece suit, white shirt, and tie. Traditionally IBM employees have worn dark suits, conservative ties, white shirts, and wingtip shoes. Jim Sherry, a salesperson for B.F. Goodrich, plastic division, calling on an IBM purchasing agent, wears the IBM "uniform" each time he calls. He desires to make the IBM officials see that "he's one of them." However, in other parts of his territory, he is known for his collection of unusually attractive ties. He is adapting his clothing to meet the expectations of his customers' images of him.[39]

You signal still more information to the client by the way you have packaged yourself. On the basis of your dress and grooming, the customer decides whether you are a formal or informal person, relaxed or apprehensive, careful or careless, conservative or perhaps a pacesetter. Remember, people prefer to do business with someone like them. So dressing the part helps you to sell. Dressing the part tastefully and carefully also builds confidence. You will find it is extremely hard to have self-confidence when you see the customer eyeing a grease spot on your slacks or a tear in your jacket. You can avoid such an uncomfortable experience by making sure your appearance is always correct.

Women in sales have a particularly hard problem of dressing appropriately because of the numerous options they have. Obviously it is easy to overdress. One thing women should not try to do is to avoid looking feminine, since this also gives rise to criticism. In jobs where reaching, stretching, or stooping is required, skirts can cause problems. Wearing light colors can be inappropriate for some types of jobs, as one saleslady for Procter and Gamble found out: "I learned very quickly that my new, white, three-piece suit was inappropriate when I spent a day on my hands and knees in a customer's dirty warehouse counting inventory. After one day it was retired. I don't know how the dry cleaners ever got the dirt out."[40] Usually a woman will find out the best information on dress from her sales manager and her peers in the company.

Grooming is an additional aspect of appearance that requires attention, since few things can be more annoying to a customer than being approached by a salesperson with bad grooming habits. One's hair, nails, weight, cleanliness, breath, and shoe condition must always be given strict attention. A customer, repelled by a salesperson's poor grooming, will not hesitate to shop elsewhere. For example, how would you react to the following salesperson (whom the authors actually encountered recently)?

Put yourself into the picture: You are shopping for a new sofa. Stopping at a dealer's showroom, you are approached by a salesman. He's wearing an irridescent blue, three-piece suit; white shirt; wide tie; and wing-tip shoes. Looking closer, you see his stringy, greasy hair, which needed cutting two weeks ago. He is so overweight that his shirt bulges under the tie decorated with grease spots. A portion of chest hair shows at his neckline, even though the collar button is fastened. Also, the inner facing of the shirt collar peeks through the material in several places around the collar. He cannot button the three bottom buttons on his vest because of his girth. Needless to say, the rest of his appearance, down to his feet, is similarly unattractive and unacceptable—as is his breath, which reeks of a steakburger loaded with onions. Staying true to form, his presentation and treatment of us as customers is congruent with his slovenly appearance. Now, would you buy from this salesman?

To sell furniture or anything else, you must be a sharp-looking, physically fit salesperson to create a favorable total image through good appearance. It is amazing how much information a person's desk, workplace, briefcase, or office communicates about that person. By simply walking into an office, even when the executive is not there, you can often discover a world of information. Is it designed as a workplace, or a showplace, or both? Is it tastefully and individually decorated to reflect the individuality of the occupant? Or is it the kind of slick, expensive-looking office that reflects the taste of a decorator? The appearance of an office may indicate the type of person who works there, whether it is occupied by a busy executive who is in full control of the job or by a mere paper shuffler . . . by one who enjoys work or hates it . . . by an iconoclast or conformist . . . by one who has original ideas or who is more comfortable with someone else's. What is true of executives' offices is equally true of their cars. Have you ever met someone for lunch, opened the door of the car, and found the floor covered with cigarette butts, crumpled maps, children's toys, and crushed containers from a drive-in restaurant? That tells you something about your friend.[41] Also, a briefcase must be neat. You might be well dressed, but if your briefcase is sloppy, papers falling out, and you are unable to find the necessary information, it is as bad as being poorly dressed or groomed. It is important that you pay attention to the image you project through appearances.

Salespeople are ultimately responsible for developing their motivational profiles of self-improvement, but you are not left entirely on your own to achieve this goal. Individual self-improvement books abound at bookstores across the nation. Many of these are offered on tape, so you can listen to them as you travel from one client to another. This practice is highly encouraged and is profitable in building and maintaining self-confidence. Companies such as Zig Ziglar Corporation, Lazer Ltd., Xerox's

Personal Selling Skills, and Wilson Learning Corporation offer specialized programs to help those desiring to achieve at their highest potential. These companies provide programmed, guided studies through readings, audio and video tapes, study guides, and exercises. Such studies are designed to increase self-confidence, motivation, and to achieve sales goals. The lack of knowledge of how to build relationships is not an excuse that many companies listen to. If they do not provide the training to correct ineffective quality relationships, it is your responsibility to learn how to build quality relationships with yourself and with others. Only you can prevent the building of successful relationships. The first step is to build a quality relationship with yourself. Then you will be capable of building one with others, both inside and outside your company.

Know that first appearances are important and often make lasting impressions. Above all, knowing what you need to know well, knowing that you know it, and knowing that it is being presented in the best possible manner will give you valuable self-confidence.

> You are nature's greatest miracle—you are rare and unique and the ultimate product of several million years of evolution. You have a greater potential than anyone who has ever lived before you. But you'll never make it sitting on your duff and telling the world how great you're going to be, starting tomorrow.
>
> **Og Mandino**

## PARTNERSHIPS

At Wilson Learning, they practice what they teach, going to great lengths to understand and respond to individual needs the same way they advise sales consultants to respond to their clients. For over twenty-five years, Wilson Learning has helped a million people in twenty-five different companies learn how to be the best they can be.

After a comprehensive diagnosis of assessing the situation, Wilson develops a sales curriculum which meets the needs of the organization's salespeople. Their three-track focus (Basic, Advanced and Manager's tracks) results in comprehensive training that has helped salespeople excel. Wilson's programs are for anyone who wants to learn how to summon inner resources, unleash creativity, and develop better and more profitable directions for themselves and their organization.

Wanting to achieve at your highest potential is a life-long process which reaps bountiful harvest of success.

*Source:* Wilson Learning Corporation, 7500 Flying Cloud Drive, Eden Prairie, Minnesota 55344-3795.

## Summary

Your success depends on your quality of relationships, including both the external and internal indicators. While your empathy, enthusiasm, and likeability are outward signs of quality, internal factors and their effectiveness depend almost entirely on the person. Refresher training programs can stimulate the desire to succeed and heighten your awareness, but they cannot set the goals, strengthen the personality, or develop the self-confidence for self-motivation.

Self-confidence and self-motivation are important to success. Each expresses how people feel about themselves. The purpose of refresher training programs is to acquaint sellers with the various facets involved in developing a quality relationship with themselves. Putting the ideas into practice depends on the individual. Each of the internal and external indicators is important in building professionalism and making one successful.

## Key Terms

contact intensity
mutual disclosure
cooperative intentions
sales slumps
refresher training
similarity
expertise
success
personality
handling rejection
external indicators
empathy
enthusiasm
likeable

positive attitude
internal indicators
self-confidence
goals
drives
goal achievement
quotas
goal achievers
goal conflict
role conflict
role ambiguity
confidence
reality anchoring
image management

## Discussion Questions

1. Discuss the external and internal indicators of a seller's relationship.
2. Compare and contrast goals and drives. What goals should salespeople set for themselves? What goals are imposed?
3. Is being a goal achiever necessary for success as a salesperson?
4. Find three periodical articles concerning role and goal conflict. Discuss how they affect quality of relationships.

5.  What is the best personality for a retail salesperson? Nonretail salesperson?

6.  Which personality traits are most important to successful selling?

7.  What is the difference between being assertive and being abrasive? Can either be a good trait for a salesperson?

8.  Comment on "Everyone likes a good joke" in a sales presentation context.

9.  Which factors express one's self-confidence? Of what importance are they?

## Decision Crossroads: Ethical Issues

1.  Encountering the sloppy salesperson described on pages 396 and 397 in this chapter, what would you do if you were the customer? If you were his sales manager? How would you do it?

2.  Describe a situation when image management could be used unfairly to influence a buyer.

## Case 14-1  **Master Lock Co.**

Tom Green is the Boseman area sales representative for Master Lock Company. Master Lock Company is based in Milwaukee, Wisconsin, and it manufactures combination and pad locks. The locks are used for various purposes, such as locking chains together, locking tool boxes, and locking gates, etc. Mr. Green was hired just one month ago, fresh out of college, and has received a two-week crash course in selling Master Lock products.

Today Mr. Green is making a cold call on James Jones. He is the owner of a small hardware and feed store in Boseman, Montana. Mr. Green happens to catch Mr. Jones as he is heading to lunch.

| | |
|---|---|
| *Green* | Is there a Mr. Jones around? |
| *Jones* | Yes. I'm Mr. Jones. What can I do for you? |
| *Green* | My name is Tom Green, and I sell Master locks. I was wondering if you would like to carry the Master Lock line in your store? |

| | |
|---|---|
| *Jones* | Well, I was just heading out for lunch. Can you come back around 4:00 this afternoon? |
| *Green* | No, I can't. I have another appointment in Butte at 4:00. |
| *Jones* | How about tomorrow morning? |
| *Green* | No. I will be on the north side of Casper. If I could have a few minutes of your time right now, I won't have to come back at a later date. |
| *Jones* | OK. Let me see what you have. (Disgustedly.) |
| *Green* | I sell the best locks in the world and just happen to have some with me. Let me show you. (Gets out his samples.) |
| *Jones* | This looks like an ordinary lock to me. What's so great about them? |
| *Green* | You can shoot right through the middle of them with a pistol and the lock will not open. |
| *Jones* | But what happens if you shoot the hook part? |
| *Green* | Hmmm . . . I don't know. I guess it will break, but if it's in the middle, it won't open. |
| *Jones* | Too bad, but I don't need any locks. |
| *Green* | Why not? |
| *Jones* | Because I've never carried them before, and I haven't had any calls for them before. |
| *Green* | Well then, you should start carrying them because you are a hardware store and people expect to find locks in a hardware store. |
| *Jones* | I don't have to carry yours or anyone else's locks if I don't want to. (Getting mad.) |
| *Green* | When people want to buy a lock, they go to a hardware store, right? |

| Jones | No! They don't. They go to Bill's Dollar Store or to K-Mart. |
| Green | But if you carried Master locks, then people would come to your store and buy them. |
| Jones | How much do they cost? |
| Green | They cost $3.00, and you sell them for $4.95. How many would you like to buy? |
| Jones | I don't want to buy any from you at that price. I can go to K-Mart for that price. |
| Green | No, you can't. |
| Jones | Yes, I can. You don't know "diddly" about locks, do you? |
| Green | I sure do. I had a two-week course on Master locks last month at the home office. |
| Jones | I'm sure you did. (Now angry.) |
| Green | Don't you want to buy some locks today? |
| Jones | NO!!! Those locks are way overpriced. (Very angry now.) |
| Green | Aw, be a sport and buy a box. |
| Jones | No way. Now get out and leave me alone. |
| Green | OK, I'm leaving. But you'll be sorry for not buying any. |
| Jones | Good; No, bye! (Pushes him out the door.) |
| Green | Bye!! (Slams door behind him.) |

### Discussion:

1. What is the matter with the salesperson?
2. What would make the salesperson get an attitude like this?
3. Devise a sales training program that would minimize this problem.

## Case 14-2  **Merck Corporation**

Sally Jackson of Merck Corporation had a miserable Friday that ended a miserable week. As she was driving home, she relived her last several calls ... "Dr. Morgan was a real grouch ... Taylor seemed to well ... come on to me ... Wow!! and Larry, the pharmacist at Druid Drug—he almost made me blow my top ... What's going on? It all seems too much. Well, after a good night's rest, I'll sort it out."

Saturday came and went, as did Sunday. Then suddenly at 10:00 Sunday night, as Sally was doing her weekly plan, she realized that she was really regretting going to work the next day. Getting out her training materials and self-help books and putting some relaxation tapes on the recorder, she began to sort out her week. Better late than never, she thought.

### Discussion:

1. What could be part of Sally's problems?
2. Pretend you are Sally. Map out a plan to keep problems from happening to the extent they have already happened.
3. What indicators could Sally look for to show that she is having the problems, not just absorbing other people's problems?

## Chapter Outline

Ethics
  Relationships Within Your Company
  Relationships With Other Companies
    and Customers
  Relationship With Society

## CHAPTER 15

# Ethical and Legal Issues in Relationship Selling

**Learning Objectives**

After reading this chapter, you should be able to:

- Explain the meaning of ethics
- Understand the ethical issues facing salespeople today
- Describe the major laws influencing selling today
- Discuss the laws that govern the behavior of salespeople
- Explain what ethical responsibilities salespeople have to themselves, their companies, and their customers
- Explain why salespeople have ethical responsibilities to their competitors.

## IN THE FIELD

You don't have to be a giant to sell to giants! Adolph Miera is a man who has shown that you don't have to be a large company to sell to the titan companies. Chemical Milling International, which Miera owns, has been a partner in the production of the Boeing 747, 757s, 767s, the Lockheed L1011, and the Douglas DC-10. His company has also been involved with the B-2 Stealth bomber, the F-18, and the F-5. His 50-person $2.5-million sales firm is a small entity in the high-powered aerospace industry.

Applying a special process to aluminum sheets used for aircraft "skins," Chemical Milling makes a product that is much lighter than conventional products without the reduction of stress caused by conventional methods. By meeting the needs of the industry Miera had targeted, Chemical was able to make its name known in the aerospace industry.

Miera used a key to penetrate this elusive market without a "big name." "The key," says Miera, "is keep your word. A lot of the time, a buyer wouldn't believe it when I'd say that our delivery is better than any competitor's. That's because many salesmen make promises, but the shop doesn't support them. When you get that first order, you deliver: even if you lose money. Too many people today turn back a job rather than lose money. Deliver what you promise, especially if it's a first order—or you'd better not show up in their lobby again."

*Source:* Norman Sklarewitz, ''Tiny Chemical Milling Wins Them with the Basics,'' *Sales and Marketing Management* 142 (February 1990). Reprinted by permission of *Sales and Marketing Management*, ©: February 1990.

Making ethical decisions is routine for the salesperson. Although never easy, sellers must judge the rightness or wrongness of their actions in every situation. Areas in which salespeople have to make periodic ethical decisions are discussed further in this chapter.

Now that the relationship with self has been built and reinforced from Chapter 14, the relationship with your company and society is important. These relationships are discussed under the topics of ethics and legal restraints.

**social responsibility**   **Social responsibility** refers to serving employees and customers in an ethical and legal manner. In today's competitive environment, some salespeople are tempted to make sales at any cost. These temptations are prohibited by new levels of professionalism that promote self-regulation as well as by laws that penalize violations. Those who do not exhibit ethical behavior may sell to a client once, but rarely are they able to establish long-term relationships. Adolph Miera (see *In the Field*) has shown that by using ethical behavior, a small company can compete for the business of *Fortune* 500 companies against the larger suppliers.

# Ethics

The rightness and wrongness of motives and behavior in dealing with others that encompasses moral principles is called **ethics.**[1] Here people choose between two or more courses of action. Ethics is an important factor in interpersonal relationships where persuasion and leadership are involved, and it becomes still more important when one person must rely on the objectivity and integrity of another person.[2] Simply stated, *ethical conduct involves an individual following established, accepted moral principles of his or her own profession.* It is also a personal view of what is right or wrong.

    Ethics provides a basis for deciding what is right or wrong in a given situation. Ethical standards for a profession are based on society's standards; most industries have developed codes of behavior that are compatible with society's standards. Abiding by these standards promotes goodwill and builds long-term relationships. The trust that these practices bring to the marketplace reduces the risk of buying. The fundamental ground rule for such a salesperson is "the welfare of the customer comes first and foremost."

    The need to make you aware of some of the ethical hazards in selling is evident in the study by *Working Woman* magazine. Of 1400 readers asked by *Working Woman* to list three places where unethical behavior often occurs, government was named by the most—66 percent, while 51 percent said sales, 40 percent law, and 38 percent the media.[3]

    Understanding ethical problems is the first step toward building a reputation for having high standards of personal integrity. Ethical problems can occur within the company, with other companies and customers, or within society.

**ethics**

## Relationships within Your Company

Why would a salesperson act unethically? Pressure from corporate superiors to meet quotas, absence of written ethical policies, and conflict between personal ethics and corporate ones are some possible reasons.[4] For example, a photocopier salesperson might face the following problems:

- Because the customer's copier is malfunctioning, the customer demands a new model as a replacement. Management, without informing the customer, will replace the copier only with a used one that looks new.

- Another customer can purchase a good, used copier at a several hundred dollar savings over the cost of a new copier, but the customer is unaware of the availability of the used machine.

### Quota Pressure

Salespeople faced by short-run goals and sales quotas may feel *quota pressure*. In succumbing to the pressure, they may ignore the customer's well-being, as in both cases above. Management may be pressuring them to get more sales "even if you have to twist arms." Do you ignore the relationship approach and persuade the customer to buy, or do you remain true to your philosophy and possibly make the sales manager unhappy? Mavericks in the corporate structure may suffer peer and managerial ostracism or even lose their jobs.[5] Those who are unethical affect the credibility and ethics of all salespeople in an industry, and the salesperson's own integrity is sacrificed. There doubtlessly will be many occasions in a selling career in which you are tempted to act against high standards of conduct, such as pressure in negotiation to "shade the truth" and close the sale. Remember Adolph Miera's advice (see *In the Field*): "always keep your word"—to yourself and to your company.

### Misusing Company Assets

Some salespeople are tempted to use company assets, such as automobiles, expense accounts, samples, and damaged merchandise, contrary to company policy.[6] These items can be used for personal gain or to influence customer's buying decisions. Using the "company car" for personal use, charging expenses that did not occur or that were for personal use, and giving credit for merchandise that was not damaged are examples of *misusing company assets* if these acts are contrary to company policy. Some of these violations of company policy also constitute violations of Internal Revenue Service (IRS) law and are punishable offenses.

### Moonlighting

Since close supervision of accomplished salespeople is not the rule, some salespeople may feel tempted to take a part-time job, be an adjunct professor at a community college, or partake in athletic pursuits during their work time. These activities are called *moonlighting*. When pursued on the seller's own time, they are perfectly acceptable with most companies. Sometimes efficient salespeople, under little supervision, find that they can effectively "call on their accounts in less time than their predecessor," giving them free time. However, this time should be spent on prospecting for new accounts, as companies request, rather than spending company time on personal activities.

## Cheating

Like misuse of company assets and expense-account fraud, cheating your company is harmful. Salespeople are often in sales contests to increase sales of certain products. Some salespeople feel justified in making *hold-back sales* (predated or postdated orders) to fit within the guidelines of the contest. Other sellers write orders for later delivery and then cancel them after the contest but before delivery. Still others overload their customers with too many products.

Other tactics involve collusion between salespeople in a sales contest or between support personnel within the company. This practice may involve helping another salesperson win, hampering others from gaining an advantage by not posting sales, or giving sales leads in a timely fashion, postponing delivery of goods until after the contest is over, or giving a salesperson an inordinate number of extra reports to fill out during a sales period. Although these tactics may increase sales in the short run, salespeople ruin their trust relationships with their customers, company, and themselves by doing so.

## Disclosure of Proprietary Information

Salespeople are privy to confidential information concerning their employers. This private information is called *proprietary information*. To salespeople who become disgruntled with the management of the company, disenchanted with company policies, or who perceive an advantage in selling a client, disclosing proprietary information to noncompany personnel might be personally beneficial. However, this information is private; thus disclosing it is similar to misusing company assets.

## Disparaging the Company

When employees become disgruntled with their company, they often start speaking poorly about it, or *disparage the company's name*. Disparaging remarks concerning your company or its employees during or after employment should be avoided. This type of behavior influences future relationships with that company and also with others who may come in contact with them. Most people look unfavorably on disparaging remarks and avoid those who make such comments.

# Relationships with Other Companies and Customers

Much of the ethical behavior in this area involves dealing with customers. Some common problems faced in the marketplace are discussed below.

## TECHNOLOGY BULLETIN

### Don't Be Blind to Technology's Pitfalls

Just because a new technology is available does not mean that it should be used. Microchips, available at $5, will play a 15-second audio message that can be used in direct mail prospecting. Audiotex invites consumers to press phone keys to respond to questions. Respondents find it easier to use than Videotex, which requires some investment and education about modem communications and computer operation. Buick's use of floppy disk technology (Technology Bulletin, Chapter 10) was desirable not only because of the diskette users' demographics but also because of their familiarity with the technology. Integrating available technologies, such as AT&T's Smart-Phone, which includes a touch-screen display and a built-in modem, may bridge the gap between Audiotex and Videotex and unite the two into a new, more powerful medium.

*Source:* M. Darrin Tisdale, "Don't Be Blind to Technology's Pitfalls," *Marketing News* 24 (November 12, 1990): 13–17.

### Business Lunch

Taking customers to lunch is one of the industry's most common, most time-consuming, and most expensive practices.

> It may be important to get the customer out of his office into a neutral, relaxed setting. When properly used, entertainment doesn't cost that much and can actually help you distinguish yourself from your competitors. For example, while calling on a construction job a couple of years ago in a remote part of Tennessee, I made it a point to take donuts to the construction site. After a while I became known as "Mr. Donut," points out Curtis Sprague of Mountain Empire Rubber and Specialty Company, Johnson City, Tennessee.[7]

While most buyers see no problem in an occasional lunch, many feel that too much dining with the same supplier can present ethical problems in future dealings. Most buyers realize that there is no free lunch; somebody pays for it in the products they purchase. Entertaining is a part of selling and should be kept on a business basis. Most business people in the United States try to keep entertaining and business separate as much as

Relationships with clients often develop beyond the office setting. Socializing with customers is the norm. In fact, some companies require their salespeople to recreate (play golf, tennis, or racketball) with their clients on company time. Salespeople must be sure that such social interaction does not lead to ethical abuses.

possible by not talking business while they entertain. However, in other countries the social customs vary. As shown in *Partnerships,* the seller often is required to conform to regional standards. This can be a problem when regional custom is to engage in an act that the salesperson's country sees as illegal.

## Misrepresentation of Information

Another ethical dilemma is the misrepresentation of information concerning your company, products, or yourself. It is tempting to exaggerate

## PARTNERSHIPS

"When in Rome . . . do as the Romans do," may mean changes in behavior for Americans interested in doing business in a multinational business. "Americans interested in doing business with Japan must realize that the Japanese are very different from Americans," says Michael Fowler, editor of *Business Tokyo.* "They do mix business with pleasure in Japan. If you are planning on selling in Japan, keep in mind that when work ends at seven or eight o'clock in the evening, it's time to socialize and strengthen friendships," he reports. Successfully doing business in other countries means adapting to the local customs as much as is ethically possible.

*Source:* "Short Takes," *Sales and Marketing Management* 142 (June 1990): 38.

claims of products, disclose proprietary information concerning new product development, or make promises that may not be kept in order to make a sale. Even a casual misrepresentation made by salespeople can put the company into court. We all know of attempts of salespeople to oversell. They exaggerate the abilities of the product and sometimes make false statements to get the sale over competitors. When Allison Farber was faced with fierce competition, ethical decisions had to be made when she felt she was unprepared for the business world (see *Partnerships,* below). Relationships are built on trust, honesty and reliability. Exaggeration or misrepresentation should be avoided in relationship selling.

> There is nothing wrong with having personal friendships with representatives of those companies with whom we do business. However, this cannot be permitted or extended to the giving and receiving of gifts. It is, therefore, against our policy for any employee to accept from any company or representative of a supplier company with whom we do business any gifts of value, including cash, merchandise, gift certificates, weekend, or vacation trips. This means, of course, returning any such gifts that may be delivered to your home or office.[8]
>
> **Robert Townsend, President Avis**

**Bribery and Inappropriate Use of Gifts.**   Using bribes to obtain business is a worldwide phenomenon.[9] In the Middle East it is called *baksheesh*, and

## PARTNERSHIPS

After working for Time, Inc. straight out of George Washington University, Allison Farber felt it was time to make more money. She then went to work for Gardner Carpets selling rugs and tile to architects, decorators, and carpet contractors in the New York and New Jersey area. Her biggest surprise was ''the amount of product knowledge that's required. Each product we sell has a different application and cost. I'm asked a lot of detailed questions. My customers rely on me to inform them correctly. If I'm not well versed, if they think I don't know what I'm talking about, they don't trust me,'' Farber says. ''I knew I'd be up against others,'' she reports, ''but, frankly, the conniving that goes on is really something else. I don't mean dishonesty—shrewdness, I guess, would be a better word.

*Source:* Arthur Bragg, ''Shell-Shocked on the Battlefield of Selling,'' *Sales and Marketing Management* 142 (July 1990): 52–53.

Some buyers' companies have policies regarding the receipt of gifts. Nevertheless, giving gifts in accordance with the buyer's company policy is standard procedure for special occasions and holidays.

in Italy it is known as "the little envelope"—*la bustarella.* The subject of bribery in sales conjures up images of sales to foreign countries, such as the Lockheed violations. Giving money or gifts to secure business is called giving *kickbacks.* Kickbacks are not limited to foreign countries. National legislation has been enacted to make this practice illegal in the United States as a method of unfair competition. There are numerous ways a salesperson may attempt to bribe a buyer. Money, gifts, entertainment, special favors, and travel may be offered.[10] There is a thin line between good business practices and the misuse of gifts. A $50 gift to a $5 million dollar customer may be merely a gift, but how do we define a $50,000 gift to a $200 million client? Many companies forbid their personnel from taking gifts over a certain described size, possibly $25. Some, such as Avis, forbid all gifts. But infractions are hard to control. For example, a sales manager for Congoleum lost his job after it was discovered that he received bribes under the guise of a consulting agreement with one of his customers.[11]

The practice of giving gifts to buyers and purchasing agents is well established, especially at Christmas time.[12] It is the inappropriate giving of gifts that is unethical. Gifts vary from wrapped bottles of liquor to hams, turkeys, or novelties, to name a few. An ethical problem arises when gift giving escalates from a pair of NFL football tickets, to a VCR, to a trip for two to Las Vegas for the agent and spouse. Table 15–1 shows

**Table 15–1**
**Gift-Taking Behavior**   What is your firm's policy for purchasing personnel to follow on accepting gifts from vendors?

| Answers | Number | Percentage |
|---|---|---|
| No gifts of any kind | 47 | 14 |
| Pens and pads but nothing of real value | 125 | 36 |
| Gifts up to $50 in value if not given often | 83 | 24 |
| Gifts from $51 to $200 in value if not given often | 6 | 2 |
| The firm's policy is that each buyer is allowed to make his or her own decision | 17 | 5 |
| Firm has no policy; thus each buyer makes his or her own decision | 66 | 19 |
| TOTALS | 344 | 100% |

Monroe Murphy Bird, ``Gift-Giving and Gift-Taking in Industrial Companies,'' *Industrial Marketing Management* 18(2): 93. Copyright 1989 by Elsevier Science Publishing Co., Inc. Reprinted by permission.

**reciprocity**

Salespeople often develop relationships with other salespeople. Ethical issues such as that of reciprocity come into focus in such relationships.

a recent study of gift-taking policies by 344 industrial purchasing agents employed in *Fortune* 500 companies.[13] Although the results are varied, the two most prominent responses are accepting gifts up to $50 or having no policy at all. Behavior of salespeople deemed ethically questionable by purchasing agents, particularly if that behavior might harm the buyer's career, has influenced the selection of that salesperson's firm as a supplier.[14]

**Reciprocity.**   A familiar business saying is, "You scratch my back and I'll scratch yours." In other words, a salesperson says "if your company will buy from me, my company will buy from you"—**reciprocity.** This practice is not unethical or illegal unless it substantially reduces competition. Reciprocity that limits competition could be a violation of the law (Clayton Act or the Federal Trade Commission Act).

Reciprocity impedes the purchasing objectives of minimizing costs and entices complacency among suppliers to call on accounts that are "locked in" to a supplier because of reciprocity. It restricts the purchasing agent's information-gathering role.

Overcoming reciprocity is difficult. Many times only proof of superiority of product, service, or faster delivery will counteract reciprocal agreements. The purchasing agents must have the ability to purchase from the best supplier to do their jobs properly. Thus they must be allowed to disregard reciprocity.

# Relationship with Society

Besides the number of issues dealing with relationships between the sales-person and the company, the professional salesperson must build rela-tionships with society. Failure of businesses and business people to act in a socially responsible manner in the past has forced legislatures to enact laws to protect the consumer. Regulations at both the federal and local level are important. Although salespeople have legal counsel with whom to discuss specific issues, a generalized knowledge of regulations can help avoid legal entanglements.

## Federal Laws

Federal regulations pertaining to marketing and selling activities include the following:

- **Sherman Antitrust Act** (1890). Prohibits (1) "monopolies or attempts to monopolize" and (2) "contracts, combinations, or conspiracies in restraint of trade" in interstate and foreign commerce.                                                               **Sherman Antitrust Act**
- **Clayton Act** (1914). Supplements the Sherman Act by prohibiting certain specific practices such as price discrimination, tying contracts, and exclusive dealings where the effect may be to substantially reduce competition or to create a monopoly.                                                          **Clayton Act**
- **Federal Trade Commission Act** (1914). Establishes a commission with broad powers to investigate and to use cease-and-desist orders to enforce Section 5, which declares that "unfair methods of competition in commerce are unlawful."                                                                    **Federal Trade Commission Act**
- **Robinson-Patman Act** (1936). Amends the Clayton Act; adds the phrase "to injure, destroy, or prevent competition"; defines price discrimination as unlawful (subject to certain defenses) and provides the Federal Trade Commission with the right to establish limits on trade discounts, to forbid brokerage allowances except to independent brokers, and to prohibit promotional allowances or the furnishing of services or facilities except where made available to all "on proportionately equal terms."                                      **Robinson-Patman Act**
- **Wheeler-Lee Act** (1938). Prohibits unfair and deceptive acts and practices regardless of whether competition is injured; places advertising of food and drugs under FTC jurisdiction.          **Wheeler-Lee Act**
- **Magnuson-Moss Warranty/FTC Improvement Act** (1973). Authorizes the FTC to determine rules concerning consumer warranties and provides for consumer access to means of                **Magnuson-Moss Warranty/FTC Improvement Act**

redress, such as the "class action" suit; also expands the FTC powers over unfair or deceptive practices.[15]

- *"Cooling Off" Rules.* Public dissatisfaction with tactics used by door-to-door salespeople caused the Federal Trade Commission and state regulators to pass rules concerning home presentations. Generally these rules state that notice of cancellation must be given a retail buyer who makes purchases of more than $25 outside the seller's regular place of business. A sale can be cancelled by written notice mailed to the seller within three business days after the transaction, thus providing a period of time to "cool off," or rethink, the purchase.

### State Regulations

Several laws, such as the cooling-off rules, are enforced at the local level. Like the federal regulations, these state and local laws are designed to minimize complaints about door-to-door salespeople.

**Green River Ordinances.**    Many municipal ordinances restrict calling door-to-door without the household's permission. It is called the Green River ordinances because it was first enacted in Green River, Wyoming in 1933. Currently these types of local ordinances make it illegal to call door-to-door without prior householder permission; restrict phone solicitations and the time of day when calls can be made; prohibit calls on holidays and calls on homes posted with "No Soliciting" signs. You should investigate the local and state regulations before attempting to make any calls outside your normal place of business.

**Doorstep Identification.**    Sellers who call on prospects at home should be prepared to verify their identity to prospects. In fact, a number of states have passed laws requiring that sellers immediately identify themselves to the person who answers the door. For this purpose, salespeople have found name badges and calling cards to be very helpful.

Most of the laws described above have had a major impact on business-to-business marketing. A salesperson knowing the laws should avoid any action that could possibly be a violation of these laws. Examples of such action might be (1) offering an exclusive price to one of several buyers and not offering it to all competitors on a proportionally equal basis **(price discrimination)**; (2) forcing a consumer to buy one product to obtain another **(tying contract)**; or (3) requiring a buyer (wholesaler or retailer) to sell only the seller's products and not sell products offered by competitors **(exclusive dealings)**.[16] Examples 2 and 3 are not illegal per se but are illegal under certain conditions, such as when used by a company that has such a large market share that competition would be injured.

**price discrimination**
**tying contract**

**exclusive dealings**

## Summary

Ethical guidelines are established by most companies. Standardized or implied practices that operate in the marketplace may tempt salespeople to compromise their integrity. Ethical, legal practices within an industry should be followed so that both the firm and the salesperson will be considered to be honest and reputable.

## Key Terms

social responsibility
ethics
reciprocity
Sherman Antitrust Act
Clayton Act
Federal Trade Commission Act
Robinson-Patman Act

Wheeler-Lee Act
Magnuson-Moss Warranty/FTC
    Improvement Act
price discrimination
tying contract
exclusive dealings

## Discussion Questions

1.  In what areas may salespeople have to make ethical decisions?
2.  Give an example of an unethical sales practice that you are aware of. Why is it unethical?
3.  Why would a company be against suppliers giving gifts to the purchasing agent?
4.  How can a seller handle a buyer who wants a kickback?
5.  What would you do if you knew that another salesperson in your company was giving gifts that were against company policy?
6.  What attributes of the selling job make it susceptible to unethical behavior?
7.  Do you think that most business lunches are used to "buy" business? Do you disagree with this practice?
8.  How much entertaining of a client should a company do? Should they give vacations or weekend trips? Sports event tickets?

## Decision Crossroads: Ethical Issues

No one wants to intimidate a prospect on a sales call, but hand out a business card with CEO or president printed on it, and that is just what might happen. Therefore Phil Pachulski, CEO of Prime Technology, Inc., a distributor of machine tools, keeps titleless cards for just such occasions.

"If hands-on plant managers and shop engineers see my title, they don't see me as their equal anymore," says Pachulski. "They think I'm a bigshot office guy who doesn't know what's going on in the marketplace."

But when he calls on big company employees to whom organizational charts are important, Pachulski presents a business card with his title on it.[17]

### Discussion:

1. Do you think this practice is unethical? Why?
2. Is Pachulski being deceptive in withholding his title?

## Case 15–1    **Allo Chemical**

Allo Company of Houston, Texas was established in 1975 by Joseph L. Allo. He instilled in his employees the motto, "Do your best, whatever it takes to get the sale." However, his motto began to fade away as his company progressed from a behind-the-scenes company to a service-oriented company. Allo Chemical Company trains its employees through on-the-job training from day 1. They are accompanied by an experienced salesperson for several weeks.

Susan Fry, a sales representative for Allo Chemical company, has just finished her training and is ready to go to work. She is about to visit Ewing Oil for the first time and is very nervous. She is standing in for a fellow sales representative, Jack Frost. Fry takes with her the professional style that she has been taught. She prepares to meet Digger Barnes. Fry steps out of her car in front of Ewing Oil. She fixes her hair and clothing on her way inside.

Barnes, the leading representative for Ewing Oil, patiently waits for the sales representative, whom he thinks will be Frost. Barnes has had dealings with Frost often and has grown accustomed to his selling style. Barnes, being one who is reluctant to change, has no idea that in a few moments tension will fill the room.

Fry enters Barnes' office promptly at 7:30 A.M., just as the previous representative had done in the past. However, in this instance, Barnes is extremely surprised by the change of representatives. As Fry walks in, tension fills the room.

| | |
|---|---|
| *Susan* | Hello, Mr. Barnes. I'm Susan Fry from Allo Chemical Company. I am replacing Jack Frost, your old representative. |

| | |
|---|---|
| *Digger* | You're doing what? What happened to Jack? (A very surprised look on his face.) |
| *Susan* | Jack was given a big promotion and was transferred to California. I am here today to introduce myself and to see if there is anything that you might need to order. |
| *Digger* | Well, you won't be getting any orders from me. (A mean, disgusted look on his face.) |
| *Susan* | Mr. Barnes, is there anything wrong with our product or service? (A hurt look on her face.) |
| *Digger* | No. There is nothing wrong with your product or service. I don't like women salespeople. |
| *Susan* | But what is wrong with women sales representatives? |
| *Digger* | Women don't know anything about the chemical business. |
| *Susan* | Mr. Barnes, I received my bachelors and masters degrees from the University of Texas. I have also worked for Allo Chemicals for over four years and have learned a lot through their training programs and seminars. (Getting defensive about the accusation.) |
| *Digger* | You graduated from the University of Texas? That's where I graduated from. Does Dr. Wilson still teach there? |
| *Susan* | Yes, and I had Dr. Wilson for several chemistry courses. He was a real influence on my career. |
| *Digger* | Dr. Wilson had an influence on my career also. Well, I guess if you graduated from UT and you know Dr. Wilson, then maybe you do know something and I could do business with you. |
| *Susan* | Thank you for having confidence in me. Now, what types of chemicals do you purchase from Allo on a regular basis, and do you need to order any today? |

| | |
|---|---|
| *Digger* | Why don't we go to the warehouse and check, and that way you can see how we handle our inventory. We can work up an order while we are down there. |
| *Susan* | Fine, let's go. |

**Discussion:**

1. How could Ms. Fry have handled this prejudiced customer better?
2. What should she be careful of on this and follow-up calls?
3. How would you have handled the situation?


## Case 15–2    R.B. Lumber

After graduating from college, Ms. Weaver obtained a position as a sales representative for R.B. Lumber, covering a four-state area. Her responsibility was to sell materials to manufacturing firms, maintain good customer contact, and collect bad debts. She knew that this job was going to be demanding, since she was the second woman hired by R.B. Lumber and only the third woman representative in the industry. Her training did not prepare her for the intimidation she received not only from her customers but also from her supervisor. Usually she could handle the lack of communication from her supervisor, but the lack of respect she received from a few of her clients was difficult. She explained to her supervisor, who had little sympathy. He asked, "How did you expect to be treated in the *man's* world?" One particular account, Pressler Inc., had a new purchasing agent, and he was not going to buy from her unless "she matched the competition's offer of a $500 rebate." She asked her boss what to do. He replied, "Do what you have to and don't get caught. That account has been with us for 10 years. I don't think any one at the home office will be happy if we lose it."

**Discussion:**

1. If you were Ms. Weaver, what would you do about how you were treated by your customers? By your boss?
2. How would you handle Pressler Inc.? What are the alternatives? What are the consequences of each alternative?

**Chapter Outline**

Overview of Time-Management
  Techniques

Planning Techniques
  Territorial Planning
  Periodic Planning

Controlling Techniques
  Daily Time Log
  Job Requirements Analysis
  Outside Influences List
  The 80/20 Rule
  The A. B. C. Method

Follow-Through Techniques
  Organizing Environments
  Daily Scheduling

Telemarketing

Avoiding Procrastination

## CHAPTER 16

# Managing Time

**Learning Objectives**

When you have completed Chapter 16, you should be able to:

- Recognize the three primary elements of time management—planning, control, and follow-through
- Describe effective time-management planning techniques
- Understand methods that sellers can use to better control their use of time
- Explain some follow-through techniques for time management.

## IN THE FIELD

*Sometimes a plant person is more responsive to customer problems than someone in sales.*

**David B. Sheldon, vice president and group executive of sales (Products Package), Ball Corporation.**

Once a salesperson establishes a relationship with a customer, we get people from all levels of our company to talk to their counterparts at the account. Plant managers visit the production lines of soft drink bottlers, for example, and engineers talk shop with engineers. This does not eliminate the sales force but enhances their productivity. Sometimes, in fact, closing the sale depends on harnessing technology to help a customer pull off a new sales promotion. The team effort in the package products group accounts for 62 percent of Ball Corporation sales.

*Source:* ``Best Sales Force Survey: Industrial Rankings,'' *Sales and Marketing Management* 141 (June 1989): 41–42. Reprinted by permission of *Sales and Marketing Management,* ©1989.

In *A Mystery of Fate,* Voltaire posed the following riddle to his friend, Zadig:

> What, of all things in the world is the longest and the
> shortest, the swiftest and the slowest, the most divisible
> and the most extended, the most neglected and the most
> regretted; without which nothing can be done and which
> devours all that is little and enlivens all that is great?

Zadig answers the riddle with the one-word response: *"time."* Voltaire continues:

> Nothing is longer, since time is the measure of eternity.
> Nothing is shorter since it is insufficient for the
>   accomplishment of your projects.
> Nothing is more slow to him that expects, nothing more
>   rapid to him that enjoys.
> In greatness it extends to infinity, in smallness it is
>   infinitely divisible.
> All men neglect it—all regret the loss of it; nothing can be
>   done without it.

> Time consigns to oblivion whatever is unworthy of being
>   transmitted to posterity, and it immortalizes such actions
>   which are truly great.
> Time is man's most precious asset.

For a salesperson, the ability to manage time well is an important input, added to the inputs of communication skills, sales training, and motivation. Making use of time effectively can lead to greater sales, more prospects, and that special commodity, time for one's self and the pursuit of happiness. This chapter will focus on understanding time management and developing techniques for planning the best use of time; for controlling one's use of time; and for following through with projects.

## Overview of Time-Management Techniques

Time is a unique resource; but it is limited, precious, moves only forward, dominates life, and can be a continuous learning experience. However, it cannot be reclaimed, and certainly there is not enough of it. "Time is money" is the old axiom that certainly applies to selling. A person working 8 hours a day, 250 days a year, will work 2,000 hours; and if that salesperson is making $50,000, an hour of time is worth $25. Adding an extra two hours of work a week could increase the income $2,500 a year.

People speak of time management, but this is a misnomer, since no one can really manage the clock. What we can learn is to manage ourselves and our lives in relation to time. One of the best ways to meet and to solve this problem is to increase our own personal effectiveness.

Effectiveness, like any skill, *can be learned.* As author Peter F. Drucker views it, "Time effectiveness is a set of 'learned' behaviors. Essentially, it is a practice and like all practices or habits, it is simple. However, the skills are hard to acquire because continual practice or reinforcement is necessary."[1]

Managing time means making the most effective use of it. What it really adds up to is the management of ourselves and of those responsible to us.[2] Time management is probably the most important input for salespeople, and they should master its three primary elements: plan, control, and follow-through. These three elements are described below:

1. *Plan.* A salesperson "who fails to plan is planning to fail." Have a daily plan of action, written statements or goals, listing what is to be accomplished during the day.
2. *Control.* Keeping on target means having clear goals and objectives about your work and even about your life. Techniques for control in-

volve monitoring one's time and productivity. Control includes planning for interruptions that come at the most inappropriate times but keeping those interruptions brief, then resuming assigned tasks.

3. *Follow-through.* Once plans have been made and monitoring functions have been determined, the seller must adopt techniques to carry out the plans and to reach the goals and objectives. Salespeople then start to work and to finish what they start. If it is impossible to complete a task, they find a good stopping point. Many salespeople acquire the bad habit of jumping from task to task and wonder why they never get anything accomplished. Following through with the plans ensures accomplishments.

## Planning Techniques

Planning time usage allows people to establish specific goals, set priorities, and determine performance criteria for self-evaluation. The old adage, "Plan your work and work your plan," is worth repeating. To a salesperson time is money. Commissioned salespeople often are surprised to realize that less than one half of their available time (39.68 percent) is spent in customer–salesperson dialogue. Approximately 20 percent of the customer–salesperson dialogue is spent in creative problem solving. Theoretically only about 8 percent of a salesperson's total time is spent creatively selling.[3] This fact makes a commissioned sales representative's time very expensive. If a salesperson averages $25,000 a year in commissions, creative selling time is worth $160.26 an hour. A salesperson who wastes time or uses time inefficiently loses potential earnings. With time being this valuable, salespeople need to maximize time spent with profitable customers and to minimize time spent with customers who offer little potential.

**territory**

Good planning of your time minimizes the distractions that inevitably occur. Formal planning practices make you more efficient, thereby enhancing your chances of success.

## Territorial Planning

A **territory** is a geographical location for which a nonretail salesperson is responsible. Its geographical size can vary according to the product(s) being sold and the number of potential customers for the product(s) in a given area. For instance, a territory for selling office machines may consist of an area the size of one city block, or a single building rising 47 stories high in a large city's business district, or it may be several hundred square miles in a sparsely populated state such as Wyoming.

The size of territories is determined by the type of product and the number of products being sold. Selling a computer to a manufacturer, for example, takes more time than selling Dove dishwashing liquid to a supermarket. Generally the more technical and expensive a product, the longer the decision-making time needed by the customer. As products become more technical, both the time and number of visits needed to complete a sale increase. The diversity of the product selection a salesperson is offering customers at each visit also lengthens the sales call time. A hardware wholesale salesperson may offer over 5,000 different products to each customer, whereas a business forms salesperson may carry only two or three dozen samples.

Two key tasks in territory time management are to forecast each customer's potential and to classify all accounts in the territory according to sales potential. Not all customers have equal potential. A recent survey showed that 75 percent of the sales in a territory comes from 20 percent of the customers.[4]

Salespeople can begin classifying each customer in a territory by *forecasting total sales potential for an established account.* This current sales potential can be used as the basis for sales quotas each year.

In an established territory, information about current customers will come from company records or from a former sales representative's files. This information is transferred to the salesperson's territory files, **tickle cards,** and contains names of key personnel, lists of products purchased by the account, estimated sales potential, and other pertinent client information, as seen in Figure 16–1.

**tickle cards**

For a new territory, the salesperson will have to create account information from scratch. By comparing potential accounts to existing company accounts, the salesperson can estimate a sales potential for a new account.[5] With or without a previously existing file, the salesperson needs a file of account cards or information from a computer file, like the one shown in Figure 16–1, for each customer in the territory.

After forecasting sales potential, the salesperson should *classify accounts according to their sales potential.* This can be done by using account cards, the 80/20 principle,[6] and Lahein's A.B.C. method (discussed later in this chapter). Looking at the forecast, assign As to the 20 percent of accounts with the greatest sales potential. Remaining customers receive Bs or Cs according to the sales forecasts. Account classifications will affect the way the salesperson plans calls in the territory.[7] For example, "A" accounts having the largest potential may require more frequent calls than "B" or "C" accounts. Experience and tenure in a territory help determine how much time each account needs. Keep in mind that competition is most intent for those accounts everyone would classify as an "A" account. Sometimes a niche strategy could therefore be effective, focusing more time on "Bs" and "Cs." When classification problems arise, managers and senior salespeople can help a less experienced salesperson determine the amount of time needed for "A," "B," and "C" customers. Account forecasts and classifying accounts by these forecasts are tools salespeople need to use to plan their time usage.

**Figure 16–1**
**Customer Tickle Card**
Customer File Card # 12

```
                        Customer File Card #12

City News Stand                              Classification: C
1414 Enos Ave.                                  Ph:  762-8943
Urbana, IL


Paul Patton — Owner
John Hawes — Worker

Personality: Gladhander — likes jokes




Buys: cigarettes, cigars, candy, pipes, watches, sundries

Note: likes quality mdse, worried about discounters

8/23/87 — said would buy Dunhill pipes Asst. #823 in Sept.
```

In addition, salespeople must plan territorial coverage for the month, weekly route sheets, and daily call plans, plus make daily appointments and follow-up calls on the telephone.[8] Travel time, call schedules, time for prospecting, and time for record keeping are items to include in each day's plan.[9]

Improved routing on sales calls in the territory increases a sales representative's time. Better use of the resources of the territorial map and daily sales call logs may point to inefficiencies in routing and scheduling or to excessive time spent on a particular customer. Some prospects, because of their potential, may need monthly sales calls, while others may need visits only every 6 to 10 weeks. This type of information can be analyzed on a computer to simplify the mathematical techniques needed to accomplish this task.[10] Other ways computers help salespeople are described in the *Technology Bulletin*.

## Periodic Planning

The salesperson needs to get a calendar, sit down with support personnel at a designated time, and organize activities each week. At the beginning

# TECHNOLOGY BULLETIN

### Software

Microsoft's new graphic Windows 3.0 shores up the greatest weakness of MS-DOS and PC-DOS, namely, poor graphics. As a sales-oriented user, TTG, Inc., Woburn, Massachusetts, recently distributed two versions of its Star Manager sales territory design and management system. With Windows 3.0, they were able to add capabilities like (1) zooming in on a selected area for a closer look, then panning for a wider perspective; (2) adding greater levels of detail as the user zooms in on a sales territory; and (3) adding or peeling away up to 10 layers of overlays when analyzing or comparing territories.

To view different files on where the salesperson stands in the sales cycle with each account, Window 3.0 has a ``memory management'' system that enables the computer to tap larger storage when running a program. Thus several programs can be run simultaneously and their files viewed on the screen at the same time by selecting the correct user-friendly icon. The use of Windows 3.0 will help salespeople better meet the needs of individual customers.

*Source:* Thayer C. Taylor, ``Software as Pretty as a Picture,'' *Sales and Marketing Management* 142 (October 1990): 94.

of each month, a representative should review what has to be accomplished; the schedule for accomplishment of activities; and who has the major responsibility for such accomplishment of tasks. Everyone likes to be informed about who is doing what, where, and when it is to be accomplished.[11] Often we can work backwards from the target date for total completion of the project, as seen in the Texas Marine Industrial Supply situation (see *Partnerships)* and to the necessary milestone dates on the calendar. For example, if a salesperson's deadline for submitting a bid is June 1 at 5 P.M. and it is known that engineering will take five days to write specifications and other delays will be three days for pricing, two days for typing, and two days for mailing, the salesperson must start on the bid request no later than May 20 to June 1—$(5+3+2+2)$ = May 20. This process is known as backward planning. If a certain task has no deadline, make one. Most people work better knowing that something has to be finished at a certain time.

### Planning for "Flexible" Time

Planning for a typical sales day schedule must include time for travel and waiting, customer presentations, service calls, reports, mail, meetings, and

**flexible time**
**rubber time**

flexible time. A basic element of planning is flexibility. Plan to have time available to take care of unforeseeable problems. This **flexible time** is often called **rubber time** because it expands or contracts as problems occur. Such time might provide a few minutes for self-motivation exercises when a day is going particularly bad. Salespeople need brief periods during the day to increase enthusiasm, to shake off critical remarks from a hostile customer, and to "get fired up." *Rubber time* might be used to listen to prerecorded motivational cassettes or to analyze the events of the day to see why things are not going as planned. Taking time to correct attitude problems can salvage a poor sales day. The time used in planning is more than offset by the avoidance of errors and frustration in the operational aspect of the task.

## Controlling Techniques

A thorough plan for the use of time on the sales job will include some criteria for measuring performance results. Monitoring or controlling functions for the seller may be the uses of a daily time log, an analysis of job

| Time | Activity | With Whom | What Accomplished |
|------|----------|-----------|-------------------|
| 8:00 | Tour through department | Alone | Good morning. Available for questions. |
|      | Read info ("In" basket) | Alone | Papers out and back in. |
|      | Phone (in) | Harry Thompson | Interrupted. He asked question. |
| 9:00 | Phone (out) | Bill James | Got answer to Harry's question. |
|      | Phone (out) | Harry Thompson | Gave Harry answer. |
|      | To Engineering | Joe Jackson | Pick up latest figures for meeting |
|      | To office (next building) | Tom Jones Charlie Miller | Deliver latest figures for meeting |
| 10:00 | Meeting | All immediate subordinates | Present pep talk |

**Figure 16–2**
**Example Daily Log for Jack White (Inside Salesman, Armour Company)**

requirements, a list of outside forces, the 80/20 rule, and the A.B.C. method of classification.

## Daily Time Log

A good way for salespeople to monitor how they are using or misusing time, as they get more experienced, is to keep a daily time log, a record of activities and their results as they occur, in terms of time elapsed during the day, rather than waiting to make records at the end of the day. Figure 16–2 shows a completed log sheet.

## Job Requirements Analysis

Another time-monitoring technique is analyzing job requirements. With this technique, the basic functions of the position are written down, as illustrated in Table 16–1. The functions are prioritized, and then compared with the actual percentage of time spent on these functions.

Table 16–1
**Proposed Time Requirements of an Industrial Sales Position**

| Priority of Importance | | Percentage of Time That Should Be Spent on Each Function (Ideal) | Actual Percentage of Time Spent on Each Function |
|---|---|---|---|
| 1. Creative selling | Face-to-face selling | 50 | 41 |
| 2. Preapproach | Traveling and writing | 15 | 34 |
| 3. "Housework" | Studying reports, paperwork, sales meetings | 20 | 20 |
| 4. Customer | Solving customer service problems | 15 | 5 |

The results of this analysis can help the salesperson better understand his/her job and consider the percentage of time spent on each function in relation to its importance. Discovering exactly how we are spending our time allows us to adapt our plans so that we control our time more effectively.

## Outside Influences List

**outside influences**
**internal influences**
**self-influenced**
**forces**

Another helpful technique is to list **outside influences,** the forces demanding our time, such as deadlines, phone calls, drop-in visitors, meetings, and, of course, interruptions, and **internal** or **self-influenced forces,** such as daydreaming, distractions, visiting, and meetings. The goal is to minimize both sources of influence by modifying our time habits. All of these influences are known as time robbers. Only by analyzing our own time usage can we know how our time is spent. From time to time everyone is plagued by time robbers. A crucial step in time management is to recognize the time robbers in your activities.

## The 80/20 Rule

**80/20 rule**

Overscheduled, overworked, and overinvolved salespeople can implement the **80/20 rule** developed by time management expert Alan Lahein and make the most of their time, energy, and talent. The 80/20 rule says: "If all items are arranged in order of value, 80 percent of the value would come from only 20 percent of the items, while the remaining 20 percent of the value would come from 80 percent of the items.[12]

The 80/20 rule suggests that accomplishing two tasks from a list of 10 will yield most (80 percent) of their total value. The objective, then, is to find these two, give them the highest priority, and get them done. It is considered safe to leave most of the other eight undone because the value derived from them will be significantly less than that from the two highest value items.

These examples, drawn from everyday life, should enable us to feel more comfortable about concentrating on high-value tasks, even at the cost of ignoring many lower value tasks:

- 80 percent of the sales comes from 20 percent of customers
- 80 percent of the production is in 20 percent of the product line
- 80 percent of the sick leave is taken by 20 percent of employees
- 80 percent of the file usage is in 20 percent of files
- 80 percent of the telephone calls comes from 20 percent of all callers
- 80 percent of the reading time is spent on 20 percent of the newspaper's pages (front page, sports page, editorials, columnists, feature page).[13]

Be careful not to get bogged down by low-value activities! You may become much more efficient by focusing on the top 20 percent, high-value tasks.[14]

## The A.B.C. Method

Alan Lahein's **A.B.C. method** can be very helpful in monitoring time management. List all the things to be done on a daily "to-do" list. Look over the list, decide which items can be delegated, and set priorities for the remaining items.

**A.B.C. method**

Mark all high-priority items with "A"; medium-priority tasks each receive a "B," and low-priority items are marked as $C_1$, $C_2$, or $C_3$. Prioritize customers by $A_1$, $A_2$, and so forth, according to their potential as buyers for that day.

Begin with $A_1$ items, and do as many of them as possible; continue down the list. Do not worry if the list is not finished.

Before you leave the office at the end of the day or the first thing the next morning, make up a new list of those "A" and "B" items that were not accomplished. Also, add items to your list as your day progresses. With use of this system, you should find that time is being organized and prioritized.

## Follow-through Techniques ▀▀▀▀▀▀▀▀▀▀

By planning the best use of time and deciding how to monitor those plans, salespeople begin to work toward the goals set forth. Organizing the environment, scheduling daily activities, telemarketing, and avoiding procrastination help sellers follow through with their plans.

## Organizing Environments

Organizing sellers' environments can make the management of available time easier. Delegating more tasks to the secretary and other office workers and prioritizing the work to be done can increase the salesperson's available time for making sales calls. One of the most valuable assets to any company and to the sales representatives is the secretary. Having a good secretary, one who is efficient and effective, can be a great help in managing time effectively. The salesperson must keep the secretary/office assistant informed about what is going on, the purpose of the work, and some of the problems anticipated. One must allow the secretary to help organize time and to make a scheduling of appointments. Most secretaries or office assistants are very competent people and are capable of doing a great deal more than we give them credit for. Realizing this fact, the manager or sales representative can allow the secretary to assume some of the salesperson's office duties, appointment calls, and verifications. Activities that waste your productive sales time often can be delegated, such as typing reports or sending appointment cards. This not only lightens a sales representative's burden but also lets the representative place proper emphasis on serving the customer's needs, on helping with maintenance of an item, or on maintaining good public relations with the customers—functions that are basic to all sellers.

Prioritize tasks according to their importance and the type of task. Rotenbury[15] suggests that saving 45 minutes per day would net one month of actual productivity by the end of the year. Here are some steps to help in setting priorities and, therefore, increasing productivity:

- *Set a deadline for every goal* to speed performance. Make the goal challenging, but be realistic. A sales goal increase of 10 percent might be challenging but not realistic during an economic recession in a territory with an 18 percent unemployment rate. A more realistic sales goal might be a 5 percent increase.

- *Do not trust your memory;* instead, carry a calendar or notebook and jot things down—ideas, assignments to be made, or "must" items to resolve—or carry a pocket recorder and dictate reminders.
- *Know the economics of each task* so that you do not use $10 of your time on a $5 decision. For example, do not spend valuable sales time filling out reports. Complete them on a plane or while waiting to see a customer.
- *Improve your reading skills* because the amount of information grows greater with each generation of computer printing. Learn to phrase read, to skim, to highlight. Get a feel for when you must read every word. Read main sentences, and if the paragraph is interesting or important, continue. Read books and reports as if reading the headlines of a newspaper. Read smarter, not harder.
- *Delegate, delegate, delegate!* Your secretary or office assistant wants to be an administrative assistant. Do both of you a favor and allow this person to achieve greater levels of accountability. You will both profit from delegation.
- *Control files*, especially the weeding of them. Your file-weeding program should operate automatically and not require "judgment" people to waste time reviewing files later. "Weed up front" by deciding what should and should not be filed.
- *Consolidate your activities* wherever possible. Try "batch processing" correspondence by handling similar letters consecutively before moving to reports. Do the same with telephone calls and other similar activities.

Meetings are time consuming, so *call them only when absolutely necessary.* When you do, be sure to:

- Preplan them
- Schedule time of each presenter
- State purpose of meeting
- Give advance notice of the meeting
- Keep it on target
- Eliminate "Mickey Mouse" chatter
- Assign follow-up duties.

Do not call a meeting as an excuse for the executive decision that should have been made originally. Clamp down on "gabfests"—starting with yourself. Consider the following:

- *Tackle your most demanding tasks in your most productive hours*—during what some people call your "prime time." Some of us work best early in the morning, others in the afternoon. You should "know thyself" and perform that way. Prime time should last 45 minutes to one hour and should be uninterrupted time—allowing you to be most productive.
- *Once you have made a decision, arrange to monitor its results, then forget it* and go on to the next item.
- *Neatness* helps, so have your workstation, tools, manual references, and frequently used telephone numbers nearby and up to date.
- *Spend some time alone each day;* your best ideas often come as a result. Stagger work hours, breaks, and lunches, if possible.
- *"No" is a very powerful word,* so learn to use it. Do not saddle yourself with unessential tasks just to be obliging. Instead, refer the requests to someone else who has the time and energy to handle the problem more efficiently and more effectively. Do not feel guilty that you must say "No." Tell the person asking for your help that you are working on high-priority items. Start with a simple but definite "No" the first time to save yourself from having to say it later because you really do not have time.
- *Do not push panic buttons,* but remember that your challenge is to fix mistakes, not to fix blame. Check whether or not support personnel are using their authority to solve problems. You are not obliged to accept "upward delegation."
- *Do unpleasant tasks as quickly as possible* by looking for mechanized but effective shortcuts. For example, using Polaroid camera pictures to capture evidence of poor working situations is infinitely better than writing a long, narrative report. After all, "a picture is worth a thousand words!"

   Tape messages for the secretary or office assistant. Photocopy text whenever possible instead of transcribing it. By attending a modern office equipment show, salespeople can learn what products could save them time.

   Finally, the preparation of formal correspondence is expensive, so at first decide: Can it be done by telephone? Could a secretary handle it? Can it be dictated? In memorandum form? Avoid lengthy handwritten text—preparation takes a long time.
- *Take time out for you, your special needs, and pursuits,* as the break can often help give you perspective, and soon you can return to your duties with a renewed sense of direction and enthusiasm for accomplishing necessary tasks.

# Daily Scheduling

Several techniques can increase the efficiency of daily scheduling. Shortening the length of the call, lengthening the work week or the work day, using travel and waiting time better, and telemarketing can dramatically improve the seller's time management.

- *Shortening a sales call* increases efficiency in daily planning. Reviewing the sales presentation may indicate time wasters. A salesperson, in analyzing a sales presentation, should ask questions such as:
  - Could time have been saved, and could I have been just as effective if I had sent information in advance?
  - Was there needless chatter during the dialogue?
  - Could I have closed sooner?
  - Did I push for a close beyond what was necessary?

  A "Yes" answer to any of these questions indicates wasted time during the sales dialogue, but use discretion.
  New salespeople often are guilty of "talking themselves out of an order." They continue to sell after the customer wants to buy. However, talking too little may indicate an impersonal attitude toward the customer. A well-planned sales presentation is like a recipe for a cake. Too much or too little of any one ingredient makes it a flop. A sales presentation characterized by idle chatter, dogged determination, or abruptness may turn a possible customer into a disgruntled, *former* prospect. Each presentation should be customer tailored to maximize the value the salesperson adds to the customer's decision-making process. A salesperson's experience and continued self-evaluation will help to make each presentation an opportunity to maximize the effectiveness of the value-added presentation.
- *Lengthening the day or the work week* gives the sales representative more time. It is tempting for a "nonsupervised" industrial salesperson to work on an "out-Tuesday–back-Friday" schedule. This provides Mondays and Saturdays for working at the office. Much support can be found for this type of schedule, since the typical salesperson bears a heavy paperwork load. Still, this schedule eliminates Monday as a selling day. Selling time is precious, and since a salesperson usually has so many other demands that cut into selling time, voluntarily surrendering a weekday would be a particularly unwise (and expensive) practice.

No longer does the salesperson have to wait until he or she gets to the office to start filling out a report or analyzing information on the office computer. Now it can be done anywhere with the laptop. This makes more efficient use of one's time, and leaves more time to meet clients.

Many other salespeople shorten their sales day by calling on customers from 9 A.M. until 4 P.M.. Knowing that many business people pride themselves on being hard workers and working earlier and later than their posted store hours, a salesperson can often create rapport with such hardworking business people by arranging earlier or later sales calls. Remember the cost per hour of your time.

- *Travel and waiting time,* which is generally considered "lost time," can be made productive. The wise salesperson makes maximum use of the time spent traveling between calls. Never forget to watch the road, but while driving you might dictate reports into an auto cassette recorder or a portable recorder for later transcription by your support personnel. Similarly, a salesperson can use an auto tape player to play motivational tapes and use travel time to turn a poor attitude into a positive one. Car phones make this time even more productive in arranging appointments and talking to the office.[16]

Time spent waiting in a lobby to see a customer can also be productive. Since salespeople must stay abreast of developments in their field and within their company and since waiting time might last as long as 30 to 60 minutes, use it to read. Keep literature, such as industry magazines, operational instructions, and inspirational articles or books in your briefcase, or carry a minicassette recorder to make personal notes for later attention.

Know when customers are available. Although purchasing agents generally work from 8 A.M. to 5 P.M., they may only see salespeople from 10 A.M. until 4 P.M. When possible, prearrange an appointment with clients. People in some professions, such as doctors, dentists, and barbers, traditionally take certain weekdays off. Salespeople, finding that time cannot be spent with particular clients on these days, can still be productive by reviewing accounts, taking inventories, putting up displays, handling complaints, or helping customers who work on these particular days and take other days off. Remember, too, that not all people in a profession take the same day off.

## Telemarketing

**telemarketing**

Although use of the telephone in sales is discussed briefly throughout the text, we feel that some emphasis is needed on the telephone and time management. **Telemarketing** is the art and science of marketing goods and services through telephone contact.[17] The cost of making outside sales calls has consistently risen, and the need to manage this increase has given rise to telemarketing. Finding it an effective way to call on ''C'' customers, to prospect, and to market directly to customers, many companies have added separate telemarketing departments to their organizations to support salespeople.

The telephone has been used to make appointments, to rearrange appointments, and to clarify misunderstood points in an order. The difference with current telemarketing is that it is used to *call* on marginal customers. Every salesperson has more potential customers than can be called on, but many more can be reached by phone than by personal visits. Routine calls for standardized materials such as coal, hardware, hydraulic fluid, and motor oil can be handled over the phone, with the salesperson making personal sales calls semiannually. In many cases this meets the customer's preferences more effectively than a personal visit call from the salesperson.

Since many salespeople lack the time to call on 100 percent of the prospective customers in a territory, telemarketing can result in better coverage of a territory. Prospecting and direct marketing by phone can be

Telemarketing can help maximize the efficiency of sales calls. This salesman handles a routine visit over the phone, saving time and money for both the buyer and himself.

very effective. Telemarketing, whether done by the salesperson or from the home office, can uncover customer interest, and the salesperson can follow up with a personal visit, if necessary.

Even telephone calls, however, can become time wasters. Managing time can be an effective way of dealing with phone calls if you will use the following general rules when making phone calls to service a customer:

- Limit the number of minutes you will talk to the caller.
- End the call honestly ("I really must go on to other tasks").
- Batch your phone calls together for a certain time of your day.
- Return calls as promised, having available the necessary information.
- Plan your telephone calls carefully. Rehearse them if necessary to ensure efficiency and completeness. Write down essential questions to ask such as *who, what, when, how much,* and *where;* and note the name, date, and telephone number of the prospective caller.
- Have files or information ready for the call.
- Jot down important points to cover in your conversation. (While similar to planning telephone calls—above, this might mean making a checklist of what must be discussed.)
- Get directly to the point; avoid excessive chit chat, which does not lead to substantive issues. An exception should be made when rapport building is important to the customer relationship.
- Summarize the call by saying, "Let me see if I understand you correctly. You want the order, when, according to the set price?"

All of these techniques will increase work habit efficiency for the salesperson, but the salesperson also must operate within a work environment.

## Avoiding Procrastination ▪▪▪▪▪▪▪▪▪▪▪▪▪▪▪▪▪▪▪▪

**procrastination**

**Procrastination**—putting off what needs to be done—could be the focus of a complete book; it is the primary nemesis plaguing effective time management. Procrastination certainly affects the follow-through stage of time management, but it also can have a detrimental effect on the planning and controlling stages. Many of us suffer from the "later syndrome"—I'll do it after lunch/tomorrow/next week/next month. It is easy to put off writing reports or making prospect calls. When the task is not accomplished, we feel guilty.[18]

Some psychologists consider procrastination a bad habit learned over a period of time. It is reinforced because there is generally no penalty involved. Herbert Tensterheim, clinical psychologist at Cornell University, says: "People know they can get away with not doing things that they have to do."[19]

What are some of the reasons for procrastinating? Most of us have long lists of our own, but here are some other possibilities:

- I don't have the skills (and am afraid to say no).
- It seems overwhelming—too difficult.
- I don't really want to (it's not really that important to me, or the chore is too unpleasant to do).
- I'm afraid of what will happen if I do—or try and fail (fear of failure).
- I won't invest time and effort.
- I can't organize it—see the component parts.
- I just can't seem to concentrate—my mind wanders and is really on other concerns.
- I don't understand it (and am afraid to admit it).
- I don't prioritize things, and everything seems equally important.
- I'm afraid it won't be good enough (so I won't do it at all).[20]

Whatever the reason for one's procrastination, it is a self-defeating cycle that can be broken by some positive actions. The first step in solving the problem is to get organized. Set up a *specific schedule* to follow. Set a particular time to do it. Say, "I will do it on Monday afternoon," and then stick with the schedule. After accomplishing it, reward yourself with a check mark, a gold star, or a treat by doing something you especially enjoy.

When planning sales presentations for a retail or wholesale dealer or even when beginning a term paper, we might put off the task for fear it will not be good enough. Rather than procrastinate, start right in and attack the task systematically. Do a rough draft of the project, then improve it. Edit it yourself or have a colleague check for "typos," errors, grammar, and syntax; polish it up with the corrections made, and complete the finished product.

Retrieve the needed information before you start your project. Get the budget, sales reports, prospectus, or whatever you need; take a deep breath and get started; and go as far as you can. If you cannot seem to get started, then work backwards if necessary, but certainly find an incentive or help to get started.

The time management commandments shown in Table 16–2 provide a synopsis of many of the techniques you will find helpful now and in the future.

Table 16–2
**Time Management Commandments**

| **Time Management Commandments** |
| --- |
| 1. Results are more important than mere efforts. |
| 2. Know how *you* spend *your* time; know how *they* spend *their* time. (Clarify your responsibilities, and have your staff clarify their own, too.) |
| 3. Small savings in significant areas can be more productive than large savings in insignificant areas. |
| 4. Do it now! (Don't procrastinate over things.) |
| 5. The purpose of gathering information is for future use; the purpose of filing is retrieval; the purpose of dissemination is for notice and action. |
| 6. One can delegate authority to perform a task but not the ultimate responsibility. If everyone is responsible, then no one is responsible. |
| 7. What *they read* is more important than what *you wrote*; what is understood is more significant than what is meant; what is *heard* is more important than what you *said*. |
| 8. What should have or could have been, isn't! Don't waste time on worry, guilt, or regret! |
| 9. Managers make history; clerks merely record it. Managers plan, improve, control, delegate, and communicate; clerks review and excuse. |
| 10. Elimination is the highest form of methods and systems improvement. Techniques and equipment are selected to meet objectives, not vice versa. |
| 11. You control the management of your time; time does not control you. |

*Source:* Adapted from Peter J. Murk, ``It's About Time and Salespeople,'' (Unpublished monograph, Ball State University, November 1983), 1–34. Used with permission.

You have seen many techniques for increasing personal effectiveness and extending selling time. Developing an efficient time-management system gives sellers more time to serve the needs of their present customers and to reach more potential customers.

## Summary

Time management is an especially important input for sales representatives because their time literally is money. By planning, controlling, and following through, salespeople can use time more effectively.

Territories may span several hundred miles and include more accounts than could be visited in one or two months. Classifying accounts and forecasting sales potential to identify priority customers along with better routing help in territorial planning. Periodic planning sessions with co-workers and making plans to use one's flexible time productively are other time-management planning techniques.

One controlling technique is the daily activity log. Once salespeople realize where they are spending time, they can adjust schedules to concentrate on the top 20 percent of their accounts. In a similar fashion, salespeople can analyze and prioritize their job requirements and the outside influences that make demands on their time. Lahein's 80/20 rule and the A.B.C. method are other devices used for controlling time usage.

Organizing environments to prevent wasting time, making daily schedules, and telemarketing help sellers follow through with effective time management. Telemarketing, for example, can extend selling time by reaching customers who otherwise would seldom be visited by a representative.

The worst enemy of effective time management is procrastination. Knowing some techniques for avoiding procrastination helps in all three areas—planning, controlling, and follow-through. While reasons for it are many, there is only one cure: put away excuses and begin the task at once!

## Key Terms

territory
tickle cards
flexible time
rubber time
outside influences
internal influences

self-influenced forces
80/20 rule
A.B.C. method
telemarketing
procrastination

## Discussion Questions

1.  What are the three main elements of time management?

2.  Pick a typical day in the week and keep a daily log. In your analysis, how can you save time? What time robbers are present in your daily routine?

3.  Explain the 80/20 rule and its use by sellers. Does the 80/20 rule really work? Investigate your life, and find five examples of the 80/20 rule.

4. Compare and contrast sales techniques for A, B, and C customers/ prospects.

5. Discuss potential uses of telemarketing.

6. Of what importance is account forecasting to saving time?

7. Analyze your day today in terms of pay-off time, investment time, organization, and wasted time. Are you spending the correct amount on each? Where do your time allotments differ?

8. What problems can occur if you try to shorten sales call time? Is the shortening that much of a problem?

9. Using the general rules for telephone calls, develop a telephone dialogue.

10. How important is procrastination to a salesperson? Is it a habit in your life? If so, how can you change it?

## Decision Crossroads: Ethical Issues

Julie was really scared. It was the end of the sales period, and she still had not been able to call on 10 customers who were on her listed territory this period. She felt overwhelmed with the time it was taking her to complete a call. Help from Bob, her sales manager, consisted of "work harder, make more calls." It seemed of little help. She seemed to be running all the time, but getting ahead was impossible. Bob kept asking her for her call reports. She had procrastinated as long as she could because she knew he would be upset if he knew she was not making all of her calls. She was evaluating her alternatives before she sent in her report.

### Discussion:

1. What are Julie's alternatives? Should she send a completed call sheet showing that she made *all* of her calls?
2. Since Julie is under pressure to make more calls, do you feel that it is ethical for her to report calling on five of the accounts she knew were at a convention for a week? What if she also knew they purchased *only* from the competition?
3. What would you do in this case? What would be the possible consequences of your actions? Would what you do depend upon how harsh the repercussions would be? Explain.

## Exercise 16–1  **How Well Do You Manage Your Time?**

Principles of time management apply during student years, just as they will in a professional career. As a student, you can develop time management habits. A good way to begin is by determining current habits. Listed below are 10 statements that reflect generally accepted principles of good time management. Circle the item most characteristic of how you perform your current job or use your time as a student. *Please be honest.* No one will know your answers except you.

1. I set aside a small amount of time each day for planning and thinking about my projects.
   0 Almost never
   1 Sometimes
   2 Often
   3 Almost always
2. I set specific, written goals and put deadlines on them.
   0 Almost never
   1 Sometimes
   2 Often
   3 Almost always
3. I make a daily "to do" list, arrange items in order of importance, and try to get the important items done as soon as possible.
   0 Almost never
   1 Sometimes
   2 Often
   3 Almost always
4. I am aware of the 80/20 rule and use it in doing my job. (The 80/20 rule states that 80 percent of your effectiveness will generally come from achieving only 20 percent of your goals.)
   0 Almost never
   1 Sometimes
   2 Often
   3 Almost always
5. I keep a loose schedule to allow for crises and the unexpected.
   0 Almost never
   1 Sometimes
   2 Often
   3 Almost always
6. I delegate everything I can to others.
   0 Almost never
   1 Sometimes
   2 Often
   3 Almost always

7. I try to handle each piece of paper only once.
   0 Almost never
   1 Sometimes
   2 Often
   3 Almost always
8. I eat a light lunch so I don't get sleepy in the afternoon.
   0 Almost never
   1 Sometimes
   2 Often
   3 Almost always
9. I make an active effort to keep common interruptions (visitors, meetings, telephone calls) from continually disrupting my work day.
   0 Almost never
   1 Sometimes
   2 Often
   3 Almost always
10. I am able to say no to others' requests for my time when these requests would prevent my completing important tasks.
   0 Almost never
   1 Sometimes
   2 Often
   3 Almost always

*To get your score, give yourself:*

   0 points for each "Almost never"
   1 point for each "Sometimes"
   2 points for each "Often"
   3 points for each "Almost always."

*If you scored:*

   0–15: Better give some thought to managing your time.
   15–20: You're doing okay, but there's room for improvement.
   20–25: Very good.
   25–30: Excellent.

## Exercise 16–2   **Priorities**

*Problem.* You (the sales manager) left Monday morning for a one-week company-sponsored training program in supervisory leadership. Your sales department was turned over to Mrs. R., but she became ill and went home. It was then turned over to Mrs. K., but her mother became critically ill and she flew home. You were called two hours ago and asked to return because of the emergency. You arrived five minutes ago. The time is

Table 16–3
**Priorities Comparison**

| Your Priority Assignment | Problem |
|---|---|
| A. ( ) | You have received a report from Miss Personnel that Mrs. L. is looking for another job outside the company. She wants you to talk to her. You figure this would take you 15 minutes. |
| B. ( ) | Mr. Big has left word that he wants to see you in his office immediately upon your return. Anticipated time: 60 minutes. |
| C. ( ) | You have some very important-looking, unopened mail (both company and personal) on your desk. Time: 10 minutes. |
| D. ( ) | Your telephone is ringing. |
| E. ( ) | A piece of equipment has broken down, halting all production in your department. You are the only one who can fix it. Anticipated time: 30 minutes. |
| F. ( ) | A well-dressed man is seated outside your office waiting to see you. Time: 10 minutes. |
| G. ( ) | You have an urgent, written notice in front of you to call a Los Angeles operator. Both your mother and the company headquarters are located in Los Angeles. Time: 10 minutes. |
| H. ( ) | Mr. Demanding has sent word that he wants to see you and has asked that you return his call as soon as possible. Time: 10 minutes. |
| I. ( ) | Miss Q. is in the women's lounge and says she's sick. She wants your permission to go home. It will take about 15 minutes to get the facts and make a decision. |
| J. ( ) | To get to your office by 1:00 P.M., you had to miss lunch. You are very hungry, but you figure it will take 30 minutes to get something to eat. |

*Source:* Adapted from Peter J. Murk, ''It's about Time and Salespeople,'' (unpublished Monograph, Ball State University, November, 1983), 1–34. Used with permission.

1:00 P.M. The day is Friday. As you walk into your office, you face 10 critical problems.

*Procedure.* These problems are listed in Table 16–3. Please read, evaluate, and give a priority number to each of them. In other words, decide which problem you should handle first, second, third, and so forth. You have only five minutes to do this. Instructor's Note: Set a timer for five minutes and read all 10 problems. Then have students assign priority numbers. If they have not finished in five minutes, they lose.

**Chapter Outline**

The Sales Manager's Job
Leadership Techniques for Sales Managers
Job Skills of Sales Managers
Planning for a Field Sales Force
    Sales Objectives
    Sales Forecasts
    Sales Budgets
    Human Resource Plans
    Determining Sales Force Size

Selecting and Preparing the Sales Force
    Selection of Preferred Traits
    Legal and Regulatory Limitations
    Recruiting

The Selection Process
Sales Training
Supervising the Sales Force
    Motivation
    Extrinsic Rewards
    Other Compensation
    Intrinsic Rewards

Sales Force Analysis
    Performance Data
    Territory Control

## CHAPTER 17

# Managing the Sales Force

**Learning Objectives**

After reading this material, the reader should be prepared to:

- Understand career paths in sales management
- Recognize the role of sales managers
- Understand the differences in compensation
- Recognize the methods of preparing sales objectives and sales budgets
- Understand the qualifications used to select salespeople
- Compare and contrast sales training program methods.

## IN THE FIELD

What differentiates a salesperson from a manager? Marvin Ball, vice president of sales for Petroleum Marketers Information Systems (PMIS), says, "Salespeople concern themselves with the products that are currently being sold. This represents but one of the manager's duties. He or she must be able to focus simultaneously on a variety of different things, like hiring new recruits, motivating the staff, and studying the market.

"Ultimately, and most importantly, it's the manager who makes the decisions about the future. Input from salespeople, customers, and research are all taken into account, but it's the manager who looks ahead and makes the decisions that affect the direction of the company."

"A manager has to know how to listen to the right people in order to determine what the market wants," explains Marvin. "Then they need to act on that information quickly and decisively."

*Source:* "What Skills Do Today's Sales and Marketing Managers Need to Succeed?" *Sales and Marketing Management* 141 (June 1989): 34.

After several years of successful selling, you may be approached by your company to consider a position in sales management. Generally, successful salespeople are asked to move into sales management positions between 5 and 10 years after joining a company. Although the skills are similar, there are differences between the two positions. And just because you have moved into management does not mean you will stop selling. Your emphasis will now be on motivating the sales force (selling your salespeople). This chapter highlights the principal areas of sales management.

> Get a minimum of 5 to 10 years of sales experience before going into sales management or marketing. If you haven't spent time in the front line with the customer, you won't have the instincts to know what they are thinking, watch them grow and change the direction of their companies, and to change the direction of your own company in response.
>
> **Theodore Atkins, executive vice president, Baldor Electric Co.**[1]

The sales manager's position differs from the salesperson's job. A sales manager's job consists of selling ideas and responsibility as well as selling salespeople on achievement. It is getting people to do what one wants and helping them enjoy it.

The third and final phase of your sales training program is the training for a sales management position, should you desire to advance into managing the sales force. Few companies have developed formalized training programs for sales management, although many companies are presently recognizing the need for such a program. **Sales management** can be defined as performing the functions of planning, implementing, and guiding professional salespeople to achieve the sales objectives of the firm. The sales manager is involved with strategic planning as well as the implementation of those plans.

Like selling, sales management can also be viewed as a process. Figure 17–1 shows the functions of a sales manager. Each function will be discussed briefly in this chapter.

The entry-level management position is generally called **field sales manager.** This manager directs the sales force, and he or she reports to a regional sales manager. A regional manager may supervise as many as six field managers in the typical large firm's chain of command.

**sales management**

**field sales manager**

## The Sales Manager's Job

Although sales managers may reach their positions because of their sales ability, as shown by Ms. Burt's example (see Partnerships), they continue to be successful only if they can become successful administrators. The job of sales manager consists basically of six traditional steps.

1. *Set goals and objectives.* Every manager must help make decisions about what is to be accomplished during the company's planning period, generally one year.
2. *Develop plans.* Plans often have their foundations in the field where the salesperson and customer carry on a dialogue. It is the field sales managers who are expected to know what is happening in their respective territories. The successful sales manager must not only have good communication with field sales personnel but also must provide field information to regional and national managers for planning purposes.
3. *Organize.* To execute plans, the sales manager must know what type of organization will perform best. Having specialized information concerning weather, transportation, and local economic and/or general economic conditions gives the sales manager unique insights into organizing the sales force into units that can produce optimal results.
4. *Direct.* The new sales manager is in a unique position. The manager no longer sells to customers but "sells" motivation to a sales force. The temptation is strong for the sales manager to become too involved in

Figure 17–1
**The Sales Manage-
ment Function**

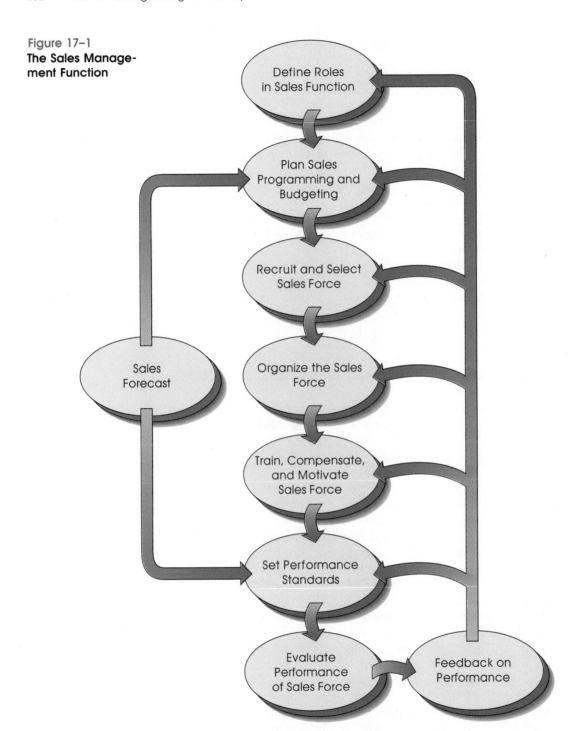

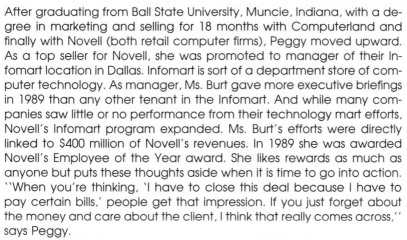

## PARTNERSHIPS

*"Customers get to know me as a person."*    **Peggy Burt,**
**Novell Corporation, a leader in computer network programming.**

After graduating from Ball State University, Muncie, Indiana, with a degree in marketing and selling for 18 months with Computerland and finally with Novell (both retail computer firms), Peggy moved upward. As a top seller for Novell, she was promoted to manager of their Infomart location in Dallas. Infomart is sort of a department store of computer technology. As manager, Ms. Burt gave more executive briefings in 1989 than any other tenant in the Infomart. And while many companies saw little or no performance from their technology mart efforts, Novell's Infomart program expanded. Ms. Burt's efforts were directly linked to $400 million of Novell's revenues. In 1989 she was awarded Novell's Employee of the Year award. She likes rewards as much as anyone but puts these thoughts aside when it is time to go into action. "When you're thinking, 'I have to close this deal because I have to pay certain bills,' people get that impression. If you just forget about the money and care about the client, I think that really comes across," says Peggy.

Ms. Burt is now Senior Manager of Sales Services, which is the executive arm of Novell for corporate executive briefings. She received the 1990 Sales Marcom award, one of the most prestigious in the industry.

*Source:* Telephone interview with Peggy Burt, January 1990.

the day-to-day customer–salesperson relations, especially when accompanying salespeople on sales calls. The sales manager's job is to teach them to sell, not to sell for them. Even though people learn from "seeing it done," people learn best from "doing it." The job is not to make sales, but to train, motivate, and direct salespeople so that they can reach their maximum sales potential.

5. *Control.* Salespeople are constantly asked to fill out reports and to maintain records that allow the sales manager to maintain control of a territory. Field sales managers also make observations by traveling with field salespeople to observe. Observation provides qualitative data, while reports provide quantitative data for control.

6. *Evaluate.* To increase the efficiency of an organization, it is necessary to evaluate progress made toward the goals set and to reward sales personnel. Quotas are easily checked by computer printouts, but salespeople and corporate goals should be evaluated by qualitative as well as quantitative standards. Goals are often unrealistic in their prediction

of economic situations. Therefore the corporate goals as well as the performance of salespeople should be subjectively evaluated. The evaluative skills of a sales manager are often a key to job success.

# Leadership Techniques for Sales Managers

Dominating the planning, organizing, directing, and controlling functions of a sales manager is leadership style. Leadership is the process by which an individual attempts to influence the action of others in a given situation. Within this definition lies the ability to be a dictator or a facilitator who controls a salesperson's actions. The influence process in sales management works this way: the sales manager influences the productivity goals of the salesperson by initiating and establishing sales goals; the salesperson tries to fulfill the needs of the customer better; the customer buys more products because his or her needs are better fulfilled by the company's salesperson. The increased sales affect the sales manager by reinforcing his or her methods.

Two types of influence relationships are built on the sources of power. The first type is based on referent power. The second type of relationship is where the party has legitimate power over the other party by virtue of position in the organization. Sources of power available to the sales manager are as follows:

legitimate power

reward power

coercive power

expert power

referent power

- **Legitimate power.** The sales manager's position in the organization is a source of legitimate power over the sales force.
- **Reward power.** The sales manager is able to award compensation for individuals' work. Rewards may take the form of money, promotions, or recognition.
- **Coercive power.** The sales manager is able to punish individuals for insufficient job performance. Punishment might mean dismissal, reprimand, or suspension.
- **Expert power.** A sales manager may have expert power because the sales force perceives the manager as a "super salesperson."
- **Referent power.** The sales manager's referent power is a direct result of sales representatives' positive and cooperative attitudes toward the manager as their leader.[2]

Legitimate, reward, and coercive power originate within the company. Expert and referent power are controlled by the individual. Referent power—respect—is the most effective power a sales manager can have, yet the sales manager has the least control over it. With referent power, the sales manager can influence a salesperson through experience and performance (expert power), compensation (reward power), and/or through criticism (coercive power). Without referent power, the other powers are somewhat neutralized. For example, if the salesperson develops a negative attitude toward a sales manager to the point that retaining his or her sales position is no longer important, reward, coercion, and expert powers are neutralized and become ineffective. The sales manager "earns" referent and expert powers from salespeople. Respect does not come with the title, and it cannot be won through reward or coercive tactics.

Effective leadership in a sales organization should be a well-matched, positive, two-way relationship between the sales manager and sales force. The strength of this relationship is built on mutual respect, caring, and understanding of each other as human beings, not as manager and subordinate. The effectiveness of a salesperson also depends on the leadership style of the sales manager.

Managers typically use three leadership styles.

1. *Achievement oriented.* The manager establishes challenging goals for the salesperson while showing confidence that the goals can be attained.
2. *Supportive oriented.* The manager shows concern for the salesperson's needs, welfare, and well-being.
3. *Instrumentally oriented.* The manager informs the sales representatives of what is expected of each of them. The manager becomes a facilitator to help the salespersons reach their goals.

## Job Skills of Sales Managers ▬▬▬▬▬▬▬▬▬

Three types of skills are needed by the sales manager.[3] They are:

1. *Technical skill.* Because selling is the required skill, the ability to be skilled in all areas of selling is required. This means not only having expertise in the selling process but also having great depth of product knowledge.
2. *Human relations skill.* The sales manager must lead, motivate, build morale, and manage conflict. Without skills in human relations, the sales manager will be ineffective and unsuccessful. There are parallels between handling conflict with a customer and handling conflict between two salespeople.

Human skills are equally important at all levels of the organization. Most subordinates single out leadership as the most important characteristic for management personnel. The importance of human relations skills is shown in the amount of time devoted to it. Time for human resource skills takes 85 percent of a sales manager's time, as shown by the following data: selling (face to face and telemarketing), 29%; administration, 24%; account service, 17%; and internal meetings, 14%.[4]

3. *Conceptual skill.* A sales manager must have the ability to see the overall scope of the total operation as well as see how each part achieves the ultimate goal. As one moves from field manager to national manager, conceptual skills become more important than technical skills. This is because field sales managers select and train salespeople, whereas national salespeople are more involved in planning to meet corporate goals.

## Planning for a Field Sales Force

Planning in sales management involves developing sales objectives, sales forecasts, sales budgets, and personnel plans.

## Sales Objectives

Once the goals and objectives of the company are established, they can be translated into marketing objectives, as shown in Figure 17–2. Marketing objectives are then translated into sales forecasts and budgets. Implementing the objectives requires the execution of market plans to reach the objective: sales. Evaluation of the sales made relative to the goals established allows the modification of future plans.

The planning function is closely related to the control function (evaluation) and depends heavily on it. One must plan to evaluate one's progress (control function) toward a goal even if the goal is accomplished. The evaluation (control) of performance allows for minimization of errors, maximization of efficiency, and effectiveness of planning. After determining the corporate marketing objectives, each area of the marketing mix will be given its set of objectives; however, the emphasis will be on the sales force. Sales objectives[5] should be established in terms of:

**contribution to profits**

- **Contribution to profits.** Cost plus markup or margin equals selling price, and cost includes the cost not only to make a product but also selling costs. Therefore the sales force can contribute a great deal to corporate profit. It can increase sales, increase profit margin on sales, and reduce selling costs. Each of these will increase the contribution to profit.

- **Return on assets managed by the sales force.** The sales force has capital invested in autos, training, and materials, etc. The return on investment of these goods can be calculated and used as a measure of efficiency.

  **return on assets managed by the sales force**

- **Market share.** A measurement of how much of the market a product has is a measure of effectiveness called market share. Although a controversy exists on whether market share increases can be attributed to advertising, sales force penetration, etc., market share is a measurable objective.

  **market share**

- **Sales/cost ratio.** Sales expenses over dollar sales volume is a quantitative measurement for determining efficiency.

  **sales/cost ratio**

Planning is a means of predicting the future. Sales management plans minimize uncertainty in the future by preparing for it. Sales forecasting involves the prediction of future events that may influence the demand for a firm's products or services. These forecasts are used to schedule personnel, production, and budgets. Sales forecasts are the basis of most quantitative planning. Forecasts are made for short-term (three to six months), medium-term (six months to two years), and long-term (over two years) periods.

## Sales Forecasts

There are two data categories of forecasting sales: qualitative data and quantitative data, as shown in Figure 17–3.[6]

### Qualitative Data

Sales forecasts using qualitative data employ either breakdown or build-up techniques. In the **breakdown technique,** the environment is forecast. This allows examination of the influence of noncontrollable variables of competition, economic conditions, technological changes, sociological and cultural changes, etc., on your company. Predictions of future events are made for the industry and the company's total sales forecast. The company's total sales are then predicted by product lines as well as individual products. The individual product forecast is broken into customer forecasts by territories, districts, and regions, etc. It is this final territorial forecast that becomes the salesperson's quota for the year.

**breakdown technique**

The **build-up technique** is a similar method of forecasting. However, the build-up technique starts with a territorial forecast predicted by the salesperson. Each territorial forecast is computed and combined in the district office. This combination plus any executive judgment revision by the district manager becomes the district sales forecast. These steps are repeated until a national forecast is obtained.

**build-up technique**

**Figure 17–2
The Relationship of
Corporate Goals to
Sales**

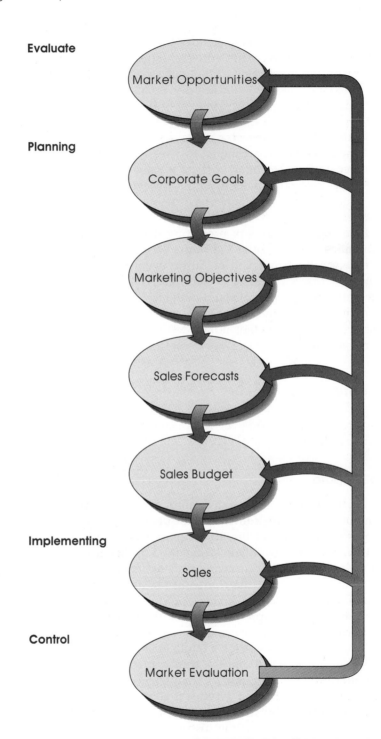

**Evaluate**

Market Opportunities

**Planning**

Corporate Goals

Marketing Objectives

Sales Forecasts

Sales Budget

**Implementing**

Sales

**Control**

Market Evaluation

Many times companies use either technique or a combination of the two in developing a sales forecast. Using both techniques may be costly in time, but it does minimize risk. Any reduction in risk requires accuracy in prediction. Accuracy has its tradeoffs of time and costs; for example, the more accurate the sales forecast, the more time and money are involved.

There are basically two types of sales forecasting models: the survey model and mathematical model. The survey model uses qualitative data, and the quantitative, or mathematical, models derive sales forecasts from the "numbers" rather than "opinions." The **survey models** include:

**survey models**

- **Executive opinion.** Several executives develop predictions of the future independently of each other.

**executive opinion**

- **Sales force composite.** Salespeople depend on their expertise as well as customer dialogues to predict sales for future years. Salespeople are often asked to participate in the establishment of sales forecasts and sales quotas. This participative management approach is called management by objectives (**M.B.O.**).[7] In a study of 202 companies, 86 percent had a policy of sales force participation in sales forecasting.

**sales force composite**

**M.B.O.**

- **User's expectations.** To determine sales forecasts, polls are often taken of a company's customers.

**user's expectations**

## Quantitative Data

*Quantitative data* employ the use of numerical data as the basis for problem solving. A brief analysis of the mathematical models includes:

- **Test markets.** These test markets are designed to provide indicators of sales success (bellwethers) for predicting sales.

**test markets**

- **Naive method.** This method assumes that a ratio of past sales to this year's sales will help predict next year's sales.

**naive method**

- **Moving average.** By minimizing the effects of the distant future and distant past, the moving average approach attempts to smooth out the extreme rates of change in the previous three to five years.

**moving average**

- **Exponential smoothing.** Like the moving average, exponential smoothing considers previous sales figures.

**exponential smoothing**

- **Trend projection.** By plotting past sales and forming a line using the sum-of-the-least-squares method, the line is projected into future periods to predict expected sales.

**trend projection**

- **Regression analysis.** This method is a statistical method that predicts sales volume (dependent variable) according to independent factors.[8]

**regression analysis**

Figure 17–3
**Categories of Sales Forecasting**

**Breakdown Method**

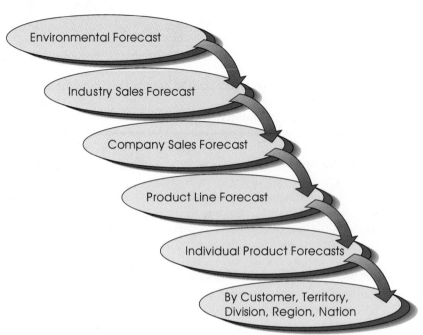

**Build-up Method**

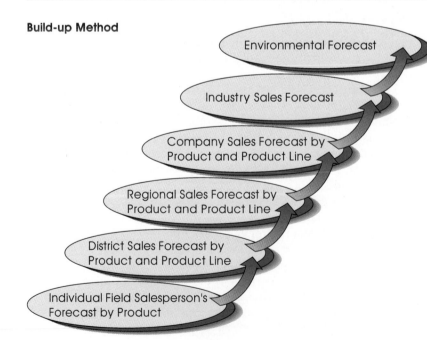

The main problem with quantitative methods is that they rely on past sales. They do not consider planned or future changes. The best forecasts for sales budgeting combine both survey (qualitative) and quantitative methods.

## Sales Budgets

Sales forecasts are used to develop a sales budget. The forecast predicts the projected level of proficiency in sales, and the sales budget projects the level of efficiency in obtaining the forecast in terms of the cost. Budgets are vital to the financial planning of a company. A **sales budget** is a record of planned sales expenses prepared on an annual basis. However, expenses are generally broken down by month and are subject to revision quarterly. The main concern in a sales budget is how much money to allocate and where to allocate these funds.[9]

**sales budget**

Historical data can be used to prepare the sales budget. Comparison with last year's budget and adjustments for perceived changes provide the basis for predicting next year's sales budget. However, the **percentage of sales method** improves on this method by using a percentage of last year's sales. As an indicator of what percentage should be used, you should look at your industry's average as an indication of the "ball park figure" that would be budgeted for an average company in the industry.

**percentage of sales method**

The percentage of sales method of sales budgeting has a disadvantage. The budget allocation moves in the direction of sales. If sales decrease, the budget decreases. This may be the time more money should be spent to encourage buying.

Once it has been determined how much to spend, it is then necessary to determine where to spend it. Various expenses that must be budgeted include:

- Training
- Sales force salaries, commissions, and bonuses
- Travel, meals, lodging, and entertainment
- Office rent and utilities
- Compensation for sales management
- Samples, selling aids, and sales equipment
- Clerical and secretarial salaries.

Budgets force managers to think and plan. They provide an aid to guide managers' decisions on allocating scarce resources to the various parts of the promotional mix. Budgeting also facilitates control of the sales operation. Although time consuming in preparation and periodic monitoring, budgets provide useful information for controlling the sales force.

## Human Resource Plans[10]

Sales-force planning is the process of determining the kind and number of salespeople needed. After determining at the corporate level the amount of sales force penetration desired and the importance of salespeople in the promotional mix, etc., an audit can be conducted for the sales force. Figure 17–4 shows details of the sales force audit. This audit allows the planning and control of not only the numbers of salespeople needed but also the type of salespeople needed.

**job analysis**

Determining the types of salespeople needed by a company is performed in a job analysis. A **job analysis** is the definition of specific sales activities to be performed and the determination of personalities and qualifications suited for the job. This is accomplished through job descriptions.

**job description**

A **job description** is a formally written statement of the nature, requirements, and responsibilities (sales volume, territory, supervisory duties, etc.) of a sales position. It is a delineation of which, when, how, and why duties are to be carried out.[11] Figure 17–5 shows a job description's five basic parts: nature of the job, principal responsibilities, duties, supervision received, and supervision exercised.

## Determining Sales Force Size

Sales force audits are used to determine the optimal size of sales force. The audit data is formulated for use in two methods of allocation, equalized work loads and the incremental method.

### Equalized Work Load

This method is designed to equalize total work so that each salesperson has the same work load, as shown in Table 17–1. After determining number of calls per year and the number of individual customer calls, the number of salespeople can be determined. For example, using the equalized work load method total sales from Table 17–1 and taking into consideration travel time and nonselling time, a salesperson might make 8 calls a day, 40 calls a week, or 2,000 calls annually. Twelve salespeople would be the size of the needed sales force because salespeople are not alike in abilities and customers do not all have the same characteristics or requirements. Sales managers have computer programs that make this task easier (see *Technology Bulletin*).

**incremental method of allocation**

Theoretically, in the **incremental method of allocation,** salespeople are added to the sales force until the incremental contribution to profit by adding the additional salesperson becomes a negative amount. To use

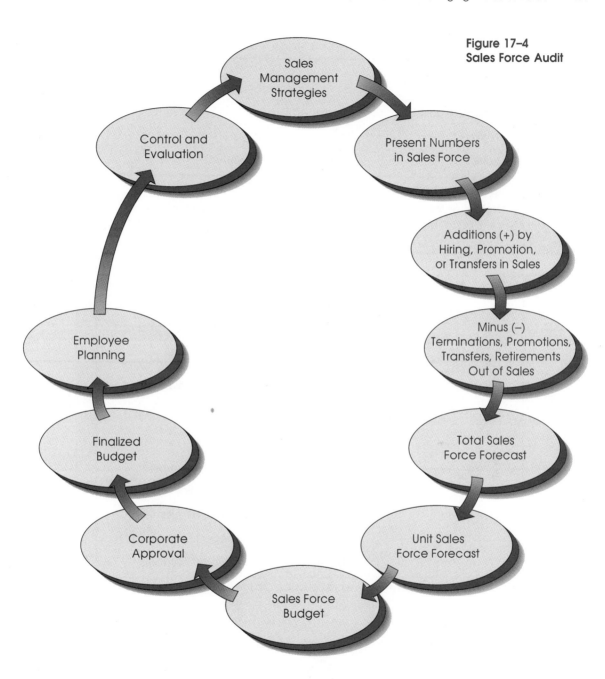

**Figure 17–4
Sales Force Audit**

Figure 17–5   **Sales Job Description**

| | |
|---|---|
| **Position:** | Sales Representative |
| **Organizational Unit:** | Copier Division |
| **Reports to:** | District Manager |
| **Date:** | (Date Description Written) |

---

| | |
|---|---|
| **Nature of Job:** | Responsible for the sales and service of copiers to new and existing accounts. Work with service representatives; determine customer's needs, problems, and potential solutions to reach assigned sales goals for specific territories. |
| **Principal Responsibilities:** | Meeting sales goals for all product lines. Maintain eight calls a day. Make follow-up calls to determine successful solution of customers' problems. |
| **Duties:** | Develop effective territory coverage resulting in high sales-call ratio. Inform management of activities by submitting daily and weekly call and sales reports to district manager. Coordinate sales and service calls into an integrated program built on service. |
| **Supervision Received:** | General and assigned tasks for each sales period. Work with district manager a minimum of one day per month. |
| **Supervision Exercised:** | Coordinate the activities of the service representative through field office. |

**Table 17-1**
**Equalized Work Load Method**

| Customer | | | Number of | Number of Calls |
|---|---|---|---|---|
| *Size* | *Class* | **Call Frequency** | **Accounts** | **Per Year** |
| Large | A | 2 per month   × | 200   = | 4,800 |
| Medium | B | 1 per month   × | 1,000   = | 12,000 |
| Small | C | 1 per quarter   × | 1,500   = | 6,000 |
| | | | 2,700 | 22,800 |

Assuming 8 calls per day per salesperson, 12 salespeople are needed to make the 22,800 calls per year (40 calls per week for one salesperson = 2,000 calls per year; 22,800 calls needed/2,000 calls = 11.4 salespeople).

this approach, the sales manager must know (1) the cost of production and distribution, (2) selling costs, and (3) the sales potential of an area. Again, not all salespeople have the same abilities, territory size, or potential customers. Therefore this method suffers, in theory, by the lack of consideration of various factors that affect the number of salespeople needed in reality.

# Selecting and Preparing the Sales Force

Regardless of which methods are used, new salespeople may need to be hired to meet the audit needs or to replace transfers and retirees. Essentially it is necessary to match salespeople with buyers. This is not to say that salespeople and buyers should be just alike. However, as pointed out earlier in the text, credibility is improved when people have similar characteristics such as age, background, training, and communication styles.

## Selection of Preferred Traits

People who have certain characteristics, such as credibility, excellent product knowledge, excellent communication skills, and certain personalities,

## TECHNOLOGY BULLETIN

### Software

Using computer mapping to plan sales territories, pinpoint direct marketing prospects, or design routes for door-to-door sellers will get a boost from TIGER. TIGER gives sellers a computer-readable (digital) map of the entire country.

Territory management, according to Donald Cook, president of Geographic Data Technology originators of TIGER, is an area where TIGER will have a dramatic impact. "The problem of unbalanced sales territories is ideally suited to a new class of geographic information systems called, 'Spatial Spreadsheets,'" he explains.

To design a territory with TIGER, the sales manager must just point a mouse to the constituent's zip codes in that area. It automatically computes spreadsheet statistics, letting the sales manager know immediately whether the sales territories are balanced.

*Source:* Thayer C. Taylor, "Put a TIGER in Your Territory Planning," *Sales and Marketing Management* 141 (July 1989): 50.

seem to be most successful.[12] A company, because of its investment in a new hire, would prefer to hire only successful salespeople.[13] Moore Business Forms reports it spends $20,000 to $30,000 per year on a newly hired salesperson during two years' training, excluding the salary of the hire.[14] It is because of this expense that the selection process is very important.

Many sales managers screen applicants on traits such as personality, maturity, appearance, empathy, and ego drive. All of these traits are often difficult to teach but very important to the success of a salesperson. **Empathy** is the ability of a salesperson to understand and relate to a customer's problems and feelings, whereas **ego drive** provides the perseverance to stay with a sale until it is finished and is the vehicle for the reward of accomplishment.[15] Although these traits are difficult to measure and require subjective evaluation on the part of the recruiter, they can be used effectively to select a superior sales force. Mr. Keller, from Merck (see *Partnerships*), has a very definite profile of a successful salesperson for Merck.

In conjunction with knowing the characteristics of those you want to hire and how many to hire, a sales manager should know the legislation imposed on recruiting. Laissez faire recruiting is prohibited by legal and regulatory restrictions.

**empathy
ego drive**

## PARTNERSHIPS

"We need to ensure that we have enough salespeople in the appropriate configurations to meet their (medical profession) needs," says Jerome C. Keller, Vice President of Sales, Merck Sharp & Dohme, Division of Merck & Company, a prescription drug company. Part of Merck's good fortune of $5.9 billion in sales last year is their self-described obsession with recruitment and training—an obsession reflected by top scores in a recent poll for their industry in recruiting and retaining salespeople. "I would have to say our major strength is that people we hire are extremely bright, have high energy levels, and are incredibly enthusiastic about the company and products we represent," says Keller.

"We prefer candidates with a background in the sciences, but we also have many with liberal arts and business backgrounds." But what they are really looking for, Keller concludes, "is the brainpower, the ability to communicate, and an ethical sort of person."

*Source:* "Best Sales Force Survey," *Sales and Marketing Management* 141 (June 1989): 47. Reprinted by permission of *Sales and Marketing Management,* © June 1989.

## Legal and Regulatory Limitations

Specific laws that influence the hiring practices of a firm are listed below:

- **Civil Rights Act of 1964.** Prohibits discrimination based on age, race, sex, color, religion, or national origin. **Civil Rights Act of 1964**
- **Fair Employment Opportunity Act of 1972.** Founded the Equal Employment Opportunity Commission to ensure compliance with the Civil Rights Act. **Fair Employment Opportunity Act of 1972**
- **Equal Pay Act of 1963.** Requires that men and women be paid the same amount for performing similar jobs. **Equal Pay Act of 1963**
- **Age Discrimination in Employment Act of 1967.** Prohibits discrimination against people ages 40 to 70 years. **Age Discrimination in Employment Act of 1967**
- **Vocational Rehabilitation Act of 1973.** Requires affirmative action to hire and promote handicapped persons if the firm employs 50 or more employees and is seeking a federal contract in excess of $50,000.[16] **Vocational Rehabilitation Act of 1973**

New laws are constantly being enacted, and current laws are being interpreted differently as times change. Therefore a sales manager must rely on the personnel office and legal counsel to ensure that no violations of legal restrictions occur during recruiting and selecting a salesperson.

## Recruiting

The organization for recruiting and selecting people varies from company to company. Whereas in large companies sales managers get involved only in the selection process, small companies generally delegate the authority to the sales manager. Recruiting is done by the personnel department.

Recruits come from inside and outside the company. Each company should look internally for people who qualify for a sales position. Many company salespeople can recommend individuals for sales positions, as they have a wide variety of contacts and acquaintances who become potential recruits. Salespeople rarely quit "selling themselves" off the job. Thus it becomes part of their personality. Therefore many acquaintances and contacts of salespeople are presold on the company already.

Company executives are another internal source for recruits. Their contacts are generally high-quality people in similar or competitive companies. Their personal recommendations, often based on friendship rather than objective evaluations, can be evaluated for their usefulness over a period of time. However, this source should not be included as the major supplier of recruiting information.

Another source of salespeople is internal transfer. Nonselling sections of the sales department as well as other departments are sources of informed recruits. Transferring people into sales is a desirable situation. Transfers are already acquainted with the company, its products, and its policies. All that is needed is an aptitude for selling. This aptitude can be tested, or a field trial can be conducted.

Outside sources are the most used sources for recruiting salespeople. Direct, unsolicited applications are an uncontrollable source of recruits. Because they are unsolicited, the "walk-in" and "write-in" inquiries for jobs should be considered "bonus" sources rather than a reliable source of recruits. The number of companies that make use of direct, unsolicited applications because they feel they show aggressiveness and initiative are as undocumented as those companies that reject this source because of a lack of qualifications. Hire the best qualified person regardless of how the application or contact is made.

Employment agencies are used by most sales managers because of their usefulness in prescreening applicants. Many agencies are paid 15 to 20 percent of the first year's salary by the person seeking the job or by the company, depending on who signs the contract. The higher the caliber of salesperson being sought, the more likely it is that the employer will pay the fee.

Sales forces of competing and noncompeting companies are another source of salespeople. Salespeople selling similar products for a competing company are excellent sources for sales personnel because of the experience they have acquired. Their experience in the same industry necessitates minimal training before placement in the sales force.

Competing salespeople are often quite costly, particularly if they are successful. Often they require premium pay to be enticed to leave their present employer. This increase in pay may cause dissension among current employees. When new employees are paid more or almost as much as current employees with similar qualifications, a morale problem called **salary compression** often occurs. It has become a problem in many industries. The premium pay for competitive salespeople not only influences salary compression but also increases the cost of sales figures that a sales manager is trying to keep low.

**salary compression**

Salespeople from noncompeting companies are often attractive recruits. They have been selling and therefore require less sales training. Often such salespeople are in "dead-end" jobs and can advance in their careers only by transferring to another company. The purchasing agent is an excellent source of names of good salespeople who call on the company. A key question for both the competing and noncompeting recruit is why the salesperson wants to leave the present employer? There are many reasons for job dissatisfaction, many of which are not the fault of the salesperson. Informal investigation into the cause of dissatisfaction may provide valuable insight about the recruit.

Executive sales clubs, such as the regional chapters of the American Marketing Association and Sales and Marketing Executives International, provide appropriate placement services. Their monthly meetings are an excellent time to meet professional salespeople who might provide the names of prospective recruits on an informal basis. Some organizations provide a newsletter or a job placement service, which should be used for recruiting.

Many companies requiring higher educational levels have turned to colleges and universities. Most of these recruits have had basic business, marketing, and, perhaps, sales training. Although the demand for college graduates varies from good to slow according to the economy, better known companies continue to go to campuses to interview. Often they will "make jobs" for well-qualified applicants.

The classified section of newspapers and trade journals has been a traditional means of advertising for recruits. Recently higher quality jobs have been advertised. Jobs for vice presidents of marketing have appeared in the *Wall Street Journal*. However, advertisements may produce an abundance of unqualified prospects. Steps can be taken to reduce the number of applicants by advertising specific job descriptions and job specifications.

However, overspecifying a job in an advertisement may scare away a well-qualified applicant.

## The Selection Process

From the pool of recruited prospects, managers must screen out candidates who do not fit job requirements. The process is a filtering system that is depicted in Figure 17–6.

After recruits are sent to a centralized location, the selection procedure begins. In the initial interview at this central location, the recruiter explains the basics of the job and asks questions. Follow-up calls or letters are sent to those who meet the screening criteria for the position, and prospects are asked to fill out an application form. Application forms are a quick method of gathering personal history in a standardized format. While showing a personal history, the application shows (1) if the person can write legibly and error free, (2) educational background, and (3) employment record of the applicant.

**Screening Interviews.**   Because interpersonal communication is important in sales, a screening interview is necessary to judge the oral communication ability of the candidate. A recruit can be asked about information that may not have been clear on the application. The recruit can also be requested to role play a selling situation. This situation requires the recruit to sell an item (ash tray, pen, eyeglasses, raincoat, etc.) to the interviewer. Often the interviewer will present problem-solving situations to the candidate and ask that they be solved. These techniques test the applicant's ability to think quickly in a stressful situation.

*Appearance* is also judged in the interview. Just as a salesperson learns to "read" a customer, recruiters learn to judge a candidate from appearance, mannerisms, and speech.

Even if a formalized "test" is not given, an informal evaluation of how the person fits the corporate image can be made. Most companies have an image they want to project. Salespeople will project that image whether or not they have formal guidelines. Unwritten "dress codes" or "images" are asserted with peer pressure and managerial "advice" on what is acceptable and unacceptable. The recruit is evaluated against the "corporate image" for its salespeople in the interview process.

Most interviews are of a patterned type, and the answers are noted by the interviewer. This provides information for later analysis. Because the selection process is a subjective process, it is important to remove as much emotion and bias as possible. Patterned interviews, standardized applications, and multiple interviews with different company employees provide a degree of objectivity to the selection process.

Figure 17–6
**Steps in the Selection
Process**

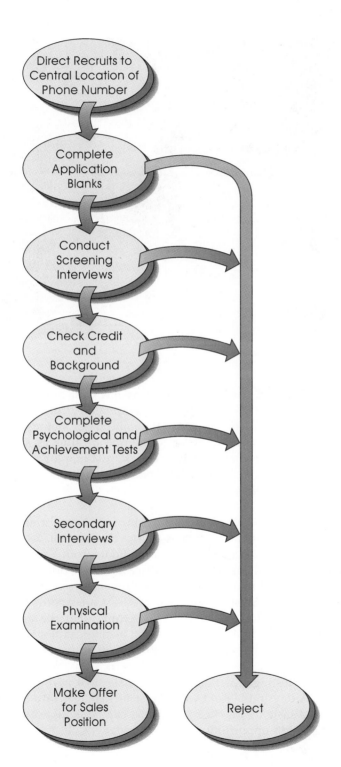

Selecting the right sales staff is very important to the success of the firm. Complete disclosure concerning all the aspects of the sales job should be spelled out to the applicant before the selection process is completed.

**Credit and Background Checks.**    Most firms check the application information. This includes checking references, employment information, and credit.[17] Not only is this done to verify the information but also to gather additional information from knowledgeable outside sources and to provide an additional degree of objectivity. Many past employers are asked, "Would you hire this person again?" A "No" response that is supportable is reason to reject a recruit.

**Tests.**    There is much disagreement on using achievement and psychological tests to select sales candidates. Many do not believe paper and pencil tests can differentiate a good sales candidate from a poor one. Others think they may be illegal because of discrimination; however, tests are legal if there is a valid relationship between the test's scores and job performance. Companies must be sure that the tests are appropriate for selecting salespeople. Also, scorers must determine that the answers are honest and not "made up." Despite flaws in testing candidates, objective measurements can help overcome the bias of interviewers or personal whims.[18]

Another testing situation of a candidate involves "riding with a salesperson." A day in the field with the sales manager or a salesperson provides added insights into the job for the candidate as well as an additional observation opportunity for the company. Calling on a difficult dealer will show how the candidate handles exposure to adverse selling conditions.

A candidate's failure at any stage of this selection process should eliminate him or her from further consideration. Candidates who pass the selection process are hired and sent to sales training.

# Sales Training

Many in-house sales training programs in smaller companies are inadequate, mainly due to the fact that some companies do not have professional sales trainers. Some outside training firms have the expertise to train and have experience with industry-specific problems or with particular types of customers. However, companies often see the main purpose of training as only motivational and thus use "rah-rah" speakers, motivational seminars, and razzle-dazzle presentations. Although useful in the short run, they are not good substitutes for adequate sales training programs. As a result, many companies must build their own programs, or use outside firms such as Wilson Learning Corporation, which customizes sales training to the users' needs.

Building sales training programs requires five major decisions: (1) aim, (2) content, (3) method, (4) execution, and (5) evaluation. The *aim* of either phase one, indoctrination training (initial), or phase 2, refresher sales training, is to increase productivity and reduce sales costs. The training needs of attenders have been thoroughly discussed in earlier chapters. Basically sales training is to teach a new salesperson how to sell. Refresher training tries to correct bad habits, reinforce good habits, increase productivity, and reduce sales costs.

Reducing sales costs and increasing productivity is no easy matter. Sales costs are high, with the average cost per industrial sales call at almost $250 and climbing.[19] To increase profit margin, sales costs must be reduced and/or sales productivity increased. The aim of a sales training program is to minimize supervision of the sales force on a daily basis through self-sufficiency.

The *content* of a sales training program varies by company. No two are alike nor should they be alike. Each program should be customized to fit the company's needs, as well as to take into account the individual salesperson's needs and background. Most, however, contain the elements discussed in earlier chapters on sales training.

After defining training aims and content, trainers must decide *methods* to be used in training. It is necessary to select the methods that are effective and to convey the desired content economically. A few methods that can be used are briefly explained as follows:

- *Lecture.* A traditional classroom method that is least effective. Average trainees can immediately recall approximately only 10 percent of what they hear in a nonillustrated lecture; therefore this method is inadequate.
- *Discussion.* Using case studies, problems in large or small groups. This method requires preassigned preparation and trainee involvement.
- *Behavioral simulations.* Trainees act out a created problem situation.[20] It tends to allow trainees to adjust to sales situations easily,[21] and allows interaction between trainees and the trainer as well as "postmortem critiques" for reinforcement. This technique is also used by having the salespeople learn selling scripts[22] or role play common sales situations with or without videotaping.[23]
- *Correspondence courses.* Trains salespeople in the basics. Few companies use it exclusively; insurance and real estate companies use it regularly. It has the advantage of low cost and uniformity, the disadvantage of lack of control and personalization.
- *Programmed learning.* Similar to correspondence courses, programmed learning, often computerized, provides faster reinforcement than correspondence courses. Otherwise, advantages and disadvantages are the same as for correspondence courses. Computerized packages of training

Sales managers are responsible for creating methods of training. These methods can get as innovative as creating behavioral situations and capturing performances on videotape.

have made great strides toward improving training programs.[24]

- *On-the-job training (O.J.T.).* Learning while working. Trainee and manager, trainee and "super" salesperson, or sales trainee being observed by sales manager are only a few of the combinations of O.J.T. The advantage of O.J.T. is "hands on" experience with immediate feedback. As soon as the trainee and manager leave the account, a critique of performance can be made either by the manager or by the salesperson.

**O.J.T.**

Generally a combination of the above methods is used. Some methods are more effective with some people than others. The use of two or more methods increases the sales training's effectiveness.

*Executing* the sales training program involves who is going to do the sales training and where it is to be handled. Training generally involves three basic sources: corporate staff trainers, regular sales force personnel, and outside training specialists. Larger companies may use all three sources, while smaller companies may use only outside sources.

Companies are divided between centralized and decentralized training. Centralized training tends to be used by larger companies that move people from all geographical areas served by the company.[25] Centralized training programs generally have excellent facilities and equipment, including videotapes, closed-circuit television, and sales laboratories for role playing. Centralization provides interaction with corporate executives, standardization of training programs, and higher training costs.

Decentralized training can be conducted anywhere. Although the costs are lower, the results are less predictable. A branch manager may have the total responsibility for training. Not being interested solely in training, branch managers minimize their interaction in the training process and negate the salesperson's enthusiasm. It is a more informal method that allows more peer motivation than centralized training.

The *evaluation* of the effectiveness of any sales training program is judged by how well it meets the sales goals.[26] Evaluation of a sales training program can be made by measuring factors before and after training on the following:

- Sales volume increase
- Average size of sales increase
- Number of calls increase
- Sales-call ratio improvement
- Customer service complaints decrease

## Supervising the Sales Force ▬▬▬▬▬

The sales manager's job does not stop with planning, organizing, and training the sales force. Directing and controlling the sales force allows the manager to make it more efficient and productive. Much of the *directing* of the sales force is done through motivation and compensation, while *controlling* is performed through periodic reviews and analysis of sales data to verify past planning and to correct future planning.

## Motivation

Just as buyers are motivated by certain stimuli, salespeople should be motivated to behave according to prescribed behavior. One field of thought on motivation suggests that motivational forces lie within the person and that a sales manager cannot motivate the individual salesperson. However, it is the responsibility of the sales manager to provide the environment through which the salespeople can motivate themselves. By either the traditional thoughts on motivation or the new ones, the sales manager is responsible for the actions of the sales force and should desire to influence salespeople through motivational techniques. Sales managers can substantially contribute to the company's profit by correctly motivating the sales force. Motivation is almost as important as efficient selection procedures in promoting success in the sales force.

Ups and downs, sales successes and slumps, are inherent in the selling job. Accompanying these highs and lows are periods of exhilarated and depressed feelings. A salesperson might interact with many pleasant, courteous people as well as belligerent, unpleasant, and rude prospects—all in the same day. Discouraged or disillusioned salespeople are often low achievers. Frustrated from various turndowns, the natural tendency is to become apathetic. Another trap is falling into a rut from making calls year after year on the same customers. This, too, can lead to low achievement levels. Motivational training is a popular alternative to firing low achievers.

All human behavior is directed toward satisfying certain needs. Why a particular person prioritizes unfulfilled needs and why a person's environmental and sociological backgrounds affect needs often remain deep inside the individual's subconscious mind. Tension from need deprivation, that is, an increase in a need's priority level, becomes the motive for behavioral action. Action reduces tension by fulfilling needs or goals.

The motivation extended by a salesperson is a function of three perceptions made by each salesperson. These three perceptions include the following observations: (1) the effort and job performance; (2) the link between job performance and rewards; and (3) the desirability of receiving increased rewards due to increased performance. The strength of the motivation to behave depends on how strongly one believes these efforts will achieve the desired performance level, and rewards must be equal to the expected reward for the effort expended.[27] The rewards affect the subsequent behavior and the subsequent performance.

# Extrinsic Rewards

**Extrinsic rewards** can be money as well as praise and recognition. The positive reinforcement theory holds that an individual's behavior is influenced by changing the work environment and praising the performance. Using praise and recognition in a regular feedback system, companies such as Emery Air Freight have used positive reinforcement to cut absenteeism by 11 percent.[28] These results are in keeping with a Conference Board Report on sales force motivation. After asking 127 senior executives to rank rewards 1 to 10 (10 being the highest ranking), the Conference Board found the top three rankings (recognition, promotion, and encouragement) to be rewards other than monetary ones.[29] It is evident that praise, recognition, and promotion are important motivators.

  To motivate the sales force effectively, a sales manager must examine individual parts of the motivational mix and determine what will motivate each salesperson. Some salespeople may be motivated by money, while others may need recognition, praise, or promotion. Specific elements of the motivational mix are described below.[30]

1. *The basic compensation plan.* Salary, commissions, and benefits.
2. *Special financial incentives.* Contests, bonuses, and promotions.
3. *Nonfinancial rewards.* Achievement awards, challenging work assignments, psychological rewards (praise, recognition).
4. *Management control procedures.* Quotas, reports, performance evaluations.
5. *Leadership techniques.* Styles, personal contact method.

An understanding of the need-satisfying behavior of a salesperson will enable a sales manager to motivate salespeople to higher efficiency and productivity.

**extrinsic rewards**

## Motivation Through Compensation

Although salespeople can be highly influenced by praise, recognition, and promotion, they may be more "money motivated" than most people, and their job subjects them to emotional highs and lows not experienced in many other occupations. Many sales force managers agree there are many other incentives besides money, but a sound compensation plan is the strongest force in motivating salespeople.

  A good compensation plan meets the following requirements:

- *Provides a living wage.* People who are worried about money matters cannot concentrate on their jobs.

- *Fits the rest of the motivational mix.* It should not conflict with the recognition need.
- *Is fair.* It should not penalize people for factors beyond their control.
- *Is adjustable.* It should provide a mechanism for adjustment when performance changes occur.
- *Is economical to administer.*
- *Implements sales goals.*

The best compensation plans generally have both fixed and variable elements. The fixed element is generally either straight salary or draw account.

The oldest form of compensation is the *straight salary*. Salary rewards people for time spent on the job. The major benefit to the company is that it is a fixed expense each year and provides maximum control over a salesperson's time. Novice salespeople often prefer to be paid this way. A straight salary is simple to administer and provides security through a steady, predictable income. However, the salesperson derives little advantage from selling more than is expected, since no financial compensation will result. The advantages of straight salary are numerous. From a salesperson's viewpoint, it develops the security of a regular income, compensates salespeople for nonselling tasks such as building displays and checking stock, and helps develop company loyalty. The advantages to the company are readily apparent. The company uses straight salary to ease the problem of recruiting new salespeople, to ensure management control over nonselling activities, and to reduce the turnover rate. However, straight salary also has disadvantages for both parties. These disadvantages include (1) limited financial incentives; (2) possible increase in fixed sales costs, since a salesperson is paid whether a sale is made or not; (3) unbalanced mix of products sold, especially if some items are more difficult to sell than others; and (4) the "weeding out" of unproductive salespeople tends to be restricted. Straight salary programs are most appropriate when it is difficult to relate the individual's sales effort to the sale of the product. Examples of people traditionally compensated by straight salary are drug salespeople for pharmaceutical companies, commodity brokers for tin or flour, and salespeople for products presold through extensive advertising efforts.

Commission salespeople are paid a percentage of their sales or gross profit. Commission is a strong incentive, but only highly skilled people and highly confident people are attracted to being paid totally on their ability to sell.

*Straight commission* is a completely variable pay plan that provides maximum incentive. The company has a system that is easy to administer. Since the company pays only when products are sold, no capital is tied up, and selling costs vary directly with the level of sales. It is an easy system to administer and is easy for salespeople to understand. The sales-people who remain with the company tend to be the most productive people. If successful, salespeople can make more money with this plan than any other. However, the straight commission plan has major disadvantages. Sales managers have little control over the salespeople in this plan. Because the company pays for sales alone, few sales managers are able to get commissioned salespeople to do nonselling activities. Commissioned salespeople tend to sell themselves rather than the company. Turnover can be excessive when the economy is bad. Because pay is directly correlated to sales, it makes sales a "boom or bust" job. When the economy is good, pay is excellent; when it is bad, commissioned sales-people demonstrate little company loyalty.

There are several *combination plans.* Each plan provides fixed and flexible elements, as described below:

- *Draw against commission.* Under this plan the salesperson is allowed to precollect commission by using a drawing account. The salesperson collects a specified amount from an account that is balanced monthly by the commission earned during the month.
- *Salary plus commission.* A fixed salary is paid to the salesperson to help control the performance of nonselling tasks as well as to provide a living wage. Incentives to sell more products come from the additional payment of commission. The commission rate depends on the products being sold, tradition, or the amount of incentive needed to "push" a product.
- *Salary plus bonus.* Like the salary plus commission, this plan provides a flexible element, a bonus. The bonus is a discretionary payment for reaching a goal and can amount to 5 to 15 percent of a salesperson's salary. For example, Mars Candy Company pays a 10 percent bonus to salespeople who make their first appointments at 8:30 A.M. each day.
- *Salary plus.* A bonus is paid to everyone in a group if all members meet the requirements set by management. This promotes team spirit plus peer pressure to do better each month. For example, C. F. Air Freight pays one bonus to individuals meeting quota and another bonus if everyone in the district reaches quota.

## Other Compensation

No discussion of compensation would be complete without mentioning *fringe benefits.* Most companies that do not rely solely on straight commissions pay some or all sales-related expenses. Typical expenses would be auto or other travel, tips, entertaining, lodging, food, telephone, and postage. The typical expense allocation in 1989 was between $4,944 for sales trainees in the services area and $19,670 for sales supervisors in the industrial goods category.[31] The Internal Revenue Service (IRS) monitors expense activities, and companies periodically check to see that salespeople are not using their expense accounts as a source of income.

Benefits may also be included to attract or reward salespeople. Fringe benefit packages may include:

- Insurance (hospital, life, accident, dental)
- Moving expenses
- Salary continuation plans
- Pension plans
- Educational assistance
- Stock purchase
- Profit sharing

Sometimes the salesperson is asked to pay a portion of the cost of a benefit to reduce its overall burden on the company. This has a reverse effect for the incentive.

**sales incentives**

One method of creating additional **sales incentives** is with sales contests. The sales contest is a special selling campaign that gives prizes and awards beyond those in the compensation plan. Generally each contest has one or two specific objectives, such as:

- Obtaining new customers
- Selling seasonal merchandise
- Promoting new products
- Obtaining more displays
- Promoting slow items into the marketplace
- Improving distributor performance.

To be successful, sales contests must reward greater sales efforts, motivate sales efforts, and assist routine sales force productivity. Rewards may be cash; prizes, such as a silver tray or country club membership; merchandise, such as luggage or a car; travel; honors, such as "Top Salesperson of the Year"; or privileges, such as special company discounts. Above all, contests must be fair and equitable. Incentives must be worthwhile, or there will be little participation.

**bonus**
**P.M. (push money),**
**or "spiff"**

A **bonus,** which is paid daily or monthly, is called a **P.M. (Push Money),** or a "**spiff.**" Often used in conjunction with sales contests, spiffs provide immediate reinforcement for sales that have been made. The closer the positive reinforcements are to the desired behavior, the more that behavior will be exhibited, according to psychologist B. F. Skinner.

The higher the margin on a product, the higher the spiff. For example, the Sealy Mattress Co., like other manufacturers, puts a "spiff" on its top-of-the-line Posturepedic mattresses.

## Intrinsic Rewards

Compensation that comes from within the individual is called **intrinsic reward.** A person who knows that he or she has performed well in a presentation or contest will feel satisfaction and a sense of accomplishment. These intrinsic feelings cannot be rewarded by the sales manager; the sales manager can give only extrinsic rewards. However, demeaning the accomplishment or failing to acknowledge it can hinder intrinsic feelings. The sales manager should establish an environment that encourages intrinsic rewards because without them morale will be low.

**intrinsic reward**

## Sales Force Analysis

To control the sales force's productivity, quantitative sales data must be gathered and examined. Sales figures may be reported in dollar figures and can be broken down by:

- Product line
- Geographical area
- Customer class
- Order sizes
- Time period
- Method of sales
- Organizational unit
- Salespeople

Sales data and reports provide the sales manager with the information needed to evaluate the sales force's performance, to motivate productivity, and to control inefficiency.

## Performance Data

Performance criteria, often called *bottom-line* data, are objective, such as:

- Sales volume (percentage increase, market share, quota)
- Average calls per day
- New customers obtained

- Gross profit by product (by customer size, by order size)
- Ratio of sales cost
- Sales orders (numbers, close ratio, goods returned)

Both quantitative and qualitative criteria discussed earlier in sales budgeting provide categories for performance evaluations. Evaluation practices vary. Some companies evaluate salespeople verbally, while others complete a formal review form. Still, memos, reports, and letters are the primary forms of communication between sales managers and the field salespeople in their territories. This is why salespeople must keep accurate and timely records of their activities. Any salesperson who does not fill out timely reports is stifling chances for promotion.

Performance can be evaluated in several ways: against quotas set in the sales planning stage, against peers' performances, or against national industry standards. Formal face-to-face evaluations generally take place once or twice a year. Informal evaluations and updates on quota achievement may come in the form of a monthly written report from the sales manager. Some small retail stores or chains that have computer capability, such as Leath Furniture chain, track sales weekly using the sales staff's records.

The basic formula for evaluating the salesperson's performance is:

$$\text{Sales} = \text{Days Worked} \times \frac{\text{Calls Made}}{\text{Days Worked}} \times \frac{\text{Orders}}{\text{Calls}} \times \frac{\text{Sales}}{\text{Orders}}.$$

Or,

$$\text{Sales} = \text{Days Worked} \times \text{Call Rate} \times \text{Batting Average} \times \text{Average Order}.$$

Sales performance is evaluated according to variables: days worked, call rate, percentage of closes, and average order size. Comparing the performances of salespeople against each other and national standards lets the manager analyze strengths and weaknesses of each representative. For example, if Joanne wrote orders for $8,550 in one month, the sales analysis for Joanne would be:

$$\text{Sales} = \text{Days Worked} \times \text{Call Rate} \times \text{Batting Average} \times \text{Average Order}.$$

$$\$8,550 = 12 \times 3 \times .38 \times \$635.$$

The company's model is:

$$\$15,000 = 24 \times 5 \times .25 \times \$500.$$

The analysis would be that Joanne (1) is only working one half the number of days required; (2) has a call rate that is only 60 percent of company standard; (3) has a percentage of closings, or "batting average," that is significantly better than company standard; and (4) closes higher-than-average orders. The challenge for the sales manager is to find out why she is missing so much work. The low call rate may be related to the number of days worked or the number of calls. Further investigation showed that Joanne was making over seven calls a day on the days she worked. To increase her productivity, theoretically, the sales manager needs to motivate her to make more calls each day. Joanne and her sales manager worked out a motivational and incentive program to inspire her to work more days and to increase her sales.

In addition to evaluating sales performance, another aspect of supervising the sales force is managing the territories.

## Territory Control

The assignment of territories is a sales control function. Territories are assigned to a salesperson by a sales manager. The chief factors of the size of a territory are the number of prospects, call frequency, call rate, class of customer, and traveling area. Once the territory is assigned, it is the responsibility of the salesperson to meet the company's sales quotas and market potential. Even though managing the territory itself is a salesperson's responsibility, the sales manager should readily equip the salesperson with the tools of territorial management.

Territories should be assigned as equitably as possible because, in theory, all salespeople are evaluated by similarity. Equality in territories provides a sense of fairness, higher morale, and greater productivity. Similar territories allow for better identification of outstanding salespeople. If the territories are similar, differences in productivity are then attributed to the salespeople.

However, equal territories may not be so common in business. A study of 80 businesses showed that the top third of the sales territories produced 55 percent of the sales of consumer goods and 65 percent of the industrial sales.[32] This closely follows the theory behind the 80/20 principle that 80 percent of the sales are made by 20 percent of the people.

Some salespeople perform better because of their territory. It is difficult to make territories equal, and often management prefers to have different-sized territories. Sales trainees are often given smaller territories. A sales manager who is not interested in comparing salespeople's productivity might match territory size to a salesperson's ability.

Territories have been used by some companies as a reward for exceptional performance. When a company has an opening in a "high potential" territory, the most outstanding salesperson in the manager's region may be assigned to it. Some companies use this reward device for all geographical areas they service. For example, one *Fortune* 500 company arranges its territories by potential sales, with the newest trainees getting the worst territories. As a more productive territory becomes available through attrition, the most outstanding trainee is given first choice of moving to it. If this salesperson turns down the ''move,'' it is offered to the next best salesperson. This happens companywide and therefore can entail several moves by several salespeople.

Regardless of how management establishes territories, the control mechanism must be consistent with the planning objectives.

## Summary

After a period of time in a sales position, the representative may be promoted into management. The sales management position functions are planning, organizing, directing, and controlling. Sales managers help set sales goals, forecast sales, develop budgets, and audit workforce needs in planning for the sales efforts of the company.

To organize a sales force, the manager recruits, selects, and trains the representatives. Sales training programs initiate the novice and re-educate and rekindle the motivation of the experienced seller. Evaluation of the training programs by the sales manager helps to ensure that they are effectively improving the personnel's sales efforts.

Once the new recruits are on the job, the sales manager becomes a supervisor, now concerned with motivation, compensation, and control of the sales force.

Matching sales representatives to a sales manager with a compatible leadership style is equally as important as hiring the ''right'' person for the sales job. Much of the quality of a company's sales performance depends on the effectiveness of the sales manager.

## Key Terms

sales management
field sales manager
legitimate power
reward power
coercive power
expert power
referent power
contribution to profits
return on assets managed by
   the sales force
market share

sales/cost ratio
breakdown technique
build-up technique
survey models
executive opinion
sales force composite
M.B.O.
user's expectations
test markets
naive method
moving average

exponential smoothing
trend projection
regression analysis
sales budget
percentage of sales method
job analysis
job description
incremental method of allocation
empathy
ego drive
Civil Rights Act of 1964
Fair Employment Opportunity
   Act of 1972

Equal Pay Act of 1963
Age Discrimination in
   Employment Act of 1967
Vocational Rehabilitation Act of
   1973
salary compression
O.J.T.
extrinsic rewards
sales incentives
bonuses
P. M. (push money), or "spiff"
intrinsic reward

## Discussion Questions

1.  List the steps of the sales management process.

2.  Discuss the six traditional steps of the sales manager's job.

3.  Explain the importance of the evaluating step of the sales manager's job.

4.  Identify and discuss the three types of skills needed by the sales manager.

5.  Why should the specific jobs of the sales manager's position be investigated before accepting a promotion as a sales manager?

6.  Discuss the relationship between planning and controlling in sales management.

7.  Cite the similarities and differences of the breakdown and build-up sales-forecasting categories.

8.  List and describe the three methods of survey forecasting.

9.  Discuss the six methods of mathematical forecasting.

10. Why is a salesperson's use of sales forecasting tools minimal?

11. Why are sales forecasts and sales budgets vital planning tools?

12. What is sales force planning, and how does it fit in with sales management planning?

13. Discuss some of the uses and importance of control.

14. List the basic elements of the motivational mix and the items considered under them.

15. Discuss the advantages and disadvantages of a straight-salary compensation plan.

16. Explain the four combination plans for compensating a sales force.
17. Discuss the basic elements of the sales performance formula.
18. Why is it important for a sales manager to assign equitable territories?
19. Discuss the three leadership styles a manager can use in supervising the sales force.
20. Why is nonfinancial compensation important?
21. What are some of the benefits that may be included in a fringe benefit package?
22. What are some methods of creating additional sales incentives?

## Decision Crossroads: Ethical Issues

1. Do you feel it is unethical for sales managers to inspect expense accounts for inaccuracies in reporting? To inspect them for appropriateness?
2. What is the social responsibility sales managers have to employees when they find an alcohol or drug problem with their sales staff? What conditions would change your mind?

## Case 17-1  Rayban Corporation

Jane Jaffe, a third-year salesperson for Rayban Corp., maker of sunglasses, is having a problem with being "at the right place at the right time." She said to Don Norris, territorial sales manager, "I never have time for all my calls. I know my customers are unhappy because either I'm there too often or not enough. What's the solution, Don?"

Don suggested she map out her territory by importance, time, and potential on Saturday. She was asked to bring in the facts and a solution by Monday.

These geographical maps shown in Figures 17–7 and 17–8, are the result of her Saturday work.

Discussion:

1. Looking at Map 1 (Figure 17–7), draw a route that can be divided into a five-week territory (calling on a person once every five weeks) that would minimize travel time and distance.
2. Using Map 2 (Figure 17–8), draw with colored pencils or pens the

route that would allow Jane to call on her accounts the required number of times during the five weeks (i.e., Mrs. K—twice; Mr. T—three times; and all others once each five weeks).

Route A = week 1 (red)
Route B = week 2 (blue)
Route C = week 3 (green)
Route D = week 4 (black)
Route E = week 5 (yellow)

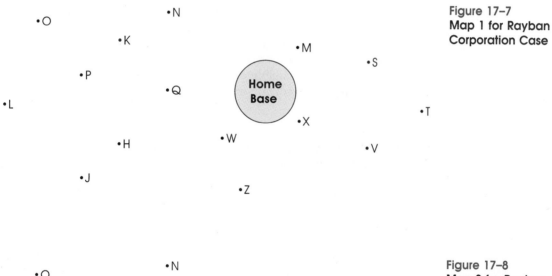

**Figure 17–7**
**Map 1 for Rayban Corporation Case**

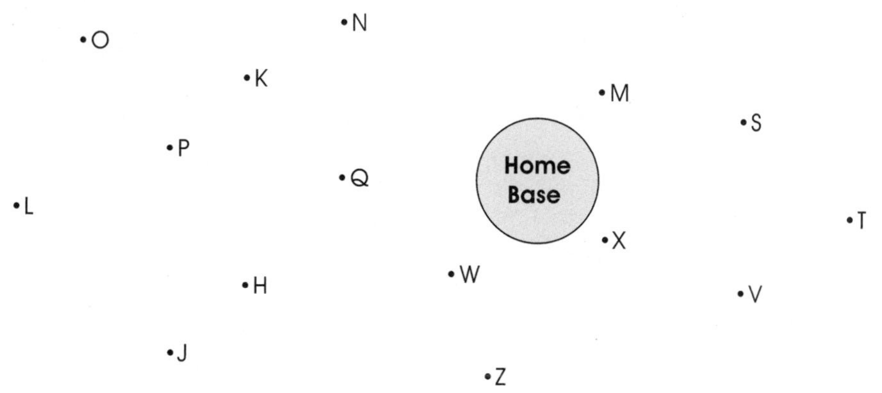

**Figure 17–8**
**Map 2 for Rayban Corporation Case**

## Case 17–2   **Hibbetts Sporting Goods**

David White is a recent marketing graduate of the University of Montana and is now working at Hibbetts Sporting Goods. David considers himself to be a very hard worker and is constantly arranging the merchandise that has been moved. He also reads as much about his products as possible. He absolutely hates standing around with nothing to do while at work. When relating to the customers, David listens as closely as he can and is quick to point out any discrepancies that he feels the customer has about the product he is selling at the time.

David began working at Hibbetts six months ago and has improved sales during his shift by 25 percent. He has done this, he believes, by trying to have an answer for every question the customer has and by constantly reading and studying the products Hibbetts has available.

Hibbetts is a local sporting goods store with five locations and carries a large variety of outdoor sporting equipment ranging from firearms to all-weather clothing for the hunter. The store itself uses only the newspaper to advertise what is considered to be mid- to upper-range prices because of the high quality of their merchandise. The store relies heavily on word of mouth advertising spawned by personalized service and the lowest prices available on name-brand products. The store itself is located down the street from a large mall.

**Discussion:**

1. How could David's attitude be found offensive by customers?
2. As a sales manager, construct a sales training program to help David.

# GLOSSARY

**A.B.C. method**   lists all the things to be done on a daily "to-do" list in order of importance.

**Active listening**   the listener directs the flow of the conversation.

**Affirmative close**   states a benefit of purchasing a product as a fact.

**Assumption close technique**   assumes the prospect is going to buy.

**Auditories**   sensors who buy, not because of what they see, but from how you talk about your products.

**Autonomously**   acting as independent agents for a company.

**Barrier selling**   selling approach that overcomes the obstacles the customer places in the way.

**Benefit**   a satisfactory fit between a product's features and a customer's needs or problems.

**Biases**   the partiality or prejudice toward one's own thinking or way of doing things.

**Body language or (nonverbal communication)**   messages composed of a combination of body features sent by means of body positions, gestures, and facial expressions that "express" the inner feelings of a person.

**Bonuses**   compensation, usually money, given for exceeding sales quotas.

**Boomerang method**   objection handling technique in which the salesperson agrees with the validity of the objection and uses the prospect's objection as a specific selling point.

**Breakdown technique**   a sales forecasting technique that begins by examining the influence of noncontrollable variables on sales and then looking at company sales.

**Breaking bulk**   a marketing function that reduces the discrepancy between the amount produced and the amount needed by consumers.

**Breaking price into smaller units**   reducing price into small units, such as monthly payments or daily usage rate.

**Build-up technique**   opposite of breakdown technique. It starts with a territorial forecast predicted by the salesperson and builds up to an environmental forecast.

**Building a mental bridge**   constructing an association between different models and their prices.

**Business-to-business selling**   selling to businesses and industry; also known as industrial selling.

**Buyers**   those who have the authority for contacting suppliers.

**Buyers' remorse**   a customer becomes dissatisfied after the purchase.

**Buying center/buying group**   an aggregation of people involved in all stages of any one purchase decision.

**Buying decision areas**   areas in which all buying decisions are made—need, source, product, time, and price.

**Buying motives**   functional/rational or psychological/emotional reasons for purchasing.

**Canned presentation**   a presentation, often memorized, that is carefully planned to include all the key selling points arranged in the most effective order.

**Career path format**   how one progresses from initial sales job to advanced positions.

**Cash discount**   reduction in price earned by the buyers who pay their bills within a stated time period.

**Center of influence**   a method of prospecting that relies on an informal referral from influential people.

**Close**   one culmination of the dialogue.

**Closing on objections or saving**   anticipated objections for which a salesperson has developed excellent answers; may be used later as an opportunity to close the sale.

**Closing rate**   the percentage of sales calls in which the call objective is achieved.

**Closing ratio**   percent of sales compared to number of sales calls.

**Closing techniques**   methods to ask for the order.

**Coercive power**   the power to punish for insufficient job performance.

**Cold canvassing or cold calling**   making calls without prior contact with the prospect.

**Combination-type closes**   use of a mixture of conclusive and composition closes to end a dialogue.

**Communication**   the two-way exchange of information.

**Company sources of information**   dissemination by manufacturers to wholesalers and retailers of literature that gives product specifications and illustrates features and benefits to prospects.

**Compensation**   what a person receives for performing duties.

**Compensation method**   objection technique in which the salesperson uses additional product knowledge to counteract the prospect's criticism.

**Competitor**   anyone who supplies goods or services that have the benefits a customer desires.

**Competitor's analysis worksheet**   provides input into other companies' viable solutions to a customer's problems.

**Complaint**   expression of customer dissatisfaction.

**Composition-type closes**   built on a series of customer–salesperson responses in which the salesperson rephrases key points to influence the buyer's decision.

**Conclusive closes**   designed to conclude the dialogue with a solution, a decision.

**Confidence**   middle state that lies between the insecure states of self-doubt, characterized by nervousness and fear of people, and ''cockiness,'' characterized by exaggerated conceit and phony exuberance.

**Connotation**   refers to the associations that are added to a word as the result of personal experience or usage.

**Consultative approach**  a "helping orientation" to selling in which clients are given information to make a decision that will fulfill their needs.

**Consumer sales or retail selling**  selling to ultimate consumers.

**Contact**  starts with an introduction followed by a warm-up period; get the buyers to talk about their buying motives.

**Contact and need assessment stage**  begins with the face-to-face meeting with the client.

**Contact intensity**  the number of contacts between buyer and seller.

**Contact stage**  designed to prepare the customer for the problem-solving mode needed in the sales presentation.

**Contingency plans**  "what if" plans—adapt to unexpected occurrences so that those in the dialogue react favorably to uncertainty.

**Continuous-yes close**  asks a series of questions posed throughout the presentation to elicit "Yes" answers.

**Contribution to profits**  cost plus markup or margin equals selling price; cost includes the amount necessary to make a product along with selling expenses.

**Cooling-off rules**  Federal Trade Commission and state laws passed to control unethical practices in home presentations.

**Cooperative intentions**  the behavior that depends on cooperation rather than competition.

**Cooperative or co-op advertising**  manufacturers sharing part of the advertising costs for their productions with retail stores.

**Cross selling**  different people in the same organization sell different, specialized services.

**Cultural influences**  multiple buying influences that emanate from outside the company or household environment but are specific to that company or household rather than to all companies or households.

**Cumulative quantity discounts**  discounts received for buying a certain amount over time: designed to induce continued purchasing.

**Curiosity approach**  an approach that immediately arouses the customer's interest, often by using a question designed to stimulate a prospect's curiosity.

**Customer benefits**  what the consumer gets from the purchase.

**Customer service**  all activities that are perceived as part of the sale.

**Daily time log**  a record of activities and their results as they occur in terms of time elapsed during the day.

**Deciders/decision makers**  those who choose among alternatives.

**Declarative knowledge**  the database used to interpret and identify clients' needs gained through experience (knowledge) according to the client's past behavior or clues from similar clients in like situations.

**Decoding**  translation of the message sent by the speaker.

**Defensive listening**  occurs when the listener considers the speaker's remarks to be a psychological threat.

**Delay technique**  used when the objection occurs before the salesperson wants to handle it.

**Denotation**  indicates the definitive meaning of the term.

**Dependent clients**  relate on a personal level; talk about themselves and the salesperson.

**Derived demand**   the demand for organizational goods.

**Differential advantage**   a unique trait used as a basis for vying in the marketplace.

**Direct-appeal close**   directly asking for the order.

**Direct denial**   method for handling invalid objections, particularly to source.

**Direct marketing or direct sales**   manufacturer sells directly to the ultimate consumer through a separate sales organization.

**Disparage the company's name**   speaking poorly about the company, generally by a disgruntled employee.

**Dominant client**   tries to control and to impress the salesperson, preferring respect and deference rather than friendship.

**Doorstep identification**   sellers calling at prospect's home may be required to verify their identity to prospects.

**Double-win philosophy**   (Denis Waitley) implies "If I help you win, I win, too." It enhanced the development of relationship selling.

**Dramatization**   a dynamic process of converting words into action—converting product features into customer benefits.

**Draw against commission**   pay issued in lieu of commission earned, to be deducted from commission at end of pay period.

**Drive or desire**   a strong stimulus that causes tension that individuals try to reduce and that forces them toward goals.

**Effective listening**   the highest level of listening. It is as if every word the person is saying is of utmost value.

**Ego drive**   provides the perseverance to stay with a buyer until the problem is solved.

**Ego involved/decisive**   customers know what they want and typically have investigated product alternatives in the marketplace before talking to salespeople. Confident of self-formed judgments, opinions, and choices, the ego-involved prospect reacts negatively to suggestions and advice.

**80/20 rule**   time management rule making the most of time, energy, and talent.

**Emotional close**   appeals to the client's emotions and desires for thrift, pride, prestige, or freedom from fear.

**Empathy**   the ability of a salesperson to understand and relate to a customer's problems and feelings. Davis distinguishes four types of empathy: (1) perspective taking, (2) fantasy, (3) empathetic concerns, and (4) personal distress.

**Encoding**   information conveyed in a common system of symbols, signs, or words.

**Endless chain**   a system of prospecting whereby the salesperson asks clients for names of others who might be interested in seeing a demonstration.

**Enthusiasm**   opposite of apathy; intense or eager interest, zeal, or fervor.

**Ethics**   the rightness and wrongness of motives and behavior in dealing with others that encompasses moral principles.

**Exclusive dealings**   requiring a buyer (wholesaler or retailer) to sell only the seller's products and not sell products offered by competitors.

**Executive opinion**   development by several executives independently of each other, of future predictions.

**Expert power**   the belief that one has some unique ability to perform necessary activities.

**Expertise**   building confidence, motivation, and learning how to handle rejection.

**Exponential smoothing**   Like the moving average, this technique of sales forecasting minimizes the fluctuations of past sales figures.

**External search**   trying to solve a problem by looking for goods or services in the marketplace.

**Extrinsic rewards**   rewards that evolve outside the person; often given by the company, such as cash awards, expense-paid trips, plaques, promotions, and election to company-sponsored achievement clubs.

**FAB technique**   features, advantages, and benefits.

**Federal Trade Commission Act (1914)**   Establishes a commission with broad powers to investigate and to use cease-and-desist orders to enforce Section 5, which declares that "unfair methods of competition in commerce are unlawful."

**Feedback**   the reaction a client might give back to the salesperson (a verbal message or a nonverbal one, as in body position and facial expression) after obtaining and decoding the message.

**Feelers**   communication types with the basic characteristics of being empathetic, of understanding their own experiences, and of being emotional and responsive to their own feelings as well as the feelings of others.

**Field sales manager**   entry level management position.

**FOB destination**   seller pays the freight to the buyer's designated location.

**FOB price**   FOB (free or freight on board) means that the freight is paid by the shipper to the location designated after the FOB term.

**FOB shipping point**   shipping costs are assumed by the buyer when it is loaded on board the transportation unit.

**Follow-up activities**   all services necessary to complete the sale and to build goodwill.

**Forestalling technique**   attempt to handle predictable objections during the presentation before the prospect voices them.

**Formula selling approach**   logical, semistructured presentation to guide the customer through a formula of five mental states: AIDCA—Attention (At), Interest (I), Desire (D), Conviction (C), and Action (Ac).

**Fringe benefits**   compensation other than monetary pay.

**Functional motives**   task-related needs.

**Gatekeepers**   people who control the flow of information to and from buying centers.

**Gesture**   any form of nonverbal expression of feelings; may include eye movement, facial expression, and body position.

**"Glad-hander"/fact finder**   basic characteristics are their information-seeking approach and their enthusiasm: they are fact finders; so preoccupied with details that making a decision may become difficult; talk about everything and frequently get "off the track."

**Goal**   a specific purpose that guides our actions.

**Goal achievement**   the accomplishment of goals.

**Goal achievers**   people who reach goals; who internally set goals above and beyond the company's goals.

**Goal conflict**   occurs because of changes in career direction or role conflict; when goals of the individual and others are not compatible.

**Green River ordinances**    municipal ordinances restricting calling door-to-door without the household's permission.

**Grouch/pessimist**    a person who has a pessimistic outlook on everything. Their bad mood will be evident, both verbally and nonverbally.

**HAIR approach**    method of handling objections by *H*earing, *A*cknowledging, *I*dentifying, and *R*ectifying them.

**Harasser**    clients who want special treatment in the area of special price concessions, gifts, or favors (perhaps personal, monetary, or sexual) or who are just hostile customers who take out their frustrations on salespeople.

**Hard-sell tactics**    typified by the back-slapping, high-pressure salesperson who will not take no for an answer.

**Hearing**    level of listening at which comprehension is accomplished to a limited degree. Bits and pieces of information are received and acted upon.

**Hidden objections**    objections, masking their "true" sentiments for one reason or another, not vocalized by the prospect.

**Hold-back sales**    predated or postdated orders.

**Household**    an individual or group of people who share a common dwelling.

**Illustrator graphic**    uses graphics or motion to depict one or more aspects of the sales presentation. Visuals such as motion pictures, slides, and maps are all potential illustrators.

**Image management**    an attempt by salespeople to influence the impression they make so that they get a predetermined, favorable response on the part of a client.

**Impulse buying**    people buying for emotional reasons, when they did not intend to buy.

**Impulsive/changeable**    a rapid talker who speaks abruptly and in clipped or incomplete sentences; often very changeable and impatient.

**Incompatible language**    speaking neither "over the head" of nor "beneath" the client.

**Incongruent value levels**    the value judgments of the salesperson and the prospect are not alike.

**Incremental method**    additional allocation of salespeople added to the sales force until the additional contribution to profit by adding the additional salesperson becomes a negative amount.

**Independent sources of information**    companies often subscribe to outside research agencies to provide market information.

**Indirect denial method ("Yes, but" method)**    indirectly denying false statements, the salesperson restates the facts in a positive manner.

**Industrial sales**    involves selling large quantities of raw goods that are standardized commodities, such as bauxite, sand, coal, and wheat to manufacturers.

**Influencers**    those who affect decisions by providing information.

**Information mode**    deals with how one processes the information gathered in the perception mode.

**Information sources**    providers of information external to the salesperson.

**Initial sales training**    sales training program that places greatest emphasis on product knowledge, selling techniques, and on learning about the company and its competitors.

**Internal indicators**    handling rejection with goals and drives, personality, and self-confidence.

**Internal or self-influenced forces**   time distractors such as daydreaming, distractions.

**Intrinsic rewards**   rewards that emanate from inside the salesperson, such as self-respect, pride, and confidence from accomplishing personal and company sales goals.

**Introductory approach**   uses a simple introduction as a client approach.

**Intuitor**   uses multiple senses to determine that the "whole is worth more than the sum of its parts" in gathering information.

**Invalid objection**   an objection based on perceived facts that are not true or are a misconception on the part of the client.

**Job analysis**   description of specific sales activities to be performed and the determination of personalities and qualifications suited for the job.

**Job description**   a formally written statement of the nature, requirements, and responsibilities of a job.

**Job mobility**   the ability to advance in an organization or move to jobs in other companies.

**Kickbacks**   giving money or gifts to secure business.

**Kinesthetics**   the characteristic of getting a "gut" feeling about decisions like whom to buy from.

**Leads**   list of possible new clients.

**Legitimate power**   the sales manager's position in the organization as a source of power.

**List price**   the published base retail price (listed in price sheets and catalogues) from which buyers may receive discounts.

**M.B.O.**   management by objectives.

**Macroenvironments or situational influences**   environments that surround all buying decisions.

**Magnuson-Moss Warranty/FTC Improvement Act (1973)**   authorizes the FTC to determine rules concerning consumer warrantees and provides for consumer access to means of redress, such as the "class action" suit.

**Manipulative methods**   result from salespeople's self-serving motives.

**Market share**   measurement of how much of the total market a product has.

**Market-oriented**   the economy controlled by the marketplace, not by manufacturers or political leaders.

**Marketing channels perspective**   how products get from the manufacturer to the consumer.

**Marketing channel intermediaries**   manufacturers, wholesalers, distributors, and retailers that perform several functions, such as buying, selling, storing, transporting, sorting, risk taking, financing, and information development, for other channel members.

**Marketing concept**   holds that the key to achieving organizational goals consists of determining the needs and wants of customers and delivering the desired satisfactions more efficiently and effectively than competitors.

**Marketing mix variables**   controllable variables of product, place, promotion, and price mixes.

**Marketing strategies**   plans that involve using marketing mix variables.

**Marketing sources of information**   publicity and advertisers.

**Markup**   amount of profit on a product.

**Missionary selling or detail selling**   trade sellers may perform detail selling activities for the wholesaler, even though they are paid by the manufacturer.

**Misusing company assets**  using company equipment without permission or contrary to company policy.

**Modified rebuy**  infrequent purchases made when products or services are needed to replace an existing one.

**Moonlighting**  taking a part-time job while being employed by another company.

**Motivation**  tension level rises to the point of recognition, forcing a person to think about satisfying that need.

**Moving average**  a method of sales forecasting that minimizes the effects of the distant future and distant past to smooth out the extreme rates of change in the previous three to five years.

**Multiple-sense appeal**  involves more than one of the five senses—hearing, seeing, smelling, touching, and tasting.

**Mutual disclosure**  establishes and maintains a climate in which buyer and seller share critical business information to solve a mutual, complex problem.

**Naive method**  assumes that a ratio of past sales to this year's sales will help predict next year's sales.

**Need analysis**  evaluation of clients needs "qualifying" through questioning and listening techniques.

**Need-satisfaction approach**  questions are used to learn a customer's needs, then product benefits are related to those needs.

**Needs**  basic forces, physiological and psychological, that motivate individuals to do something.

**Net price**  price clients pay after all discounts and allowances are deducted.

**Noncumulative quantity discounts**  one-time reductions in price for purchasing large amounts.

**Neurolinguistic programming (NLP)**  based on recognizing and then appealing to the dominant mode of perception used by another person.

**New buy**  a purchase situation in which no previous buying experience is available.

**Noise**  a distortion or disruption in the communication process.

**Nonvisual people (verbal)**  are able to imagine or pretend from a verbal description.

**Nonmanipulative approach**  clients achieve satisfaction, appreciate the services performed by the salesperson; builds trust in and gains respect for the seller.

**Nuclear families**  the traditional family—father, mother and children living together.

**O.J.T.**  on the job training.

**Objection**  an expression of confusion, doubt, or disagreement with the statements or information presented.

**Objections to price**  preconceived miscalculations (or misconceptions) of the relationship between value and cost by the client.

**Observation method**  obtaining names of potential customers through visual sighting.

**Open-ended questions**  questions that require more response than yes or no.

**Organizational buying**  a firm's purchasing goods and services to be used in making other goods as well as purchasing goods to be resold.

**Organizer graphic**  provides a story form of illustration.

**Other orientation**  an attitude of concern more for satisfying the customers' needs than promoting one's product regardless of the circumstances.

**Outside influences**   external forces demanding our time, such as deadlines, phone calls, drop-in visitors, meetings, and interruptions.

**Overcautious/think it over**   customer type who appears unsure and consistently seeks advice from others.

**P. M.s (Push Monies) or "spiffs"**   money given to a sales force to promote specific products to be sold during a sales promotional campaign.

**Passive listening**   encourages the customer to take charge of the conversation rather than be directed by the seller's comments.

**Percentage of sales method**   sales forecasting method that uses a percentage of last year's sales as a predictor of sales increases for the coming year.

**Perception mode**   the processes by which one gathers information; becoming aware of objects, occurrences, or ideas.

**Performance criteria**   measurement of efficiency, often called "bottom-line" data.

**Person-to-person communication**   one's effectiveness depends on his or her ability to adapt personal communication style to each buyer and seller. It is this person-to-person interaction that makes a professional seller.

**Personal sources of information**   information that comes from family and friends, fellow salespeople, sales managers, repair personnel, and customers.

**Personality type**   communication styles of thinkers, feelers, intuitors, and sensors.

**Persuasion**   an open appeal, either rational or emotional, to influence someone into action or belief.

**Persuasive approach**   the selling style based on an open appeal, either rational or irrational, to influence someone into action or belief.

**Positive attitude**   that frame of mind that allows you to accomplish whatever you want because you know that you can create the opportunity and make it happen.

**Positive choice close**   presents the client with two alternatives to purchase. Do you want A or B?

**Postconsumptive activities**   services that come after the product is consumed.

**Praise approach**   use of affirmation to compliment the client during the approach.

**Preconsumptive activities**   services that take place before the product is used.

**Predispositions**   attitudes of people to act in certain manners, as in a psychological contract or attitude.

**Premium approach**   the giving of gifts to establish a favorable atmosphere.

**Price**   value of a product or services negotiated between the buyer and seller.

**Price discrimination**   offering an exclusive price to one buyer out of several buyers but not offering it to all competitors on a proportionally equal basis.

**Price–quality relationship**   method of handling a price objection that shows "you get what you pay for."

**Primary information**   first-hand information.

**Problem-solving approach**   approach that uses a statement that other clients have faced to begin the contact.

**Problem-solving style**   purpose of the sales call is not just to satisfy the salesperson's need to make a sale but also to satisfy customers' problems, unfulfilled needs, and wants. It involves more two-way communication in the form of probing questions between the salesperson and the customer than in persuasive selling.

**Procrastinations**  strong buying signals that are denied by the client.

**Procrastinator/look around**  customers who put off making decisions because it necessitates foregoing all other possible choices.

**Procuring agent**  governmental purchasing agent.

**Product approach**  customer approach that places the product in the hands of the consumer.

**Product as an investment**  justification of cost of a product through long-term value.

**Product knowledge**  includes information about company history, product information, present and future product promotions, the firm's pricing policies, etc.

**Products**  bundles of benefits that customers seek to fit their needs.

**Professional selling**  an interpersonal communicative process designed to influence the buying decision process.

**Professional sources of information**  consumer groups and government agencies.

**Promotional allowances**  monetary or free goods (for example, $100 promotional allowance/or buy 12 cases, get 1 case free); compensation used to promote the products in the market place.

**Promotional mix**  a component of the marketing strategy that includes selling, advertising, public relations, and sales promotion.

**Proprietary information**  confidential information concerning a company that belongs to that company.

**Prospect**  a qualified buyer.

**Proxemics**  study of space and the movement of people within it; four types of proxemics are physical, psychological, territorial, and contact.

**Psychological contract**  the mental image or predisposition of how others should behave before and during the sales presentation. It consists of *expected* verbal remarks and body language messages sent by means of body positions, gestures, and facial expressions.

**Psychological motives**  nontask related reasons for action.

**Purchasing agents**  buyers for manufacturing firms.

**Qualified prospect**  a client who needs, can benefit from, can afford, and has the authority to buy a product.

**Qualifying prospects**  locates and separates prospects from "suspect" clients.

**Qualitative data**  employs either breakdown or build-up techniques.

**Quantitative data**  employs the use of numerical data as the basis for problem solving.

**Quantity discounts**  used to entice one to make larger purchases.

**Question approach**  normally consists of giving an interesting fact about the product offering, then following up with a question.

**Quota pressure**  short-run goals and sales quotas felt by salespeople.

**Quotas**  goals expressed as dollars of sales, units of sales, number of customer calls, or number of demonstrations per time unit.

**Reality anchoring**  having a realistic view of your ego.

**Reciprocity**  mutual buying agreements (I'll buy from you if you'll buy from me).

**Referent power**  the degree to which each party trusts and identifies with the opposite party.

**Referral leads**  prospective customers' names obtained from present customers.

**Refresher sales training**   training during a sales career meant to correct bad habits and to encourage more "closings" through improved selling techniques.

**Regression analysis**   a statistical method of determining a sales forecast that predicts sales volume (dependent variable) according to independent factors.

**Relationship**   is *E*stablished by developing *M*utual, *B*eneficial, *E*mpathetic *R*apport built on trust (*EMBER*).

**Relationship selling (consultative approach)**   an interdisciplinary approach concerned with understanding buyer and seller interactions, using principles learned from education, psychology, social psychology, sociology, and communication. It integrates all adaptive approaches into one style by building a continuing alliance between the consultative salesperson and the client to achieve maximum satisfaction in the allocation of customer resources and by satisfying customers' needs for information.

**Relevant field**   the accumulation of experiences each person has (work experience, educational background, socioeconomic status, cultural biases, and social skills that accumulate to comprise one's character and personality).

**Retail selling**   involves selling to the ultimate consumer.

**Retailer**   the only marketing channel intermediary that sells goods directly to the ultimate consumer.

**Return on assets managed by the sales force**   sales efficiency technique that evaluates the sales force with the capital invested (autos, training, and materials, etc.) in the sales force.

**Review of the buying decision (RBD)**   reviews the buying decision areas of need, product, source, price, and time.

**Reward power**   the power to award compensation for an individual's work.

**Risk**   perceived risks in financial, physical, social, performance, and psychological well-being and loss-of-time areas.

**Robinson-Patman Act (1936)**   amends the Clayton Act. Adds the phrase "to injure, destroy, or prevent competition"; defines price discrimination as unlawful (subject to certain defenses).

**Role ambiguity**   conflict between the role management wants you to play and how you see the role.

**"Rubber time"**   time flexibility that expands or contracts as problems occur.

**Salary compression**   new employees are paid more or almost as much as current employees with similar qualifications.

**Salary plus commission**   wages figured by giving a predictable amount plus a percentage of sales or profit.

**Sales budget**   a record of planned sales expenses, prepared on an annual basis.

**Sales force composite**   predicting future sales by talking with the sales force.

**Sales incentives**   additional compensation for sales performance beyond the normal compensation.

**Sales management**   performing the functions of planning, implementing, and guiding professional salespeople to achieve the sales objectives of the firm.

**Sales manuals**   company-supplied information containing complete advice on making the sales talk and on the sales job in general.

**Sales meetings**   a sales program by a company designed to provide salespeople with information.

**Sales plan**   the strategy a salesperson follows to meet the client's anticipated needs.

**Sales portfolio**   contains material to make a presentation.

**Sales presentation**   a sequential process whereby the salesperson presents product benefits and gets feedback on each one before proceeding to the next benefit.

**Sales refresher training**   the sales training program that shifts the focus to improving sales techniques by correcting inefficient sales skills that may have developed and learning new sales-motivating techniques.

**Sales resistance**   conflicts impeding a customer's buying process manifested in prospect's words and body language.

**Sales slumps**   nonproductive sales periods that may result in bad sales habits.

**Sales/cost ratio**   sales expenses over dollar-sales volume is a quantitative measurement for determining efficiency.

**Salesperson franchises**   relationships between client and salesperson in which there is total accountability and support is present.

**Salesperson's appearance**   a reflection of the salesperson's self-image.

**Salesperson's manner**   reflects how the salesperson sees himself or herself.

**Salient need**   the need uppermost in the mind of the client entering into a dialogue with a salesperson.

**Secondary information**   second-hand information.

**Selective attention**   the extent to which one decides what to pay attention to after selective exposure.

**Selective comprehension**   information understood from the information that was attended to.

**Selective exposure**   receivers of information, both the salesperson and the client, choose what they will expose themselves to.

**Selective perception**   process of screening out irrelevant information during the decoding process.

**Selective retention**   information stored in memory.

**Self-concept**   how one views oneself.

**Self-oriented approach**   the selling (hard-sell and persuasive types) style in which the salesperson treats customers as an object.

**Selling**   a face-to-face, interactive dialogue between two or more people.

**Sensor**   uses a predominate sense—hearing, seeing, smelling, touching, tasting—to gather information.

**Sherman Antitrust Act (1890)**   prohibits (1) "monopolies or attempts to monopolize" and (2) "contracts, combinations, or conspiracies in restraint of trade" in interstate and foreign commerce.

**Showboating**   dramatizing a feature in such a way that it illustrates the demonstration's effects rather than highlights the product's feature.

**Showmanship**   uses dramatic ways to show how features benefit the consumer.

**Silent**   customer type who is reluctant to discuss situations and the points that the salesperson is making.

**Similarity**   building empathy, likeability, and perseverance.

**Similies**   words that show the feature so well that the customer can see it.

**Single obstacle close (SOC)**   a lingering objection on which a close may be based.

**Skeptic/chip on shoulder/arguer**   customer type who doubts everything discussed; takes issue with everything, making cutting and sarcastic remarks about selling in general, your company, your products, and even you.

**Slow-methodical/hesitant**   customer type who is slow to react; may be misinterpreted as an inability to think, but there is no relationship between an individual's being methodical and being able to think and communicate.

**Social responsibility**   serving employees and customers in an ethical and legal manner.

**Source approval**   a client's questioning the validity and reliability of the salespeople, the information they offer, and their company.

**Source credibility**   believability and trustworthiness the salesperson builds with clients; the extent to which one is perceived as knowing the right answer and being willing to communicate it (i.e., how much believability does this person have?).

**SPIN questioning technique**   a multiple question technique used by Xerox to verify precall strategy. *SPIN* stands for (1) *S*ituation, (2) *P*roblem, (3) *I*mplication, and (4) *N*eed-payoff; relies on asking these four types of questions in a specific sequence.

**"Spotters" or "bird dogs"**   salespeople who use the telephone to arrange appointments for other salespeople.

**Standardized commodities**   goods that are purchased in large bulk and are graded, such as sand, coal, lumber.

**Standing room only (SRO)**   using a close that puts time limits on the client.

**Statement approach**   uses a product benefit statement to make contact.

**Status groups**   reflect a community's expectations for lifestyles among each social class; restrict behavior among individuals of different groups.

**Stereotyping**   generalized expectations.

**Straight commission**   wage paid by a percentage of sales or profit sold by the salesperson.

**Straight rebuy**   purchases made when much previous purchasing experience is available and no new alternatives are considered.

**Straight salary**   an annual wage, such as $25,000 a year.

**Strategy**   a plan designed from precall information that will best meet the needs of the client.

**Strategy formulation**   systematically analyzing and classifying buyer input data into contingency plans of action.

**Subscription services**   companies who provide information on future events in various industries by subscription.

**Success**   the achievement of one's ultimate goal that gives to each individual a high level of personal satisfaction.

**Survey approach**   uses information gathering as a means of making an initial contact.

**Survey models**   predicting future sales by questioning various publics.

**T-account or summary of benefits technique**   going over each major point one by one, getting agreement on each point before moving on to another in graphic form.

**Telemarketing**   selling over the phone.

**Telephone selling**   telemarketing.

**Teleprospecting**   telephoning for an appointment.

**Territory**   a geographical location for which a nonretail salesperson is responsible.

**Test markets**   sales predictors that pretest products by measuring their sales in special markets before market introduction.

**Thinkers**   individuals who have the basic characteristics of being logical, prudent, objective, analytical, and rational and of preferring alternatives in their information procession.

**Third party**   receptionist, secretary.

**Tickle cards**   salesperson's territory files, which contain names of key personnel, lists of products purchased by the account, estimated sales potential, and other pertinent client information.

**Time objections**   center around the immediacy of a prospect's need satisfaction.

**Trade discounts**   used to compensate marketing middlemen (wholesalers and retailers) for the services they perform. This discount is usually stated off the list price.

**Trade sales**   selling products that will be resold.

**Transition**   moving from the contact/need assessment into the sales presentation.

**Trend projection**   sales forecasting that plots past sales and forms a line using the sum-of-the-least-squares method. The line is projected into future periods to predict expected sales.

**Trial close**   solicits additional customer inquiries in an attempt to finalize a sales presentation. A barometer to determine the "rightness" of the time to ask for the order.

**Trust link**   the bond, built on honesty and source credibility, between the salesperson and client.

**Trustworthiness**   a component of credibility.

**Turnover**   a product's salability, or how well it will sell.

**Tying contract**   forcing a consumer to buy one product to obtain another.

**Ultimate consumer**   the "end user" of a product; also called a consumer.

**Users**   people who work with the products and services purchased.

**User's expectations**   sales forecasts made from polls taken from a company's customers.

**Valid objection**   objection that concerns a correct observation of fact that exists from the salesperson's viewpoint.

**Value-added sales presentation**   sales presentation developed to educate clients about all possible alternatives to solving their need(s). It adds value to a client's decision process by providing information from one source rather than the need to gather information from multiple sources.

**Visually-oriented person**   must see things to understand and to appreciate a description.

**Want**   a means for satisfying needs.

**Warm-up**   a short period of discussion after the initial interaction; designed to establish rapport and develop a two-way discussion.

**Wheeler-Lee Act (1938)**   prohibits unfair and deceptive acts and practices regardless of whether competition is injured.

**Wholesalers/distributors**   "add value" to a product by performing the duties of "breaking bulk," "creating an assortment," then reselling goods to other channel members.

**"Why" technique**   allows the salesperson to clarify the reasoning behind the objection and lets the prospect provide additional information about the buying decision.

**Win-lose philosophy**   a self-oriented selling style permeated by the salesperson *winning* by persuading the customer to buy. The customer *loses,* since the purchase may be made because of the persuasive abilities of the salesperson rather than by solving the client's needs.

**Zone price**   the price based on geographical location.

# Notes

## CHAPTER 1

1. Al Urbanski, "Americas Best Sales Force," *Sales and Marketing Management* 140 (June 1988): 39.
2. J. Barry Mason, and Hazel F. Ezell, *Marketing: Principles and Strategy* (Plano, Tex: Business Publications, 1987): 15.
3. William C. Moncrief, "Five Types of Industrial Sales Jobs," *Industrial Marketing Management* 17 (May 1988): 161–167.
4. "Sales Talk," *Sales and Marketing Management* 141 (November 1989): 132.
5. Jane Easter Bahls, "A Demanding Customer," *Nation's Business* 78 (March 1990): 29; and Don Hill, "Who Says Uncle Sam's a Tough Sell?" *Sales and Marketing Management* 140 (July 1988): 56–60.
6. Martin Evert, "This is the Ultimate in Selling," *Sales and Marketing Management* 141 (August 1989): 238.
7. "Sales Talk," *Sales and Marketing Management* 141 (April 1989): 48.
8. "Sales and Marketing Management Survey of Selling Cost," *Sales and Marketing Management* 142 (February 26, 1990): 75.
9. Thomas L. Quick, "The Best Kept Secret for Increasing Productivity," *Sales and Marketing Management* 141 (July 1989): 34–38.
10. "Job Outlook," *American Salesman* 35 (March 1990): 12.
11. Bill Brown, personal interview with author, Tuscaloosa, Al; June 15, 1990.
12. Porter Henry, *Secrets of Master Sellers* (New York: AMACOM, 1987), 29.
13. J. Barry Mason, and Hazel F. Ezell, *Marketing: Principles and Strategy* (Plano, Tex: Business Publications, 1987), 454.
14. Philip Kotler, and Gary Armstrong, *Marketing: an Introduction*, 2nd ed. (Englewood Cliffs, NJ: Prentice-Hall, 1990), 352.
15. Alan J. Magrath, and Kenneth G. Hardy, "Factory Salesmen's Roles With Industrial Distributors," *Industrial Distribution* 16 (August 1987): 163–166.
16. "Sales and Marketing Management Survey of Selling Cost," *Sales and Marketing Management* 142 (February 26, 1990): 75.
17. "Job Outlook," *American Salesman* 35 (March 1990): 12.
18. Somerby Dowst, "Good Salespeople Make the Difference," *Purchasing* (February 23, 1989): 19–21.
19. Art Palmer, and Robert Morey, "Retail Sales Clerk Evaluation Methods," *Developments in Marketing Science*, edited by Jon M. Hawes and George Gilisan (Akron, Ohio: Academy of Marketing Science, 1987), 300–334; and Malcolm H. Kirkup, and C. Dennis Anderson, "The Role of the Dealer in Farmer's Purchase Decision," *European Journal of Marketing* 21 (1988): 231.

20. "Job Outlook," *American Salesman* 35 (March 1990): 12.
21. Harry R. Davis, personal interview with author, J.C. Penney, Atlanta, Ga, June 5, 1990.
22. Milan Moravec; Marshall Collins; and Clinton Tripodi, "Don't Want to Manage? Here's Another Career Path," *Sales and Marketing Management* 142 (April 1990): 70–76.

## CHAPTER 2

1. L. A. Davis, personal interview with author, Department of Marketing, Youngstown State University, Youngstown, Ohio, August 23, 1990.
2. Lawrence B. Chonko, and John F. Tanner, Jr., "Relationship Selling at Trade Shows," *Review of Business* 12 (Summer 1990): 13.
3. Denis Waitley, *The Double Win* (New York: Berkley Books, 1985), 15.
4. Thomas N. Ingram, and Raymond W. LaForge, *Sales Management: Analysis and Decision Making* (New York: Dryden Press, 1989), 21.
5. Philip Kotler, *Marketing Essentials* (Englewood Cliffs, NJ: Prentice Hall, 1989), 15.
6. Anthony J. Alessandra, and Phillip S. Wexler, with Jerry D. Dean, *Nonmanipulative Selling* (Reston, Virginia: Reston Publishing, 1979), 3.
7. Sharon G. Johnson, "Consulting as Marketing Management," *Journal of Small Business Management* 19 (October 1981): 10.
8. Philip Kotler, *Marketing Management: Analysis, Planning and Control,* 6th ed. (Englewood Cliffs, NJ: Prentice Hall, 1988), 15.
9. Sharon G. Johnson, "Consulting as Marketing Management," *Journal of Small Business Management* 19 (October 1981): 12.
10. Steve Zurier, "Consultative Selling is Here!" *Industrial Distribution* 79 (July 1990): 49.
11. Rosann L. Spiro, and Barton Z. Weitz, "Adaptive Selling: Conceptualization, Measurement, and Nomological Validity," *Journal of Marketing Research* 27 (February 1990): 61–69.
12. "The Five Step Customer Care Course: Action Skills to Sales Excellence," *Personal Selling Power* 9 (November–December 1989): 26.
13. Thomas L. Powers; William F. Koehler; and Warren S. Martin, "Selling from 1900–1949: A Historical Perspective," *Journal of Personal Selling and Sales Management* 8 (November 1988): 11–21.
14. Thomas L. Powers; William F. Koehler; and Warren S. Martin, "Selling from 1900 to 1949: An Historical Perspective," *Journal of Personal Selling and Sales Management* 8 (November 1989): 11–21.
15. Steve Zurier, "Teamwork Leads to Sales Paydirt," *Industrial Distribution* 78 (August 1989): 41.
16. Philip Kotler, *Marketing Essentials* (Englewood Cliffs, NJ: Prentice Hall, 1989), 15.
17. William A. O'Connell, and William Keenan, Jr., "The Shape of Things to Come," *Sales and Marketing Management* 142 (January 1990): 36.
18. Thomas Peters, *Thriving on Chaos* (New York: Alfred A. Knopf, Inc, 1988).
19. David M. Szymanski, "Determinants of Selling Effectiveness: The Importance of Declarative Knowledge to the Personal Selling Concept," *Journal of Marketing* 52 (January 1988): 64–77.

20. Robert E. Speckman, "Strategic Supplier Selection: Understanding Long-Term Buyer Relationships," *Business Horizons* (July–August 1988): 75–81.

21. John A. Quelch, *How to Market to Consumers* (New York: John Wiley and Sons, 1989).

22. Steve Zurier, "Inside Sales Tape Gives Tips On Problem Solving," *Industrial Distribution* 79 (January 1990): 69.

23. Michael H. Hayes, and Steven W. Hartley, "How Buyers View Industrial Salespeople," *Industrial Marketing Management* 18 (July 1989): 73–80.

24. Steve Zurier, "Team Effort Earns Construction Sales," *Industrial Distribution* 79 (May 1990): 59–60.

25. Somerby Dowst, and Ernest Raia, "Teaming Up For The '90s," *Purchasing* 108 (February 8, 1990): 54–59.

26. Robert E. Speckman, "Strategic Supplier Selection: Understanding Long-Term Buyer Relationships," *Business Horizons* (July–August 1988): 75–81.

27. Michael H. Morns; Ramon Avila; and Alvin C. Burns, "The Nature of Industrial Source Loyalty: An Attitudinal Perspective," *Developments in Marketing Science,* edited by Kenneth D. Bahn (Miami, Fla: Academy of Marketing Science, 1988), 333–337.

28. Charles D. Bodkin, and Camile D. Schuster, "A Preliminary Investigation of the Prediction for Adaptive Behavior and Sales Success," *Developments in Marketing Science,* edited by Kenneth D. Bahn (Miami, Fla: Academy of Marketing Science, 1988), 291–295.

29. Don Wallace, "The Heart Of A Sales Call," *Success* 37 (May 1990): 34.

30. Thayer C. Taylor, "Anatomy of a Star Salesperson," *Sales and Marketing Management* 138 (May 1986): 49–51.

31. Jon M. Hawes; C. P. Rao; and Kenneth E. Mast, "Consumer Perceptions of the Importance of Salesperson Attributes," *AMA Educator Proceedings,* edited by Susan P. Douglas and Michael R. Soloman (Chicago: American Marketing Association, 1987): 113–118.

32. Harris M. Plotkin, "What Makes A Successful Salesperson," *Training and Development Journal* (September 1987): 54–56.

33. James R. Moore; Donald W. Eckrich; and Lorry Thompson Carlson, "A Hierarchy of Industrial Selling Competencies," *Journal of Marketing Education* 8 (Spring 1986): 79–86; and H. Michael Hayes, and Steven W. Hartley, "How Buyers View Industrial Salespeople," *Industrial Marketing Management* 18 (May 1989): 73–80.

## CHAPTER 3

1. Mervin G. Morris, Speaking at the 1981 national meeting of the National Retail Merchants Association.

2. Stephen C. Buschardt; Aubrey R. Fowler, Jr.; and Sukumar Debnath, "Sales Force Motivation: A Theoretical Analysis," *Human Relations* 41 (December 1988): 901–913.

3. James Block, personal interview with author, Roerig Division, Pfizer Pharmaceutical Inc., Birmingham, Alabama, October 12, 1990.

4. "What are the Best Ways to Break in New Salespeople," *Sales and Marketing Management* 142 (July 1990): 20.

5. Warren S. Martin, "Good Salesperson is a 'Problem-Solver,'" *The Birmingham*

*News* (June 13, 1988): 5B.

6. Parisian, Inc., Annual Report 1986, 5.

7. John F. Tanner, Jr., "Leadership Through Quality," *Journal of Personal Selling and Sales Management* 10 (Winter 1990): 49–51.

8. Jay Van Natter, personal interview with author, Pfizer Pharmaceutical, Indianapolis, Indiana, May 1983.

9. "Survey of Selling Costs," *Sales and Marketing Management* 141 (February 17, 1989): 11.

10. "Survey of Selling Costs," *Sales and Marketing Management* 142 (February 23, 1990): 73.

11. Larry Osterman, telephone interview with author, Director of Sales Personnel, Procter and Gamble Co., Cincinnati, Ohio, June 1984.

12. Steve Zurier, "Sales Training Is for Life," *Industrial Distribution* 79 (September 1990): 41.

13. Ramon A. Avila, and Edward F. Fern, "The Selling Situation as a Moderator of the Personality-Sales Performance Relationship: An Empirical Investigation," *The Journal of Personal Selling and Sales Management* 3 (November 1986): 53.

14. Helen Keller, *The Faith of Helen Keller*, edited by Jack Belch (Kansas City, Mo: Hallmark Cards, Inc., 1967), 43.

## CHAPTER 4

1. William M. Kincaid, Jr., *Promotion: Products, Services and Ideas*, 2nd ed. (Columbus, Ohio: Merrill Publishing Company, 1985), 5.

2. Harish Sujan; Mita Sujan; and James R. Bettman, "Knowledge Structure Differences Between More Effective and Less Effective Salespeople," *Journal of Marketing Research* 25 (February 1988): 81–86.

3. Raymond L. Horton, *Buyer Behavior: A Decision Making Approach* (Columbus, Ohio: Merrill, 1984), 100; and J. P. Kotter, "The Psychological Contract: Managing the Gaining-up Process," *California Management Review* 15 (February 1973): 91–99.

4. Isabel Briggs Myers, *Gifts Differing* (Palo Alto, Calif: Consulting Psychologist Press, 1980), 1–217.

5. I. B. Myers, *The Myers-Briggs Type Indicator* (Palo Alto, Calif: Consulting Psychologists Press, 1962).

6. Richard Bandler, and John Grinder, *Frog Into Prince: Neuro-Linguistic Programming* (Moab, Utah: Real People Press, 1979).

7. Information for this discussion of Neuro-Linguistic Programming comes from Kerry L. Johnson, *Subliminal Selling Skills* (New York: Anacom 1988); Richard Bandler, and John Grinder, *Frog Into Prince: Neuro-Linguistic Programming* (Moab, Utah: Real People Press, 1979); and Gary Dischtenberg, "You See What I'm Saying?" *Successful Meetings* 37 (November 1988): 100–101.

8. William G. Nickels; Robert F. Everett; and Ronald Klein, "Rapport Building for Salespeople: A Neurolinguistic Approach," *Journal of Personal Selling and Sales Management* 3 (November 1983): 1.

# CHAPTER 5

1. Donald E. Peterson, "Consumer Preferences Must Be Reflected in Every Level of Corporation," *Marketing News* 128 (December 11, 1981): 13.
2. Cynthia Hamilton, and Brian H. Kleiner, "Communication: Steps to Better Listening," *Personnel Journal* 66 (February 1987): 20.
3. Timothy D. Schellhardt, "Talk, Talk, Talk, Talk: Try A Little Listening," *The Wall Street Journal,* March 22, 1990: B1.
4. John Johns, "Verbal and Nonverbal Communications," A workshop, Ball State University, Muncie, Indiana, October 31–November 20, 1981.
5. Charles L. Lapp, "Are You Listening," *American Salesman* 30 (November 1985): 26–30.
6. Kaylene C. Williams; Manfred Maute; and Rosann Spiro, "Communication Style in Sales Interaction: Consequences and Antecedents," In *Proceedings of the AMA Educators' Conference 1985,* edited by R. F. Lusch, et al. (Chicago, Ill: American Marketing Association, 1985), 238.
7. John E. Swan; Frederick Trawick; and David W. Silva, "How Industrial Salespeople Gain Consumer Trust," *Industrial Marketing Management* 14 (August 1985): 204.
8. John O'Shaughnessy, "Selling as an Interpersonal Influence Process," *Journal of Retailing* 47 (Winter 1971–72): 38.
9. Arthur Bragg, "Put Your Program To The Test," *Sales and Marketing Management* 142 (February 1990): 10.
10. Arthur R. Miller, "Are You a Lousy Listener?" *Industry Week* 226 (August 1985): 44–45.
11. Porter Henry, *Secrets of the Master Sellers* (New York: American Management Association, 1987), 140.
12. Ray L. Birdwhistell, cited by Mark L. Knapp, *Essentials of Nonverbal Communication* (New York: Holt, Rinehart and Winston, 1980), 15.
13. Norma Carr-Ruffino, *The Promotable Woman: Becoming a Successful Manager* (New York: McGraw-Hill, 1982), 114.
14. M. L. Patterson, *Personality, Roles, and Social Behavior,* edited by W. Ickes, and E. S. Knowles (New York: Springer-Verlag, 1982), 141–164.
15. Adapted from Gerhard Gschwandtner, "Nonverbal Selling Power," *Training and Development Journal* (November 1980): 62–64.
16. William J. Seiler; E. Scott Baudhuin; and L. David Schuelke, *Communication in Business and Professional Organizations* (Reading, Mass.: Addison-Wesley Publishing, 1982), 111.
17. William J. Seiler; E. Scott Baudhuin; and L. David Schuelke, *Communication in Business and Professional Organizations* (Reading, Mass.: Addison-Wesley Publishing, 1982), 112.
18. Gerhard Gschwandtner, "Nonverbal Selling Power," *Training and Development Journal* November 1980: 62–64.
19. Myles Martel, *Before You Say a Word: The Executive Guide to Effective Communications* (Englewood Cliffs, N.J.: Prentice-Hall, 1984), 27.
20. Kenneth J. Gergen, and Mary M. Gergen, *Social Psychology* (New York: Harcourt Brace Jovanovich, 1981), 218.
21. Mark L. Knapp, *Essentials of Nonverbal Communication* (New York: Holt, Rinehart and Winston, 1980), 144.

22. L. B. Gschwandtner, "John Cleese: Brings His Unique Body Language Savvy to the Sales World," *Personal Selling Power* 9 (November/December 1989): 8–12.

23. Kenneth J. Gergen, and Mary M. Gergen, *Social Psychology* (New York: Harcourt Brace Jovanovich, 1981), 83.

24. Kenneth J. Gergen, and Mary M. Gergen, *Social Psychology* (New York: Harcourt Brace Jovanovich, 1981), 14.

25. Mark L. Knapp, *Essentials of Nonverbal Communication* (New York: Holt, Rinehart and Winston, 1980), 154.

26. Mark L. Knapp, *Essentials of Nonverbal Communication* (New York: Holt, Rinehart and Winston, 1980), 132.

27. Mark L. Knapp, *Essentials of Nonverbal Communication* (New York: Holt, Rinehart and Winston, 1980), 134–35.

## CHAPTER 6

1. Kate Bertrand, "Rep Quality Top Buyer Value," *Business Marketing* September 1989: 40.

2. Michael D. Hutt; Wesley J. Johnson; and John R. Ronchetto, Jr., "Selling Centers and Buying Centers: Formulating Strategic Exchange Patterns," *Journal of Personal Selling and Sales Management* 5 (May 1985): 33–40.

3. Peter H. Bloch; Daniel L. Sherrell; and Nancy M. Ridgeway, "Consumer Search: An Extended Framework," *Journal of Consumer Research* 13 (June 1986): 119–126.

4. John L. Haverty, "A Model of Household Behavior," In *1987 AMA Winter Educator's Conference,* edited by Russell W. Belk, et. al. (Chicago: American Marketing Association, 1987), 284–289.

5. U.S. Bureau of Census, Current Population Reports, Series P–25, No. 986 Series A assumptions (reflecting recent changes in marriage and divorce trends) 1989.

6. Gregory P. Shea, and Richard A. Guzzo, "Group Effectiveness: What Really Matters?" *Sloan Management Review* 28 (Spring 1987): 25–31.

7. Alan J. Dubinsky, and Thomas N. Ingram, "A Classification of Industrial Buyers: Implications for Sales Training," *Journal of Personal Selling and Sales Management* 3 (Fall/Winter 1981–1982): 46–51.

8. Donald W. Jackson; Janet E. Keith; and Richard K. Burdick, "Purchasing Agents' Perception of Industrial Buying Center Influence," *Journal of Marketing* 48 (Fall 1984): 75–83; and W. E. Patton, III; Christopher P. Puto; and Ronald H. King, "Which Buying Decisions Are Made By Individuals and Not by Groups?" *Industrial Marketing Management* 15 (May 1986): 129–138.

9. Wesley J. Johnson, and Robert E. Speckman, "Industrial Buying Behavior: A Need For An Integrated Approach," *Journal of Business Research* 10 (1982): 135–145.

10. Joe Agnew, "Home Shopping: TV's Hit of the Season," *Marketing News* (March 13, 1987): 20.

11. George M. Fodor, "Applying Basics Wins Core Customers," *Industrial Distribution* 79 (May 1990): 84.

12. Rowland T. Moriarty, and John E. G. Bateson, "Exploring Complex Decision

Units: A New Approach," *Journal of Marketing Research* 19 (May 1982): 182–191.

13. Alvin J. Silk, and Manohar U. Kalwani, "Measuring Influence in Organization Purchasing Decisions," *Journal of Marketing Research* 19 (May 1982): 165–181.

14. Wesley J. Johnson, and Robert E. Speckman, "Industrial Buying Behavior: A Need For an Integrative Approach," *Journal of Business Research* 10 (1982): 135–145.

15. James F. Engle; Roger D. Blackwell; and Paul W. Minard, *Consumer Behavior* (Chicago: Dryden Press, 1990), 170.

16. William O. Bearden, and Michael J. Etzel, "Reference Group Influence on Product and Brand Purchases," *Journal of Consumer Research* 9 (September 1982): 185.

17. H. H. Gard, and C. Wright Mills, *From Max Weber: Essays in Sociology* (New York: Oxford University Press, 1946), 193.

18. Max Haller, "Marriage, Women and Social Stratification: A Theoretical Critique," *American Journal of Sociology* 86 (1981): 766–795.

19. James F. Engle; Roger D. Blackwell; and Paul W. Minard, *Consumer Behavior* (Chicago: Dryden Press, 1990), 170.

20. Barbara C. Perdue, "The Size and Composition of the Buying Firms' Negotiation Team In Rebuys of Component Parts," *Journal of the Academy of Marketing Science* 17 (Spring 1989): 121–128.

21. Paul A. Dion, and Peter M. Banting, "Industrial Supplier–Buyer Negotiations," *Industrial Marketing Management* 17 (February 1988): 43–48.

22. R. W. Lawson, "Group Cohesiveness and Conformity," *Quarterly Review of Marketing* 10 (April 1985): 1–6.

23. P. Filiatrault, and J. R. Brent Richie, "Joint Purchasing Decisions: A Comparison of Influence Structure In Family and Couple Decision Making Units," *Journal of Consumer Research* September 1980: 325–332.

24. Erin Anderson; Wujin Chu; and Barton Weitz, "Industrial Purchasing: An Empirical Exploration of the Buying Class Framework," *Journal of Marketing* 51 (July 1987): 71–86.

25. Donald W. Jackson; Janet E. Keith; and Richard K. Burdick, "Purchasing Agents' Perception of Industrial Buying Center Influence," *Journal of Marketing* 48 (Fall 1984): 75–83.

26. A. H. Maslow, *Motivation and Personality*, 2nd. ed. (New York: Harper Brothers, 1970), 51–53.

27. Gabriel Biehal, and Shankar Dipankar, "Consumers' Use of Memory and External Information in Choice: Macro and Micro Perspectives," *Journal of Consumer Research* 12 (March 1986): 382–405.

28. David T. Wilson, "Industrial Buyers' Decision Making Styles," *Journal of Marketing Research* 8 (November 1981): 433–436.

29. Thomas J. Reynolds, "Implications for Value Research: A Macro vs Micro Perspective," *Psychology and Marketing* 2 (Winter 1985): 297–306.

30. Michael J. Ryan, and Marcus B. Holbrook, "Decision Specific Conflict in Organizational Buying Behavior," *Journal of Marketing* 46 (Summer 1982): 62–68.

31. Paul A. Dion, and Peter M. Banting, "The Purchasing Agent: Friend or Foe to the Salesperson," *Journal of the Academy of Marketing Science* 16 (Fall 1988): 16–22.

32. David A. Lax, "Optimal Search In Negotiation Analysis," *Journal of Conflict Resolution* 29 (September 1985): 456–472.
33. B. C. Perdue; R. L. Day; and R. E. Michaels, "Negotiation Styles of Buyers," *Industrial Marketing Management* 15 (August 1986): 171–176.
34. Daniel Kahneman; Paul Slovic; and Amos Tversky, eds., *Judgement Under Uncertainty: Heuristics and Biases* (Cambridge, England: Cambridge University Press, 1982).
35. Rowland T. Moriarty, and Robert E. Speckman, "An Empirical Investigation of the Information Sources Used During the Industrial Buying Process," *Journal of Marketing Research* 21 (November 1984): 137–147.
36. Christopher P. Puto; Wesley E. Patton; and Ronald H. King, "Risk Handling Strategies in Industrial Vendor Selection Decisions," *Journal of Marketing* 49 (Winter 1985): 89–98; and Jon M. Hawes, and Scott H. Barnhouse, "How Purchasing Agents Handle Personal Risk," *Industrial Marketing Management* 16 (November 1987): 287–294.
37. James R. Lumpkin; John C. Crawford; and Gap Kim, "Perceived Risk as a Factor in Buying Foreign Clothes—Implications for Marketing Strategies," *International Journal of Advertising* 4 (No. 2 1985): 157–171.
38. See R. J. Lutz, and P. J. Reilly, "An Explanation of the Effects of Perceived Social and Performance Risk in Consumer Information Acquisition," In *Advances in Consumer Research* (Urbana, Ill.: Association for Consumer Research, 1973), 393–403; and Ugur Yavas; Maurice G. Clabaugh, Jr.; and W. Glen Riecken, "A Preliminary Investigation of Perceived Risk Differences in the First Order and Second Order Retail Markets," In *Proceedings of the Academy of Marketing Science* (Dallas, Tex: Academy of Marketing Science, 1981), 64–67.
39. Robert B. Settle, and Pamela L. Alreck, "Reducing Buyers' Sense of Risk," *Marketing Communications* 14 (January 1989): 34–40.
40. Jon M. Hawes; Kenneth E. Mast; and Scott H. Barnhouse, "Perceived Personal Risk: An Examination Across Demographic Groups of Purchasing Executives," *Developments in Marketing Science Vol. 9* (Miami: Academy of Marketing Science, 1988), 328–332.
41. Janet Wagner; Richard Ettenson; and Jean Parrish, "Vendor Selection Among Retail Buyers: An Analysis by Merchandise Division," *Journal of Retailing* 65 (Spring 1989): 58–79.
42. Donald W. Jackson, Jr.; Janet E. Keith; and Richard K. Burdick, "The Relative Importance Of Various Promotional Elements in Differential Industrial Purchase Situations," *Journal of Advertising* 16 (Fall 1988): 34–45.
43. Michael J. Ryan and Marcus B. Holbrook, "Decision Specific Conflict in Organizational Buying Behavior," *Journal of Marketing* 46 (Summer 1982): 62–68.
44. Melvin R. Mattson, "How to Determine the Composition and Influence of a Buying Center," *Industrial Marketing Management* 17 (August 1988): 205–214.
45. Richard G. Newman, "Single Sourcing: Short-term Savings Versus Long-Term Problems," *Journal of Purchasing and Materials Management* 25 (Summer 1989): 20–25.
46. John L. Graham; Dong Ki Kim; Chi-Yaun Lin; and Michael Robinson, "Buyer–Seller Negotiations Among the Pacific Rim: Differences in Fundamental Exchange Processes," *Journal of Consumer Research* 15 (June 1988): 48–54.

47. George M. Zinkhan, and Ali Shermohamad, "Is Other Directedness on the Increase? An Empirical Test of Riesman's Theory of Social Character," *Journal of Consumer Research* 13 (June 1986): 127–130.

## CHAPTER 7

1. "Sales Talk," *Sales and Marketing Management* 141 (August 1989): 84.
2. Bill Kelley, "Picking the Best From The Rest," *Sales and Marketing Management* 141 (July 1989): 28–30.
3. Marvin A. Jolson, "Qualifying Sales Leads: The Tight and Loose Approaches," *Industrial Marketing Management* 17 (August 1988): 189–196.
4. Libbie Bramson, "Making Sales a Partner in Lead Generating Programs," *Sales and Marketing Management* 142 (July 1990): 94–95.
5. Ted Pollock, "Sales Ideas That Work: 15 Ways To Get A Larger Order," *American Salesman* 34 (March 1989): 24–29.
6. Bill Kelley, "Picking the Best from the Rest," *Sales and Marketing Management* 141 (July 1989): 28–33.
7. Douglas M. Lambert; Howard Marmorstein; and Arun Sharma, "Industrial Salespeople as a Source of Market Information," *Industrial Marketing Management* 19 (October 1990): 141–148.
8. Judith J. Marshall, and Harrie Vrendenburg, "Successfully Using Telemarketing in Industrial Sales," *Industrial Marketing Management* 17 (February 1988): 15–22.
9. Herbert E. Brown, and Robert W. Bruce, "Telephone Qualification of Sales Leads," *Industrial Marketing Management* 16 (August 1987): 185–190.
10. Thomas J. Peters, and Robert H. Waterman, Jr., *In Search of Excellence* (New York: Warner Books, 1982), 157–159.
11. Harvey B. MacKay, "Humanizing Your Selling Strategy," *Harvard Business Review* 88 (March–April 1988): 36–47.
12. Richard Cardozo, and Shannon Shipp, "New Selling Methods Are Changing Industrial Sales Management," *Business Horizons* (September–October 1987): 23–28.
13. Harvey B. MacKay, "Humanizing Your Selling Strategy," *Harvard Business Review* 88 (March–April 1988): 36–47.

## CHAPTER 8

1. Gilbert A. Churchill, Jr.; Neil M. Ford; Stephen W. Hartley, Jr.; and Orvile C. Walker, Jr., "The Determinants of Salesperson Performance: A Meta-Analysis," *Journal of Marketing Research* 22 (May 1985): 103–118.
2. David M. Szymanski, and Gilbert A. Churchill, Jr., "Client Evaluation Cues: A Comparison of Successful and Unsuccessful Salespeople," *Journal of Marketing Research* 27 (May 1990): 163–174.
3. Barton A. Weitz; Harish Sujan; and Mita Sujan, "Knowledge, Motivation, and Adaptive Behavior: A Framework for Improving Selling Effectiveness," *Journal of Marketing* 50 (October 1986): 174–191.
4. Larry Wilson, *Changing the Game: The New Way To Sell* (New York: Fireside Books, 1987), 180–197.
5. Elizabeth Conlin, "Roadside Research," *Inc.* 12 (April 1990): 29.
6. David M. Szymanski, "Determinants of Selling Effectiveness on Evaluation

Strategies," *Journal of Marketing* 52 (January 1988): 68.

7. Barton A. Weitz; Harish Sujan; and Mita Sujan, "Knowledge, Motivation, and Adaptive Behavior: A Framework for Improving Selling Effectiveness," *Journal of Marketing* 50 (October 1986): 174–191; and David M. Szymanski, "Determinants of Selling Effectiveness on Evaluation Strategies," *Journal of Marketing* 52 (January 1988): 64–76.

8. Gerald Gschwandtner, "Nonverbal Selling Power," *Training and Development Journal* (November 1980): 62–64.

9. Ronald H. King, and Martha B. Booze, "Sales Training and Impression Management," *Journal of Personal Selling and Sales Management* 6 (August 1986): 51–60.

10. Kerry L. Johnson, "Prospects Trust People Not Products," *Personal Selling Power* 10 (May/June 1990): 44–45.

11. Paul H. Schurr, and Julie L. Ozanne, "Influences on Exchanges Processes: Buyer's Preconceptions of a Sellers Trustworthiness and Bargaining Toughness," *Journal of Consumer Research* 11 (March 1985): 939–953.

12. Edith Cohen, "A View from the Other Side," *Sales and Marketing Management* 142 (1990): 112.

13. Larry Wilson, *Changing the Game: The New Way To Sell* (New York: Fireside Books, 1987), 191.

14. Kate Reilly, and Eric Baron, "Teaching Salespeople the Five 'W's' and the 'H' of Sales Call Planning," *Business Marketing* 72 (August 1987): 62–66.

15. Siew Meng Leong; Paul S. Busch; and Deborah Roedder John, "Knowledge Bases and Salesperson Effectiveness: A Script-Theoretic Analysis," *Journal of Marketing Research* 26 (May 1989): 164–178; and Thomas W. Leigh, and Patrick F. McGraw, "Mapping the Procedural Knowledge of Industrial Sales Personnel: A Script-Theoretic Approach," *Journal of Marketing* 53 (January 1989): 36–47.

16. Information for this area synthesized from Rom Zemke and Kristen Anderson, "Customers From Hell," *Training* 27 (February 1990): 25–30; and C. Winston Borgen, *Learning Experiences in Retailing* (Santa Monica, Calif: Goodyear Publishing, 1976), 271–293.

17. Jacquelyn Denalli, "Dealing With Angry Customers," *American Salesman* 34 (May 1989): 16–19.

18. "Lifestyle Segmentation Approach To Selling Stresses Customer-Orientation," *Bank Marketing* 22 (April 1988): 30.

19. Steve Zurier, "To Script, Or Not To Script," *Industrial Distribution* 78 (September 1989): 63.

20. Marvin A. Jolson, "Canned Adaptiveness: A New Direction for Modern Salesmanship," *Business Horizons* (January–February 1988): 7–8.

21. Marvin A. Jolson, "Canned Adaptiveness: A New Direction for Modern Salesmanship," *Business Horizons* (January–February 1988): 12.

22. Harvey B. MacKay, "Humanize Your Selling Strategy," *Harvard Business Review* 67 (March–April 1988): 36.

23. David M. Szymanski, and Gilbert A. Churchill, Jr., "Client Evaluation Cues: A Comparison of Successful and Unsuccessful Salespeople," *Journal of Marketing Research* 27 (May 1990): 167.

24. Steve Zurier, "Training Program Teaches Step-by-Step Sales Approach," *Industrial Distribution* 78 (October 1989): 53.

# CHAPTER 9

1. William Keenan, Jr., "Back On the Fast Track Again," *Sales and Marketing Management* 141 (November 1989): 32.
2. Linda Lynton, "The Fine Art of Writing A Sales Letter," *Sales and Marketing Management* 140 (August 1988): 51–55.
3. Donald Austerman, "Writing Sales Letters That Really Sing," *Sales and Marketing Management* 141 (February 1989): 40–44.
4. "Drop a Line," *INC.* 11 (May 1989): 123.
5. Bill Kelley, "Is There Anything that Can't Be Sold by Phone?" *Sales and Marketing Management* 141 (April 1989): 60–64.
6. Roy Schwartz, "Telephone Sales Tips," *American Salesman* 32 (May 1987): 13–15; and Emile van Westerhoven, "Telemarketing: Finding a Needle in the Haystack," *European Research* 15 (May 1987): 78–80.
7. Howard Fejertag, "Cold Call Sales Approach Will Result in Hot Prospects," *Hotel and Motel Management* 203 (January 11, 1988): 30.
8. "Skills in Cold Calling Boosts Sales Productivity," *American Salesman* 34 (October 1989): 10.
9. "Start Your Day With a Sale," *Managers Magazine* 63 (March 28, 1988): 16.
10. Robert E. Krapfel, "Customers Complaint and Salesperson Response: The Effect of Communication Source," *Journal of Retailing* 64 (Summer 1988): 181–198.
11. "Four Strategies For Creating A Lasting Impression," *Personal Selling Power* 9 (November/December 1989): 17.
12. "Not By Any Other Name," *American Salesman* 33 (March 1988): 7.
13. Adapted from Joseph W. Thompson, *Selling: A Managerial and Behavioral Science Approach* (New York: McGraw-Hill, 1973), 383.
14. "On the Floor Sales," *INC.* 12 (August 1990): 108.
15. Deborah Gordon, "Mastering the Gentle Art Of Probing," *American Salesman* 33 (May 1988): 12–13.
16. Neil Rackman, *Spin Selling* (New York: McGraw-Hill, 1985).

# CHAPTER 10

1. Gregory R. Glan, "Rating Your Performance," *Specialty Salesman* 10 (January 1980): 59.
2. "How to Prepare An Effective Sales Presentation," *American Salesman* 33 (December 1988): 20.
3. "Sale Talk: Pep Up Your Presentation With An Anchor," *Sales and Marketing Management* 142 (January 1990): 84.
4. Telephone conversation with Jay VanNatter, Pfizer Pharmaceutical Company, June 1987.
5. Jeffery P. Davidson, "Use High Impact Visuals," *Industrial Distribution* 77 (May 1988): 34.
6. Richard Kern, "Making Visual Aids Work For You," *Sales and Marketing Management* 141 (February 1989): 45–48.
7. Jack Falvey, "Does Your Company Need First Aid For Its Visual Aids," *Sales and Marketing Management* 142 (July 1990): 97.
8. "A Picture is Worth 1,000 Salesman's Words," *Sales Management* 125 (May 28, 1973): 3.

9. Jack Falvey, "Does Your Company Need First Aid For Its Visual Aids," *Sales and Marketing Management* 142 (July 1990): 99.

10. Richard Kern, "What to Look For in a Portable Video System," *Sales and Sales Management* 140 (July 1988): 43.

11. Stephen S. King, "It's Show Time for Business," *Nations Business* 77 (April 1989): 54–58.

12. Richard Kern, "Making Visual Aids Work For You," *Sales and Marketing Management* 141 (February 1989): 45–48.

13. Dawn Bryan, "Using Gifts to Make the Sale: If Holiday Gifts are Good For Business, Why Not Keep Giving Throughout the Year," *Sales and Marketing Management* 141 (September 1988): 18.

14. Michael L. Rothchild, and William C. Gadis, "Behavioral Learning Theory: Its Relevance to Marketing and Promotion," *Journal of Marketing* 45 (Spring 1981): 70–73.

15. Richard Kern, "Making Visual Aids Work For You," *Sales and Marketing Management* 141 (February 1989): 45–48.

16. "Giving Great Presentations," *Success* 37 (May 1990): 30.

17. Adapted from Neiman-Marcus Sales Training Manual (Dallas, Texas: Nieman-Marcus Publishers, 1986).

18. "Giving Great Presentations," *Success,* 37 (May 1990): 30.

19. Anthony J. Alessandra, and Phillip S. Wexler, *Non-Manipulative Selling* (Reston, Va: Reston Publishing Company, 1979), 111–118.

## CHAPTER 11

1. Robin T. Peterson, "Sales Representatives Utilization of Various Widely-Used Means of Answering Objections." In *AMA Educator Proceedings*, edited by Susan P. Douglas, and Michael R. Soloman eds. (Chicago: American Marketing Association, 1987), 119–122.

2. "Breaking Down the 'No' Barrier," *American Salesman* 34 (June 1989): 3.

3. Ralph L. Day; Ronald E. Michaels; and Barbara C. Perdue, *Industrial Marketing Management* 17 (May 1988): 154.

4. Robert B. Settle, and Pamela L. Alreck, "Risk Business," *Sales and Marketing Management* 141 (January 1989): 48–52.

5. "Dealing With The Objection—How Savvy Are You?" *Managers Magazine* 3 (November 1988): 30.

6. Camile P. Schuster, and Jeffery E. Danes, "Asking Questions: Some Personal Characteristics of Successful Sales Encounters," *The Journal of Personal Selling and Sales Management* 6 (May 1986): 17–27.

7. William R. Soukup, "Supplier Selection Strategies," *Journal of Purchasing and Materials Management* 23 (Summer 1987): 12.

8. Joyce Neu; John L. Graham; and Mary C. Gilly, "The Influence of Gender on Behavior and Outcomes in Retail Buyer–Seller Negotiation Simulations," *Journal of Retailing* 64 (Winter 1988): 427–451.

9. "Making the Price Right," *Business Marketing* 74 (June 1989): 37.

10. Peter J. D. Carneval, "Time Pressure and The Development of Integrative Agreements in Bilateral Negotiations," *Journal of Conflict Resolutions* 30 (December 1986): 636–659.

11. Richard Kern, "The Art of Overcoming Resistance," *Sales and Marketing*

*Management* 142 (March 1990): 101–103.

12. Roger M. Pell, "The Road to Success is Paved with Objections," *Bank Marketing* 22 (February 1990): 16.

13. W. H. Krause, "Improving the Productivity of Your Manufacturer's Representatives," *SAM Advanced Management Journal* 42 Spring 1985: 32–36.

14. Richard Kern, "The Art of Overcoming Resistance," *Sales and Marketing Management* 142 (March 1990): 103.

## CHAPTER 12

1. Abner Littel, "Sales Consultants Solve Prospect's Problems," *Personal Selling Power* 10 (May/June 1990): 48–49.

2. Gerhard Gschwandtner, "Closing Sales Via Body Signals," *Marketing Times* September–October 1982: 12–13.

3. Gerhard Gschwandtner, "Closing Sales Via Body Signals," *Marketing Times* September–October 1982: 12–13.

4. Staff Report, "Eight Techniques To Close More Sales—More Often," *Personal Selling Power* 9 (November/December 1989): 33.

5. Staff Report, "Eight Closing Techniques To Close More Sales—More Often," *Personal Selling Power* 9 (November–December 1989): 33.

6. Art Palmer, and Robert Morey, "Retail Sales Clerk Evaluation Methods," In *Developments in Marketing Science,* edited by Jon M. Hawes, and George B. Glisan (Akron, Ohio: Academy of Marketing Science, 1987), 330–334.

7. W. L. Colwill, "Fear of Success in Women, Organizational Reality of Psychological Mythology?" *Business Quarterly* 49 (Fall 1984): 20–21.

8. Walter J. Sheilds, "Closing the Sale," *Insurance Sales* 130 (February 1987): 20–22.

9. "Is Your Sales Personality Costing You Sales?" *American Salesman* 34 (September 1989): 27–29.

10. Staff Report, "Selling Today," *Training and Development Journal* 41 (March 1988): 38–41.

11. "Sales Talk," *Sales and Marketing Management* 141 (February 1989): 82.

12. Personal Interview with Anna Workman, retired comptroller, Sherman Distributors, Urbana, Illinois, 1990.

## CHAPTER 13

1. Nathan J. Muller, "Taking Care of Business Means Taking Care of People," *Business Marketing* 72 (June 1987): 74–75; Barbara Bund Jackson, "Build Customer Relationships That Last," *Harvard Business Review* (November/December 1985): 120–128.

2. Maurice G. Clabaugh, Jr., J. Barry Mason, and William O. Bearden, "Consumer Alienation and Causal Attribution as Moderators of Consumer Satisfaction/Dissatisfaction and Complaint Behavior," *Proceedings of the Third National Conference on Consumer Satisfaction/Dissatisfaction and Complaint Behavior 1978* (Chicago: Indiana University, 1978), 2–6.

3. Steve Zurier, "Get More Sales Out Of Existing Accounts," *Industrial Distribution* 78 (March 1990): 67.

4. "The Sales Arsenal," *Success,* 37 (May 1990): 38.

5. "Sales Talk," *Sales and Marketing Management* 141 (January 1989): 88.

6. Richard Kerndt, "Sales Talk," *Sales and Sales Management* 141 (January 1989): 88.

7. Somerby Dowst, "Buyers Give Honors to Quality Salesmen," *Purchasing* 19 (August 20, 1989): 63.

8. Windy S. Baker, and Richard S. Wellins, "Customer–Service Perceptions and Reality," *Training and Development Journal* 42 (March 1990): 50.

9. Clabaugh, Mason, and Bearden, Ibid., 4.

10. Erich Birch, "Sales Talk," *Sales and Marketing Management* 141 (January 1989): 88.

11. "Most Consumer Complaints Fall on Deaf Ears: Survey," *Marketing News* 14 (February 2, 1980): 5.

12. "The Sales Arsenal," *Success* 37 (May 1990): 38.

13. Jeffery Senne, "Customer Service: The Other Face of Sales," *Bank Marketing* 21 (November 1989): 8.

14. William Keenan, Jr., "The Difference in Selling Services," *Sales and Marketing Management* 142 (March 1990): 48–52.

15. William A. O'Connell, and William Keenan, Jr., "The Shape of Things to Come," *Sales and Marketing Management* 142 (January 1990): 36–41.

16. Richard Marcus, *Building Your Sales With Your Client Book* (Dallas, TX: Neiman-Marcus, 1981), 14.

17. Stanley A. Brown, "The I.D.E.A. Shows You Must Reach For Excellence," *Marketing News* 23 (November 20, 1989): 8.

## CHAPTER 14

1. Larry Wilson, *Changing The Game: The New Way to Sell* (New York: Simon and Schuster, 1987), 235.

2. Oliver E. Williamson, "Credible Commitments: Using Hostages to Support Exchange," *American Economic Review* 73 (Fall 1983): 519–40.

3. Oliver E. Williamson, "Credible Commitments: Using Hostages to Support Exchange," *American Economic Review* 73 (Fall 1983): 519–40.

4. V. J. Derlega; B. A. Winstead; P. T. P. Wong; and M. Greenspan, "Self-Disclosure and Relationship Development: An Attributional Analysis," in *Interpersonal Process: New Directions in Communication Research*, M. E. Roloff, and G. R. Miller, eds. (London: Sage Publications, Inc., 1987).

5. J. E. Swan; I. F. Trawick; and D. W. Silva, "How Industrial Salespeople Gain Customer Trust," *Industrial Marketing Management* 14 (Summer 1985): 203–211.

6. Lawrence A. Cosby, and Nancy Stephens, "Effects of Relationship Marketing on Satisfaction, Retention, and Prices in the Life Insurance Industry," *Journal of Marketing Research* 24 (November 1987): 404–411.

7. Raymond Dreyfack, "The Selling Edge," *American Salesman* 34 (December 1989): 23–26.

8. Lawrence A. Crosby; Kenneth R. Evans; and Deborah Crowles, "Relationship Quality in Services Selling: An Interpersonal Influence Perspective," *Journal of Marketing* 54 (July 1990): 68–81.

9. Dan C. Weilbaker, "The Identification of Selling Abilities Needed for Missionary Type Sales," *Journal of Personal Selling and Sales Management* 10 (Summer 1990): 54.

10. Rosann L. Spiro, and Barton A. Weitz, "Adaptive Selling: Conceptualization, Measurement, and Nomological Validity," *Journal of Marketing Research* 28 (February 1990): 63.

11. Mark H. Davis, "Measuring Individual Differences in Empathy: Evidence for a Multi-Dimensional Approach," *Journal of Personality and Social Psychology* 44 (January 1983); 113–126.

12. Mark W. Johnston; Joseph F. Hair, Jr.; and James Boles, "Why Do Salespeople Fail," *Journal of Personal Selling and Sales Management* 9 (Fall 1989): 53–58.

13. Gilbert A. Churchill, Jr.; Neil M. Ford; and Orville C. Walker, Jr., "The Determinates of Salesperson Performance: A Meta-Analysis," *Journal of Marketing Research* 20 (May 1983): 103–118.

14. Norman Vincent Peale, *Enthusiasm Makes the Difference* (Englewood Cliffs, NJ: Prentice Hall, Inc., 1967), 13.

15. Frank Bettger, *How I Raised Myself From Failure to Success in Selling* (Englewood Cliffs, NJ: Prentice Hall, Inc., 1949), 10–11.

16. Personal Interview with Hayden Schuetts, Director of Personnel Training, AJF Leasing Corporation, October 26, 1990.

17. Arthur H. McMahon, "How Jack Zufelt Turns Salespeople Into Top Producers," *American Salesman* 34 (July 1989): 21.

18. Denis Waitley, *Seeds of Greatness* (New York: Pocket, 1983), 27.

19. Stephen C. Bushardt; Aubrey R. Fowler, Jr.; and Sukumar Debnath, "Sales Force Motivation: A Theoretical Analysis," *Human Relations* 41 (December 1988): 901–913.

20. Denis Waitley, *Seeds of Greatness* (New York: Pocket, 1983), 116.

21. Charlotte D. Sutton, and Richard W. Woodman, "Pygmalion Goes to Work: The Effects of Supervisor Expectations in a Retail Setting," *Journal of Applied Psychology* 74 (December 1989): 943–950.

22. William L. Cron, "Industrial Salesperson Development: A Career Stages Perspective," *Journal of Marketing* 48 (Fall 1984): 41–52.

23. William L. Cron, "Industrial Salesperson Development: A Career Stages Perspective," *Journal of Marketing* 48 (Fall 1984): 41–52.

24. Douglas C. McClelland, *Motivating Economic Achievement* (New York: Free Press, 1969).

25. William L. Cron, "Industrial Salesperson Development: A Career Stages Perspective," *Journal of Marketing* 48 (Fall 1984): 41–52.

26. Douglas N. Behrman, and William D. Perreault, Jr., "A Role Stress Model of the Performance and Satisfaction of Industrial Salespersons," *Journal of Marketing* 48 (Fall 1984): 9–21.

27. David N. Behrman; William J. Bigoness; and William D. Perreault, Jr., "Sources of Job Related Ambiguity and Their Consequences upon Salesperson's Job Satisfaction and Performance," *Management Science* 27 (November 1981); 1246–1260.

28. Lewis Carroll, *Alice's Adventures in Wonderland,* rerpint (Berkley, CA: University of California Press, 1982), 42.

29. Dick Semann, "The Magic of Goal Setting," *Cleaning Digest* 11 (September/ October 1981): 2.

30. Ronald H. King, and Martha B. Booze, "Sales Training and Impression Management," *Journal of Personal Selling and Sales Management* 6 (August 1986): 51–61.

31. Ramon A. Avila, and Edward F. Fern, "Selling Situation as a Moderator of the Personality-Sales Performance Relationship: An Empirical Investigation," *Journal of Personal Selling and Sales Management* 7 (November 1986): 53–63.

32. Mark W. Johnston; Joseph F. Hair, Jr.; and James Boles, "Why Do Salespeople Fail," *Journal of Personal Selling and Sales Management* 9 (Fall 1989): 53–58.

33. William L. Cron; Alan J. Dubinsky; and Ronald E. Michaels, "The Influence of Career Stages on Components of Salesperson Motivation," *Journal of Marketing* 52 (January 1988): 78–92.

34. Denis Waitley, *Seeds of Greatness* (New York: Pocket, 1983), 46.

35. Ajay K. Kohli, "Some Unexplored Supervisory Behaviors and Their Influence on Salespeople's Role Clarity, Specific Self-Esteem, Job Satisfaction, and Motivation," *Journal of Marketing Research* 22 (November 1985): 4–24.

36. George A. Lucas, Jr.; A. Parasuraman; Robert A. Davis; and Ben M. Enis, "An Empirical Study of Salesforce Turnover," *Journal of Marketing* 51 (July 1987): 34–59.

37. Clyde E. Harris, Jr., and Rosann L. Spiro, "Training Implications of Salesperson Influence Strategy," *Journal of Personal Selling and Sales Management* 1 (Spring–Summer 1981): 10–17.

38. Howard Scott, "The Power of Self-Confidence," *Salesman's Opportunity* (March 1980): 33.

39. Personal Interview with Jim Sherry, B. F. Goodrich, June 1983.

40. Personal Interview with Cathy Watts, Proctor and Gamble, March 1985.

41. Maurice Clabaugh, "Image and the Salesperson," a working paper, Ball State University, Muncie, Indiana, January 25, 1983, 4.

## CHAPTER 15

1. Thomas R. Wotrumba, "A Comprehensive Framework for the Analysis of Ethical Behavior, with a Focus on Sales Organizations," *Journal of Personal Selling and Sales Management* 10 (Summer 1990): 29–42.

2. Joseph A. Bellizzi, and Robert E. Hite, "Supervising Unethical Sales Force Behavior," *Journal of Marketing* 53 (April 1989): 36–47.

3. Lloyd Shearer, "Eyes on the World," *Parade Magazine* (November 4, 1990): 8.

4. Arthur Bragg, "Ethics in Selling. Honest!" *Sales and Marketing Management* 138 (May 1987): 42–44.

5. Alan J. Dubinsky; Eric N. Berkowicz; and William Rudelius, "Ethical Problems of Field Sales Personnel," *MSU Business Topics* (Summer 1980): 12.

6. Joseph A. Bellizzi, and D. Wayne Norvell, "Personal Characteristics and Salesperson's Justifications as Moderators of Supervisory Discipline in Cases Involving Unethical Salesforce Behavior," *Journal of the Academy of Marketing Science* 19 (Winter 1991): 11–16.

7. Steve Zurier, "Partying's a Whole New Ballgame," *Industrial Distribution* (August 1990): 37.

8. Robert Townsend, *Up the Organization* (New York: Alfred A. Knopf, 1970), 66.

9. Kern Berney, "Finding the Ethical Edge," *Nation's Business* 75 (August 1987): 18–24.

10. Linda Lynton, "The Dilemma of Sexual Harassment," *Sales and Marketing*

*Management* 141 (September 1989): 67–71; Maureen P. Woods, and Walter J. Flyn, "Heading Off Sexual Harassment," *Personnel* 66 (November 1989): 45–49.

11. "A Legal Tangle over a Tale of Bribery," *Sales and Marketing Management* 135 (November 11, 1985): 56.

12. I. Fredrick Trawick; John E. Swan; and David Rink, "Industrial Buyer Evaluation of the Ethics of Salesperson's Gift Giving: Value of the Gift and Customer vs. Prospect Status," *Journal of Personnel Selling and Sales Management* 9 (Summer 1989): 31–37.

13. Monroe Murphy Bird, "Gift-Giving and Gift-Taking in Industrial Companies," *Industrial Marketing Management* 18 (Fall 1989): 91–94.

14. I. Fredrick Trawick; John E. Swan; Gail W. McGee; and David R. Rink, "Influence of Buyer Ethics and Salesperson Behavior on Intention to Choose a Supplier," *Journal of the Academy of Marketing Science* 19 (Winter 1991): 17–24.

15. Philip Kotler, and Gary Armstrong, *Marketing: An Introduction* (Englewood Cliffs, NJ: Prentice-Hall, Inc., 1990), 129–130.

16. Louis Stern, and Adel I. El-Ansary, *Marketing Channels*, 2nd ed. (Englewood Cliffs, NJ: Prentice-Hall, 1982), 364–399.

17. "Hands on: A Manager's Notebook," *INC.* 11 (July 1990): 94.

## CHAPTER 16

1. Peter F. Drucker, *The Effective Executive* (New York: Harper & Row Publishers, 1967), p. 25.

2. Paul J. Meyer, "Making Every Moment Count," *Sales and Marketing Management* 132 (March 17, 1980): 48–49.

3. Thomas C. Reinhart, and Donald R. Coleman, "Using Independent Reps: Why Now," *Sales and Marketing Management* 128 (June 7, 1982): 44.

4. William A. O'Connell, "The Shape of Things to Come," *Sales and Marketing Management* 142 (January 1990): 36.

5. John Canning Jr., "Value Analysis of Your Customer Base," *Industrial Marketing Management* (Fall 1982): 89–93.

6. Andris A. Zoltners, and Prabhakant Sinha, "Sales Territory Alignment: A Review and Model," *Management Science* (November 1983): 1237–1256.

7. Alan J. Dubinsky, and Thomas N. Ingram, "A Portfolio Analysis to Account Profitability," *Industrial Marketing Management* (Summer 1984): 33–41.

8. A. Parasuraman, "An Approach for Allocating Sales Call Effort," *Industrial Marketing Management* (Winter 1982): 75–79.

9. Tom Eisenhart, "Drawing a Map to Better Sales," *Business Marketing* (January 1990): 59–61.

10. Kate Bertrand, "Speak Now, Or. . . .," *Business Marketing* (January 1990): 68–71.

11. Carl K. Clayton, "How to Manage Your Time and Territory for Better Sales Results," *Personal Selling Power* 10 (March 1990): 46.

12. Alan Lahein, *How to Get Control of Your Time and Your Life* (New York: Peter H. Wyden, Inc., 1973), 3.

13. William J. Tobin, "80–20 or Perish," *Sales and Marketing Management* 134 (August 13, 1984): 16.

14. Peter J. Murk, "It's About Time and Salespeople," (unpublished Monograph, Ball State University, November, 1980), 18.
15. Harry C. Rotenbury, "On Time—Time Management and Scheduling," *Management World* 8 (May 1979): 24–25.
16. Mel Mandell, "Car Phones: Should You Pick Up Now?" *Sales and Marketing Management* 140 (September 1988): 44–51.
17. "Telemarketing Rings in New Business Era," *Advertising Age* (January 27, 1986): 52.
18. Charles Smith, "Procrastination," *American Salesman* 34 (August 1989): 10–11.
19. Simi Horitz refers to the work of Herbert Tensterheim, Associate Professor of Clinical Psychology at New York Hospital, Cornell Medical Center, Ithaca, NY; see Horwitz's article "How to Stop Procrastinating," *Family Weekly Magazine* (September 27, 1981): 12.
20. Adapted from Peter J. Murk, "It's About Time and Salespeople," (unpublished Monograph, Ball State University, November 1983), 1–34.

## CHAPTER 17

1. William Keenan, Jr., "Back on the Fast Track Again," *Sales and Marketing Management* 141 (November 1989): 35.
2. John R. French, and Bertram Raven, "The Bases of Social Power," in *Group Dynamics,* edited by Dorium Cartwright and Alvin F. Zander, 2nd ed. (Evanston, IL: Row, Peterson and Co., 1960), 607–623.
3. Alan J. Dubinsky and Thomas N. Ingram, "Important First-Line Sales Management Qualifications: What Sales Executives Think," *Journal of Personal Selling and Sales Management* 3 (May 1983): 18–25.
4. William O'Connell and William Keenan, Jr., "The Shape of Things to Come," *Sales and Marketing Management* 142 (January 1990): 39.
5. For results of empirical research in these areas see Alan J. Dubinsky and Thomas E. Berry, "A Survey of Sales Management Practices," *Industrial Marketing Management* 11 (1982): 133–144; and Donald W. Jackson, Jr.; Lonnie L. Ostrom; and Kenneth R. Evans, "Measures to Evaluate Industrial Activities," *Industrial Marketing Management* 11 (1982): 269–274.
6. For different classification schemes and more detailed discussion of individual forecasting methods, see David M. Georgoff and Robert G. Murdick, "Manager's Guide to Forecasting," *Harvard Business Review* 64 (January–February 1986): 113–118 and J. Scott Armstrong; J. Brodie; and Shelby McIntire, "Forecasting Methods for Marketing: Review of Empirical Research," *Singapore Marketing Review* (March 1987): 7–23.
7. Mark R. Edwards; W. Theodore Cummings; and John L. Schlacter, "The Paris–Peoria Solution: Innovation in Appraising Regional and International Sales Personnel," *Journal of Personal Selling and Sales Management* 4 (November 1984): 27–38.
8. Adrian B. Ryans, and Charles B. Weinberg, "Territorial Sales Response Models: Stability over Time," *Journal of Marketing Research* 24 (May 1987): 231.
9. Nigel F. Percy, "The Marketing Budgeting Process: Marketing Management Implications," *Journal of Marketing* 51 (October 1987): 45–59.
10. Much of this discussion in this section comes from Alan J. Dubinsky and

Richard W. Hansen, "The Sales Force Management Audit," *California Management Review* (Winter 1981): 86–95.

11. Herbert M. Greenberg, and Jeanne Greenberg, "Job Matching for Better Performance," *Harvard Business Review* 58 (September–October 1980): 128–133.

12. Jack Shewmaker, "The Master Sellers," *Nation's Business* (November 1988): 20–30.

13. Ronald E. Goldsmith; Kevin M. McNeilly; and Frederick A. Russ, "Similarity of Sales Representatives and Supervisor's Problem-Solving Styles and the Satisfaction–Performance Relationship," *Psychological Reports* 64 (1989): 827–832.

14. Personal Interview with Dale Peterson, Moore Business Forms, Indianapolis, Indiana, May 1990.

15. Jeanne Greenberg, and Herbert Greenberg, "Avoid Costly Mistakes—Follow These Steps to Identify Good Salespeople," *Marketing News* (March 15, 1985): 33.

16. J. Michael Munson, and W. Austin Spivey, "Salesforce Selection That Meets Federal Regulation and Management Needs," *Industrial Marketing Management* 9 (February 1980): 10–12.

17. Liz Murphy, "Did Your Salesman Lie to Get His Job?" *Sales and Marketing Management* 139 (November 1987): 54–58.

18. Samuel J. Maurice, "Stalking the Hire-Scoring Salesperson," *Sales and Marketing Management* 137 (October 7, 1985): 63–64; George B. Salsbury, "Properly Recruit Salespeople To Reduce Training Costs," *Industrial Marketing Management* 11 (April 1982): 143–146; Richard Kern, "IQ Tests for Salesmen Make A Comeback," *Sales and Marketing Management* 140 (April 1988): 42–46.

19. William O'Connell and William Keenan Jr., "The Shape of Things to Come," *Sales and Marketing Management* 18 (January 1990): 39.

20. Larry J. B. Robinson, "Role Playing as a Sales Training Tool," *Harvard Business Review* 65 (May–June 1987): 34–35.

21. Ronald H. King, and Martha B. Booze, "Sales Training and Impression Management," *Journal of Personal Selling and Sales Management* 6 (August 1986): 51–60.

22. Thomas W. Leigh, "Cognitive Selling Scripts and Sales Training," *Journal of Personal Selling and Sales Management* 7 (August 1987): 39–48.

23. "Video Assists in Medical Products Sales Training," *Marketing News* 20 (October 10, 1986): 14.

24. For reviews of software packages see, Robert H. Collins, "Sales Training: A Microcomputer–Based Approach," *Journal of Personal Selling and Sales Management* 6 (May 1986): 71–76; and Robert H. Collins, "Artificial Intelligence in Personal Selling," *Journal of Personal Selling and Sales Management* 4 (May 1984): 58–66.

25. Charles M. Futrell; Leonard L. Berry; and Michael R. Bowers, "An Evaluation of Sales Training in the U.S. Banking Industry," *Journal of Personal Selling and Sales Management* 4 (November 1984): 40–47.

26. Alan J. Dubinsky, and William A. Staples, "Sales Training: Salespeople's Preparedness and Managerial Implications," *Journal of Personal Selling and Sales Management* 2 (Fall 1981/82): 24–31.

27. V. Vroom, *Work and Motivation* (New York, NY: John Wiley Publishers, 1964), 1–20.

28. "Where Skinner's Theories Work," *Business Week* (December 2, 1972): 64–65.

29. "Those Inflation Blues," *Sales & Marketing Management* 123 (November 12, 1979): 24.

30. Charles Futrell, *Sales Management: Behavior, Practice, and Cases* (Hinsdale, IL: Dryden Press, 1981), 298.

31. "Sales and Marketing Management Survey of Selling Cost," *Sales and Marketing Management* 142 (February 26, 1990): 75.

32. Harry D. Wolfe and Gerald Albaum, "Inequality in Products, Orders, Customers, Salesmen, and Sales Territories," *Journal of Business* 35 (July 1982): 300.

# Name Index

## A

## B

## C

# Subject Index

expert, 147, 294, 455
legitimate, 455
referent, 147, 454, 455
reward, 455
Pre-approach stage, 179–185
Pre-call plan, 260–261
Pre-close
conclusions, 362–364
dialogue, 362–363
Pre-consumptive
activities, 359
conditions, 359
Predispositions, 83–87
Pre-Industrialization Period, 41
Pre-presentation information,
260–262
Presentation, 262–268
as a road map, 263–264
delivery, 264–265
directing, 281
dramatization, 264–265
prepare for, 281
Price
discrimination, 416
negotiations, 299
objections techniques, 299,
308–311
breaking price into smaller
units, 309
building a mental bridge, 309
presenting the product as an
investment, 309
price-quality relationship,
299, 308–309
Pricing policies, 61–62
cash discount, 62
FOB destination, 61
FOB price, 61
FOB shipping point, 61
List price, 61
Net price, 61
Trade discounts, 62
Zone price, 61
Problem recognition, 151
Procrastination, 440–442
Procuring agents, 12
Product
demonstrations, 273
differentiation, 296

knowledge, transfer of, 58–61,
264
Promotional
allowances, 62
departments, 171–172
Proposal(s), 153
acquisition of, 153
analysis of, 153
Proprietary information, 409
Prospecting, 168–185, 439
Proximics, 277–279
Psychological
contract, 83, 195–196, 241
influences, 146
motives, 145
Purchasing agents, 12, 357

**Q**

Qualified
buyer, 249
prospect, 180
Qualifying the prospects, 238–239
Quantity discounts, 61
cumulative, 61
noncumulative, 61
Quantity needed, 151
Questioning mode, 243
Questions, 242–246
encouragement, 243
exploratory, 242–243
HAIR approach, 302
multiple questioning technique
(SPIN), 243–246
open-ended, 243
reflective, 242–243
why? 302–303
Quota pressure, 408
Quotas, 408, 427, 453, 459, 478,
482

**R**

"Reading" the client, 116, 241
Reality-anchoring, 393
Reciprocity, 142, 414
Recognition, 7, 417

Recruiting, 468
Referral leads, 173–175
Relationship(s)
building, 194–198
external indicators, 384–386
internal indicators, 387–398
management, 358
selling, 30–36
traits of, 46–47
with other companies and
customers, 409–414
with self, 283–298
with society, 415–416
within your company, 407–409
Relevant field(s), 79, 84
Responding, 82
Retail salespeople, 9
Retailer, 17
Revitalization of consumerism, 42
Reward(s), 7
extrinsic, 7, 477–481
intrinsic, 7, 481
Risk, 148–149
Robinson-Patman Act of 1936,
415
Role
ambiguity, 389
conflict, 389

**S**

Salary compression, 469
Sales aids, 263, 268–274
types of, 268–274
illustrator, 268–269
organizer, 268–269
using effectively, 274
Sales budgets, 461–462
percentage of sales method,
461
trend projection, 461
Sales departments, leads from,
169
Sales force
allocation, 465–466
equalized work load, 465
incremental method of,
465–466

## Photo Credits, Continued